Rowland Gibson Hazard

Freedom of Mind

Rowland Gibson Hazard

Freedom of Mind

ISBN/EAN: 9783337285951

Printed in Europe, USA, Canada, Australia, Japan

Cover: Foto ©Lupo / pixelio.de

More available books at **www.hansebooks.com**

FREEDOM

OF

MIND IN WILLING;

OR,

EVERY BEING THAT WILLS A CREATIVE
FIRST CAUSE.

BY

ROWLAND G. HAZARD.

NEW YORK:
D. APPLETON AND COMPANY,
443 & 445 BROADWAY.
LONDON: 16 LITTLE BRITAIN.
1865.

Entered, according to Act of Congress, in the year 1864, by
D. APPLETON & COMPANY,
In the Clerk's Office of the District Court of the United States for the Southern District of New York.

PREFACE.

THE public mind is at present so engrossed with other pursuits, and so satisfied with its progress in them, that there is little room to hope that it will bestow much attention upon the subject of this volume. Physical Science and Material Progress are now the absorbing objects of effort. To these all utility is ascribed, to the exclusion of the Metaphysical, which lies under the imputation of being both uninteresting and useless. Why this opprobrium and whence the general neglect, the absolute indisposition, to inquire into the structure and conditions of our spiritual being, which, as the source of all our power and all our enjoyments, one might naturally suppose would most interest us, and at the same time, by its mystery, most excite our curiosity? That the discoveries in Physics, so varied and so magnificent, have largely contributed to our material comforts, have feasted the intellect and even regaled the imagination, is undoubtedly one cause of this neglect of the science of mind. But there are other reasons, among which we may mention the real difficulties of the subject. These are of two distinct kinds; first, those of ascertaining the truths; and second, those of imparting them after they have been ascertained. The first of these are, in some respects, peculiar. We want to examine that which examines; we want the mind to be employed in observing its own action, *i. e.*, we want it to be doing one thing when it is of necessity doing another. A further difficulty, even in the investigation of the phenomena of mind, arises from the fact that the language applied to metaphysical science is very imperfect as an instrument of thought. The science of mind has very little language of its own, and in adopting for it what has been formed and fitted to another department of knowledge, much confusion and error result. The ambiguity, or various meanings of the terms, so often mislead the investigator himself, that he is not unfrequently obliged to relinquish the instrumental aid of words, and directly examine his original ideas and conceptions of the subjects of inquiry. The difficulty of imparting the results in a language so imperfect is obvious, and is increased when it has been discarded in reaching them.

But, with all this inappreciation of its benefits and all its recognized difficulties, Metaphysics has its peculiar attractions. The questions of every child, the yearnings of the adult, though in expression only occasionally gleaming through the settled gloom of discouragement and despondency, still manifest the fervid curiosity in regard to that *mysterious invisible*, which knows, thinks, feels and acts; and even in those too busy, too sluggish, or too hopeless to put forth an effort to gratify it.

The reason of its being neglected lies not so much in its want of attraction, as in the prevailing idea of its inutility; and this idea, though now magnified by temporary causes, has a foundation in the fact, that no investigation of the nature of our faculties and powers, mental or physical, is essential to that use of them which our early existence demands. For this we have the requisite knowledge by intuition. We can use our powers without studying either Anatomy or Metaphysics. It is not, then, surprising that we should early direct our attention to the study of those extrinsic substances and phenomena of which more knowledge is obviously and immediately useful. The want of satisfactory results has also had its influence; and perhaps there is no question, the discussion of which has tended more to bring upon Metaphysics the reproach of being unfruitful, than that of the "Freedom of the Will." The importance of removing this grand obstruction to the progress of ethics and theology, is appreciated only by those who in their researches have encountered it. They alone have caught glimpses of the radiant fields of speculation which lie beyond; and most men regard the speculations upon it, not only as having furnished no new truth, but as having obscured what was before known.

Whatever opinion may be formed of the success or failure, of my effort to elucidate this subject, I trust it will be admitted, that the arguments I have presented, at least, *tend* to show that the investigation may open more elevated and more elevating views of our position and our powers; and may reveal new modes of influencing our own intellectual and moral character, and thus have a more immediate, direct, and practical bearing on the progress of our race in virtue and happiness, than any inquiry in physical science.

CONTENTS.

BOOK I.
FREEDOM OF MIND IN WILLING.

PAGE

CHAPTER I.—OF THE EXISTENCE OF SPIRIT, ... 1

Postulates of the argument—Knowledge, thought, sensation, emotion, want and effort recognized as in one combination ; one mind—Each of such combinations, associated with a particular form, constitutes what each denominates I —Idea of form not essential to our idea of spirit, or intelligent being—Certain sensations, which we *can* and *do* ourselves produce ; some of the same kind, which we know that *we* do not produce, and, attributing to others, get the idea of other finite minds ; and others, which we cannot produce ; and thus get the idea of Superior Power—This power really infinite, or to us the same as if it were so—We thus come to know ourselves, our fellow beings, and God, as CAUSE.

CHAPTER II.—OF THE EXISTENCE OF MATTER, ... 5

We know of it only by our sensations—Sensations not conclusive proof of its existence—Sensations may be the thought and imagery of the mind of God directly imparted to us—In either case they represent His thought, and are equally real—That they are thought and imagery directly imparted to us, the more simple hypothesis, and more in accordance with our own conscious powers—Matter not necessary for Spirit to act upon—This illustrated by geometrical science—To ignore matter would simplify the question of freedom of the mind and make creation more intelligible—Not sufficient proof to warrant this course ; but, in either case, the phenomena are the same, and matter is unintelligent and inert.

CHAPTER III.—OF MIND, ... 9

Its attributes and its faculty of will—Its sensations and emotions not dependent on its will—Its knowledge also not so dependent—But act of will may be essential to the acquisition of knowledge—Feeling a property, or susceptibility, rather than a faculty—Ability to acquire knowledge a capacity, or sense, rather than a faculty—Object of act of will always is to produce some effect in

CONTENTS.

PAGE

the future—Supposed faculties of mind, other than will, all but names of some form of knowledge, or of some mode of effort to acquire it—All knowledge, in the last analysis, a simple mental perception—Objection, that these supposed faculties sometimes seem to act of themselves, considered—Definition of knowledge and of metaphysical certainty.

CHAPTER IV.—LIBERTY, OR FREEDOM, ... 19

Opposing terms, compulsion, control, constraint, and restraint—That which controls its own action, acts freely.

CHAPTER V.—OF CAUSE, ... 21

Cause used as that which produces change—Four distinct *conceivable* kinds enumerated—Two of them material, and two intelligent.

CHAPTER VI.—OF THE WILL, ... 24

Confusion in treating will as a distinct, active entity—Will defined as the power or faculty of the mind for effort—Mind cannot be inert cause—Mind has two distinct spheres for its activity; in one, it seeks to learn what is, and in the other to influence the course of events in the future—These connected by the mind's prophetic power.

CHAPTER VII.—OF WANT, ... 27

The term want used to express the conscious condition of the mind, and not the thing wanted—A mere sensation, or emotion, or its absence, is not in itself a want—The idea of change an essential element of want—Primary and secondary wants—Natural, acquired, and cultivated wants—Natural wants not the result of volition—Acquired want results from some increase of knowledge—Influence of want on will not varied by the cause of it.

CHAPTER VIII.—OF MATTER AS CAUSE, ... 32

All changes in matter must arise from motion in it—Cannot move itself, and hence cannot be cause, except by first being in motion—Can it thus become cause? If so, as it may have been in motion from eternity, may always have been cause—Other questions upon which this depends—If motion gives it causative power, that power is diminished in producing effects; and hence, in an eternity, must be reduced to an infinitesimal—Matter in motion subjected to intelligent control—Matter cannot be made cause by impressing laws upon it—Matter an instrument, a means, by which one intelligence communicates with, or produces effects upon another—If matter be cause, its effects cannot affect the freedom of the mind in willing, any more than the effects of intelligent causes can—Action of mind on matter—Independent action of matter.

CHAPTER IX.—OF SPIRIT AS CAUSE, ... 42

Spirit is an indispensable, if not the only cause—Relations of the finite to the Supreme Intelligence, as cause—Creative powers of the finite mind of man similar to those of the Infinite—Man has no faculty by which he can create, or even conceive of the creation of matter as a distinct entity, and there is no necessity, or reason to suppose that God has—The human mind, within the

PAGE

sphere of its knowledge, with a coördinate finite presence, is creative—Its incipient creations are conceptions of its own mind—Its creative power exerted in the same manner as that of the Infinite—Creative power of man may be secondary in its character—That is, moulds its conceptions in the same material which God has previously used for a like purpose—Our own ideal conceptions distinguishable from the external creation only by their subjection to our will—God's conceptions, or creations, also subject to change or annihilation by His will—Man's limited power to transfer the conceptions of his own to other minds—Finite mind can create not only new forms and new combinations, but new thought and new beauty.

CHAPTER X.—FREEDOM OF INTELLIGENCE, ... 51

The question should be, not, *Is the will free?* but, Does the mind will freely? —The willing distinct from its sequence or effect—Connection between volition and its effect—Intelligence must have an object for acting, rather than not acting—This object must be an effect which it *wants* to produce ; must arise from a *want*—With this want must be associated knowledge of the means of its gratification—Action different under different circumstances, and the first step must be to examine, or to ascertain the circumstances, and this fact is probably intuitively known—Want and knowledge the source in which volitions originate and receive their direction—Sources of volition resolvable into an active being with knowledge and want- Want and knowledge may be without volition—A want may itself be the object wanted—We do not make, but find knowledge ; and for intuitive knowledge do not have to seek—Deliberation necessary in applying acquired knowledge—Without the knowledge of a choice in means, the first perceived would be adopted—Experience teaches deliberation—Deliberation still but the application of knowledge to action—Deliberation is the considered application of knowledge, leading to a judgment—Time devoted to it decided by the mind—Mind can arrest its impulse to gratify its want by the first perceived means, to consider its proposed action—This power makes one distinction between instinctive and rational actions—We do not make any effort for what already is—Every effort is a *beginning* to do, and is an exercise of creative power—Finite mind has creative powers, and capacity to use them—Circumstances, examination of which is essential to proper effort—We never will to do what we know we cannot do—Mind does not always adopt the easiest mode of attaining the ultimate object of its effort—Illustration from the want of food—Efforts must be in a certain order, otherwise abortive—Effects of a series of finite efforts as clearly manifest design as the planetary system—Deliberation illustrated—We do not will as to what is past, but to produce some effect in the future—Mind forms preconceptions of this future effect of effort—To will requires a prophetic view of the future, making a broad distinction between intelligent and unintelligent cause—The mind's prophetic power fits it for a *first cause*—The *mind* must determine what change it will try to produce—For this, if want and knowledge were not fixed and independent of will, the data would be insufficient—If want and knowledge not fixed, the mind must form hypothesis to act upon—No power, ignorant of the want and the perceptions of the agent, could determine the will of that agent —That want and knowledge are not subject to the will, facilitates the mind in the exercise of its freedom in willing—Whether the mind's preconceptions are realized by its own power, not material to the question of its freedom in will.

A*

PAGE

ing—Finite mind exerts its creative power in same manner as the Infinite—Each, respectively, subject to its own conditions—Conflicting wants and wants of activity and repose (note)—Supposed commencement of creation—A creative God must make effort—Intelligence a cause, which produces various effects—Another step in creation supposed—Every creative act a *beginning* of a new creation—Supreme Intelligence acting with coëxisting blind causes—Acting also with coëxisting intelligent causes—In either case, must will freely—Amount of its power makes no difference to the *freedom* of intelligent being in willing—Nor does the amount of its knowledge—Hence, the finite intelligence may be as free as the Infinite—One intelligence may shape circumstances to influence the will of another, which may be effective if that other acts freely—The period of creation at which the finite mind begins to act does not affect its freedom—Every act of will the same, in some respects, as a first act—Is the finite mind, in willing, controlled by any other power?—Conceivable modes of external control—These modes considered—Influence of other intelligences—Influence of circumstances—If mind wills at all, it must will freely—Same result more concisely reached through the logical relation of terms.

CHAPTER XI.—INSTINCT AND HABIT, ... 98

The sphere of liberty varies in different orders of intelligence—Each equally free in its own sphere of knowledge—Matter has no such sphere, and hence, if it had the essential attributes, could manifest no freedom—Being, with sensation, but no want, could not will—Knowledge, to be available for willing, must extend to the future—The lowest order of intelligence, admitting of will, is that with one want and one known means of gratifying it, and this intuitive—Instinctive action still voluntary and free—And free, not merely as not counteracted—In the instinctive, the spheres of knowledge and freedom reach their minimum, but are still coëxistent—But for the element of knowledge, instinctive action would be mechanical—*Conceivable* that first instinctive actions may be mechanical—Knowledge that we can will, and how to will, and that by will we can produce change in ourselves, could not be taught by practical examples, but must be intuitive—Hence, not mechanical—All the requisites of will incorporated in our being—Instinct may bring the infant within easy effort of its object—Absence of deliberation in intuitive action—Muscular action the basis of our plans for external change—Bodily movement always instinctive—This is the point from which instinctive and rational actions take their departure—In the instinctive, not only the mode of making the action, but the plan, the successive order of volitions, is intuitively known—Inferior free agents may still subserve the purposes of a superior—Conflicting modes and wants are cases for the exercise of judgment—Imitative actions diverging from instinctive—Distinguishing features of instinctive action—Some cases of rational action liable to be confounded with instinctive—When we are conscious of forming a plan of action this does not occur—When we work from memory of a plan, intuitive or acquired, it is HABIT—Peculiar characteristics of habit—Similarity of instinctive and habitual action—Analogy of habitual to mechanical action—Rational actions, in becoming habitual, approach the instinctive—Customary actions belong to the same group—Recapitulation of actions, mechanical, instinctive, rational, customary, and habitual—Habit has same relation to

CONTENTS. xi

PAGE

action that memory has to knowledge, and depends on memory and association—That habit applies to actions which we have most frequent occasion to perform, increases its benefits, yet often regarded as a vice of the mind—Reasons why it is so regarded.

CHAPTER XII.—ILLUSTRATION FROM CHESS, ... 126

Known laws of the game somewhat analogous to intuitive knowledge—First moves *may* be habitual—Subsequently the player deliberately forms preconceptions and compares them—Does not examine every possible move, but determines how long to examine by an exercise of judgment—Each volition to move the same as if he had never before moved—A more complicated game supposed, more nearly resembling that of real life—The skilful succeed against many opponents ; and Infinite Wisdom would accomplish Its end though opposed by any number of finite intelligences, all acting as freely as itself—The uninitiated see no order or design in the game—It is a creation having its own laws—Automaton chess-player—But for the uniformity of God's actions, the efforts of finite agents would be impossible—Case in which, by the laws of the game, only one move is possible, and analogous cases in real life—Compliance with the laws of the game, as with the laws of God, may become habitual, but this does not conflict with freedom—Influence of law on individual action—The word law, in such cases, used in two distinct senses, but the knowledge of the law, in either sense, important in deciding our efforts.

CHAPTER XIII.—OF WANT AND EFFORT IN VARIOUS ORDERS OF INTELLIGENCE, ... 136

Want requisite to all but the lowest forms of animated existence—Imputation of want to the Supreme Being—A sole first cause, without want, would immediately become inert—Intelligence must have a retaining power and some adaptation to put its retained power in action—If matter is cause, no application of a self-moving power to it is possible—If the activity of any intelligence ceases, it cannot put itself in action again—No intelligent being can do anything unless it makes effort to do something—Want rouses the mind to effort, but does not direct the effort—Effort the condition of cause in the Infinite as in the finite being—Some cause with power to produce change, which it does not of necessity immediately exert, is necessary—Mind and matter in motion the only such causes conceivable—The existence of God cannot, of itself, be the cause of anything which ever began to be—Effort makes the distinction between that condition of a being in which it seeks to produce change and that in which it does not—If in the Supreme Being there is no such distinction, all effects must be independent of His action—Reasons why it is thought Omnipotence may produce effects without effort—Omnipotence has its bound in the absolutely impossible—Want has with it the germ of its own gratification—Man may design change, and make effort to actualize his design, though no other intelligence or power in existence—The *mode* of connection between volitions and their sequences not important to the act of will.

CHAPTER XIV.—OF EFFORT FOR INTERNAL CHANGE, ... 145

Question stated—Do we produce the sequences of volition?—The important fact is, that our volitions are necessary to them—*Effects* of effort for internal change as uniform and as inscrutible as for external—We can induce spiritual as well as physical want, but cannot *directly* will either into existence—Increasing our knowledge the only means for this, and, though it may sometimes have the opposite effect, is still the only mode—Constitutional occurrence and recurrence of our spiritual wants—Want the source of effort for internal changes in all intelligent beings—General moral evil and individual depravity—Man's knowledge infallible as to what, for him, is morally right—Directs his efforts for internal change by means of his preconceptions—In forming these, need not recognize existing circumstances—An advantage of the purely ideal conceptions—In the moral nature the willing is the consummation, and hence, in it, mind is a *supreme* creative first cause—Distinction between effort in the moral sphere and out of it—A man who does not want to be pure and noble may begin with the want to want to be pure and noble—Virtue all lies in the effort, and not in its sequence—Not any present moral wrong in want, or knowledge, and hence all moral right and wrong concentrated in the act of will—Efforts to be pure and noble may become habitual—We may indirectly discard a want—A being with no want for what is unholy cannot be unholy—Cannot will what is contradictory to its own nature—Though many of our moral wants are innate, they may be cultivated, enabling us to influence our moral characteristics at their source—Conclusion from the foregoing, that man in the sphere of his moral nature is a supreme and a sole creative first cause—Man's will infinite, but limited in its range, because his power of conception is finite—This power may forever increase—Man responsible and accountable for his acts of will.

CHAPTER XV.—CONCLUSION, ... 161

Recapitulation of the previous results and leading positions—Wants seemingly insignificant may be the basis of contests for the mastery of empires—Man bountifully provided with wants—Physical wants temporary—Made less inconstant by the secondary want of acquisition—They are preliminary to the soul's progress, teaching effort; though this provision is often counteracted by acquisitiveness with a material bias—Spiritual want essential—Early ideal constructions and influence of the romantic passion—" Castle building "—The interest which attaches to the products of our labor—Influence of wants not left to accidental occurrences—Recurrence of both spiritual and bodily wants amply provided for—Each has within himself an inchoate and, to him, a boundless universe, which is his especial sphere of creative action—Constructing this universe within himself the principal, if not the sole end of life.

BOOK II.

REVIEW OF EDWARDS ON THE WILL.

INTRODUCTION, ... 173

CHAPTER I.—EDWARDS'S DEFINITION OF WILL, ... 177

Edwards's definition of will—He identifies volition with choice and preference, and willing with choosing and preferring—His definition admits of vari-

PAGE

ous constructions—Confounds the process of choosing with the result of the process—Also asserts that an act of choice is a comparative act of the mind—Proof that the comparative act is not itself the act of choice, and that the choice, which in some cases is the result of a comparative act, is not an act of will, but is knowledge—The choice to will preceding the act of will considered—Edwards's definitions of choice as an act of will, and also as the result of a comparative act, involve an absurdity—In making choice an act of will, he makes it the last act of the mind in relation to the effect intended—Cases mentioned by Edwards in which the soul would rather *have* or *do* distinguishable, and the question whether choice is ever an act of will, examined—Edwards's use of the word choice confounds the understanding with the will—Further proof that choice is knowledge, and not act of will—Sophism admitted by making choice a synonym for will—Difficulties encountered by Edwards, growing out of his definition—Difference in a man's preferring to walk and preferring to fly—Edwards constrained to admit exertion, but having no space between choice and effect, must crowd it into one or the other—My views applied to explain the difference of the cases of preferring to walk and preferring to fly—Edwards's intention to use the word choice in its popular sense—Recapitulation.

CHAPTER II.—LIBERTY AS DEFINED BY EDWARDS, ... 201

Edwards asserts that the only liberty in man is power " to *do* as he pleases," or " conducting as he wills "—This places liberty in that in the doing of which we are not conscious of having any agency—In this case the mind has no liberty in willing, and the definition begs the question—The hypothesis that the willing is itself a doing considered.

CHAPTER III.—NATURAL AND MORAL NECESSITY, ... 204

Edwards's definitions of these terms—Much confusion from vague use of some of the terms—Every intelligent being with will a distinct cause—Hence our will cannot change the course of nature, except by being an independent cause—God's action or the counter-willing of finite minds may, either of them, control or influence the effect intended by another, without interfering with the freedom of that other in willing—The argument is rather against the freedom of man in *doing* than in *willing*—Edwards's definition admits three distinct intelligent causes, each acting freely—The term "*necessity*" used in different senses in defining natural and moral necessity—Edwards makes "motive" a cause, producing volition, or makes human volitions the direct action of God—The argument from these definitions stated—The hypothesis, that the same causes of necessity produce the same effects, essential to it—It assumes that human volitions are a part of a necessary chain of events—Yet asserts that the mind encounters difficulties in bringing them to pass—The assumption that the human will is finite shown to be an error, and especially if it is "*choice*"—Supposed difficulty in willing examined, and found not to be in the willing, but in finding or knowing what to will—The martyr and the craven equally free in willing—Difference in action indicates difference in character—Modes in which we form our own characters and aid each other in doing it—The difficulty spoken of by Edwards consists in the conflict between present pleasure, and right or future good—That a man may will against such convic-

PAGE

tions may prove that he is not pure and wise, but not that he is not free—The particular cases of moral inability stated by Edwards—Examination of those cases—All analogous to those of inability to will, because there is no want—Inability to will what we do not want to will is not against freedom—No reason to suppose that a *previous* bias or inclination will prevail over the present in the act of will—If it does, it is because the biased or inclined mind itself controls the act of will—As in the case of "nature of things," Edwards makes "habit" a power, or cause—No certainty and no necessity that habits will continue—Habits of a man influence his act of will only in case he wills freely —Man is said to be a slave to his habits; reasons why—The argument from moral necessity only proves that a man wills in conformity to what he wills, and natural necessity only implies that he cannot always execute what he wills.

CHAPTER IV.—SELF-DETERMINATION, ... 233

The argument against the self-determining power of the will irrelevant to my position—Edwards's statement of his argument against the soul's determining its volitions *in* the exercise of its power of willing—From which it can only be inferred, that whatever is true of acts of will is true of acts of choice— Changing the word "*in*" to "*by*" vitiates the argument—Confusion from using choice as the process of choosing, and also as the result of the process, and "mind" and "will" as equivalents—Edwards does not recognize mind as cause—There must be something to move the mind, as it does not act without a reason—Edwards finds this prime mover in his "motives;" I have ascribed it to "want"—Control, by a previous act of will, fatal to freedom in the present act—Edwards's favorite reductio ad absurdum that a self-determined or free act admits of no first free act, fallacious.

CHAPTER V.—NO EVENT WITHOUT A CAUSE, ... 240

Edwards says he applies the word cause to what has no positive influence— This facilitates his proof, but makes it unavailing for his purpose—Edwards's positions being admitted, if mind is itself cause, they prove its freedom in willing—He assumes that the cause of a volition must be not only without the volition, but without the mind that wills—If the act of mind, as cause, must have a cause, for the reason that everything which begins to be must have a cause, there can be no first act of cause—The soul itself, being the cause of its volitions, is not, in them, the subject of effects which have no cause—The question why the soul exerts such an act and not another considered—Examination of Edwards's position that "activity of nature" cannot be the cause why the mind's action is thus and thus determined—This argument also vitiated by changing *in* to *by*, or by assuming that of two terms expressing the same thing one is the cause of the other—Volition cannot be determined by the "past."

CHAPTER VI.—OF THE WILL'S DETERMINING IN THINGS INDIFFERENT, . 259

Edwards's statement of the question imperfect, though warranted by extracts from his opponents—As he states it, *one* thing is indifferent, and *another* chooses—Other of his arguments founded on his assumption that will and choice are identical—His use of the phrase "determining power" ambiguous, applying either to mind or will—Another statement of the argument—Ed-

CONTENTS.   xv

PAGE

wards supposes the mind to devise a way of getting itself out of a state of indifference, and illustrates by the touching of one of the squares of a chess board—His argument denies that the mind can get itself out of a state of indifference, yet begins by showing how it can do so—Mind's doing, indirectly by volition, what it cannot do directly, is not against its freedom—In this case such indirection (the giving itself up to accident) does not obviate the supposed difficulty, but increases it—Just as difficult for the mind to determine what accident as what square of the chess board—Edwards might as well have made the movement of the finger as the movement of the eye determine the square to be touched—In either case, the difficulty of indifference may recur—There is the same difficulty of indifference in applying the accident, even if it can be selected—The whole causal efficacy must be, not in the accident, but in the rule which the mind makes to apply it, in doing which it again encounters indifference—The mind can as well make the rule to touch a particular square without the accident as with it—The whole efficacy of the proposed plan is in the mind's *governing itself* by an arbitrary rule which itself has created—The indirection would not aid the argument for necessity, but these supposed cases of indifference militate against it—If choice, among the objects of effort, is essential to will, a man never could will if there was only one object—Not necessary to an act of will that we should select, or choose even, among objects which we know to be different—The bearing of the views elicited in Book I. on this question—Similarity of cases of indifference and those of *wanting* to will—The apparent analogy of Edwards's mode of deciding them to that of deciding between parties having equal claims—But this would as well be accomplished by a direct act of will—If decided by lot, or accident, an arbitrary rule must still be made—Analogy of the cases of indifference to matter kept at rest by equal counter forces.

CHAPTER VII.—RELATION OF INDIFFERENCE TO FREEDOM IN WILLING, . 284

Edwards uses the term indifference as directly opposed to preference—His argument against the soul's sovereign power in certain cases, only proves that if the soul wills when it does not will, then its willing is not wholly owing to itself—Much confusion from using the term inclination as identical with will, and yet as something which goes before it—Another of his arguments only proves that the mind is not free in willing when it is not willing at all—And this and the subsequent reasoning only proves that the mind cannot both will and not will at the same time—His statement that a *free* act of will cannot immediately arise out of a state of indifference, considered—He assumes that choice is a necessary element of free will—Argument thus far avails only on certain inadmissible premises, and has little application to my positions—For the purposes of this argument, Edwards's assumption that choice is a pre-requisite of a free act of will may be admitted—Form in which this admission may be most plausibly used against freedom—The essential element of free action is not choice, but self-direction—Suspending volition—Edwards assumes that suspending volition must be an act of volition—If so, the mind never can stop willing, for suspending its willing is only another willing—Even then the mind could suspend action in one direction by acting in another—And liberty in every action might still be maintained—What is meant by suspending an act of will—Illustrations from reading aloud—Do we will either to will or not

PAGE

to will ?—Nearest approach to willing to will is when we want exercise for the faculty of will and act capriciously—Indifference indicates the point of departure from the passive to the active state ; perfect in the non-active state of profound sleep—Vigilance of the mind as to changes about it which may call for effort—Effort to find what changes are taking place, or what action these changes require, is ATTENTION—To know these changes does not always require effort—Changes often occurring and requiring no action, as the striking of a clock, are immediately forgotten—Reason why monotonous sounds favor reverie and the concentration of the mind in abstract thought.

CHAPTER VIII.—CONTINGENCE, ... 313

Treated by Edwards in Part II., sections 8 and 9—If mind is the cause of its acts of will, then Edwards's argument only proves that they are necessarily connected with mind, and not that mind is not free—Edwards absurdly argues that the mind is not free in the act of willing, because the act of will is connected with the mind—His argument also involves the contradiction that mind is not free, because it cannot be otherwise than free—In chapter xiii. applies similar reasoning to prove that if the will controls itself it cannot be free, because controlled by itself—Fallacy of this and preceding argument—From the position that every effect is dependent on its cause, Edwards infers, not that the *effect*, but that the action of the *cause* is necessitated—Necessary futility of reasoning on his statement, which really only asserts that a man wills what he wills—The hypothesis that there are other mental faculties which influence the will considered in its relation to the mind's freedom in willing—Edwards's argument denies the possibility of this ; but with more reason it might be said that all cause is of necessity free—Even matter in motion is not constrained or restrained till it comes to the producing of an effect—Any force or power subject to extrinsic control is an implement rather than a cause—Essential difference in the freedom of intelligent and material causes.

CHAPTER IX.—CONNECTION OF THE WILL WITH THE UNDERSTANDING, . 323

Sometimes the last dictate is neither an act of will nor followed by an act of will—If will is choice, it never follows the last dictate of the understanding—If it does, still not against the mind's freedom or self-determining power in willing—Edwards attempts to prove that the will, as a distinct entity, is not free—Act of will not always necessary to the mind's attention—Mind may begin by an effort to obtain the requisite knowledge, or may direct its action by a simple perception of it—Edwards's position in regard to the will's following the last dictate of the understanding really confirms the freedom of mind in willing.

CHAPTER X.—MOTIVE, ... 327

Statement of Edwards's argument on motive—Varies his definition of will to accommodate the argument—His argument, even admitting his definition of will, is still fallacious—His definition of motive amounts only to "that which is a motive is a motive"—As impossible to deduce any new truth from such definition as from the expression "whatever is, is"—The argument, as he states it, does not contravene that of his opponents—The difficulty is radical, arising from defining motive not by what it is, but by what it must do—To

PAGE

conform to the definition and admit the deduction of necessity, the motive must control the mind—The motive cannot itself determine that it is the strongest—This must be done by the intelligent being that wills—His positions involve an infinite series with no beginning—That the mind has in itself, or its own view, a motive, no reason why it does not act freely—Whether motives prove necessity or freedom must depend on their character or influence—Edwards uses "motive" sometimes as meaning the *mind's view* of an object, and at others the *object* viewed—The assertion that the mind is governed by its own views affirms its freedom—The point that, if the mind determines itself by its own view, the object viewed is still essential to that view, considered—The existence of objects of choice cannot be a reason why the mind does not will freely—Freedom does not imply a power to make existing circumstances different from what they are at the time—Classification of objects, which may possibly be motives, under Edwards's definition—These considered in their order—Vague popular notions in regard to the influence of circumstances—Particular cases, as stated by Edwards, make motive the mind's view of the future effects of its own action—Inquiry as to the meaning of "previous tendency"—The argument again leads to an infinite series, and makes the act of (will) choice before that by which the mind chooses has acted—In Edwards's system, motive, or previous tendency of motive, must be an act of choice springing directly out of a state of indifference—Same difficulty in regard to motive which Edwards finds in regard to will—This difficulty attaches to every system which does not recognize a self-moving power or cause.

CHAPTER XI.—CAUSE AND EFFECT, ... 364

The argument of Edwards assumes that the same causes of *necessity* produce the same effects—If the same cause never acted twice there could be no application of the rule—The law is deduced from observation, and cannot be of metaphysical necessity—No reason to suppose the law goes farther than our observations indicate—That there is no general rule without exceptions, conflicts with it—No reason to suppose that God may not vary from any law of uniformity which he has established for His own government—That He is omniscient obviates the *necessity* of trying different modes—In mind, observation does not indicate any such law—To all appearance, different minds act differently, and even the same mind changes its mode in similar circumstances—No case can arise for the application of the rule to mind—Under such rule a sole First Cause never could have produced but one effect—The application of this rule to intelligent cause denies any continuing power to produce changes in the universe—As applied to God, the rule can only mean that He has adopted uniform rules for His government—The finite mind, after having tried one mode, may, upon the recurrence of the same circumstances, try another—As used by Edwards, the law of cause and effect involves an infinite series with no beginning of action—There must be some cause which has power to change itself as cause, or to vary its effects—Changes in matter must be referred to an intelligent will—Some things may have been made not uniform, to vary the problems of life, for the development of the finite intelligence—No difficulty in supposing that the finite mind may be a first or originating cause—If mind is cause, the necessity of volition as its *effect* does not prove that mind is not free—The *uniformity* of God's action is necessary to and argues the existence of

PAGE

finite free agents—The argument that, if the same circumstances occur a thousand times to mind in the same condition, its action will be the same, examined.

CHAPTER XII.—GOD'S FOREKNOWLEDGE, ... 384

Edwards argues that the acts of the will must be necessary, because God foreknows them—Unavailing reply to this—An event foreknown by infallible prescience must be as certain in the future as if known by infallible memory in the past, and God's *foreknowledge* of *free volitions* is contradictory—The other link in the argument of Edwards, that God *must* foreknow, denied—Edwards's position that, without foreknowledge of men's volitions, God could not be able properly to govern the universe—His argument goes rather to disprove freedom in executing the volitions than in the volitions themselves—God, foreknowing all the effects of human volition which are possible, can provide in advance for any contingence—That He may do this without deviating from uniform modes of action, illustrated by an automatic chess-board—He may also deviate from such uniformity in miracles—And, in many things, we do not know that He has established any uniformity—Foreknowledge, for the purpose of making seasonable provision, not necessary when the power is infinite—Foreknowledge of God has the same relation to His actions that preconceptions of man have to his.

CHAPTER XIII.—CONCLUSION, ... 401

Recapitulation of the argument—Edwards's erroneous and incompatible definitions of Will and Choice—His favorite reductio ad absurdum and various sophisms founded on these errors—His error in defining Freedom—His argument from Moral Necessity and Moral Inability, and supposed difficulties in willing—His argument from the connection of volition with a prior cause—Motive—Habit as a motive—Assumption that the same causes necessarily produce the same effects—Indifference and Contingence—Last dictate of the understanding—Willing in cases of indifference—Foreknowledge—Edwards's idea of it would deprive God of the highest attributes of creative intelligence.

BOOK I.

FREEDOM OF MIND IN WILLING.

BOOK I.

FREEDOM OF MIND IN WILLING.

CHAPTER I.

OF THE EXISTENCE OF SPIRIT.

EVERY argument has its postulates. We cannot reason from the known to the unknown, unless something be first known. Of all that we believe, nothing is more certain than the existence of belief itself, constituting knowledge; and, of this knowledge the belief that there is some existence which believes, stands in the first rank; and, next in order, a belief in a plurality of existences, which, of necessity, implies that each of the existences, constituting this plurality, has peculiar and distinguishing characteristics, otherwise it would be identical with some other existence. It would not add to the number of existences; and, if none possessed distinguishing attributes or conditions, there could be only one existence. In such case, if space is a necessary existence, all other existence would become impossible. Even if space were homogeneously filled, that which fills must, in some way, be different from that which is filled. Time itself would be excluded. It may then reasonably be assumed not only that the belief in the plurality of existences itself exists, but that it is well founded. In this plurality there is nothing of which we have more convincing proof than of the existence of sensation, emotion, want, and of effort to supply want, of all which we are conscious.

Perhaps we cannot logically deduce from this any separate existence, which knows, feels and acts, but it is at least certain, that this knowledge, sensation and effort are, in some way, so far associated as to justify us in speaking of them as one combination; and, in doing this, each individual combination of them is denominated a spirit, an intelligence, mind, or soul, of which the attributes of knowing, feeling and acting are distinguishing characteristics. As present with this mind, or soul, yet distinct from it, we associate the idea of a particular *form*, which, with the soul, constitutes what each expresses by the term, " I." This idea of form is not essential to our conception of mind, or spirit, the attributes of which may be conceived of as entirely independent of such association, or as purely intelligent being, or beings.

Among our sensations are some which each individual finds he can himself produce. He can, by certain efforts, produce the various sensations known as muscular movements, the sound of a bell, &c.; and hence knows his own power to produce effects. But he finds the sensation is sometimes produced without any effort of his own, and hence he infers a cause, or power without himself; and most naturally attributing the effect to a power similar to that which in himself produces similar effect,—to another finite intelligence,—he gets the idea of the existence of other finite minds. It is, perhaps, hardly necessary here to remark, that although through the sensations of sight we may have an immediate perception of other *forms* like our own, still, the belief that other similar *beings* are associated with, or represented by such forms, is an inference from the visual sensation, in connection with other facts. We draw no such inference from our image in a mirror, or from any other object known to be lifeless, however nearly resembling the human form.

But, among our sensations, are some, which we find we have no power to produce, or very insufficient power; and hence we infer the existence of a power without ourselves, greatly exceeding our own; so incomparably surpassing it, that we term it *infinite*. Strictly speaking, the evidence as first presented to us, only proves the existence of a power capable of producing the sensations of which we are conscious; but every new observation revealing greater and greater power, and power far beyond what we had previously conceived, lays the foundation for a belief that the power is unlimited, and that any apparent limitation to it is in our own finite powers of observation and conception. Or, to put it in another form, the constant effect of the enlargement of our own observations and conceptions having always been to make the limit of this external power appear more remote, there is no reason to suppose that a further enlargement of them, to any finite extent, would bring us nearer to that limit; and hence, so far as our experience goes, we may, if not with strict logical accuracy, yet without danger of its leading us into philosophical error, apply the term *infinite* to the Supreme Intelligence. A power, which can accomplish everything conceivable to us as within the province of power, is, to us, the same as if it were infinite. It has, for us, no conceivable limit.

The inference, by which the finite intelligence argues the existence of other similar intelligences, is not one of absolute necessity; for all the phenomena,—the sensations,—which he ascribes to their agency, may be produced in him by the Infinite,—the greater including the less. But the exhibition of weaknesses and imperfections like his own, and which are incompatible with the Infinite; and the repeated coincidence, or frequent association of these phenomena with the presence of forms similar to, yet differing more or less from that which he associates with his own being, and in which changes resembling his own external actions take place, give preponderance to the hypothesis of the existence of *other* and numerous finite intelligences, distinct from his own. In the absence of any reason to the contrary, it is rational to suppose things *really* to be as they *appear* to be.

So far, then, we may be said to have arrived at the knowledge of the existence of our own finite intelligence; of other similar finite intelligences; and of the Supreme, or Infinite Intelligence. We have come to know ourselves, our fellow beings, and God, as powers producing certain effects, as being CAUSE.

CHAPTER II.

OF THE EXISTENCE OF MATTER.

WE know nothing of matter except by the sensations, which we impute to its agency, mediately, or immediately; and as those sensations can exist in the mind without the intervention of the external, material forms, or forces, to which we impute them, the sensations are not conclusive evidence of any such external existence. In dreams, and especially in nightmare, we have as vivid sensations of what we afterward find had no corresponding external materiality, as we ever have under any circumstances. If this arises from the excited action of our own memory and imagination, it merely proves that the mind, under certain conditions, has a power of reproducing what has before been impressed upon it by some external power, and at the same time of varying the combinations in which they before existed. This does not conflict with the position that, as the sensations may exist without the intervention of matter, the sensations are not evidence that matter exists.

All the sensations which we attribute to matter, are as fully accounted for by the hypothesis that they are the thought, the imagery of God *directly* imparted, or made palpable to our finite minds, as by the hypothesis of a distinct external substance, in which He has moulded this thought and imagery. If God, with design, created or fashioned matter in the forms presented to us, then these forms are but the result of thoughts and conceptions existing, or which existed in His mind; and the only question is, does He impart or impress them directly and immediately upon our finite minds; or indirectly and mediately, by first writing, picturing, moulding, or carving them out in a distinct substance called matter? In either case it is to us equally *real;* the sensations, by which alone we know these, to us, external phenomena, being the same. The hypothesis that the material forms are but the imagery of the mind of God made palpable to us, is the more simple of the two, and makes creative attributes more nearly accord with powers which we are ourselves conscious of exercising.

We cannot infer the existence of matter as an entity distinct from spirit, from any necessity of spirit for something to act upon; our conceptions of it serving for this purpose, as well as any such distinct existence could do; and, indeed, being all that we can employ the faculties and attributes of spirit upon. The whole science of Geometry, which, being the science of quantity, or extension,—one of the attributes of matter,—may be deemed as emphatically a material science, is entirely founded on such conceptions; and, in fact, on such conceptions as we get no accurate sensations of from without; for, not to insist that no one ever had a sensation of such abstractions as a mathematical point, or line, we may assert that no one ever had a sensation from matter of a perfect mathematical form, for instance, of a perfect circle. It is a conception of the mind, and for the purposes of mathematical reasoning, is a *creation* of the mind, brought into existence by actualizing this conception in a definition; and for these purposes, whatever conforms to that definition is a circle, and what does not so conform is not a circle. The reasoning is wholly based on the *definition* of our *conceptions* of form, and not on any actual existence, or sensation of such forms in matter, which are never sufficiently accurate to rest such reasoning upon; and hence, mathematics is really a hypothetical science, and would be equally true if there were no material forms even bearing any resemblance to the conceptions of the mind brought out in its definitions. The science of mechanics, too, is founded on our *conceptions* of resistance and forces, as solidity, inertia, momentum; and does not involve the question as to what these forces really are.*

To adopt the hypothesis, that our sensations of what is external are but the conceptions of God, made directly palpable to us, and ignore matter entirely, would free the subject of the *freedom of intelligence* from some apparent, if not real difficulties; and would, at the same time, avoid much confusion, which I apprehend has been occasioned by the close and various associations of matter with spirit. We should then have only to consider the action of intelligence in its finite and infinite forms. But as either hypothesis accounts for all the phenomena, the fact that one is more simple and that it makes the process of material creation more comprehensible to us is not, perhaps, even with our experience in dreams, a sufficient reason for presuming that matter does not exist as an entity distinct from mind

---

* See Appendix, Note I. at the end of the volume.

and with the properties which our sensations indicate. We may remark, however, that, supposing the Infinite Intelligence to fashion and control this matter, it would make no difference as to the question of our freedom; for, in that case, the real phenomena would be the same,—the thought and imagery of the mind of God—and the only question would be as to which of the two modes He has adopted in communicating that thought and in making that imagery palpable to us. We may further remark that, with the testimony of our senses on the one hand, and on the other, the consideration that the *imagery* of the mind of God is not in itself intelligent, but an effect of intelligence in action, we may assume, in either case, that matter is in itself unintelligent and inert. Admitting, then, for the purposes of the argument, the existence of matter as distinct from spirit, we will, in a subsequent chapter, inquire how far it can produce effects, or be CAUSE.

CHAPTER III.

OF MIND.

MIND has feeling, knowledge, volition. It is susceptible of sensation and emotion; has a simple perceptive attribute by which it directly acquires knowledge; and a faculty of will, through which it manifests its power to produce, or to try to produce change.

Our sensations and emotions are not dependent upon the will. We hear the sound of a cannon, whether we will to hear it or not; and can neither avoid, nor produce the emotions of joy or sorrow by merely willing it. We may, by effort, bring about the conditions precedent to a particular sensation or emotion; but, the conditions being the same, whether they exist by our own act, or from some other cause, makes no difference as to the effect.* Our knowledge is also independent of the will. We cannot know, or believe anything by simply willing to know, or believe it. If I have a sensation of seeing a tree, I cannot by any act of will believe that I have no such sensation, or that I have the sensation of seeing a rock instead. So, too, if in the relations of my ideas, I perceive certain truths, as that $2+2=4$, I cannot at will disbelieve or not know such

* See Appendix, Note II.

truths. By will I can bring about the conditions favorable to the increase of knowledge, but I cannot thus determine what shall become known. I may, by effort, remove an external obstruction to sight and thus be enabled to see what was behind it; but I cannot, by will, determine what it is that I shall then see. So also I may by effort arrange and compare my ideas, so that some truth, which before was hidden, will become obvious; but I cannot will what that truth, when discovered, will be. In both of these, and in all other cases, the discovery of the objects, or of the abstract truths, and the consequent addition to our knowledge, is, in the last analysis, a *simple mental perception;* and all our efforts to acquire knowledge are only to make such external changes in matter, or so to arrange our ideas, as to bring the truth within reach of the simple perceptive attribute of the mind.

From the foregoing it appears that feeling, whether in sensation or emotion, is rather a *property*, or *susceptibility*, than a *faculty* of being. So also the ability to acquire knowledge is a capacity, or a sense, rather than a faculty.

Our sensations, emotions, and knowledge, at the time being, are actual present existences, in common with all others now actually existing,—independent of the will. Having become existent, whether by the agency of will, or otherwise, such existence cannot, by will, be changed, *in the present*, any more than what existed in the past can be so changed. Whenever we seek to produce any change, it must be with reference to the future, and this is always by will. Whenever by the exercise of our own power we try to influence the course of events, we will. When by effort we recall the knowledge of the past, the *recalling* is still an event *future* to the effort.

There are other attributes, or modes of mind, which are often spoken of as if they were distinct faculties, or active agents, having *power* of themselves to *do* certain things. In this category we may embrace memory, judgment, reasoning, imagination, conception, and perhaps, also association. These are all names of some form of knowledge, or of some mode of mental action to acquire, or reproduce it. The forms of knowledge, to which they are applied, are actual present existences, not subject to the will. Our memories of the past, our observation of the present, and our anticipations of the future are all, when reached, but present knowledge. When, from any cause, the knowledge of the past, the present, or the future is perceived by the mind, it is a simple mental perception. When we make effort to produce such changes, internal or external, as will bring any knowledges within the mind's view, it is an act of will, a trying to *do* something. So that, in all cases, the names of these supposed faculties only indicate actual existing knowledge, or its acquisition by simple mental perception, or by acts of will to produce those changes which will bring knowledge within reach of this simple mental perception. These acts of will differ from each other either in their mode, or in their object. Memory, for instance, is but a condition, and a necessary condition, of knowledge of the past. Without it such knowledge could not exist. In this sense it is only an expression of one form of our knowledge. To say, *I remember an event*, is to say, *I know an event in the past.* If, from any cause, an event of the past comes before the mind it is then a simple mental perception. When we make effort to bring an event of the past into the mind's view we call it an exercise, or *effort* of *memory*, and this, of course, is an act of will, a *trying to do* this thing.

So likewise the term judgment may express the mind's conclusion as to the equality, or superiority of one thing, or method as compared with another ; or as to the truth, or error of a proposition. And such conclusion is a simple mental perception ; while any effort in comparing, examining, &c., by which we seek to bring about the conditions favoring such perception, is called an exercise, or effort of judgment, which, is another act of will.

The same may be said of reasoning, imagining, conceiving, &c. In the sense in which these are spoken of as faculties, or powers, they are but names of varied modes of effort, or of efforts for *different objects*, made by the same unit-mind, manifesting its power to produce change by its efforts, or acts of will.

Whether these supposed faculties are but names of varied acts of will, or otherwise, does not really affect the question of the *mind's freedom* in action; for, whether it act by a faculty called will, or by a faculty called judgment, would not affect its freedom in action so long as the faculty by which it thus acted pertained to its own being. If the question were, whether the will, considered as a distinct entity, were free, it might become important to inquire if there were any coördinate powers of mind by which it could be controlled. The introduction of these supposed faculties, as distinct powers, does, however, tend to complicate and confuse the argument as to the mind's freedom. In confirmation of the views already stated, it may be observed, that if acts of will are but efforts of the mind, and these faculties are exerted by the mind, it follows that they but indicate, or name different acts of will, or efforts of the same unit power—mind.

In further illustration that they are but names of these varied efforts, I would remark, that the *immediate object* of every act of will is to move some portion of the body, or to influence mental activity. In either case we are conscious only of the effort and the effect, and though we speak of bodily and mental efforts, we still recognize them *all* as efforts of the mind. In so speaking, we distinguish them not by the active agent, which is the same in all, but by the *immediate* object of the effort, or by the subjects of it, which, in some cases, are but instruments to accomplish remoter objects. Thus, when movement of the body, or of any portion of it, is the object, we speak of bodily, or muscular effort, and subdivide into efforts of the hand, the foot, &c.; while those efforts, of which the mind is the subject, we designate as mental efforts; and, as in these we are not conscious of distinct members as the *subjects* of our action, we subdivide, or classify by the *objects* sought, as efforts of memory, of judgment, of imagination, &c.*

By the phrase *bodily effort* we cannot mean to assert that the body is an active agent, itself making effort, but only that its movement is the *object* of the mental effort; and, in as close analogy to this as the case permits, the expressions, efforts of memory, of judgment and imagination, &c., only signify that the object of the effort is to remember, to judge, to imagine,

---

* See Appendix, Note III.

&c. In all, we recognize but varied efforts, or efforts for different objects, by the same unit-mind, without the intervention of any other powers; and all these efforts are but manifestations of the mind's action, varied in conformity with the objects, or changes it seeks to produce.

It may be objected to this dispensing with these alleged faculties, and considering them merely as names designating different modes of effort, or efforts for different objects, that they sometimes seem to act of themselves. Of this, memory is the most marked example. Our memories seem to rise unbidden before us, and in an order which we do not control. Now, as a present sensation is known by means of simple mental perception, without effort, it may so happen that the circumstances, which exist without our agency, may also bring the knowledge of the past within the reach of this same perception. This appears to be effected mainly, if not wholly, by means of association, which is an arrangement, or classification of our knowledge in conformity to some observed relation, as that of cause and effect, or of antecedent and consequent; or of some resemblance, in which last may be included similarity as to time, or place; and, by a slight extension, this will also embrace *contiguity* in time and space. But whatever the rule, or principle of association, it seems that through it, an idea, or sensation in the present may suggest others in the past without any effort. The sensation I now have of a tree in sight recalls, or causes me to remember a sensation I had last week of a tree then in sight; and this again suggests the fruit I saw upon it, &c. In this case, through external agencies—agencies not of the mind—the past knowledge has been brought within reach of the simple mental perception. As in the case of simple sensation, the mind has been the recipient of knowledge without any active agency of its own; and hence the case affords no ground to suppose an active agency in its memory, or in any other of its attributes.

These views seem to justify the conclusion that the mind has but one real faculty, or power to do anything, and this faculty is designated by the term *will;* that with this power it has a susceptibility to feeling, and also a capacity, or sense of simple mental perception, through which it becomes the recipient of knowledge; and that all knowledge, whether the result of preliminary effort, or otherwise, in the last analysis is a simple perception of the mind, and that all preliminary effort for its acquisition is only to bring about the conditions essential to such perception. We know that we have certain sensations without effort. We attribute some of these to the instrumentality of the bodily senses; but the sensation is in the mind; and it is not the bodily sense that *knows* of its existence. Nor does it require any act of will to know it; on the contrary, we cannot, by will, avoid knowing it. Here then is a faculty, or capacity of knowing; of simple mental perception, or assimilation, as independent of the will as sensation itself.

To proceed one step further; it is not the *bodily* sense which knows the *difference* between the sensations of black and white; or of sound and color; and we still are not *conscious* that to know this requires any effort. If we regard general and abstract ideas, instead of sensations, we may perhaps without previous effort know that what is, is; that the whole is greater than its part; that two parallel lines cannot cross each other; but we do not thus know that all the angles of every plane triangle are equal to two right angles; to ascertain this, requires effort.* There must then somewhere be a point at which acts of will become necessary to our acquisition of knowledge; but the mind cannot by such action determine, or vary the facts, or its own conclusions in regard to them. If it could, it would then have no idea of absolute truth. The last result; the finality of the process—the assimilation—being thus independent of the will, must come by the attribute of knowing, i. e. by simple mental perception; and the object of the effort of the mind is to recall and so vary and arrange either its previous knowledge, or things external to it, that the truths sought will come within the range and scope of its simple perceptive power; such effort, however, is not always needed, sensation sometimes performing this office, or the truths being in themselves obvious to simple perception, without effort. For instance, if an effort to remember is the effort to find some idea, which by association will recall, or lead through other associations to some particular knowledge of the past, this suggestive idea may sometimes be brought to mind by external events through sensation, without our effort; or it may arise in some train of thought, which we are pursuing for another purpose, without any intention or any effort to recall the past knowledge. In both cases the knowledge of the past is brought within reach of the mind's simple perceptive sense without effort for that end; and the memory *appears* to act spontaneously as an independent power. The facts, however, do not

* See Appendix, Note IV.

really conflict with the hypothesis that what we term an effort of memory is but a mode of effort of the mind, and that, in its efforts for recalling the past, prying into the future, or investigating abstract truth, it but exerts its own unit-power in different modes, and does not put *other* powers in action for that purpose.

When, for the purpose of ascertaining truth, or of determining action, we call up and examine other knowledge, we deliberate; and any conclusion, to which we thus come, is a judgment. This process may involve a secondary one of examining, or comparing various simple perceptions, which have resulted from various views of the subject, or from views of different portions of it. We often, and sometimes from the urgencies of the case, examine very hastily, while at others we do it very thoroughly. This leads us to speak of hasty conclusions and deliberate judgments, the latter being the result of the more full examination of our knowledge relating to the subject. Though this judgment is a result of an effort in the examination of our knowledge, it is immediately incorporated with and becomes a portion of it; in this respect not differing from facts, or any other addition to our knowledge, acquired by mere observation, or simple mental perception without previous effort. From the nature of the examination, or of the subject itself, these judgments vary from the slightest shade of probability to that of demonstrative certainty; and induce various grades of belief, from that of mere conjecture to confirmed knowledge; but, such as they are, we are often obliged to act upon them from want of time, or of ability to obtain better.

Of knowledge, obviously an important element in all intelligent cause, I will further remark, that I deem the term, in strict propriety, applicable only to those ideas, or perceptions of the mind of which we entertain no doubt; and that it is applicable to such, even though they are not conformable to truth; for, if we cannot say that we know that of which we have no doubt, there is nothing to which we can apply the term, and it is useless. This is liable to the objection that we may *know* what is not *true*. Knowledge is a certain condition of the mind; and there is no difference in this condition, whether we have an undoubted belief that $7 \times 6 = 41$, or that $2 \times 2 = 4$; the *knowledge* that $2 \times 2 = 4$, and the *fact* that $2 \times 2 = 4$, are distinct; and to make the latter a condition of the former is to define, or describe one thing, by attributing to it what belongs not to it, but to another distinct thing, which is unphilosophical, and leads to confusion.

When, however, I speak of the use which the mind makes of its knowledge in connection with its faculty of will, it is generally more convenient to embrace, in the one term, all its opinions and beliefs of every grade of probability, which, in the absence of certainty, it is often obliged to make the basis of action; and, in such cases, I use the term with this latitude.

Metaphysical certainty applies to that order of ideas and perceptions, or to that order of expressions, which we perceive to be necessarily true in their own nature, and the denial of which involves an obvious absurdity, or contradiction.

CHAPTER IV.

LIBERTY, OR FREEDOM.

These terms are, perhaps, as well understood as any by which we could directly define them. The opposing terms are compulsion, control, constraint and restraint; and when the term necessity, as the antithesis of liberty, or freedom, is applied to the action of the mind in willing, it must imply that such action is compelled, controlled, constrained, or restrained.

The question may arise, whether that which controls itself is free, or whether the fact of its being controlled, even though by itself, renders it not free. This question, in our present inquiry, concerns the action of the mind in willing; but we may say, generally, that everything, in moving, or in acting; in motion, or in action, must be directed and controlled in its motion, or in its action, by itself, or by something other than itself; and that, of these two conditions of every thing moving, or acting; or in motion, or action, the term freedom applies to the former rather than to the latter; and if the term freedom does not apply to that condition, it can have no application to the acting, or the action of anything whatever. And hence, self-control 'is but another expression for the freedom of that which acts, or of the active agent; and this is in conformity to the customary use and the popular idea of the term freedom.

CHAPTER V.

OF CAUSE.

The word Cause is variously used. I shall use it, in what I deem its most popular sense, as meaning anything which produces change. In this sense, four distinct kinds of causes are *conceivable:*

First, such as are both unintelligent and inactive; as a rock, which arrests the motion of a moving body, causing it to stop, or alter its direction. These we will call *inert* causes.

Secondly, unintelligent, but active causes; as a heavy body in motion, moving others in its course, but which does not intend, or know the effects it produces. These are *motor* causes.

Thirdly, causes which produce changes by their activity, and which are not only conscious of the changes, when produced, but can anticipate the effects of their activity, yet do not plan, or design the means, or modes of producing these effects; as the lower forms of intelligent agents. These are *instinctive* causes.

Fourthly, causes which produce changes by their activity, and not only anticipate and know the effects of their activity, but design and form plans to produce them. Of these God is the type. They are *originating*, or *designing* causes.

We might have divided the third class, making two others, one merely knowing the effects after they occur; the other only anticipating them; but as we know of none in which the two are uncombined, there is no necessity for including them in our classification.

I mention the four varieties, just named, as *conceivable* and as embraced in the popular notion of cause. Whether they are all real causes may be a question for further inquiry.

We have then, of material causes, two kinds, inert and motor. The inert becomes cause only by being first acted upon by the active, or motor cause. Each motor may also be inert cause in relation to other motor causes, as when one motor impinges against another, the effect, in some cases, may not be influenced by the motion of this other, but be the same as if it were inert.

We have of intelligent causes also two kinds, the instinctive and the designing. The former of these also becomes cause only by being first acted upon by the latter. The instinctive must first be informed by the designing cause, before it can become cause itself. The designing may include, or be associated with the instinctive; and, sometimes acting without exercising the faculties by which it is *capable* of designing, manifest itself at such times only as instinctive cause.

A definition, or statement is sometimes spoken of— I think improperly—as a cause, of which the logical consequence is the effect; as, for instance, the equality of the four sides of a square *causes* those opposite each other to be parallel. Such consequences are necessary, self-existent, or co-existent truths; which are *found*, or *discovered*, and not *caused*.

When we speak of *time's changes*, the expression is elliptical. We do not mean that the changes are effected by time itself as a cause; but by those causes of which the effects are gradual, and perceptible only after the lapse of some considerable periods of time.

CHAPTER VI.

OF THE WILL.

It is not unusual to speak of the will as a distinct entity, possessing and exercising certain powers. This produces much confusion in the argument on the "freedom of the will." It is obviously the *mind* that wills, as it is the mind that thinks; and we might with as much propriety speak of a thought, which thinks, as of a will, that wills. In treating of mind (Chap. III.) I have already stated that there is a passive state, in which, without any active agency of its own, it may be the subject of sensations, and the recipient of knowledge. Also, that in another condition it seeks, or endeavors to produce change by the active exercise of its power. In this the mind is said to will. Of these two conscious states of its existence, that of activity—that in which it strives to produce change—is a state of willing. The mind's willing, or its act of will, then, is the mind's effort; and WILL *is the power, or faculty of the mind for effort*. It is not a distinct thing, or instrument, which the mind uses, but is only a name for a power, which the mind possesses; and an *act of will* is that action, or mode in which intelligence exerts its power to do, or to try to do, and manifests itself as cause. The willing, or act of will, is the condition of the mind in effort, and is the only effort of which we are conscious. In each individual the efforts are all by the same active agent—by the intelligent being—by the mind—but are classified as bodily and mental efforts; the former being subdivided into efforts of the arm, the lungs, &c.; and the latter into efforts of memory, of judgment, of imagination, &c.*

Mind—intelligence—has no property, or attribute by which it can be inert cause. It may be the passive subject of change by other active agencies, but can itself be the cause of change only by the *exercise* of its power, i. e. by an *effort*. The existence of any mind with certain powers, may be among the circumstances which other intelligent agents take into consideration in their action, but it is only by its own effort that itself can *do* anything—that it can of itself produce any change, or be CAUSE. †

The mind has two very distinct spheres for the exercise of its activity—for its effort. In one it seeks to acquire knowledge; in the other to mould the future. In the first it analyzes, combines and compares its ideas; observes the present external; recalls the past, and, by this use of its present knowledge, acquires more. It can thus not only learn abstract truths, but is enabled, with more or less of certainty, to anticipate the course of events, and to perceive in what it would, by effort, try to alter that course. In both cases it seeks to affect the future; but in one case the effect is confined to changes in its own knowledge, to ascertain, or find what now is, has been, or will be; in the other, it seeks to affect the succession of events, to change what now is and influence what will be.

* See Appendix, Note V. † See Appendix, Note VI.

By means of its prophetic power, the mind reaches into that future in which by effort it seeks to produce effects. The success, or failure of the effort, however, cannot in any way affect the effort itself, which already has been. To the effects which the mind, by its activity, or effort, produces, it has the relation of cause, whether these effects were, or were not intended.

By its influence upon the future, however proximate, by its active agency in creating that future, mind manifests its originating, creative power. In this, its finite sphere, every finite intelligence, of every grade—having the faculty of will—is a finite first cause, as the Supreme Intelligence is Infinite First Cause, in its sphere of the infinite. The inquiry as to the truth of this position is involved in the question, *does the finite intelligence will freely?* which we are hereafter to examine.

CHAPTER VII.

OF WANT.

THE term *want* is probably better understood than any word, or phrase, which we could select to define, or explain it. Nothing is better known to us than our wants. We must, however, in the use of the term, carefully distinguish between the want and the thing wanted; between that present feeling, or condition, which is a state of want, and which we already have, and that which will gratify the want, and which, as yet, we have not. It is to the present condition, that I apply the term. We feel a painful sensation, or emotion, and *want* such *change* as will give relief. We find that we are ignorant on a point upon which knowledge is, or may become useful, and we *want* to know; and when, either from past experience, or intuition, we are conscious of the *absence* of a sensation, we may *want* that sensation.

A sensation, or emotion is not, in itself, a want; it may exist without any corresponding want. We may be content with it as it is. Nor is the perceived absence of a sensation, or emotion, of itself, a want; for we may be content with such absence. To get rid of an unpleasant sensation, which we have, or to induce an agreeable one, which we have not, are often the *things* wanted, but are not *themselves* the want. We have the sensation of hunger, and want food, but neither the sensation, nor the food is itself the want. In this case the food is the thing wanted, and the sensation is one of the conditions which causes us to want. This sensation, or emotion, in this, as in other cases, is to us an extension of knowledge, which requires on our part no effort.

That the idea of change is essential to the want is very obvious in cases in which some absent sensation is the thing wanted. When a present sensation is the subject, the want must either be to continue, to discard, or to modify that sensation; and even the want to continue requires the knowledge, or idea of possible change. So, too, an emotion is not in itself a want; a joy, which so satisfies the mind that it neither desires, nor thinks of change, cannot be said to be a want. And there is a grief—a holy and unselfish grief—of the elevating and hallowing influences of which we are so conscious, that we would not banish, or modify it. Our admiration may be so pleasurably excited by what appears to us already perfect, that no change is suggested, or wanted in the sensation, or the object. Wonder, of itself, involves no idea of change, and no want; and, under the emotion of awe, we reverently shrink from all thought, or anticipation of change.

Want involves an idea of change. We must, at least, be able to conceive that by some change in what exists, the pain we feel will be discarded, or the knowledge which we seek, or the pleasure we covet be acquired; though we may not know by what means the desired change is to be effected.

The existence then, of this idea of change, seems in

all cases to be an essential element of want. A man, entirely satisfied with things as they are, cannot properly be said to have a want. It is true, we say, that such a man *wants things to remain as they are.* The expression is really equivalent to saying he wants nothing, i. e. does not want—he is content. If it really expresses any want, it is the want of such change as will ensure things remaining as they are, and relieve him of any apprehension that they may not so remain. This can amount to no more than that, to make certain the continuance of some things as they are, he wants change in some other things; which is to say, he is not satisfied with things as they are.

It may be convenient to classify wants into primary, or those the gratification of which is the final object, or end in view; and secondary, or those which relate only to the intermediate *means* of such gratification, and to what is not in itself wanted. A man, in imminent danger, to get to a safe place, may want to walk, though every step is painful: to reach the place of safety is the primary want; to walk, in such case, the secondary. The lust of power is, perhaps, always a secondary want; being wanted not for itself, but as a means of gratifying other wants. These secondary wants, however, seem also to belong to the mind's perception of the means of gratifying its primary wants, and, as such, may with as much propriety be classified with its knowledge as with its wants. They are knowledge, or at least belief, that by some act, perhaps not in itself wanted, that which is wanted may be attained.

Again, wants may be divided into natural, acquired and cultivated. Natural wants are those which are innate, constitutional. Hunger, or the want of food is a natural want. But we may want to be hungry for the sake of the enjoyment which attends its gratification; and this want to be hungry, supposing it to grow out of the acquired knowledge that hunger is a basis of the enjoyment, may be said to be an acquired want. If we take exercise, or adopt other means to induce the want of food, such want may be said to be a cultivated want; and from this low, material form, our cultivated wants may rise to the most ethereal aspirations of our æsthetic, moral and religious nature. We speak of them merely as cultivated, for they still have their root in the constitution of our being; and we only use our knowledge of means to bring them out, or give them vitality and force, when they would, otherwise, be dormant or sluggish.

That which we have spoken of as a secondary want, is a consequence of our perception of what is necessary to gratify a primary want; and is thus the offspring of the primary want, and the knowledge of the means of gratifying it. As our primary wants and knowledge may exist without our volition, the consequent secondary want also may. We cannot, by an act of will, directly change the perceived fact, or our knowledge of the means essential to a particular result.

The natural, or innate want is obviously not an effect of volition. An acquired want must result from some increase of knowledge. If we made effort, and increased our knowledge for the purpose of acquiring this want, we must have previously wanted it, and the acquired want, in such case, was, before its acquisition, the thing wanted, and not the want which we sought to gratify. If we accidentally acquired such want without intending it, it has come without our willing it; and though it may have been a consequence of our efforts for some other purpose, it is such a consequence as we did not foresee, and for which we have made no effort. It may be such a result as, had we foreseen it, we would have opposed; but not having foreseen it, it is an effect, which we have neither favored, nor opposed. As the influence of an actually existing want upon the will is not varied by the source, or cause of its existence, it will not, in treating of it in this connection, often be necessary to allude to these distinctions.

CHAPTER VIII.

OF MATTER AS CAUSE.

WHATEVER changes take place in matter must arise from its motion, either massive, or atomic. But matter has no power to move itself; and hence cannot become cause of such change, except by first being in motion; and, even if imbued with locomotive powers, would have no knowledge to direct its movements to produce any *given* effect; and, if possessing both these attributes, being destitute of sensation and emotion, would have no inducement to make effort to produce any effect, supposing it also to have a faculty of will. It is plain then, that matter cannot be an originating cause, even of its own movements; and hence, if changes in it ever had a beginning, they must have originated with intelligence. I say, if they ever had a beginning; but we have still to inquire whether matter, even if once put in motion, could produce effects, or change other matter, or be affected, or changed by other matter, from the mere circumstance of its being itself in motion; in short, whether, in motion, matter becomes *cause*, originating effects, or prolonging, or extending the effects of any intelligent action, which may have put it in motion. The mere change of place by motion* cannot

---

* See Appendix, Note VII.

be considered as an *effect* of motion, but, rather, as the motion itself. If it is an effect of motion, cause and effect are here blended in one. The only reason why matter in motion can become cause of any other effect than that which took place immediately on the commencement of its motion, is, that by time and motion the circumstances become changed, though matter cannot intend, or know of this change. If, with motion, it can become cause, then, though it never could have commenced its own motion, yet, as in considering intelligence as cause, we are obliged to regard it, in the abstract, as a necessary existence, which had no beginning, so we might also suppose that matter had been in motion from eternity, and hence always had in itself causative power.

Whether matter in motion, can of itself produce effects, seems to depend mainly on another question, viz.: Does matter in motion, of necessity, have a tendency to continue in motion, or to stop the moment it is relieved from all impelling power? If I throw a ball, after it leaves my hand I can no longer control it; I make no effort to control it; it continues to move even though my attention is wholly withdrawn from it. But whether it does so move, because to stop requires change which, being mere matter, it cannot effect; or whether it continues to move in conformity to a law, which the Supreme Intelligence has adopted for its own government, and by which, in certain cases, it uniformly executes the decree, or causes certain effects to follow the effort of the finite mind, even after that effort has ceased; in brief, whether it continues to move by its own inherent material force, or by the action upon it of an invisible intelligence, or cause, is a question, which I can find no means of determining.

A particle of matter can begin no change in itself. When put in motion does it require change in itself to stop, or to continue its motion? If the former, then a moving body has in itself the amount of power which is required to stop it; and when it comes in collision with another body, as the two, by a law of metaphysical necessity, cannot occupy the same space, some effect must be produced; for instance, if moving in opposite directions, in the same line, one must be stopped, or turned back, or if the forces are equal we may, perhaps, infer that both must of necessity stop.

The ball thrown obliquely, after leaving my hand, if in vacuum, moves in a parabolic curve; or if resisted by the air, in an irregular curve. This, in either case, involves a continued *change* of direction, and it may be asked how matter, undirected by intelligence, can conform its changes of direction to these curves, or indeed, how change its direction at all? If, however, matter in motion has power to stop, retard, or change the motion of other bodies; or is liable to be stopped, retarded, or changed by them, it is conceivable, as has been suggested, that such change may be produced, and the projectile kept in the particular curve by particles of matter moving through space, and impinging on one side of the projectile, while the earth protects the other side from similar influence; once admit the self-existent, or inherent force, and its application is quite conceivable. The line of motion is changed from the parabolic to the irregular curve by the body itself impinging against the particles of the atmosphere.

As any force of matter in motion depends upon its

OF MATTER AS CAUSE. 35

supposed tendency to continue in motion; and it being evident that some of the bodies, coming in direct opposition to each other with equal force, must be stopped; and that matter has no power to put itself in motion again, it follows that the power of that portion thus stopped is annihilated; and the power of matter being thus continually diminishing, must, with *sufficient time*, be eventually destroyed, or, at least, be reduced to an infinitesimal quantity.*

But, if matter is an originating cause, or power, independent of intelligence, it must, as we have before shown, be so in virtue of having been in motion from all eternity; and hence, there having been *sufficient time*, its power, from the cause just mentioned, must have been destroyed. It follows then, that any power which matter may *now* have, in consequence of its being in motion—supposing it to have any—must be either the result of its having been put in motion within a finite time by intelligence, or from intelligence subsequently sustaining and renewing the motion, which may have been from eternity.† If this supposed power of matter in motion were left to act uncontrolled by intelligence, its blind activity would accelerate its self-destruction, and must, in some instances, counteract itself by opposition, while in others its effects would be increased by co-operation of the forces. The observed uniformity of material effects is inconsistent with this blind exercise of power; indicating that, even if matter now has, or has had power of itself, as cause, to produce effects, it has been subjected to an intelligent control—to a designing cause—and that all such effects are *now* the result of intelligent action.

* See Appendix, Note VIII. † See Appendix, Note IX.

The argument on this point may be thus stated: admitting the existence of matter as a distinct entity; and that it has always existed, we know, as a fact of observation, that the motion of one portion is always affected and often destroyed in producing effects upon other portions. Now, further admitting, that its original state was that of motion, it must always have been with its present conditions, or the original conditions of its motion must have been changed. If it commenced with the present conditions, which would continually lessen its motion, then, with sufficient time, and an eternity must be sufficient, its motion would be destroyed, or reduced to an infinitesimal and inappreciable quantity; and hence, on this supposition, the interference of some other—of intelligent cause—must have been necessary to sustain any appreciable power in matter, as cause.

And if we adopt the other hypothesis, that its motion was originally subject to other conditions than those which are now observed, then this change in its conditions, or mode of action, could not have been effected by matter itself, but must be attributed to intelligence, as the only other conceivable cause. So that, whether matter in motion was, or was not, originally subject to its present conditions, its present influence, by means of motion, must result either from intelligence sustaining its motion, or from its controlling that which is inherent. And, except on the hypothesis that the tendency of matter once put in motion is to continue in motion and not to stop, this control by intelligence must be direct and immediate; for upon no other hypothesis can intelligence make matter a means of producing or even of prolonging effects, after its own action upon it is discontinued. The matter would stop when that action left it, and no change would take place in it till further action of intelligence again moved it.

Nor, without the further hypothesis that the effects of matter in motion are necessary, can we either suppose that without the power of selection—without purpose—these effects would either be uniform, or yet vary in any respect. They must arise from the necessities of the case; as, for instance, the impossibility of two impinging bodies occupying the same space; and some effect must thus be absolutely necessary, or none would be produced. Still, as in most, if not all conceivable cases, more than one effect seems possible, as when two bodies impinge, both may stop, or one turn back; some power which can select, seems essential to the uniform ordering of the effects. This consideration exposes one difficulty in supposing that which is unintelligent to be cause at all; or to be anything more than an instrument used by an intelligent cause. Nor could intelligence make matter cause, or increase its causative power, and make it capable of selecting its own effects, or of beginning a change, or a series of changes, by impressing laws upon it for its government; for, to be governed immediately by law, presupposes a knowledge of the law, *i. e.*, intelligence on the part of the governed.

If all matter were at this moment quiescent, it could not of itself, in virtue of any law, begin a change. To do this it must move itself. But more especially could it not so move itself as to produce a particular effect at a particular time. This would require it not only to have power to move itself, but to *know when* to move, and *how to direct* its movement; all which, as matter is inert and unintelligent, is contradictory, and hence impossible even to infinite power. All that can be meant when we refer an event to the "nature of things," or to the "laws of nature" is, that the intelligence, which causes these events, is itself the subject of laws, under which it acts uniformly in its changes of matter; and all those changes in matter, which begin to be, must be attributed to the action of spirit; and, of course, such of them as are not caused by a finite, must be referred to the action of the Infinite Intelligence. And however difficult the conception may at first appear, there seems no way to avoid the necessity of this constant exercise of creative energy to begin change, or produce uniform results; or the conclusion that every particle which floats in the breeze, or undulates in the wave; every atom which changes its position in conformity to the laws of electrical attraction and repulsion, or of chemical affinities, is moved, not by the *energizing*, but by the *energetic* will of God.*

From these views we may infer that matter cannot, without the aid of intelligence, be an *active cause* even of changes in itself. It can produce no activity in itself, and any imparted activity is diminished in producing effects; nor can it, even if in virtue of a derived activity it becomes an active cause, select and effect such changes as will conform to the will and wants of intelligence; nor yet directly impart activity to it as one body appears to do in regard to another; though, as desirable, it may be the object, and, as admitting of desirable changes in itself, it may be the subject of intelligent action. Any observed changes of matter

* See Appendix, Note X.

vary the circumstances presented to the intelligence, which, in virtue of its power to judge of and to conform to these circumstances, varies its action accordingly. In this way, one intelligence having the power to produce changes in matter, may, by such changes, influence the action of another intelligence; but, in such case, matter is but a means, a mere instrument, by which one intelligence communicates with, or produces effects on another, and not a *cause* of those effects.*

It is true that we loosely speak of matter, or of circumstances, as cause; and to this we have been led by observing the uniformity with which certain phenomena follow certain conditions, or changes of matter. We generalize the facts, deduce the law, and then ascribe directly to that law what we should ascribe to the intelligence whose uniform action makes, or is the ground of our inferring, the law. Science has now made us so familiar with these generalizations, called secondary causes, that we habitually accept them as the ultimate of our inquiries, without tracing them to a first cause, that can begin a series of effects.

Even supposing that matter has been in motion from all eternity; that the tendency is to continue in motion and not to stop; and consequently that it has power to produce effects, and that this power continues undiminished through all time; still, as these effects must be necessary effects, and matter has no power to vary them, they may be of necessity, as they are in fact, uniform, not less so than if produced in conformity to the laws, which the Supreme Intelligence, on the other hypothesis, has adopted for his government of matter; and hence, by observation, we may learn

* See Appendix, Note XI.

equally well to calculate on the certainty, or probability of the effects; and, as in either case they make but a part of the circumstances on which the finite intelligence acts, whether the causes of these circumstances are material or intelligent, can make no difference to the intelligent cause, which is to act in conjunction with such other causes, or in view of the changes by them, which it can anticipate. The change of circumstances actually produced, or expected, will have the same influence on the mind in willing, or upon its freedom in willing, if produced by the one cause as if by the other.

If all matter were quiescent, then the action of intelligent cause to produce change on it would be to move it. If it were in motion, producing changes in an established order, which the acting intelligence could anticipate, then the action of the intelligent cause must be to vary this established order; and the problem, as to its proper action to produce a given result, becomes more difficult and intricate, requiring the exercise of more contrivance, or of judgment to determine that action; but whether that established order of external changes arises from the *necessary* effects of matter in motion, or from the *free* efforts of some intelligent cause, designing such uniformity as will admit of its effects being anticipated, can make no difference to the intelligence, which makes effort to vary that known established order.

Again, if all matter were quiescent, it could not begin motion in itself, and, of course, could not be cause. If it were in motion, it could not determine or select its own effects, and if certain consequences of necessity resulted, it would have no power to vary, or to produce changes in those consequences, and so far could not be cause. That which produces effects, which it cannot but produce, must be constrained to produce them by some power which it cannot control; and, in such case, the power which constrains is more properly the cause, and the subject which is constrained, its instrument.

It appears, then, that matter cannot possibly be cause, except by means of motion; and whether it can then become cause depends upon the question, as to its tendency to continue in motion, or to stop, which is undetermined. But if, with motion, it has power to effect change, still, every application of that power to an effect, diminishes it; and as to make matter an independent cause, and not merely an instrument used by some other cause, we must consider it as having been in motion from all eternity, this diminution by use must have exhausted its causative power; and further, that in any event, if matter be quiescent, or if it be in motion, producing changes in a necessary established order, it cannot be a cause of changes either in that quiescent, or yet in the established order of changes; or begin any new series of changes; and that, to effect such changes, or to begin any new series of changes, spirit is the only competent power or cause.

CHAPTER IX.

OF SPIRIT AS CAUSE.

In postulating thought and effort, we have already assumed the inherent activity of spirit, that is, its power to produce changes, or, at least, to endeavor to do so. If we have now shown that matter cannot, in the proper sense of the word, be cause, or have an inherent and inhering power to produce change, or that it could not retain such power; and that it cannot originate or begin a series of effects, or, of itself, have retained any power to continue an established series, or yet to alter such established series; we must infer that spirit, if not the only real, is an indispensable cause.

The question next arises, whether this causative power of spirit is all concentrated in one Supreme Intelligence, or whether there is a sphere in which the finite intelligence is also an active, originating cause, using its attributes to create, or change, uncontrolled by the Infinite, or any external power. This question is closely connected with the main question which we are to consider, and, at this stage of the argument, we can only state our position, viz. :

That one Supreme Intelligence has power, and, if He chose, might exert the power to create and sustain all that exists in the sphere of the infinite. But that, within this infinite sphere, He has allotted a finite sphere for the action of finite intelligences; that He has adapted that sphere to the action of such finite intelligences, by furnishing it with circumstances, and by conforming His own actions to such uniform modes, that the finite intelligence, acting either through the power of the infinite thus *uniformly* exerted, or with reference to His future action, may be able to anticipate the result of its own efforts, and to direct those efforts, or to will, accordingly. The human intelligence thus acts freely with the assent and co-operation of the infinite; unaided by which, though possessed of powers *similar* to the infinite, its action would be restricted within very narrow limits.

Let us more particularly note this similarity of kind and variation in degree. God is omnipotent; man has finite power. God is omniscient; man has finite knowledge of the present and past, and can, in some degree, anticipate the future. God is omnipresent; man has faculties by which he can make everything within his finite sphere of knowledge, past, present, and future, present to himself; and, therefore, may be said to have a finite presence commensurate with his knowledge, *i. e.*, man has a finite presence, which has the same relation to omnipresence, that his knowledge has to omniscience.* God has a creative power, and this seems to be fully embraced in the faculties of thought, imagination, and conception, with the power of fixing the thoughts, imaginings, and conceptions, in His own mind, and making them palpable to others, either immediately, by transferring this thought and imagery directly to finite minds, or mediately, by depicting or

---

* See Appendix, Note XII.

forming them in matter, and thus making them palpable to other intelligent, percipient beings. If matter, as a separate substance, exists, and was not created by, but is co-eternal with intelligence, then all the creative power of God, as manifested in the material universe, may be confined to mere *changes* in matter; and man has the same power in a finite measure. If there is no such separate existence as matter, then material creation is but the imagery of the mind of God made palpable to us; and man here, also, has the same creative power in a finite measure. The creation of matter, as a substance distinct from spirit, seems to be entirely beyond the power of man. He has no faculty even to conceive of any possible mode of such creation. But, as all material phenomena can be as well accounted for, without supposing matter to be created, by either of the two modes just suggested, *i. e.*, either by considering matter as co-external with spirit, or as an emanation, or a mere effect of the action of intelligence, we cannot, from its existence or phenomena, infer that it was created. And if we cannot conceive of any possible mode of its creation, nor infer such creation from its existence, nor from any of the phenomena of its existence, we can have no proof that any being possesses the power to create it; and the phenomena of the material creation furnish no proof of any great attribute of the Infinite mind, which is not also found, in some degree, in the finite.

Whether, then, we adopt the one or the other of the two hypotheses of creation just alluded to, the creative power of any being, so far as we can have any knowledge of it, is all embraced in these two powers, to both of which knowledge is a prerequisite,—first, that of thinking, imagining, or conceiving the forms, appearances, relations, and changes, which constitute creation; and secondly, that of impressing these forms, and appearances, and relations, and changes upon its own and upon other minds. The finite mind has both these powers in a limited degree, and, we should say, the latter in less proportion than the former.

The finite intelligence can collect all within its sphere of knowledge, and, by analyzing and recombining, form for itself such a new creation at will, as, on deliberation, its judgment or fancy may dictate. It forms this creation first in idea, in its own mind, and then decides whether or not to make further effort to give permanency, or outward actuality, to these internal creations. The limit of its knowledge is the boundary of that finite sphere, in which the finite intelligence, with its co-ordinate finite presence, is creative with its finite power and its fallibility, as the Supreme Intelligence, with its omnipresence, its infinite power and its infallibility, is creative in its infinite sphere.

Every time a finite intelligence, by an act of will, forms a conception of thought, things, and circumstances, in new combinations, or in new relations; that is, every time, by effort, he conceives change in the phenomena within his finite sphere of knowledge, it is to him a new creation of his own, which, by other efforts, other exercise of will, other creations, he may, at least in some cases, make palpable or depict to other intelligences.

I will add that this creative power is exerted by the finite in the only way in which we can conceive of its exercise by the Infinite Intelligence, and under the same conditions. Either must exert the power from a desire to produce some change, from a feeling of want. By means of its knowledge, or by the exercise of its knowing faculties, it is enabled to form conceptions of the effects of its contemplated efforts before it puts them forth, and to vary these conceptions till it finds one adapted to the want; and, in the case of the finite mind, one which it supposes is within the scope of its finite means and power to actualize by its finite efforts. This often makes a very complicated problem, in which all the powers of the mind find an appropriate and improving exercise. It is in the mind's preconceptions of the effects of its efforts, in relation to its previous wants, that it finds the *reason* for its action.

It may be said, that the creative power in finite intelligences is of a secondary character, and limited to producing changes, or new combinations, in the creations of the Supreme Intelligence. In regard to matter, if a distinct entity, this is merely saying that we mould our thoughts, or conceptions in the same material which God has previously used for a like purpose. Any of us can imagine a landscape, and vary it as we choose. We can even imagine a universe, and one varying from that which is the subject of our observation. We can conceive of one in which all the bodies should be in the form of cubes, cones, double cones, or prisms, &c., &c., and all stationary, or moving in orbits, hexagonal, or epicycloidal, &c., &c.; and this, for the time being, is, to him who conceives it, a new creation, perhaps distinguishable from that creation which, not resulting from his own efforts, is *without* him, only by the fact that one is subject to be changed or annihilated by his own effort or will, or by his ceasing to will, and the other is not. If the material universe is but the thought and imagery of the mind of God, made directly palpable, it no doubt is in the same manner subject to change and annihilation by an act of His will, or a suspending of it. So far as the individual is concerned, the imagery, which he, by his finite powers, has willed into existence, is, while he so wills its existence, a real creation.* But when we attempt to transfer this imagery of our own to other minds, we find that our power of doing so is very limited in regard to the amount of imagery we can so transfer; the completeness or precision of the transferred images, and the number of other minds upon which we can impress them. Though we may have created the imagery by a direct act of will, we cannot thus transfer it to other minds, but only by slow, circuitous and tentative processes or efforts; some, however, doing it with much more facility than others.

We can, by effort, change matter with more or less of accuracy, in conformity to certain ideas in our minds; and the change, under certain conditions, will be impressed on the minds of some others. The rudest and least gifted intellect can do something of this; while superior genius is able, not only to conceive of the grand, the beautiful, the tranquil, or the terrific, but to make these creations recognizable and enduring by so portraying them in language, picturing them on canvas, or carving them in marble, that they will long be palpable to many other minds. But, to make the conceptions of a Raphael thus palpable, requires an almost countless number of efforts, before the pre-requisite conditions, by which it is perfected and exhibited on the

* See Appendix, Note XIII.

canvas, are completed—before his creation becomes a palpable, tangible reality to other men; though superior intelligences may have perceived the original formation, as it existed in his mind, without the aid of the external means, by which it penetrates through our obtuseness.

The finite intelligence may create new forms and new combinations. It can conceive a pleasing landscape, and therein create not only new combinations, but new thought and new beauty, and exhibit it to others. The poet, through the medium of language, does this. The painter, with his pencil, also. The florist, with his spade, does the same. All create new forms, new combinations, new beauty; and, by their different modes, impress their creations on other minds.

The efforts of the florist are *most palpably* made in reference to the aid of the Supreme Intelligence, acting by uniform modes, of which he has acquired a knowledge, and by which his own designs are executed,—his finite efforts made effective. But the painter is really hardly less dependent upon this same extrinsic aid, for the successful exhibition of his ideal creations, in a tangible form, to others.

The poet, though still dependent on this uniformity for the means of making his conceptions palpable, seems to be less so than either of the others. There is less intervening between his conceptions and our perceptions of them. He issues the fiat, " let there be light," and his creation flashes upon us. It is in the purest forms of poetry—those in which the words seem to vanish and leave the unalloyed thought and imagery of the poet, as if flowing directly from his mind to our own—that we can most readily realize that mode of creation in the Supreme Intelligence, which we have supposed to be a direct impression of the creative conceptions of the Infinite upon the finite mind.

Whether our mental creations are made palpable by means of some direct, but unperceived connection between our efforts and their outward manifestation, or through the uniform modes of God's action, is not material as to the question of our power to make them manifest. If such manifestation only follows our efforts, it identifies the *power to produce the effect*, with our *power to make the effort*. But the finite mind, in its present condition, can thus impart, and give, even a qualified durability to a very small portion of its conceptions. Whether, in a farther stage of its progress, this means of imparting to others will be increased, as its present disproportion to our powers of conception would seem to indicate, is a question not within the scope of our present inquiry; and we content ourselves with the conclusion, that here and now, the finite mind of man, made in the image of God, has finite powers corresponding to omnipotence, omniscience, omnipresence, and other creative attributes of the Infinite; and, so far as we can know, exerts these powers in the same mode and under the same conditions; that is, it has wants, it has a faculty of effort, or will, by which to endeavor to gratify those wants; and it has knowledge, which enables it to form preconceptions of the future effects of those efforts, and to judge as to what effort to make, and thus determine that effort and the consequent effect, as in itself A CREATIVE FIRST CAUSE.*

* See Appendix, Note XIV.

Whether the finite mind, in the exercise of these powers, is independent of, or is controlled by the Infinite, or by other powers, or forces, is a question involved in that of *the freedom of the mind in willing*, which we will now proceed to consider.

CHAPTER X.

FREEDOM OF INTELLIGENCE.

As the will is very frequently spoken of as a distinct entity, so, as a logical consequence, it is not uncommon to speak of the "freedom of the will." This opens the way for the argument, that the will is dependent upon, and is controlled by the mind; and, hence, is not free, producing much confusion; whereas, the real question, and that which involves the important consequences of human responsibility, regards only the freedom of the being that wills—whose responsibility is supposed to be affected by the condition of freedom, or necessity. The inquiry should then be, not is the will free, but, *does the mind, the soul, will freely?*

In reference to this question, it is not material whether the effect we seek to produce when we will, follows our volition, or not. We may not have the *power to do* what we will, and yet may *freely will to do*. There may be no such connection as we supposed between the volition and the intended result; our knowledge may have been deficient, our deductions erroneous. If that result was in any degree dependent on other causes or forces, as the motion of matter, or the action of other intelligences, we may have been mistaken in our anticipations of those movements or actions; or have made wrong inferences, as to their influence or effects. However this may be, it is manifest that the subsequent result cannot control the volition, which already is, or has been; the *actual* effect cannot control its cause, after that cause has been exerted. Of that mysterious connection between the effort and its consequences, we know nothing beyond the fact that, under certain conditions, the latter more or less uniformly follow the former. If, in a normal and natural condition of my being, I will to move my hand, it moves. If I will to throw from it a ball, the ball moves and even continues to move after my mind has ceased to act in regard to it. Now, whether the movement of my hand, and of the ball, while in it, arises from some direct, but latent connection between my mind and my hand; and whether the ball continues to move, after my mind has ceased to will in regard to it, in virtue of some power inherent in matter or some *necessary* principle of motion; or whether, all beyond my willing is to be ascribed to the action of some other intelligence, ever present and ever active and efficient, are questions which I have already alluded to as undetermined. The last we know of our own agency in producing change, is our act of will, or effort to effect it. We know that the change follows this willing with more or less of certainty; but why it so follows we do not know. We may intuitively or experimentally foreknow what effects will probably follow certain efforts, but, beyond the effort, we know nothing of ourselves as the cause of these effects.

For every intelligent act, or every act of an intelligent being, as such, there must be an object, a reason for its acting, rather than its not acting. To suppose intelligence to act, and yet not know any object or reason for its acting, is to suppose it to act without intelligence, and if there is no intelligence involved, or concerned in the act, the action, if any there can be, must be wholly independent of the intelligence; or, which is the same thing, of any exercise of intelligence by the intelligent agent or being; which, in the case of its willing, would involve the contradiction of its being passive in its own action. It would also make a case in which that which is unintelligent moves itself.

To suppose any being to will any particular act, and yet know no reason or object for that act, is either to suppose a change, or an effect, without any cause; or that this act of will is directed by some cause, without the being that wills. But, as will hereafter more fully appear, there is no possible way in which any power, external to the agent that wills, can affect the direction of this willing, except by causing him to know some reason, or object for such direction.

Intelligence in acting, then, must have an object. The object of its action must be an effect which it *wants* to produce. The mind, acting intelligently, will not make an effort, or will to produce an effect, which it does not *want* to produce. Every volition, then, must arise from the feeling or perception of some want, bodily, or mental; otherwise there is no object of effort. This want may be that of food, of knowledge, of muscular movement, or of mental effort, in some of the various modes before indicated, or merely a want of change from the present state of things. But though the want suggests change, it does not indicate the mode of effecting it.

A mere sensation, or perception, attended by a

desire for change, but with no knowledge as to the mode of producing that change, points equally in all directions, furnishing to the mind no indications of the means of effecting the change. It, so far, furnishes no ground or reason to the mind to suppose that effort is the means, or that any particular effort will tend to the desired effect, any more than to the contrary. The mind must have some additional knowledge as to the mode. With the want, which, as before stated, is compounded of feeling and the knowledge that *some* change is desirable, must be associated the further knowledge of *what* change, and the means of effecting that change. The knowledge that effort is the means by which we must effect change generally, is innate; as probably also all that knowledge which is essential to existence, and especially that which is thus essential in the earlier stages of being. If the first want is that of breath, or of food, the knowledge of the means of gratifying it probably accompanies the want. The infant breathes, and knows, at least, how to swallow, if it does not also know how to find the source of its nourishment in its mother's breast, and later in life want is developed, with which, without any agency of our own, is associated the knowledge of the mode of its gratification.

Again, as the circumstances under which the want may exist may be very different, there must be some power of adaptation to them. Suppose, for instance, a man being hungry, knows that by walking a few steps to the north he can find bread to relieve his want; but he becomes hungry when he is in a different position, requiring him to walk a few steps south to get the bread. The first step, in such cases, when the knowledge is not an immediate mental perception, is to examine the circumstances. This is a preliminary effort of the mind to obtain more knowledge with which to direct its final action. But this effort also requires some previous knowledge. We must know something before we *will* to know more. As preparatory to such effort, we must at least know that more knowledge is desirable, and that to examine is the mode of acquiring it. And this previous knowledge must either be intuitive, or acquired through the senses without effort. In the latter case its acquisition would be merely accidental, and the mere passive observation of events is so entirely different from an effort to examine, that the latter could never be inferred or learned from the former; and if so, then the knowledge that we must examine the circumstances, in order to know how to adapt our final effort to them, is probably intuitive. If it is not, the infant, in *seeking* its mother's breast, must do it by knowledge *imparted to it* in *each particular case* as it occurs, and adapted to the peculiar circumstances of that case. If we suppose it only to know the mode of muscular movement, and that, under any circumstances, it may succeed, by moving its head, or turning its eyes, first in one way and then in another, till it finds the right direction, such movements of the head, or of the eye, are but modes of examining the circumstances in regard to which there must have been some pre-existing knowledge, at least, that by such movements there is a possibility of finding the object sought, *i. e.*, must know that an *effort to examine* is the mode of attaining its object. If the mind has no knowledge in any degree, —no expectation—that by effort it can accomplish the object, it is, to it, the same as if it had no object of its effort. It may be only the knowledge, that we need more knowledge properly to direct the effort to gratify the want, or that, by effort, we may possibly effect some change, which change may possibly be a desirable one. With such certainty, probability, or hope, we make the effort, *i. e.*, *we will*.

We have here, then, in want and knowledge combined, the source in which volitions originate, and the means by which mind, in virtue of its intelligence, gives them direction. Without want, the mind would have no object to accomplish by effort; without knowledge, it would have no means of directing its efforts to the accomplishment of that object. Without want and knowledge, the mind would never manifest itself in effort, or self-action; and hence, if without them it could be cause at all, it would be only blind cause, like matter. Its want furnishing an object of action, and its knowledge, enabling it to determine *what* action, are all that distinguish the mind from unintelligent cause, or force; for even if without them it could will at all, it would will blindly, as matter moves, and without any more reference to its effects. As want is compounded of feeling and knowledge, these sources of volition are resolvable into an intelligent or knowing being, with a faculty of will and a susceptibility to feeling; in other words, into a *cause*, which itself perceives the effect it would produce, *i. e.*, what it would do, or at least try to do; knows the means, and is conscious of its ability to do, or to try to do it; and at least believes that its effort may possibly be successful.

The want does not, generally, arise from our volition. We may want, we do want, without effort to want. The mind could not begin its action by willing a want, unless there was first a *want* of that want. As already shown, without some want to be gratified by its act of will, the mind would not will at all. It would not will for the mere purpose of exercising its will, unless such exercise of will were itself a previous want; the want must precede the action of the will to gratify it, and must, in the first place, come by the act of God, immediately, or mediately through the constitution of our being. As we may want without effort, so also we may *know* that we want without effort, for we cannot want without knowing it. It has before been shown that the want itself involves the knowledge of a desirable change, and that some of our knowledge, and especially some of that which we acquire through the senses, comes to us not only without effort, but could not be prevented by our direct effort. Any intuitive knowledge which we may have, must also exist in us without effort to obtain it.

To these pre-requisites of effort—want and knowledge—no antecedent effort, then, is necessary. They may both exist without it. We cannot directly will either; but may will to use means by which to produce them in us. It is not necessarily, by an act of will, that we see and thus *know* that a heavy body is approaching us, or that we *know* that we are in danger from it, or that we *want* to avoid it, or that we *know* the means of avoiding it, and how to adopt the known means, *i. e.*, to make an *effort to move*. With such knowledge and want, the first effort of the mind may be to make the bodily movement; but, if we suppose it not yet to know in which direction to move, but to know that the mode of learning this is to examine the circumstances, *i. e.*, by further observation or reflection, then its first effort will be to examine.

A want may itself be the object wanted; we may *want* a want, as we *want* an apple; and the *want* that already is, may be the occasion of our willing in regard to the attainment of the want, which is the object desired; as the *want* of the apple is the occasion of the effort to obtain the apple. For instance, we may *want* to be hungry, *i. e.*, *want* to want food, that we may enjoy the pleasure which arises from gratifying hunger. In such case we must distinguish between the secondary want, which, like the apple, is but the object of our effort, and that primary *want*, which excited us to make the effort, and for the gratification of which the secondary is required. As the apple is not itself the want, but the thing wanted, so also, in the case just supposed, the hunger, or want of food, is not itself the want, but is the thing wanted. But, though we do not make, or cause, this primary or exciting want, it is *our* want that we feel, and not the want of another. The same of knowledge; we do not make the fact, or the truth, or the evidence of it. The most we can do is to seek that which already is; and the moment we find, or know it, it is our knowledge, let the source from whence derived be what it may. For intuitive knowledge we do not even have to seek.

The want is, while it lasts, a fixed existence in the mind, demanding effort for its gratification or relief.* The knowledge becomes a portion of the mental apparatus, by which the mind directs its efforts; every increase of its knowledge increasing its means of accomplishing its purposes and enabling it to direct its efforts

---

* See Appendix, Note XV.

with less of fallibility to the desired resu.ts. To make knowledge most available, or useful, often requires thought, reflection, or deliberation in its application. An exciting want may be accompanied with a consciousness that our knowledge is insufficient, and, in such case, the secondary want of more knowledge intervenes. We want to ascertain the circumstances, or the best mode of proceeding under them, and our effort is first directed to obtain this knowledge. We examine, we *deliberate*, and thereby reach a conclusion or judgment. These judgments are but the knowledge, certain or otherwise, as to what is, or what we should do; acquired by preliminary efforts for this object. We observe, we examine, and so arrange our ideas, that the knowledge sought may come within the scope of simple mental perception. As a basis of the whole proceeding, however, there is always a want; and, of course, with this want as one of its elements, some knowledge (at least the knowledge that by effort more knowledge may be obtained) which required no effort. The feeling, which is one element of the want, is constitutional; and the knowledge, which is the other element, is in the first instance either innate, or acquired by simple perception, without effort. The preliminary efforts of the mind to obtain knowledge to use in directing its final effort, are but parts of a plan, embracing a series of efforts, to accomplish the final end it has in view.

As preliminary to that final act of will, or series of acts, by which the primary exciting want is to be gratified, the mind may have to decide—

1. Between its conflicting wants.
2. Between various objects; the obtaining, or effecting some one of which is essential to the gratification

of its want; and this is always a change, or effect to be produced in the future.

3. Among various possible, or conceivable, modes of producing this effect in the future.

4. Whether to make the effort to produce the effect, or not; and then, if the mind so decides, it proceeds to make the effort in conformity to the preferred mode to produce the selected effect, to gratify the chosen want.

The preliminaries, as above, may be settled in *other* order, and may not *all* of them be requisite to every final act of will. The fourth decision seems to be very closely associated with the final act of will; and, perhaps, liable to be confounded with it. But a decision or judgment is but a particular form of knowledge, which is often the result of acts of will, but cannot itself be such act, or effort. The final act of will comes after the decision to do. If the process ends with the *decision* to do, there is no room for the *willing* by the mind, to do that which it has thus decided to do; and the whole matter is as completely ended by a decision *to do*, as by a decision *not to do*. The difference in the two cases is, that a decision to do is followed by a further action of the mind to execute its decision and effect change in the future; and a decision not to do is a finality, leaving the mind in a state of quiescence, and not of action. If the decision is itself the act of will, we have nothing to mark the difference in the subsequent mental conditions of action in the one case, and of repose in the other.

We may suppose a being to know that there are, or may be, several modes of gratifying a want, and yet not know that there is, or may be, a choice among them. Such a being would, no doubt, on feeling the want, adopt the first means it perceived of gratifying it, as though it knew and could know no other. If, in so doing, it adopted the worst mode, it would have been better not to have known it. We all know that this disadvantage sometimes occurs to us when acting too hastily, without sufficient deliberation, and this experience teaches us the necessity of deliberately examining the facts and the probable results of action, before we act. In the same way, too, we learn that of several wants there may be a choice as to the order in which they shall be gratified, or whether they shall be gratified or not. Hence, from experience, or that knowledge which comes after effort, we learn the importance of using, before an effort, what knowledge we then have; and thus, with the want and knowledge which alone were sufficient to enable the mind to will, and to will intelligently, is associated deliberation, which is a preliminary effort of the mind to obtain more knowledge to enable it to will better and *more* intelligently in its final action, *i. e.*, to produce the desired result of gratifying the want more certainly, more fully, or with less collateral, or consequential disadvantages. Deliberation being thus but the application of our knowledge, in an effort to obtain more knowledge, cannot be considered as a new, but as the same element, used in a preliminary, or intermediate effort, induced by the want of more knowledge. In its every act of will not purely instinctive, or habitual, the mind applies its knowledge, or some of its knowledge, in devising, or adopting a mode of gratifying its want; and must take *some time* to make the application at all;* and the ex-

---

* See Appendix, Note XVI.

tended deliberation is only devoting more time to make that application more perfect, or to obtain more knowledge to apply. The deliberation is only an examination of our knowledge, generally resulting in a judgment, but is sometimes fruitless. It may be exhaustive, but more frequently it is not, and the quantity of time which shall thus be devoted, in any case, is also a matter for the mind to judge of and to decide, at any point, by the knowledge which it then already has. If we *want* food, it will not be advisable to spend a month in considering whether it is best for us to eat beef, mutton, or venison; and yet, perhaps, less time would not suffice for a *thorough* examination. In such cases, the mind judges for itself, bestowing such time as, under the circumstances, seems to it desirable; the exercise of a proper judgment, in this respect, combining prudence with decision. That the mind has the power to arrest its impulse to gratify its want by the first means it perceives, to consider or examine whether there are not better means; or whether it is proper that the want be gratified at all, by whatever means it may have at command; is a very important fact, making, perhaps, the foundation of one essential difference between instinctive and rational action.

In turning from the want, knowledge, and the application of the knowledge, or deliberation, which precede, to that effect, which the mind seeks to accomplish by its effort, constituting its object, we may remark, as an obvious fact, we might say, a truism, that *we do not make any effort for what already is.* Hence, a beginning, or a design to do what might not otherwise be done; an endeavor, or attempt to bring to pass what before was not; to originate some change, which otherwise might not occur, seems involved in the very idea of effort. In this view, every volition is an exercise of the creative power of the intelligence that wills; and when successful, results in a creation, formed, with more or less skill and wisdom, from the unarranged materials existing in the chaos of circumstances, which this same intelligence perceives, examines, compares, analyzes, and combines in idea, before its final volition is decided upon,—before it determines by what actual construction of these materials it can best effect its purpose,—by what means it can best gratify, or relieve the want, which excited it to action.

We have seen that the finite intelligence has all the powers essential to creative action, and also the knowledge required to direct these powers. Hence it may of itself use them with intelligent aim. To direct our first efforts, we have sufficient intuitive knowledge, and when this, with any accumulations passively acquired by the knowing sense through external sensation, will not avail, we know that the mode of obtaining more is by an effort to examine.

Among the circumstances, the examination of which by the mind may be essential to its proper exercise of these powers, must be included not only the actual present existences around us, but our recollections of past observation and reflection; our anticipations of the future; our knowledge of the experience of others and of what others may be doing, or expected to do; and, especially, of those laws, or uniform modes, by which the Supreme Intelligence regulates His acts of change; and by, or through, or in conformity to which our own volitions are made effective. Among the circumstances, our opinion as to our ability to execute this or that design, will largely influence us as to the effort we conclude to make. Whether that opinion is, or is not correct, is not material to its influence on the volition. The mind will, in this respect, be influenced in its action by the internal existing belief,—the present known—and not by the external future *fact*, which is unknown, perhaps unanticipated, or even disbelieved.

We never will to do, what we know we cannot do. To will an act, I must first *know* what act to will. If no particular act appears to me as better adapted to produce the desired effect than another, there is no reason why I should adopt one act rather than another; and, in such case, my knowledge would only indicate trying any act out of the infinite number of conceivable acts. But, if I know that there is *no* act that will produce that effect, there is no reason why I should will at all. I could just as well will without any want, as to will when I knew the act of will would have no influence on the want. Under such circumstances there can be no decision of the mind to act, and nothing to be executed by an act of will. The *decision* to will, is a portion of the mind's knowledge; and to say one cannot decide to will to do what he knows that he cannot do, is merely saying, that he cannot reconcile the contradiction, and know that he will do what at the same time he *knows* he cannot do. The effort, or trying to do, involves some expectation of doing. If I know the *nature* of the act, which, if my power were sufficient, would produce the effect, but know that my power is not sufficient, I know that willing such act cannot avail. I, in effect, know that it will no more produce the effect, than any other act, however different its *nature*. Under strong impulse, men sometimes seem to make efforts which they know will be insufficient to produce the desired effects. Strong emotion often finds relief by expression in unavailing words; and a like relief is derived from expression in unavailing action. Such relief may be the end rationally designed, or, perhaps, in such case, action is instinctive. If a friend asks me to push aside a mountain of granite, I say I cannot do it; and if, in compliance with his request to try, I push against it, I still do not will to move it; but the whole object of my effort, and what I will, is to push against it to please him, and this I pre-perceive to be possible. A man, who can demonstrate the impossibility of duplicating the cube, or of contriving a perpetual motion, may yet will to exercise his wits upon these problems. His effort, however, is not to solve the problems, but, perhaps, by exercise to improve himself in geometry and mechanics; or to amuse himself thereby. Sometimes persons, in moments of frenzy or desperation, *appear* to attempt impossibilities. This *appearance* may arise from various causes. In a pressing exigency, when there is nothing but what is highly improbable, things highly improbable may be attempted. This is expressed in the ancient adage, "A drowning man will catch at a straw." Or, the object sought may have taken such strong hold on the imagination, or may so exclusively absorb the attention, that the obstacle to its attainment, the impossibility, though ever so palpable to others, is overlooked by the actor. A man in battle, surrounded by an army of his enemies, may act as if to cut his way through them, rather than passively meet the fate he knows to be inevitable; but, in this case, what he really seeks and wills is not to cut his way through the army, but something else; perhaps to destroy as many of the enemy as possible; or to get that relief, which effort gives by its excitement and by withdrawing his thoughts from his impending doom. Again, the *habit* of resistance, or of effort in similar, though less hopeless cases, may have its influence on the action willed. (Of the influence of habit, I shall have occasion to say more hereafter.) So, too, it seems certain, that our belief as to the degree of certainty with which we can attain an object, is one of the circumstances generally taken into the view of the mind in forming its judgment as to what it will try to do, or in what mode it will attempt it. The mind may not always adopt the easiest mode of reaching the ultimate object of its effort. It may be indifferent as to the amount of effort, and hence not seek the easiest mode; or it may prefer to make more effort than is necessary, and adopt the mode which will embrace this intermediate with the ultimate object; but it must always seek to adopt a mode by which what it wants will be accomplished; and, in doing this, the mind must itself judge of the mode, or modes, which it knows, or which, when not immediately apparent, it finds by a preliminary act of search, and, in view of all the circumstances, including its own power, and the pleasure or pain of exercising that power, decide whether to adopt any one, and, if so, which one.

These views show the necessity of want and knowledge as pre-requisites to any effort of the mind. It is, perhaps, sufficiently evident that the mind will make no effort to do anything which it does not want done; also, that it will make no effort to do what it wants done, if it knows that such effort will not produce any desirable result; or even when, without this negative certainty, it has no affirmative faith, or hope of such a result.

But, more fully to explain, let us suppose another case. A man feels a sensation, and with it has certain knowledge, constituting a want, say of food; the intuitive knowledge which, in the first stage of his existence, indicated the mode of gratifying this want, no longer avails him, and his acquired knowledge must be brought into requisition. But he knows of no way of ministering to the want by a direct act of will. He knows that this is impossible, and he now *wants* to make such effort as will lead, though indirectly, to the desired result. He *knows* that, by examining the circumstances, the means may, perhaps, be found; and he now *wants* to examine. This he has the power to do, and on doing it, he finds, from immediate perception, or from the memory of previous perceptions, that there is bread in the baker's shop over the way, or, at least, a probability of its being there; but he knows of no way of obtaining it by a direct act of will, without being first near to it; and he now *wants* to be at the baker's shop; still, he knows no mode of accomplishing this end by a direct act of will; but he knows that by a direct act of will he can make and govern the movements of his limbs so as to walk there; and he now *wants* to walk there. To meet this want, he has the requisite knowledge and power; he can will and successively continue to will the movements necessary to walk, and commencing with these, he goes through the several stages of moving himself to the baker's shop, obtaining the bread and applying it to relieve his sensation of hunger. At every stage there was a *want* demanding effort, but no *direct effort* to relieve or gratify the want, until it was reduced to one in which there was corresponding *knowledge*—knowledge of a means, of a plan, by which a series of acts of will, in proper order, would accomplish it. The wants, which arise in forming this plan, are all *secondary* wants, and may be embraced in the want of the mind to apply its knowledge, or to obtain more knowledge to apply.

The contrivance, or design, by which the finite mind finds means to reach indirectly, what it cannot by a direct act of will, is one mode in which it manifests its creative power. It is conceivable, that a man with his mind engrossed by some absorbing subject, and at the same time feeling hungry, might have his notions so confused as to move his teeth to chew before he put the food between them. Perhaps most persons have experienced something analogous to this, and all can readily perceive how abortive such efforts must be. Hence we see that, to produce any given effect, it is important that the efforts should be in conformity to some pre-existing plan or design. A single want may thus require not only a number of acts of will, but that they shall be in a certain consecutive order; and a little system, as clearly manifesting the orderly arrangement of designing cause, as our planetary system, be created before the original want, which induced the effort, is gratified; these little separate systems, going to form that universe which every man, by the exercise of his creative powers, is gradually constructing, and in which, as in the stellar universe, some of its constituent parts are continually being formed, while others, having fulfilled the purposes of their existence, are obliterated. If, in the case just stated, we suppose the man to know, not that there is bread over the way, but that there is a baker's shop a short distance in one direction, where there may be bread; and another shop, farther off, in another direction, where there is a greater probability of finding it; also, that in another place beef may be had, and fruit in another, then the judgment must be exercised; the mind must seek, by examination, to find the best mode of effort to get the bread, or to determine whether, in view of all the circumstances, the effort should not be to obtain the beef, or the fruit instead. In such case there is more extended *deliberation.*

We have already remarked that we do not make effort, or will as to what now is; neither do we will as to what is past. The object of our effort is always to influence that which is to be—to produce some effect in the future. What already is, or has been, has no other effect upon our decision as to the effort to be made, than as our memory of the past and perceptions of the present increase the knowledge by which we are better enabled to judge as to what effects we should seek to produce in the future, and add to our power and means to produce them. In other words, this knowledge enables the mind to form those preconceptions of the effect of any contemplated effort, which are essential to its decision, or judgment, as to what effort it should put forth. The object of willing being always to produce some change in the future, this preconception of the effect of the willing on that future is obviously a very important element. If a man could not anticipate some desirable change as the result of his effort, he would not, as a rational and intelligent being, put forth the effort. He could have no object of effort and no reason for making it. To will, then, requires that, by means of our knowledge of the past and present, intuitive or acquired, we be able to obtain a prophetic view of the future. This is true of the effort to form these preconceptions. When they are not obvious to simple mental perception, effort is required to form them, and the mind must have some faith, that by effort in examining, it can get the foresight—the knowledge required to form them, or so arrange its knowledge that such preconceptions will become apparent. The knowledge, that by examination we can get the knowledge requisite for action, as before suggested, is essential to our first actions, and is probably intuitive.

As a conception, poetic or logical, of the effects of any contemplated efforts upon the future, is thus essential to the effort, a being, with only sensation and a knowledge of the past and present, would not will. It is only by the God-like power of making the future present, that intelligence, Infinite, or finite, in the exercise of its will, becomes creative. By means of this power of anticipating its effects, the mind, in willing, is influenced by the anticipated creations of its own action, while those creations are still in the future, making a very broad distinction between intelligent and any conceivable unintelligent cause.

It is this fact, that intelligent cause is influenced by its preconceptions of its own effects, that fits it for FIRST CAUSE; for that which is thus, as it were, drawn forward by the future, needs no propulsion from the past; that which is moved by inducements before it, does not need a motive influence behind it; that which acts from its own internal perception of the effects of its own action upon its own internal, existing want, does not require to be first acted upon by extraneous, external forces. It is essential that the want exists, but not material to the action how it came to exist. If the mind is moved to exert its causal influence in acts of will, by the consideration of the effects which will *succeed*, and not by what has *preceded* its action; it cannot, up to the point of effort, but be a first cause, and, as such, an independent power, freely trying to do its finite part in that creation of the future, which is the object of its effort. In the *past* it has acquired the knowledge which aids its judgment as to the effect of any contemplated action under the *present* circumstances.

The problem which the mind has to determine, in such cases, and which the mind alone must determine, is this: given, a certain want, or, which is the same thing, a certain change to be wrought out in the future; and, with this, certain facts, constituting whatever knowledge the mind has from memory of the past, or observation of the present, including, of course, all instruction, from any source, human or Divine, up to the moment of deciding; to determine by what change in the future the want may be gratified; and then by what effort, or series of efforts, this gratifying change may be effected. If the want and the existing circumstances, or facts, were not already fixed and determined, and, as such, not subject to the will, we should have, for finding the required volition, only variable and unknown data. There would be nothing fixed, or known as a basis of calculation, and the problem would be as indeterminate as that of constructing a triangle with three unknown sides. If the want were not fixed, the problem would still be indeterminate. The mind, that does not know what it wants, is not prepared to determine its action. Or, if we suppose the want and the knowledge of it to be fixed, but all other knowledge to be dependent on the will; then the mind would, by an act of will, have to fix this other knowledge of the past and present before it could make it available in determining its course as to the future. The mind, in such case, would have to assume the facts and truths, by its own creative acts for its present purpose, make them fact and truth in some fixed form; it would be acting upon an assumed basis, upon mere hypotheses, and the action founded upon such assumptions might prove to have no adaptation to the actual existences. No sane man would, from such process, expect other than imaginary or hypothetical results, admitting of actual application only when the actual existences *happened* to correspond with the assumed hypotheses. He might, in this way, plan action without reference to any actual, existing circumstances, or to any changes, which other causes might be affecting; but the chance of his plan being applicable to the actual existences, would be inconceivably small. With the want and knowledge both given, the mind has only to determine their relations to the contemplated acts, to make the problem analogous to that of constructing a triangle, knowing two sides and their relations to the other. It becomes a determinate problem, but it is the mind's knowledge, including that of its want, which thus makes it determinate; and the mind itself, by the use of its knowledge, actually determines it. If we do not know the existing facts or circumstances, which relate to our action, we seek by a preliminary act to find them. The mind may be in doubt as to some, or all of the data, or knowledge, upon which it bases its constructions; and, so far, the result will be doubtful and the problem be determinate only within the limits of certain probabilities; or it may be mistaken in the data, either as to the facts, or the relations, and, so far, the result may be erroneous, and the act of will have no tendency to produce the expected result; or there may be a want of power to produce the effect willed. However this may be, however perfect or imperfect the solution—the mind, with such means as it has, must itself resolve this problem, growing out of the relations, indicated by its own knowledge, between its own want and the conception which it forms of the future effect of certain of its own acts of will, and determine the result or act of will, or that result, that act of will, will not be determined. No other power, material or intelligent, could possibly determine it without knowing both the want, and the perception of the relation between the contemplated action and the want, which exist in the mind of the agent willing. This could be only by one who knows all our wants, "to whom all hearts are open, all desires known." On this point, of the possible control of the finite will by the Supreme Intelligence, we have already made some suggestions, and shall consider it more fully in another place.

From the views just stated it appears that, if the want and knowledge of the mind were subject to, instead of being independent of its will, they would have to be fixed by specific acts of will before any other act of will could be determined; and the fact that the want and knowledge of the mind are not subject to the control of its will, instead of involving necessity as at first glance one might suspect, is really essential to the freedom of the mind in determining its action; or, at least, facilitates the exercise of that freedom. That we have want, know our want, and the means or mode of gratifying that want, cannot militate against our freedom in the use of that knowledge, to gratify the want. The want is the original incentive to that effort, the direction of which the mind determines by means of the relations which it perceives between its wants and its preconceptions of the future effects of this effort; among such conceptions selecting, or choosing, for actualization, that one which, in its view, is best adapted to its purpose of gratifying, or relieving the want. It is in the forming of such preconceptions, as will probably answer the purpose, in the accuracy of these preconceptions, or their conformity to the effects that will actually be produced, and in selecting among them, that the mind manifests its ability in action.

Whether or not these preconceptions are realized by the power of the mind in effort, is not material. It is sufficient that its effort is a pre-requisite to such realization. Up to the point of and including the effort, the finite mind, in its own sphere, so far as we can know, exerts its creative powers in the same way as the Infinite, and as freely. It has a want; forms a preconception of what changes will gratify the want; what effort, or succession of efforts, will produce these changes; and makes the efforts, or wills these changes. The only necessity or restraint, differing from that of the Infinite, which the finite mind is under, arises, not from a difference in the kind, but in the limited quantity of its power. It cannot do what it has not power to do; it cannot act from considerations, which it does not perceive or apprehend; or upon knowledge which it does not possess; *i. e.*, the finite mind cannot reconcile contradictions. But neither can the Infinite. In this respect they are, if not on the same, at least on similar footing. The finite mind cannot be infinite, and the Infinite cannot be finite; and this difference in condition makes a corresponding difference in the contradictions, to reconcile, or to overcome which is, to each, impossible. If no intelligence can will to do what it knows that it cannot do, then the Infinite cannot will to do anything which is really impossible to it; while the finite, being limited in knowledge, *may* will to do what, to it, is impossible, and even what is absolutely so; for the very reason that it does not know the impossibility, or the fallacy in its perception of some apparent means; and hence, the finite mind may will in some cases in which, if omniscient, it could not.*

Having now premised that the finite intelligence has the powers essential to creative acts of will, and that it has a finite sphere commensurate with its knowledge, in which it has a finite, all-pervading presence; and in which, so far as we can know, its creative powers are exerted in the same manner as those of the Supreme Intelligence are, in His infinite sphere, let us suppose a commencement of creation.

The one first cause—the Supreme Intelligence—exists, and must have power to act, to will to do, or nothing would be done, or even attempted. This, in It, must be a fundamental condition of its existence. It must, originally, as a part of the constitution of its Being, know how to exert at least some of its powers, as the same knowledge is constitutional, or innate in the active finite intelligence. This Supreme Intelligence, then, is about to act for the first time. Its object is to

* See Appendix, Note XVII.

produce some effect, some change. To do this must require action of some kind on its part; for, if the effect can take place without any such action, it can take place as well without its agency as with it; and the effect is not the effect of its agency. To produce an effect, even Omnipotence must exert its power—it must put forth effort, it must *will*. A creative God cannot be an inert Being, wholly passive, and yet manifest creative power. Such an idea cannot be conceived without violence to all our notions of power. Power itself does not act, but the *being* that has power, acts and must exert its power—must put forth effort, or the power will not be exerted, will not produce any effect. Such a Being, then, is about to exert its causative or creative power. If there is no matter—nothing but this one intelligence, there is manifestly nothing extraneous to itself to oppose, to determine, or even to influence its action; and it must, therefore, be free to exert its power as itself may determine. It must itself determine this first act, or it cannot be determined. Nor is it difficult to see how this may be done. The Supreme Intelligence exists with its wants, its knowledge, and power; its knowledge including the mode of using that power. It wants to create; it has the knowledge of means; the wisdom to select and to adopt those means; and the power to apply them, so as to produce the creation or change wanted. There being no opposing force, the first creation, the first effect of its effort, must be in conformity to its design, if that design be within the province of its power to accomplish. If it could have but one want, and only the knowledge of one way to gratify that want; if, in intelligence, there was no principle of adaptation to new circumstances, then, even this Supreme Intelligence could produce but this one effect, or, at most, but duplications of it. From the fact that intelligence has a variety of wants; also a variety of knowledge, or the faculties to acquire it; and that, from its variable knowledge, it can select for use that which it deems best suited to the occasion, it becomes a variable cause, adapting itself to the want and the circumstances existing in its view; each new want, with every increase of its knowledge, and every combination of want with knowledge, becoming, in its view, a reason for new and different effects by the active intelligence, which thus becomes a multiple cause, producing varied effects. Suppose, then, the first want which actuated the Supreme Intelligence to have been gratified; that want can no longer exist; and, it being a fundamental property of intelligence to want change, or to want to do; a new want arises. It may be only a want of variety, or of exercise for its faculty, but another new creation, or effect in the future, is required to gratify this want. This second creation must have some reference to the first. The first has changed the conditions, and a different combination of circumstances enters into the decision as to the mode in which the second want is to be gratified. This, however, does not interfere with the *freedom* of the active agent, but only varies the circumstances under, or upon which it freely exerts its active power. It contemplates another creation—no less a new creation than the first, but begun or conceived under different circumstances, which the intelligence takes into account as a portion of its knowledge, by which it determines as to what is best to be done, and what the best means to do it. It is the same as though it had now to act for the first time, and found the circumstances, as they now are, to act upon, or to consider in its action. That by previous action it has itself made, or contributed to make, the circumstances what they are, has nothing to do with the proper action under them. The date, or the cause of their existence, cannot affect the result, all that enters into the deliberation being their actual present existence; so that every successive act of the creative intelligence is the same as the beginning, or, we may say, is the beginning of a new creation, made in reference to what already exists.

So also if, when intelligence was first to act, it found matter coexisting; and further, that this matter was in motion and blindly producing changes in itself; this would vary the circumstances under which the intelligence would act, but could not affect the freedom of its action. To this uncalculated and uncalculating state of things, it would bring the new element of intelligent action, and, from the chaotic confusion of numerous blind forces, educe the order, the unity of a designing cause. The *design* must be all its own, for no variety, no quantity of blind causes, or forces, could make a design, *form a preconception*, or be in any way influenced by, *what, as yet, is not*. For a similar reason, the effort to fulfil the design must be its own effort. Blind forces, cannot conceive or will at all, much less will in conformity to, or in the order of a preformed, or preëxisting design or plan, which it cannot form, or know, but the design may be wisely so formed, that some, or all of such forces, if any such be possible, may coöperate with the effort of the intelligent cause to actualize its designs or conceptions. The effort must, however, be to make the effect different from what it may be obvious that all such forces combined will do; otherwise it is but an *effort to accomplish nothing;* which is an absurdity. When, then, the design is such, that all the blind forces, unchanged, obviously *aid* in its accomplishment, the design must include something in addition to what the designing agent perceives these forces would themselves accomplish. Such forces may be auxiliary to the power of the Supreme Intelligence, or may present circumstances to be changed and impediments to be overcome; but evidently, for reasons above stated, do not interfere with His freedom of *design* or *effort*, though, if His power were not infinite, they might prevent the actualization of the design, or frustrate the effort. If infinite, this could only occur in case the design were so unwisely formed as to involve contradiction, as the making, on a plane surface, of two hills without a hollow. Such contradiction an infinitely wise Being would avoid. We have now supposed the Supreme Intelligence acting as the only cause, and also in connection with any blind causes.

If we suppose one of the creations of the Supreme Intelligence to be a subordinate, finite intelligence, and this created intelligence to act freely as cause, producing its own effects, independent of the Supreme Intelligence, and without Its prescience, then the Supreme Intelligence must, in its subsequent creations, make these new circumstances, this new cause, with its own uncertainty, or ignorance of the effects which this cause may produce, a part of the foundation of its own action; as the finite intelligence, in its action, has reference to its own uncertainty and ignorance, as to many events depending on the action of the Infinite, of which it has no certain prescience. Some of these, however, we rely upon with implicit faith; as the rising of the sun; others, as the changes of the weather, are to us very uncertain; and we must sometimes provide, in our designs or plans of action, for numerous contingencies, which we cannot certainly foreknow. This very uncertainty makes one of the circumstances which we have to consider in determining what, in view of all combined, we will try to effect. If there is any such uncertainty in the mind of God, as to human actions, it will be but one of the circumstances which He will consider in determining His own action. His designs, His efforts, though they may be made in reference to the existence of this finite cause, are not made, either wholly or in part, by it; they are still his own designs, his own efforts, freely made. The existing finite intelligence not only has not *sufficient power* to coerce or control the *freedom* of the infinite, as to its *designs* and *efforts*, but it has no *tendency* to do so. The mere changing of the circumstances upon, or in view of which the Supreme Intelligence acts, even though such change could, in some unseen way, frustrate the effort, could not affect the freedom of the design, or of the effort. Among, or upon one set of circumstances, His designs and efforts would be as free as among another set; though some combination of circumstances may, to any but the infinite, *require* less, and some *admit* of less deliberation, than others. The Supreme Intelligence, then, whether acting as the only activity in the universe, or in connection with matter in motion, or with inferior intelligence, must will without constraint or restraint—must will freely.

Nor can the *amount of the power* of the intelligence make any difference in regard to the *freedom* of its efforts. The mind's own estimate of its power, may be one portion of the knowledge by which it judges as to what effort to make. If mistaken in this, it may make efforts which are unavailing. Still, this does not show any want of freedom in its *willing*, but only a want of power to *do what it wills*. That it can *will to do* even what it *cannot do*, is rather an indication of its freedom in willing than otherwise. If, in conformity to a stringent logic, we suppose God to have no more power than is required to do what we see He has done, such limitation could not affect His freedom in the exercise of that power. Neither can the *amount of knowledge* have any influence on the *freedom* of the effort, but only upon the *wisdom* of the design, or of the effect intended. With inadequate knowledge we may not form full and correct preconceptions of the effect, or of the mode of producing it, and hence be liable to err in our judgment as to the wisdom or propriety of the contemplated change, or to mistake the means of producing it, but this does not effect our freedom in the attempt.

It seems to be a self-evident proposition, that the Supreme Intelligence, acting alone as the only existing cause, must act freely; and the views just stated, in connection with those before presented, in regard to spirit and matter as cause, show that this freedom is not —at least not necessarily—affected by the amount of the power, or of the knowledge of the intelligent cause; nor by the coexistence of other causes, material or intelligent. If, then, neither the amount of the power, nor of the knowledge of the willing agent, nor the coexistence of other causes, influence the question of the freedom of the agent in willing; and man, as we have shown, is creative in that finite sphere, in which, with finite power, he is present to all that he knows; as God is creative in that infinite sphere in which He is omnipotent and omnipresent, we must infer that man *may* as *freely* exercise his finite creative powers in his finite sphere, as God does His infinite powers in His infinite sphere; and, that every act of will is a new and independent movement, and, as it were, a fresh beginning of a new creation, evolved by the mind from the new combination of circumstances in view of which it wills. Each individual intelligence wills as in its view of the circumstances it deems best; and though these circumstances may be the result, the composition, of the previous action of itself and of all other intelligences, and any other possible causes, still, as no such action can change the present state of things, at the present time, each intelligence acts, so far as external circumstances are concerned, as if, at the moment of its action, all other powers were quiescent and itself the only active power in existence. What the others have already done, or may be expected to do, are but portions of the circumstances upon which the mind acts in judging, or deciding, as to the effort it will make, if any. In re gard to its own efforts, then, the finite mind, so far as external events, circumstances, and coexisting causes are concerned, at the moment of willing, may be as free as if no other intelligence or force existed; and hence, may will freely, though other forces may frustrate the subsequent *execution* of what it wills. One intelligence may to the extent of its power, shape the circumstances with a view to *influence* the will of another; but this is presuming that the other wills freely. If that other does not, there would seem to be no use in presenting to it the newly adjusted circumstances to influence its will; no reason to suppose that its will could thus be influenced by any change of circumstances produced by other intelligences, or other causes.

In connection with the argument that, as the freedom of the mind in willing is not affected by the amount of its power, or knowledge, the finite mind may will as freely as the infinite, the foregoing views suggest that it makes no difference at what period of creation the finite mind begins to act. Suppose it, first having acquired knowledge, to have been quiescent for ages, and again to begin to act at this moment, and that previous activities, having brought creation to its present state, should all cease to act, except those agencies, whatever they may be, which execute the decrees of the human will, leaving nothing but this one finite mind, with its wants, faculties, knowledge, and the surrounding circumstances; these latter all quiescent in the state to which the recent activities brought them. This one finite mind could make effort to change these circumstances, in the absence of all other active influences, as well as with their presence; and, in their absence, there being nothing else, must itself direct the effort, which must be directed, and is consequently free in making that effort, and especially as there is nothing to oppose, to constrain, or control it in so doing. However small its power to will, that power must be sufficient to overcome no obstruction. The circumstances do not make the effort, or any part of it. In order to form a preconception of the effect of any contemplated effort to change the present, the mind must consider what now is, and hence acts in reference to what already is; but mere circumstances, having in themselves no power, no self-activity, cannot act upon anything, and can only be acted upon. The finite mind, then, under such conditions, being, by the hypothesis, the only activity, the only power capable of producing change, or capable of making effort to produce change, must be wholly unimpeded in such effort, and must determine its *effort*, without extraneous aid or hindrance. Nor can it make any difference, if we suppose the other activities to be reinstated. They cannot alter the past, nor can they in the *present moment*, alter the *present*, whatever already is, though its existence commenced in the present instant, is as surely existent as if it commenced its existence ages before. The reinstating, then, of these other activities, at the instant that this supposed *one* finite mind wills, cannot, at that instant, alter the circumstances, except as their own existence is a fact added to the knowledge of this one mind, and, thus far, may vary its action; but cannot, as before shown, affect its freedom in acting. From this fact, that no cause can alter what is at the instant, in the same instant—or make things as they are, and, at the same time, different from what they are—every act of the intelligent being, finite or infinite, is the same as a first act of such being, under such circumstances as it might find coexisting, and, in the absence of all other activities, forces, or causes; and further, as the number of coexisting circumstances does not affect the mind's freedom in choosing among them, or in combining them, or in considering their relations to its efforts, or in its preconceptions of the effects; and the quantity of the agent's power does not affect its freedom in using what it has; every effort of the finite mind may be as free as the first creative act of the Infinite, even supposing It to have then been the only existence.

These considerations serve to show that the finite

mind *may* will freely; and we shall next inquire as to whether it is controlled in willing by any other power.

The only essential elements in willing which are *within* the mind, and yet are not the mind's action, are want and knowledge. The want does not itself will. It does not direct the will; for it has not the knowledge by which alone this can be done. The knowledge does not will, nor, itself, direct the will; for knowledge, if considered as an entity distinct from mind, is not, in itself, intelligent, and cannot even know the want to the gratification of which the effort must be adapted. It is also obvious that no want, or combination of want with knowledge, can will. The effort and its direction, or determination, must be by that which is cognizant of both the want and the knowledge, and perceives the relations between them; that is, by an intelligent being, or agent.

In regard to external control, I will further observe that the only conceivable modes in which the mind of any finite intelligent being, as man, can be influenced from without itself, in its act of will, are,

First, by some other intelligence, cause, or force acting directly upon his will, and, as it were, taking the place of his mind, and using his will to accomplish its own objects; or,

Secondly, by such other intelligence, cause, or force acting directly upon that man's mind and, by controlling its action, through it control his will; or,

Thirdly, by so changing his knowledge, including the knowledge of those sensations and emotions which are elements of want, that in consequence of this change of knowledge, he comes to a different result, and wills differently.

As the power of matter, if it have any, must be limited to changing the circumstances and thus changing the knowledge on which, or in view of which, we act, it can only influence us in the last of the three modes, and hence may be excluded in considering the other two.

The first of these involves the absurdity of making the will a distinct entity, separable from the particular mind with which it is usually associated, and liable to be used by any other intelligence, that can get possession of it.

If the will is not a distinct entity, but is a mere quality, property, faculty, or attribute of a mind; or a result or condition of its activity; then, when we destroy its connection with that mind, or with its activity, the will vanishes as completely as the image in a mirror, when the object is removed from before it; and there is no will left to be thus controlled by another intelligence, or other external force. Upon the hypothesis that my will is a distinct entity, or a separate portion of my mind, it is, perhaps, conceivable that such will, though controlled by another, may be so connected or associated with my mind, as in some sense to be said to be my will; but even then, the *action* of that will, thus controlled by another, cannot be my action; the effort, the willing through, or by means of, that will, is not my willing, but it is the effort, the willing of that other intelligence, which thus uses my will and acts through it; and, in such case, my mind makes no effort—I do not will at all. Hence the question, as to whether I will freely or not, cannot arise in this case.

In the second case, if another intelligence *directly* controls my mind, and causes it to will without any reference to my own views, my own knowledge, then my intelligence has nothing to do with the willing. I am not then the intelligent being that wills, or the agent that acts, but am the mere *instrument* which some other active agent uses, as it would an axe, or a lever, to accomplish its own purposes. The willing, thus *directly* controlled by external power, may be in opposition to that which I perceive would accomplish what I want. If the external power perceives in me certain conditions of want and knowledge, and conforms the forced action of my mind to them, it is thus conformed by the volition of the external power, and not by my action. The extrinsic agent perceives the conditions, and their relations to the action, as the sculptor perceives the aptitudes of a block of marble, in which he works out his own designs. So, if my mind is constrained in its act of will by external power, my own want and knowledge, my perception of means to ends, my preconceptions of the effect, have no more to do with the coerced action, than the form of the block of marble has with the action of the sculptor. The act is not the action of my intelligent being. It is not *I* who *act*, but some other being, which, in acting, uses me as its instrument. I am, in such case, no more than an *inert something*, acted upon by intelligence, which is not of me; and I in no wise differ from unintelligent substance, except, in being conscious of the changes thus wrought in me by a power without me.

In neither of the first two of the three supposed cases of control of the will of any being by the action of extraneous power; viz.: that directly exerted on the will, or that on the mind, to compel, or constrain its act of will, can there be any willing by that being to be thus controlled. In these cases, such being does not itself act, but is only a passive subject, acted upon by some external power, though still having the capacity to feel, and to know, the changes thus produced in it. There may still be a being with sensation and knowledge, but no will.* Hence, the moment we reach the point of controlling the will, in either of these two modes, there is no willing of the being to be controlled. It may further be remarked that, even if such extrinsic control and willing were compatible in themselves, we neither know, nor can conceive of any mode in which extrinsic power could be directly applied either to will or to mind.

In regard to the third and the only other conceivable mode, there are various ways in which the knowledge of one intelligence may be increased or changed by another. In relation to external circumstances, this may be done by adding to or altering the actual existing circumstances, which is an exercise of creative power, finite or infinite, so that other intelligent beings, perceiving this change, will, in virtue of their intelligence, their power to adapt their efforts to circumstances by means of their knowledge, will differently from what they would have done but for such addition, or change of circumstances. Even finite mind may so influence the infinite.

In regard to those abstract ideas, and the perceived relations among them, which are not influenced by extrinsic changes—in regard to what is true or false—the views and knowledge of one finite mind may be changed through the action of another mind in statement, illustration, argument, &c.; but the finite intelligence can-

* See Appendix, Note XVIII.

not thus influence omniscience. But such change of knowledge in any mind, from any cause, whether by the action of others or by its own efforts, or directly through its own simple perceptive attributes without aid or effort, is not the willing of that mind; it is not such willing in any one of these cases of change of knowledge, more than in the others; and the only reason why, in either case, such change in the mind's knowledge has any influence on its willing is because it *freely* conforms its action to its knowledge—to its perceptions of the fitness of the action to the end sought. If the circumstances themselves be altered, this is not of itself altering the will, and no alteration can take place in it, except as the mind acts upon its perceptions of the altered circumstances, and that, under a *different view* of the circumstances, whether produced by an actual change in them, or by argument, or otherwise, the mind may *will differently*, or make a different effort in consequence of the change in its knowledge, is no evidence that it does not will freely, but, on the contrary, such change of its act of will to conform to its own views, or its own knowledge, indicates its own unrestrained control of its own act of will; and, as already intimated, if it does not will freely, there is no reason to expect any change of its will, by changing its view of the circumstances, either by direct action on the mind, or indirectly, by actual change of the circumstances viewed. If it does not will freely, that which is desirable, if it have any influence at all, may influence it in the same way as that which is undesirable; and if this lack of freedom extends to the internal, as well as the external, even a man's own virtuous emotions, or proper wants, may be the foundation of vicious voluntary efforts; all of which is not only contrary to observed fact, but is self-contradictory and absurd.

These considerations, touching the influence which may be supposed to arise from the mind's view being affected by change of circumstances, are equally applicable, if the circumstances change in any other way, or are changed by any other cause than another intelligence; and even if they change themselves—if any such changes, or modes of change, are possible. Even if matter or circumstances are an independent cause, producing effects, it can produce no other effects on the mind's action than may be produced by intelligent cause changing the circumstances in view of which the mind acts; and hence the reasoning just herein applied to the influence of other intelligent causes on the will, applies also to any which are unintelligent.

The mind, in determining its own action, may consider what any other cause may be expected to do, and, in willing accordingly, still will freely. The mind, in willing, builds the future upon the present circumstances, and is thus active in a sphere which circumstances have not yet reached. It uses the circumstances as means, and in the absence of such means, may not be able to effect what it might effect with them.

In regard to this influence of circumstances, we may further observe, that if any future event is necessarily connected with any *circumstance*, or with any *thing* in the past or present, and comes to pass of necessity from such connection, then the circumstance, or thing, is itself the cause of that future event, which must thus come to pass in virtue of such connection without any act of will. If it be said that the *act of will* is itself that event which is thus so connected with the past or present circumstance or thing, that it comes to pass in virtue of such connection, then the circumstance, or thing, is the cause of such act of will, and is the power which produces it, and the being, to whom the act is attributed, really makes no effort, he acts no act of will, there is no willing by him. Again, the instant that, in the past or present, with which such act of will is necessarily connected, comes to pass, the act of will, being of necessity connected with it, also comes to pass, and they are really simultaneous; and every act of will necessarily dependent on the past or present must, at any subsequent instant of time, have actually taken place, and no new act of will could grow out of this past. If the act of will has no such *necessary* connection, but subsequently becomes so connected, then the new connection is a change, requiring a cause, which did not of necessity produce its effect at the instant the past circumstances came into existence; but this must be a cause which can originate and begin subsequent action, *i. e.*, a cause which is at least so far independent of these past circumstances, that it need not act in immediate connection with, or as a necessary consequence of their existence. But, if the effect of these past circumstances may be deferred for one moment, it can be for another and another, and so may never be, and hence is not a *necessary* effect. From what has just been said, it is evident that no new effect can come from past existences, till some new cause has connected such effect with such past existence, and hence it follows, that an act of will never can be the *necessary* effect of anything in the past, or have any connection with it, till the action of some efficient cause makes the connection, and, in such case, the cause which makes this connection is really the cause of the act of will. Now the only conceivable modes in which the effects of a cause can be continued in time, after the cause has itself ceased to act, are by means of matter in motion, and by intelligence retaining or recalling the effects by memory, and thus, as to itself, making them still present. But matter in motion cannot will or select, decide or determine, among the various conceivable possible volitions; and though it may be a link in the connection between a past event and a volition, the last and essential link is made by the mind itself. The nature of the circumstances cannot enable them to make a necessary connection, or to decide when and where it shall be; their nature can have no influence on the mind in willing till it knows their nature, and it is thus only through the cognition of the mind itself, that they have any influence on the act of will; and the real connecting cause is intelligence,—mind;—and the past circumstances, including any movements of matter, only furnish the knowledge, or reasons, for its action in willing. These positions confirm the conclusion we before reached by another mode, that every act of will is, in itself, a beginning of action.

Again, if the past is a *necessary* cause of volition in a mind, then, as to this mind, there always is a past, it must be constantly willing, which is contrary to the known fact. If it be said that, though the past does not of necessity always produce a volition, yet, whenever a volition does occur, it is, of necessity, so connected with the past as to be controlled by it, then, as the circumstances cannot themselves select and determine when this connection shall, and when it shall not be, we must find some other cause for this connection, and our previous reasoning upon this connecting cause recurs. Even if we suppose this subsequent connection to make *the effect*, *i. e.*, the act of will, necessary; it does not follow that *the cause*, which, by this connecting, produced the act of will, was necessitated in its action by the preëxisting past; but, on the contrary, it has been shown that, if so, all the possible acts of will must be simultaneous with the supposed past existence, which is thus presumed to cause and necessitate them, and no new act of will, or any other effect, could thereafter arise, as the effect of such connection with the past.

From this reasoning it also follows, that there must be some cause, which does not, of necessity, produce its effects *immediately;* but, as just stated, if the effect of a cause may be deferred one instant, it may be deferred another and another, and so on forever, and hence such cause may never produce its effect; and this must be a cause, a power, which, so far as the past is concerned, may act, or not act. Mind, intelligence, is such a power, and it is conceivable that matter in motion may be, both admitting the intervening of time between any two *extrinsic* changes which they may produce by their continuous activity; and these are not merely the only causes that we know of as admitting of this deferred effect of their activity, but the only real causes of any kind, that we can conceive of. If the activity—the motion—of matter ceases, it requires external force, again to put it in motion. If the activity of spirit ceases, it requires some change within, or without itself, which it feels or perceives—some want—to rouse it to activity. It seems *conceivable*, that these two kinds of causes may act and react upon each other, at least thus far, that intelligence may put matter in motion, and thus make it a cause of change, and that the changes caused by matter in motion may furnish the occasions or the reasons for the action of intelligent cause. It is not, however, conceivable that matter can act directly on the will of any intelligence, but, only by changing the circumstances, occasion it to want, or if listless and inert, remind and call its attention to the conditions of want. And this is only so to alter its knowledge, that its own action, freely conformed to its own knowledge, will be different from what it would have been but for such changes by matter. The same is true of all changes or circumstances external to the mind whose action is thus influenced, and which are produced by any cause extrinsic to it, or even by itself. It is the changed knowledge that the mind uses to determine its action, without regarding how it became changed.

If matter in motion, or any other unintelligent cause can change the circumstances, the changes can of themselves produce only the same subsequent effects as if such changes were the results of intelligent cause. In the one case it would be cause doing without design what, in the other, cause did with design. No such causes of change in circumstances, and no such change of circumstances, can act directly on any will without making that will its own; and can only influence another to will differently by, in some way, changing its knowledge; and this it may do by actually changing the circumstances which the mind views, or the mind's view of the same circumstances without any change in them. This is the limit of the power of circumstances on the mind in willing, *and all their power*, as already shown, *depends on the mind's ability to will freely*— to direct its own action in conformity with its own knowledge.

In many cases, in which the act of will is supposed to be controlled by circumstances, the influence is not ascribed to any existing circumstances, but rather to the fact, that certain circumstances do not exist. When such non-existence is recognized by the mind before its act of will is determined, it makes a portion of the knowledge by which its effort is influenced or determined, but, when it is not recognized, it may only influence the *effect* of its effort. In the case of non-existence, it is obvious that the mind is influenced in its effort, not by the non-existent thing, but by its own knowledge of such non-existence, and of the consequences attending it, and it is also true, in the case of any external existence, that the mind is influenced in its efforts, not by the thing itself, but by its knowledge of the existing thing, and of the consequences attending it. The thing itself, if unknown, would have no effect upon the mind, or upon its effort; and it is only by changing its knowledge, that changes in circumstance have any influence whatever on the mind's action; and change of effort, upon changed knowledge, as already shown, does not conflict with freedom of effort.

If there were no past or present circumstances— nothing external to itself—for the mind to know, or even if there were none known to it, its only act of will or effort would be to create something out of nothing—to begin a primary creation. In doing this it would not of course be controlled by existing or past circumstances. And, if we suppose events and circumstances already existing to be in action and producing effects, then, the only reason for the action of an intelligent will must be, either to arrest or to vary those effects, or to produce other wholly independent effects. These last must be by the mind acting independently of the existing circumstances, excepting so far as it perceives that they will not produce the effects; and in this case the mind directs its own action or effort, by means of its own knowledge of the end wanted and of the modes of reaching it; or, in other words, perceiving that no other causes are producing the desired result, the mind exerts its own causative power to do it.

In the other case, when the mind seeks to arrest or to vary the effects of the supposed action of circumstances, its effort must be to resist or control their influence; which is the reverse of control of the mind by the circumstances. If, however, it be supposed that the effort, or volition, is one of the effects of the action of the circumstances, there being but one effect, and that effect not a thing, in itself, but merely a change in the condition of a thing or being, such change, or such effort, or volition, must be the effect of its cause. And hence, in such case, the effort or volition is the effort or volition of the circumstances, and not of the being with which it is associated, and argues nothing against the freedom of that being when it exerts its power to produce an effect—when it does will.

A man may *will* to give a beggar a shilling, and unexpectedly find he has no shilling to give. He freely willed to give. He acted upon his knowledge,—belief,—that he had the shilling, the means of producing the future effect which he designed; but, in the *execution* of that design he was frustrated by the actual existing circumstance. It is in the *doing* what he wills, and not in the *willing*, that a man may be *directly* controlled by the external circumstances.

Of the three and only conceivable modes of influencing the mind in willing, from without the mind that wills, two of them are inconsistent with any exercise of its will, and the other is effective only in case the mind wills freely. If, then, in willing, it is influenced by something extrinsic, it must, to be so influenced, will freely; and if, in willing, it is not influenced by anything extrinsic, it must, in such act, be wholly under its own control, and, of course, be free in such act of willing; so that, if a mind wills at all, it must will freely.

The same result, in terms, is more concisely reached thus. For a man to will and yet not will freely, is to will as he does not will; is to be willing when he is unwilling, which is a contradiction. Reasoning, then, directly upon the *nature of the things* involved in the inquiry, or from the logical relations of the terms by which those things are represented in the common discourse of men, we reach the same conclusions, that the mere act of willing implies a free action, involving the necessity of freedom in the agent willing; and that to will, and yet not will freely, involves a contradiction; and hence, the only question left, in regard to the freedom of the human intelligence in willing, is, does it will? This we assumed as a fundamental premise of our argument, and, if our reasoning is correct, the conclusion that the mind wills freely is within our postulate.

Necessitarians assert that the existence of such freedom is neither true in fact, nor even possible. I shall notice their arguments in Book II. of this work.

CHAPTER XI.

INSTINCT AND HABIT.

It appears, then, that every being that really wills, must will freely. The sphere of its free activity may be more or less circumscribed, varying with the extent of its intelligence, from the lowest, most sluggish form of sentient life, to that of the most vital and ethereal spirit—from the contracted world of the monad, to the illimitable sphere of the Supreme Intelligence. Throughout this infinite range, each, in its own sphere, is equally free. If I want a piece of metal, and, from deficiency of knowledge, know only tin and lead, I cannot will to have gold; and yet, as to the obtaining of tin or lead, my efforts may be as free as though I knew all the metals. Within this limit of my knowledge I am as free to will, as if I were omniscient. If I have knowledge of other metals, but also know that I have power to obtain only tin or lead, I will not make the effort to obtain gold; but as to tin and lead, I may will as freely as if I were omnipotent.

Mere matter—unintelligent, having no will—must be wholly controlled, in its *changes*, by some power without itself; all *real* changes in it, except the subsidiary effects of the finite, must be referred to the action of the Supreme Intelligence. Or if, in any sense, matter can be said to produce change, by being itself in motion, such change is, and, as before shown, *must be* a necessary consequence of such motion, which the matter has no power to prevent or to vary. It has no knowledge, and, so far as its own movements, independent of any present action of intelligence, are concerned, is wholly controlled by the past. In short, it has no will, no self-control, and hence no inherent or real liberty. And if it had, having no knowledge, it would have no sphere in which to manifest it. If to senseless matter we add only sensation, it could feel, but not will. It might suffer, and yet could not know that any change is either possible or desirable. As yet it *knows* no *want*, and must passively suffer or enjoy its sensations. If now, adding want, we suppose a being capable of conceiving that by change its suffering may be diminished, or its pleasure enhanced, it may then want change; but if it have no knowledge as to what change will produce the effect desired, or knows no real or supposable mode of producing such change, it still cannot will. With the addition of such knowledge, will becomes possible, though it does not follow of necessity; otherwise, it would always immediately follow, and there would be no opportunity for the mind to select as to the different wants, or as to the different means of gratifying the same want; the first want felt, with the first known means, would immediately determine the volition; and no exercise of the judgment, no deliberation as to different wants and modes, would be possible, which is contrary to known facts. To be available for effort, the knowledge must extend to the future. A being which does not perceive enough of the future to conceive that the effect of its action will, or may be, to gratify its want; for instance, that taking food may relieve its hunger, cannot be said to act, to eat, from any intelligence of its own; and, in such case, some power without it must move it to action if it be moved.

It lacks an essential element of creative, or first cause; it does not form a preconception, perfect or imperfect, true or false, of the effect of its effort. It can have no design, no purpose, no intent, no end in view; and hence has no inducements to effort. It is evident, that to will to do anything requires an idea, a preconception, of *the* thing, or of something to be done; to make an effort and have no object of effort; to will and not will *anything* is an impossible absurdity. Such a being, though it might still have sensations in the present and memories of the past, yet, perceiving no relation of these sensations and memories to the future, would have no means within itself of foreknowing the effects of its efforts on the future, or that there would be any effect whatever; and would not will as to that future. It would have no will. It has no knowledge except as to the past and present; it is not, in any sense, in the future, and cannot act in the future; its whole sphere of thought and activity is confined to the past, bounded and separated from the future by the present. It cannot change the past and any effort in regard to it, as to remember, or to recombine what it remembers, is really an effort to produce a *future* effect. It cannot will any effect, or change, as to the past or present; and thus, having no knowledge available for willing, its sphere of free activity, always commensurate with that knowledge, is reduced to nothing. All changes in, or of such a being, must still, like those of unintelligent matter, be effected by some power without itself, with only this difference, that the being may feel and recollect the changes, and matter cannot. There is no conceivable way in which such a being could manifest its sensations and memories; and, unless the external power, acting upon it, caused it to exhibit the phenomena we usually attribute to internal power —to will—such being would appear to us the same as senseless matter, moved only by external forces. If all finite intelligences were of this order, any real changes in matter could only be by the will of God. The same also of a being with sensation, but no power of voluntary action—no will; and a being with no knowledge of good and evil,—using these terms in a large sense,— would have no choice as to its sensations, no want, and no will. In such beings all change must be either immediately or mediately by the act of God. The necessity of this control by the Supreme Intelligence, to the preservation of the being, or to any change in it, diminishes as the being derives or acquires power itself to contrive those plans, which are essential to its existence and well being.*

The lowest order of intelligence, then, with which will is compatible, is that in which there is only one want; with the knowledge of only one means of gratifying it; and that knowledge wholly intuitive. We say intuitive, because this implies less intelligence than acquired knowledge; which presupposes an ability to learn by observation, or by rational process. Even to act from knowledge acquired by simple observation, requires an inference; whereas this inference, or rather the idea or fact inferred, may itself be the subject of the intuitive knowledge. For instance, if I have ob-

* See Appendix, Note XIX.

served that, when at one time I willed to move my hand, it did move; I may, from association, expect, or, having some previous idea of the uniformity of cause and effect, infer that when again I repeat the effort, the effect *may* be the same; whereas, the knowledge that willing the movement of the hand is the way to move it, may be directly imparted intuitively. In the former case I have to devise the plan to reach the end from my own knowledge; in the latter, the plan of effort is previously devised for me. The sphere of effort, as also of freedom, in a being with only one want and one known means of gratifying it, would be limited to gratifying its only want in the only mode known to it, or not gratifying it at all. It is still a sphere commensurate with knowledge. The gratification of its want would still depend on its own effort, without which its want would not be gratified. To reduce this to its lowest terms, we must suppose the being having only one want and an intuitive perception of only one mode of gratifying it; also to have no knowledge—no thought —that it may possibly be better not to gratify it. If, in this hypothesis, we increase the number of wants, and suppose that only one of them arises at a time, it makes no material difference. In each case, as it occurs, it is still one want, one known mode of change, and no knowledge, or thought that it may be better not to adopt that mode, or to make no effort to produce that change. If more than one want arise at once, or if the being knows of more than one mode applicable to the want, it must select among them; it must compare and judge, requiring that mode of effort, which is known as an exercise of the rational faculties; but, under the condition above named, no comparison is instituted; there is no occasion, no room for the exercise of the rational faculties. Now all animals, so far as we can ascertain, come into existence with wants, and some *one known mode* of gratifying each want, and no thought that it may be better not to gratify it; and hence, requiring no additional knowledge to direct its effort, and of course no exercise of the rational faculties, no deliberation to obtain it; and this is INSTINCT.

Instinctive action still involves a free effort of intelligence, though it precludes the exercise of the rational faculties in devising the mode of effort, or in selecting from different modes already devised by itself, or by others. Having the want, the requisite knowledge of the means, and the power to use the means, or to make an effort, it makes that effort. The effort in such case is spontaneous; no deliberation being required; but there is still an effort. It may, perhaps, be certain, that under those conditions such being will make the one particular effort, the only one known to it; but this is not because it is *constrained* to make, but, because it is in no way *restrained* from making such effort. It feels the want, has the power to gratify it, knows how, and being free to exert its power, does itself exert it. The effort still is the actual, the uncontrolled, the free effort of the being that makes it, and without which effort the effect would not be produced. That it has no knowledge of any other effort, does not affect its freedom in making that which it does know. It is not as in the case of matter which some other power has put in motion and directed—the freedom of which, if it can have any, consists in the absence of any obstruction, or counteraction—for in instinctive action intelligence still uses and directs its own powers, and, without such *self-*

movement, there would be no exercise of its powers. That the knowledge by which it directs such exercise or effort is intuitive and not acquired, cannot affect its freedom in using its knowledge for directing its efforts, or for any other purpose. In either case, once in possession, it is equally knowledge, and the mind's own knowledge. An act of will is the *primary* self-movement of the mind, and not an antecedent cause of it. The effect, or sequence which it, as a first cause, produces, is some change of body or mind. In an act of will or effort, the agent, even when he knows only one mode of action, is free in a different and wider sense than that of not being counteracted in an action which some external power has imposed upon him.

The agent willing is free to make and to direct the effort which it does itself make. If there be nothing in existence but himself acting through his will, and his want and knowledge, which are independent of his will, the effort may yet be made. The want itself cannot know, or apply the knowledge. The knowledge itself cannot know the want and adapt the effort to it, nor could both combined. This must be done by something which is not only conscious of both the want and the knowledge, but is capable of perceiving the relations between them,—by the intelligent being,—and, as there is no other existing activity (for by our hypothesis there is no other existence of any kind but the one active being, the want, and the knowledge), the act must be wholly its act; and, there being no other power, it must act without restraint or constraint, it must act freely. Under our theory of instinctive action, the knowledge being reduced to the least quantity with which will is compatible, the spheres of freedom and of will there reach their least assignable limits, but are still coexistent; and, like the decreasing quantities of the differential calculus, retain their relations to each other, even in their infinitesimal forms; and when freedom vanishes, the will of necessity vanishes also; and this occurs when the knowledge of the future is reduced to zero, admitting of no preconception of any change to be willed, or made the object of effort. It will be observed, then, that the only essential difference between the observable *phenomena* of mechanical and of instinctive action, arises from the incorporation into a vital being of one iota of knowledge,—the knowledge of one means corresponding to one want. Without this, even if a being had sensation and memory, its instinctive movements must be produced *without any effort of its own* by some external power; and, whether the subject thus moved be that of being with spirit, bones and muscles, or that of stars and planets, such movements are purely mechanical. The proximity of the two, separated only by this single step, has caused confusion in regard to them, and led some to doubt, whether what we class as instinctive actions are not, really, mechanical. And it seems quite conceivable that the first instinctive movements, as, for instance, that of the infant in obtaining food, are not preceded by any act of its will, but that all the movements of its muscles to that end are as immediately produced by the Supreme Intelligence, without the action, prior or present, of the infant's own will, as are the beginning of movements in lifeless matters; that these first motions of the infant may be but God's teaching; his mode of practically and directly imparting the knowledge, which is essential to its existence, till, by imitation, or other means, it learns to evoke, or to invoke the same effects by its own efforts; as a tutor, with his own hand, sometimes guides that of his pupil, to teach him how to write. If it has not the knowledge that it *can* will, and also *how* to will, by intuition, it must, in some way, acquire it before it can itself will, either freely or otherwise. It *seems* quite *conceivable* that this and other intuitive knowledge may be thus practically taught us, and especially in regard to our bodily movements; and yet, on closer examination, we may find that this is *practically impossible*, and that such knowledge must be taught, or must consist in an *idea, or conception of the mode directly imparted as such*, and not derived from the observation of external movements of our own bodies, or those of others. The *moving* of the hand by external force is so entirely distinct from the *internal effort* to move it, that the knowledge of the latter could no more be obtained from the former, than the idea of weight from color. Nor could I ever learn to move my hand by will, from seeing another person move his hand,—for the process of will by which he does it, is not cognizable by the senses through which alone I could learn it in observing the external. All that I could possibly learn from seeing another person move his hand, by will, or from having my own hand moved by a force exerted through the will of another, would be the velocity and direction of its movements, and not the *process of will* by which it was so moved. Still less could I get this idea of movement by will, from any movement of my hand by an external force, which I did not refer to any act of will whatever. Nor can the mind first get this idea by the application of its reason to such external phenomena; for no one has ever yet discovered any rational connection between the effort and the movement.

The mind, then, does not get this knowledge of muscular movement at will, by observation, and must get it by intuition; and by it we know only the fact without any rationale of it. It must be an ultimate idea directly imparted to us, and we may, with the first want of muscular action, be supposed to know the *mode* as well as at any subsequent recurrence of such want. There is nothing gained by supposing the first muscular movement to be mechanical, or the effect of external power. The facts in regard to a want which comes into existence after we have become capable of observing, confirm the conclusion that such knowledge is directly imparted to us, and that all that is voluntary in subsequent action, is voluntary in the first instance; that it is our effort, and is not the *direct* effect of the external power which imparts this knowledge. The change in our knowledge is only a reason for changing our own efforts.

By the same mode of reasoning it may be shown, that we must also intuitively know the mode of putting our mental faculties in action; and as every effort we make is, in the first instance, to affect some portion of either our body or mind, we are justified in regarding all these early actions, which we term instinctive, as the consequence of the effort of the being to gratify its want by a mode intuitively known to it; and with a preconception, at least, of the proximate effects of that effort; and hence, as really voluntary and not mere mechanical acts, from which, indeed, they are sufficiently distinguished by the existence of the effort and its prerequisites, want and knowledge.

If there are any such movements of the body produced by external power, as have just been mentioned as *conceivable*, they are as purely mechanical as those of inert substance.

In nature, when God works out his own plan, the action is called *mechanical*. When he imparts the knowledge of a plan to a finite being that works it out, the action of this being is *instinctive*.

The uniformity and symmetry which we see in crystals, are God's perfect work, and rank with the *mechanical*. The bee, in forming its cells, though it executes with less nicety and precision, works from a plan equally uniform and equally symmetrical, which God has furnished to it, and its action is *instinctive*. It knows the plan, but probably does not know why it is preferable to others. Some of its advantages were unknown, even to scientific men, until revealed by the application of the differential calculus.

We have, then, incorporated in our beings, in the first instance, the power to will; the want, which requires the exercise of that power; and the knowledge which is requisite to its early and very limited exercise; also the knowledge that by will we can put in exercise those mental faculties by which we may come to more perfect knowledge, which sometimes itself gratifies the want and at others reveals the action apposite to the want. We also thus have the knowledge of the first step into the external by muscular action.

The power to will, a want, and corresponding knowledge of means to gratify it, are constitutional elements of every creature that wills; and such creature can at once will, and will freely, because it is constitutionally such a creature as it is.

Instinct may teach the infant only sufficient to enable it to come within the reach of easy effort to accomplish its object; and this may be designed to induct it into a habit of making effort, thus subserving a double purpose. If this be so, it will not materially vary the previous results.

The instinctive actions, then, being voluntary, in what respect do they differ from other acts of will? The whole phenomena of most voluntary actions, as observed in the adult man, are embodied in the want, the knowledge, including the preconception of the future, the deliberation, the volition, and the effect. The distinction we are seeking is not in the faculty of will itself; we have not two wills. It is not in the want, for the same want may often be equally gratified by the instinctive, or by other modes. It cannot be in the volition, for the same volition may arise in instinctive, as in other modes. It must then be in one or both of the other two elements—deliberation and knowledge, that is, in knowledge itself, or in the mode of obtaining, or of applying it. Now, one of the most obvious peculiarities of instinctive action is the absence of deliberation, or of any exercise of the judgment, or rational faculties, in devising or selecting means; and this condition of absence, as we have just shown, can be perfect only when the knowledge of the mode of action is *intuitive*.

In further confirmation of this we may remark that if, on any particular occasion for action, we have not the requisite knowledge, we must, in some way, acquire it; and in its acquisition, or in its application, or in both, must use our rational faculties.* We have also

---

* See Appendix, Note XX.

shown, that the mode of producing bodily movements by will, must be intuitively known; and that this knowledge is simply of the fact, without any such rationale of it as will enable us to vary the mode by any mental process. We know but one mode, and this knowledge is intuitive. In the first applications of this knowledge, we do not know that there may be some reason for not making the movement, and such action then is purely instinctive. As, in our efforts to produce external changes, we always begin with bodily movements, they form the substratum of our plans of action for such changes. In these plans we subsequently learn rationally to combine muscular movements to produce desired results, for which our intuitive knowledge is insufficient. Our plan may embrace certain particular movements, the order of which we arrange; but we do not attempt to arrange, or plan the mode of producing these particular movements. When, subsequently, we have learned to look about us to see if there is sufficient reason for not making the contemplated movement, and have decided that there is not, we are in the same condition as if we had no knowledge, no thought, that there might possibly be such reason. In the last analysis, the bodily movement itself is always instinctive; there is no plan, no deliberation, no exercise of judgment, as to the *mode* of making it; but only as to the particular movements, or series of movements, to be effected by the known mode; and the intuitive knowledge that by will we can produce muscular movement, is the starting point of all our efforts for external changes.

From this one common point both instinctive and rational actions take their departure. In the instinctive, the plan of action, or the successive order of the series of volitions required to produce the intended result is also intuitively known, is so imparted, either mediately or immediately, that it is the same as if incorporated in the being, and requires no rational process to ascertain it. The whole plan may be known at once, or only each step, singly, as it is reached. In either case it still requires the exercise of the will to act out the plan thus furnished to it, without which the knowledge even of the whole plan, though associated with a want demanding its execution, would not avail.

The kid, the moment it is born, can rise upon its feet and go directly to the food its mother supplies. It must not only know that by volition it can produce muscular movement, but it must know what particular movements to make, and the order of their succession. It works from a plan furnished to it, and not designed or contrived by itself. As, by its will, it still produces effects in the future, it is creative, but in an inferior degree. It creates, as the most untaught laborer, who removes the earth from the bed of a canal, has an agency in creating the canal, though he acts only under the direction of the superior intelligence, which designed and comprehends the whole structure. The inferior free agent, while executing all within its own sphere of action,—all the plan which itself *forms*, or *apprehends*—may subserve the purposes of a superior intelligence and help to execute its higher designs. But the intuitive knowledge of a mode of producing bodily movement, except when mere bodily movement is itself the primary want, would answer no purpose unless the knowledge of the particular bodily movement, or series of movements, required to reach the end, is superadded. If this is intuitive also, requiring no exercise of the rational faculties, no deliberation as to the plan, or order of successive efforts, then the action, or series of actions, is purely instinctive. But to shut out all ground for the exercise of the rational faculties, there must, as before stated, be only one want, one known mode of gratifying it, and no knowledge or thought that it may possibly be better not to gratify it.

If we suppose an intuitive knowledge of two or more *modes* of gratifying the same want, or that there are conflicting *wants*, we have a case for the exercise of the judgment. In the former of these cases, the mind may be said to be confined to the two or more modes. It has not designed or planned either of them; but it may design and plan, and must decide as between them; and then the subsequent action becomes, so far, a rational one; and, if the decision is not immediately obvious to the knowing sense, deliberation—effort to examine and obtain more knowledge—with consequent delay, becomes an element in the mental process of determining the final effort. The same is obvious in the case of conflicting wants; and we may remark that any indisposition to the effort, or a disposition to be passive and inert, is a conflicting want.

When the plan of action was before unknown, and yet is obvious to simple mental perception, without preliminary effort to acquire it, the case approaches very nearly to that of action from a plan intuitively known, if, indeed, it can be practically distinguished from it.

Another easy divergence, from the purely instinctive, seems to be that in which the knowledge of the required change, or series of changes, instead of being intuitive, is derived from the simple observation of such external changes, or movements as we can see others make, requiring only to be imitated. This differs from the intuitive, in requiring an effort of attention to observe the movements or their successive order; and an exercise of the rational faculty to infer, that as we have the power to move our muscles, we may therefore be able to make similar movements, and that they will lead to similar results. We might thus learn to apply our knowledge of muscular movement by will; though, as already shown, we never could acquire this knowledge by merely observing others.

As distinguishing features of instinctive action, we have, then, the absence of any plan, design, or contrivance, *on the part of the active being,* to attain its end; and, in place of such contrivance of its own, the knowledge of a plan directly imparted to it, ready made, requiring no contrivance of its own, and no deliberation.

The circumstances under which such actions are most conspicuous, perhaps the only cases of purely instinctive action in human beings, occur in the infant, when its whole attention is absorbed by the want of the moment, when its knowledge is limited to its intuitive perception of only one mode of gratifying that want, and it has yet no thought that it may be better not to gratify it. In brutes it continues more prominent, because they learn less of other than the intuitive modes. It seems, too, not improbable that, with the deficient ability to plan rational modes of action, the necessities of existence may require an increase of the intuitive modes; but if our distinction is well founded, we cannot deny rational actions to most of the inferior animals, or even that a large portion of their actions are of this class, though more alloyed with the instinctive, than those of man. The hungry dog, acting instinctively, would not hesitate to seize the joint of meat he sees before him in his master's kitchen; but he learns that, in the presence of the cook, the effort to get it may be unsuccessful, or be attended with unpleasant consequences, and he governs himself in conformity to this acquired knowledge, including his consequent preconceptions of future effects, and foregoes the effort to appropriate the meat. If, in view of the circumstances, he plans to wait the absence of, or in some way to induce the cook to let him have the meat, he exhibits still more of rational design than by simple forbearance. Though instinctive action is thus less conspicuous, as the acquired knowledge increases, it is conceivable that a being with any amount of such acquirement may act without using it to contrive means, and may wholly disregard any plan it may have previously contrived for similar occasions. In man, a want may be so imperative or so absorbing as to exclude all others; and also all comparison of the different modes of gratifying it; and all deliberation as to whether to gratify it or not; and, in such cases, he acts as a being having only one want, one means of gratifying it, and no knowledge or thought that it may be better not to gratify it; if the one known means has to be found, the action is a rational one; but if it is intuitively known, all the conditions of purely instinctive action are fulfilled. Cases in which our rational actions thus approximate more or less nearly to the instinctive, occur when we are under the influence of some absorbing passion, as, for instance, of fear excited to terror, in sudden fright, and we yield to the impulse to flee from whatever has terrified us. If, in so doing, the mode is immediately perceived, or if it is a result of our own efforts in searching out and designing a plan of action, but, under the excitement, so instantaneously formed and applied that the element of deliberation is very minute, the action will be liable to be confounded with the instinctive, though properly belonging to the rational.

That we flee *from* danger, and not *toward* it, indicates the formation of a *plan* of action *founded on our perception of the circumstances*. We may intuitively know that to avoid being burned we must move from the fire, and how to so move; but we must still perceive—know—where the fire is, and the combination of the two knowledges *may* be by a rational process. In other words, the knowledge of the general facts may be intuitive, and their application to particular cases rational. In running from a fire, we may fall down a precipice of which we well knew, but did not take time to embrace the knowledge in our deliberation, or use it in the preconception of the effects of our action.* When we are *conscious* of forming the plan of action at the moment, however quickly, we are in no danger of confounding it with the instinctive. The distinction, however, is practically not always obvious, and especially in those cases in which the plan of action is easily and quickly formed. The movement of the jaw, to relieve the pain occasioned by the pressure of a person's own teeth on his finger, would, no doubt, be deemed by some an instinctive action; but there have been cases of idiots who did not know enough to do this, though they had all the intuitive knowledge requisite to make the movement, as evinced by their voluntarily making it whenever they ate; showing that, at least in them, an *inference from the peculiar circumstances of the case*

* See Appendix, Note XXI.

—more knowledge—was required to enable them to *apply* their intuitive knowledge of the mode of moving the jaw, in such way as would relieve the pain of the finger. It may be as difficult for such an idiot to form a plan for extricating his finger, as for a horse to plan to extricate his foot when it gets entangled in the halter. The pain being in his finger, he, not improbably, seeks to move and thus to effect change in it, as the horse pulls on his entangled foot for relief; in both cases, from not knowing *plans adapted to the circumstances*, aggravating the difficulty. In such persons, the intuitive knowledge may be less than in some others; but the *particular point* at which the intuitive must be aided by the acquired, is not material to the illustration.*

Though, in terms, the rational may be clearly defined by the formation of a plan of action by the active being; and the instinctive, by the plan of action being furnished to it by intuition, ready formed; yet practically we do not always readily perceive the exact boundary between them.† They are often blended, and perhaps the rational always embraces something of the instinctive. We may rationally plan a series of successive muscular movements in a certain order, but, as before stated, the mode of making each of the movements by will is always instinctive. The same rule will also apply to the use of our mental powers by a prearranged plan.

The mode in which the knowledge of a plan of action is acquired does not affect the action itself. Once acquired, whether by the teachings of the Infinite, or of a finite intelligence, or by our own rational investiga-

* See Appendix, Note XXII.   † See Appendix, Note XXIII.

tion, or by simple perception, the acting from it is the same; and, having memory, we can repeat or reënact the same, by mere association with our wants knowing when to repeat it. The instinctive and the rational both admit of being thus repeated by memory and mere imitation, though neither memory nor imitation could have had any part in our first instinctive actions, for there were then no actions to remember or to imitate; and when ever the young intelligence begins to work by memory of a plan adopted in previous acts, instead of one known by a direct intuition applicable to the case, it begins to be the subject of HABIT. The same of those actions which we have ourselves designed, however complicated, however much contrivance and ingenuity they may have originally required, when, after frequent repetition, we perform them in proper order by memory instead of by a reference to the original *reasons* of that order, they, too, have become HABITUAL.

The peculiar characteristic of habit seems to be that we become so familiar with the plan by which the desired result is to be reached, that, at every stage of it, we know what to do from what has already been done, and do not have to form a preconception of the future, or, at most, not more of it than the next immediate act, or even recur to any preconception previously formed of it; we do not have to perceive the connection of the immediate act contemplated with the end sought. We may merely recollect that, on previous like occasions, we did thus or so with satisfactory results; and that, after such an act, such another act immediately follows. We do it by rote. Suppose a man, who is accustomed to walk in a certain path from one place to another, wishes to go to some other place, requiring him to diverge from the familiar track. If, on reaching the point of divergence, he fails to look at the portion of his plan, which is yet in the future, but, as on former occasions, directs himself in each successive act by reference to the preceding one, or by mere association with it, he will take the old path, and will not discover his mistake until he looks to the future and refers to his preconception of the result intended, and of the means of attaining it. This *habitually* pursuing an old plan when a new one had been designed, is matter of common experience. As a consequence of this working from memory of an old plan, instead of one newly formed for the occasion, there is in habitual action little, if any, need of deliberation, or for the exercise of the rational faculties. As, in the case of instinctive action, there is also in the habitual, a plan ready formed in the mind, and though it may be there, by our own previous efforts, instead of by intuition, it subserves much the same purpose. Perhaps the only essential difference is, that the intuitive knowledge *may* embrace that of the occasions for adopting the particular plan; and in adopting our own previously formed plans, we have always to determine by an exercise of judgment the proper occasions for their application. This, however, as already suggested, may sometimes be necessary also in regard to the application of a mode, or a series of actions intuitively known as the means of reaching an end; and in the habitual, after we have decided to adopt the mode, or series, we pursue it without further deliberation, or exercise of the judgment in going through the successive steps. Again, as before observed, the occasion upon which to use a known plan, either intuitive or acquired, may be suggested by its mere association with recurring circumstances, and, if that examination of our knowledge, which results in a judgment, is an element of association, such examination, or exercise of the rational faculties in comparing and judging is often so slight, or so instantaneous as to be almost unnoticeable. We observe, then, how nearly habitual action brings us back from the rational to the instinctive; and in this we may find the significance of the common saying that "habit is second nature." The instinctive also resembles the habitual in this, that it is not *essential* in either that we should ever know, at one time, any more of the plan than the connection between the action just done and the one next in order. The bee, when it has constructed one side and one angle of its cell, *need* not know that it will require five more such sides and angles to complete it. The most that is essential to its subsequent action is the knowledge that the next step is to make another like side and angle; and so in the habitual, all that is requisite is the recollection of what action comes next, and then again the next.

We find another similarity in the fact that, in resorting to an habitual mode, even though originally acquired, and especially if then adopted after full deliberation, the mind may again use it, as if it were the only one possible; just, as in the first instinctive action, it adopts the one and only known mode, which it has by intuition. With these points in common, the instinctive may glide easily into the habitual. By repetition in practice, the *memory* of the consecutive order of the actions may take the place of the *direct knowledge* of that order.*

Though more unlike, rational actions become habit-

* See Appendix, Note XXIV.

ual by the same process—by the repetition, on like occasions, of the series of efforts embracing the plan of action, till we distinctly remember the routine of the successive efforts, and can go over them in the same order, without reference to the end or the reason of such order. In the habitual, as already intimated, the mind may determine each successive action, not by its perception of its connection with the future, but by association with that which is past; and this analogy of such actions to the movement of a material body by a force behind it, without itself perceiving its course in the future, has probably favored the popular application of the term mechanical to habitual actions, which was naturally enough suggested by the comparatively small amount of mental effort they require.

It is obvious that a very large proportion of the actions of adults are habitual, and that our rational actions, in becoming habitual, approach so nearly to instinctive, is probably one cause of that difficulty in distinguishing the instinctive from the rational, which is so general; a difficulty which may be further increased by the instinctive also actually becoming habitual, the two thus blending together and becoming undistinguishable in one common reservoir, from which the main current of our actions subsequently flows, and through which it is often difficult to trace their respective sources.

Customary or imitative actions also belong to this group. When we do anything merely because it is customary, we adopt the plans or modes of action which we have seen others adopt, without ourselves contriving, and sometimes without even perceiving the reason why others have adopted them. In regard to instinctive, habitual, and customary actions, the question may arise whether it may or may not be better to class those in which we perceive the reason of the plan at the time of action, with the rational actions. There is evidently, in this, a distinction for which philosophical accuracy requires a corresponding difference in expression.

To recapitulate; mechanical action, or material movements and changes, are either God's action, immediate or mediate, upon his own plan—a part of his rational actions; or, as seems to be conceivable and more in conformity to the popular idea, the *necessary* consequences of blind causes, as of matter in motion, which can have no plan.

Instinctive actions are the efforts of a finite intelligent being, conformed by its intelligence to the plan which God has furnished, or furnishes to it, ready formed.

Rational actions are the efforts of an intelligent being, finite or infinite, in conformity with a plan, which itself has contrived, by means of those faculties, which make a part of the constitution of its being, derived or underived.

Customary or imitative action is the action of a finite being in conformity to a plan which it has derived from its observation of the action of others.

Habitual action is the action of a finite, intelligent being, in conformity to a plan which it has in its mind, ready formed, with which practice has made it so familiar, that each successive step is associated with, and is suggested by those which precede it, requiring no examination as to its influence, or its connection with the desired end, or effect in the future; whether that plan was originally instinctive, rational, or customary.

In regard to habit, I would further remark that it has, in some respects, the same relation to action, that memory has to knowledge. They are both retaining powers. As memory of the results of former investigations, or of former observation, obviates the necessity of repeated investigation or observation to enable us to *know*, so habit obviates the necessity of examining as to the probable result of the different proposed *acts*, or of repeating the experiments required in the first action, and which, with the caution then requisite, rendered it slow and tedious, compared with the facility acquired after practice has made us familiar with the order of the successive efforts, and rendered us fearless of any latent consequences, the apprehensions of which, in the first instance, would induce careful examination of our preconceptions of the future effects. Habit seems to be mainly dependent on memory and association. The first time certain circumstances occur, if we have not the knowledge of the mode of action intuitively, we have to examine, compare, judge, and perhaps resort to experiments as to how we shall act; when they recur, we may adopt the former modes implicitly, if the result was then satisfactory, or with such modifications as experience may suggest; and repeat the experiments, with variations, till we have got what we deem the best. When, from the plan adopted on a former occasion, gratification has resulted, a recurrence of similar circumstances suggests, by association, the want of like gratification. This want is also intensified, not only by the recollection of the former pleasure, but the mind, being relieved from the labor of a particular examination of the means and of devising a plan; and also from apprehension as to unseen consequences, which rendered circumspection necessary in the first instance, may direct its attention to the expected gratification, and be almost exclusively absorbed by it.* In regard to any action requiring several successive efforts, as, for instance, walking, a man with full strength, unless knowing by intuition not only the mode of making the particular muscular movements, but their proper respective *order and force*, would, probably, in a first effort to walk, have to proceed very slowly, giving a conscious, attentive, tentative effort to each movement, and perhaps then not always succeed in practically doing as he desired; but, by repeated experiments, he learns the proper order and degree of the movements, and by repetition becomes able to make them without any conscious thought as to the order, degree, or result, each effort suggesting the succeeding one, as a letter of the alphabet, after much repetition, suggests the one which follows it. If, by memory, we retained the knowledge of the letters of the alphabet and of their order of succession only long enough for the occasion, we should have to relearn, every time we had occasion for such knowledge; and but for the retaining power of habit, we should have either to study or experiment in regard to every particular act, not instinctive, and as to the order of any instinctive series of actions, as often as the same might be required to reach the desired result. Habit is but a substitution of the memory of former results of investigation, and experience for present investigation and trial; those former results being suggested by association with like circumstances. In other

* See Appendix, Note XXV.

words, it is memory, aided by association, and applied to actions, when like occasions for them recur. In cases to which it is applicable, habit thus relieves the mind of nearly all the mental labor requisite to action—that of investigating the circumstances and forming its creative preconceptions in the future, and thus facilitates our advancement in action; making it easy for us to do that which we are accustomed to do, whether right or wrong.

While habit thus facilitates effort, it also enables us readily to select from among passing occurrences those which require attention or effort, and to dismiss others almost without notice. When we have no special occasion to know the hour, the striking of a clock, which is constantly repeated within our hearing, makes so little impression, that it is not recollected a moment afterwards. We know from repeated observation that we need not attend to it. It awakens no interest, no want, in us. Ask a man who has just looked at his watch, for the time, and, in a majority of cases, he cannot tell you. He *habitually* saw the time, as indicated on the dial plate, and inferred that the hour of his engagement had not yet arrived, or found that it suggested nothing to be done, and immediately dismissed the whole matter. He can give no account of what passed in his mind. Perhaps a little more of memory of the process so instantaneous would reveal to him that he merely saw that a certain hour had *not* arrived, rather than what the present time was. The want for which he made the effort to look at his watch was satisfied by the former, and he had no interest to know or to retain the latter.

That habit especially applies to those actions which

we have most frequent occasion to perform, increases the benefits we derive from it. It seems, however, to be frequently regarded as a vicious element of mind. This, probably, often arises from only looking at its power to perpetuate or facilitate actions which are wrong, overlooking its influence on those which are right, and may be confirmed by the further consideration, that retaining the old habit enables us to dispense with new acquisitions and with new efforts, thus fostering indolence; and that which legitimately furnishes the great means of progress in action, thus perverted, enables a man to forego the efforts, which are the very germs of this progress. He has become familiar with one course of action—*habit* has made it easy to him; it no longer requires the examination, the experimental efforts, the circumspection, which are necessary to learn and apply new methods. He has also learned the gratification arising from the habitual course, and does not know, and does not seek to know, that by pursuing a different course he may obtain a higher, more permanent, or more unalloyed gratification, or, at least, has not so brought the knowledge home to his affections, and into such practical form, as to induce a want for such higher gratification. Being slothful, the higher and higher wants, which with efforts for progress are continually evolved in the mind, are undeveloped, and remain in their original chaotic state, without the sphere of his efforts, in a region which he has never attempted to penetrate, and, by the exercise of his creative powers, to reduce to order.

CHAPTER XII.

ILLUSTRATION FROM CHESS.

As a partial illustration of some of the foregoing views, let us suppose two persons, A and B, to be engaged in playing chess; and as there is no conceivable necessity for *supposing* any other intelligence to do, or to have done, anything in relation to the game, we may, so far as the players and their efforts are concerned, assume that none others exist. The players have no intuitions of the game; but the knowledge of its laws, indicating what moves can and what cannot be made, having been taught them by others, without any contrivance of their own, is somewhat analogous to that intuitive knowledge which is the foundation of our early actions; and the unreflecting spontaneity with which a young player avails himself of an opportunity to take a valuable piece, without reference to future consequences, has some resemblance to instinctive, undeliberative action. The first move to be made by A is, so far as the position of the pieces is concerned, to be made under precisely the same circumstances as has been every other first move, which he has ever made, and he may now make his *habitual* move without reinvestigation, and each player continues to do this until the combinations become such that past experience can no longer avail. Or either may try an entirely new first or subsequent move, and test its advantages. In any case, however, both the players soon come to new or unremembered combinations. A has just moved, and may be supposed to be passively waiting the move of B, who is now the only active intelligence, and is to will his next move in view of the new circumstances which the last move of A has presented, and which circumstances cannot now be changed until after himself wills and makes his move. His primary *want* is to checkmate his opponent; but, in view of the *circumstances*, he *knows* that, in conformity with the laws of the game, he cannot gratify this want by any move now possible. He then *wants* to make the move which will most tend to checkmate. This secondary want induces him to make an effort to ascertain what move will best fulfil this condition. He examines, he *deliberates*—that is, he makes an effort to obtain more knowledge, with which to direct his final effort, or move; and then, by means of his knowledge of the present position of the pieces, and his power of forming an idea of the future, including his conjectures of the subsequent move of his opponent, he compares his preconceptions of the possible or probable result of various moves; and having, by that use of his knowledge which results in a judgment, selected among them, wills, or puts forth the final effort in conformity to that judgment. He does not fully examine all the possible results of every possible move. This would make the game insufferably tedious, indeed, impossible to be played in a lifetime; but the time he will give to deliberating is also a matter for him to judge of, or decide by his knowing faculty; and, in fact, he often moves with a consciousness that his examination is very imperfect. Of two or more moves, he may not have decided which is best; but, the fact is, he does decide to adopt one, and as, by the hypothesis, there is no other existing intelligent activity to decide for him, he must, in such case, himself decide which to adopt. So far as his present volition and act are concerned, it is the same as if he had never before willed or acted. That he has contributed, by his previous moves, to make the circumstances as they are, does not now affect the considerations by which his present move is to be determined. For the purposes of this action, he *begins* with the circumstances as they now are, and is precisely in the same situation as if he found the game in that condition and was (being already possessed of the same knowledge of the past and present, and with the same power of anticipating the future) to move for the first time. Every time he wills, or puts forth an effort, making or planning a move, is a new and distinct exercise of his creative energy; and the effect is a new creation, evolved from the new circumstances, sometimes getting existence only in the conception of his own mind, and sometimes actualized, or made palpable to others, in the altered position of the piece moved.

We might suppose a more complicated game, in which several persons moved at the same time on one side, each having to take into account not only the probable future moves of the several opponents, but, also, the simultaneous moves of his several coadjutors; and this would more nearly resemble the complicated game of real life. But though, in real life, many may move at once, yet, to each individual, certain circumstances are presented for him to act upon at the moment of willing; and whether, at that moment, these circumstances are fixed, or are still flowing by the influence of some other intelligence or force, is but a circumstance to be taken into view in willing, as also the anticipated future action of other intelligences; as the future possible or probable moves of one party at chess are taken into account by the other in determining his own move. If we look for the *cause* of the move, we refer it immediately to the will of the mover; and if we seek the *reason* why he willed this and not some other move, we may, in most cases, by making such an examination of the circumstances as we suppose he made prior to moving, form a conjecture, in some cases amounting almost to certainty, in others only to the smallest degree of probability; while, in some instances, we may fail to discover a probable or even a supposable reason. The same thing occurs in real life, showing that we differ in our knowledge, or come to different conclusions from the same premises. One man may better understand the game of life, or see farther or more clearly into the future, than another. Some can successfully compete with several skilful chess players, or can ably direct several distinct games at once; and so some men are a match for many others in some of the rivalries of active life, and accomplish their ends in competition with numerous opponents. In a game of diplomacy, a Talleyrand or Metternich would succeed against most men, many men combined, or in separate games with each at the same time. And a Being of infinite power and wisdom would accomplish His purposes, though opposed by any number of finite intelligences, all exerting their finite power as freely as He His infinite.

To one uninstructed, the chess board with a game

partly played out, would appear a mere confusion, without any more arrangement than a child discovers in the position of the stars; and the moves would seem to him as arbitrary and erratic as the motions of planets and comets did to the early pastoral astronomers; but on ascertaining and applying the laws of the game, the element of design immediately appears, and an harmonious system is evolved from the apparent chaos. It is a creation—a very tiny creation—in which the finite intelligence has as *freely* exerted its creative power in devising and assigning the laws of the movements of the game, and in moving the pieces in conformity to those laws, as the Supreme Intelligence exerts its infinite power in making laws and moving the universe in conformity with them. The inventor of the game has, in fact, created another sphere for the exercise of human activity; like the great sphere of God's creation, conditioned by certain laws, which, for the purposes of the game, must be regarded as inviolable as if decreed by infinite wisdom, and enforced by infinite power. It is a sphere in which many of the same processes of mind, which are common in active life, are brought into play, and in which are formed habits of effort, of deliberation, or the investigation of intricate combinations, preparatory to action; and perseverance in effort under circumstances apparently the most hopeless; and in which many of the emotions of real life, as hope, fear, despondency, the feeling of disappointment, the sense of superiority, the humiliation of defeat, the pride of victory, also have place.*

If we suppose only one intelligent being to be engaged in the game, with an automaton chess player so

* See Appendix, Note XXVI.

contrived that the automatic moves will be in conformity with the laws of the game, we shall have a case analogous to that of the finite intelligence acting with reference to the anticipated action of the infinite, uniformly conforming to certain laws, the consequences of which can be only partially known, or vaguely anticipated by the finite. But for this uniformity in the Divine action, our position, in the efforts of life, would be that of a person who should attempt to play chess with one who was wholly regardless of the laws of the game. In such case, all effort in investigating, planning, designing, and moving would be useless; the game would be impossible. And so in the affairs of real life; but for the recognized uniformity in the action of the Supreme Intelligence, there would be no reason or ground for the efforts of finite free agents.

In chess it often happens that, in conformity with the rules, only one move is possible; for instance, when the king must be put out of check, and there is only one move by which it can be done. This resembles some cases of supposed necessity in the voluntary efforts of real life. By the *laws of the game*, the player is confined to one move, and has no liberty to will any other. But there is no conceivable case in which the mind is, or can be, compelled to will at all, and this apparent want of liberty or analogy to it, in chess, is merely an inability in the agent to conform to laws which he has voluntarily adopted for his own government, and, at the same time, not to conform to them; which, so far from detracting from a man's freedom in determining his own volitions, is essential to it; for if, at the same moment that he either decided or willed to conform, he could also decide, or will, not to conform, and the two mental efforts were to go forth simultaneously, his power would be completely neutralized. It is a mere inability to work contradictions, and cannot even be regarded as a deficiency of *power*, for no increase of power tends to give such ability. In the case supposed, the effort of the player to make a particular move is made to depend on his knowledge of the laws of the game, and any other knowledge which may lead him to *want* to conform to them; and such government of himself to gratify this want, by the aid of any knowledge he may have, does not make a case varying from those which we have before considered. The laws of the game are certainly not more obligatory upon him than the just demands of his country, or the laws of God, or his own convictions of right. In all such cases, the existence of such obligation, or of any conclusions, or inferences from them, are but circumstances to be considered by the mind in determining its efforts; but do not affect its freedom in making the efforts, the making, or not making of which still depends on itself.

The memory of the conclusions of former examinations of the circumstances, of which these laws form a portion, may enable a man to dispense with present examination, and act from habit. In chess, each player tacitly pledges himself to conform to the laws of the game; and a man, on full deliberation, may resolve always to conform his efforts to the laws of God, and, in both cases, his compliance may become habitual, so that he ceases to deliberate, or to form new plans of action, spontaneously adopting the old; but this substitution of the result of a former for a present examination, does not conflict with freedom, but is itself an act of freedom. If the mind's predetermination to be governed by certain laws, or in certain circumstances to act in certain uniform modes, could be regarded as a voluntary curtailment of its liberty, that which was thus abandoned could be voluntarily resumed, and the mind, by its own act, regain its entire freedom; but the freedom of the mind is as apparent in the voluntary curtailment, as in the reëxtension of its sphere of effort. But, in adopting such laws or modes, the mind does not, by its free effort, curtail its freedom, but uses its knowledge of general rules to lessen the deliberation required in each particular case as it occurs, or to direct its efforts in cases for which its knowledge, if it did not embrace these laws, or general rules, would be wholly inadequate. That God wills to conform His action to certain laws or uniform modes, does not impair His freedom.

In regard to the influence of law on individual action or effort, we would remark generally, that matter cannot know the law, and, therefore, cannot govern itself by law; that an intelligent being, knowing the law, and not *willing* to be governed by it does not so govern himself; but that, in both instances, the movements or actions of the matter, or of such non-willing being, if made to conform to the law, must be so conformed by some external power, to which the law is a rule of action. If the intelligence making or promulgating the law enforces it by an exercise of its own power, then the law is only a law to itself, and the will of a controlled being has no part in it, and has no more to do with the result of a law thus enforced, than a heavy stone has to do with the effects of gravitation. A law made by one being for the government of another, and not enforced by direct application of power, must depend for its efficiency upon the will of that other. He may will to obey it, because, having examined the particular law, he deems it good in itself; or because it is dictated by a being in whose wisdom and beneficence he confides. In the latter case he *adopts* the rule, because he perceives that it is a particular case of a more general rule, on which he has before decided.

In all cases of government by law, we are influenced, not by the existence of the law, but by our preconceptions of the effects of breaking the law, or of conforming to it. It may be that we perceive it will grieve or offend one whom we love; or it may be the consideration of more direct personal consequences, distinctly and directly apprehended, or inferred from the attributes of the law-maker. The knowledge of the law is always such an addition to our knowledge as enables us better to preconceive the future, and especially in regard to what others, in certain contingencies, will do; but, in the mind's application of this knowledge, to determine its own efforts, there is nothing conflicting with its freedom in willing. If it wills in conformity to the law, it is just as free as if it wills in opposition to it. The word *law*, in such connection, *seems* to be used in two distinct senses; the one indicating a rule by which causes are governed in producing effects; the other expressing a mere uniformity of such effects. But the observation of this uniformity of effects is perhaps but a mode in which we learn the law of the cause which produces them; as, for instance, by our observation of the changes in the material universe, we come to know the laws which God has adopted for His own government in producing these changes, and the two senses of the term become blended in one. But be this as it may, the knowledge of such laws, whether they are the mere uniformity of the effects, or those invariable rules or modes which an intelligent cause adopts in producing them, enables us better to preconceive the effects of our efforts, and, of course, to determine them more wisely; or, at least, more certainly to produce the effect intended.

CHAPTER XIII.

OF WANT AND EFFORT IN VARIOUS ORDERS OF INTELLIGENCE.

From the foregoing views it follows that want, often regarded as a weakness, or defect, is really requisite to all but the lowest forms of animated existence. It is necessary to all intelligent activity, and hence, essential to all the enjoyment which arises from the exercise of our faculties and from that conscious progress, or that satisfaction in the performance of duty, which attends our proper efforts. It is necessary to elevate us above the condition of mere sensitive and sensuous being; and, as no intelligent being will make effort to do what he does not want to do, it is thus necessary, with a metaphysical necessity, which even Omnipotence could not obviate.

If these views are well founded, God Himself cannot be active, or make any progress, or produce change in anything except by being the subject of want; and, in every order of intelligent being, *to want* is as essential to the exercise of a free creative energy, as *to know*.

This imputation of want to the Supreme Being, to some may seem irreverent, and especially to those who habitually regard it as an imperfection. Let such consider that we know God only by the attributes which He manifests in action, or by the effects of His action;

that we cannot conceive of Him as destitute of qualities; and that the simplest and most evident affirmation which we can make, touching the exercise of His active power, is that He doeth that which He *wants* to do.

Nothing, by the mere fact of existence, can be a cause of any effect *after* such existence began; for all the effects of which its *mere existence* is the cause would take place the instant it came into existence, and all its causative power would then be exhausted and cease. It could produce no further changes even in itself; and hence, a sole first cause, without any want to excite it to effort, would immediately on coming into existence, become inert. Such existence, then, would not act on anything, but would become mere material to be acted upon.

It is only by the faculty of effort that intelligence rises above this condition; and this faculty, to be available for such elevation to us, without direct, extrinsic aid, must either be continuous, or we must have a retaining, internal power, with some adaptation to put this retained power in action. In mind, one or the other of the required conditions is fulfilled by the constant, or by the recurring influences of want, which is the only mode known to us, and perhaps the only one which is conceivable, for exciting the voluntary action of an intelligent being, and moving it from a quiescent state. If we ever become quiescent, we cease to be cause, and this want must then become manifest by some change effected by some active cause without us, the effect of which, from the constitution of our being, we may recognize without effort of our own; and the fact is, we cannot always prevent such cognition. If our mental activity ever entirely ceases, it must then be as if we had no mind, and we must be *re-minded* before we can again become an active cause; and this, as before suggested, may be done by want in us, produced by causes to the action of which our own efforts are not essential.

If matter in motion is cause, its power, while it has any, is continuous and ready to be exerted whenever the occasion for it occurs. Being unintelligent, no application of self-moving power to it is possible; having no mind, it cannot be *re*-minded.

It must be true of every intelligence, of whatever order, that if its activity entirely ceases, it cannot, of itself, put itself in action, till some extrinsic activity has, in some way, acted upon it; and the only condition upon which a sole First Cause could entirely suspend activity, without annihilation, would be by its first creating other cause, which would continue to be active independently of the creative cause, and which, by producing some subsequent change, would react upon and arouse the now dormant cause which by previous activity created it. There is, however, no reason to suppose that the supreme First Cause ever becomes quiescent; and it is even doubtful whether the finite mind ever does. It is only certain that we do not always *remember* in what we were active, or that we were active in any wise.

No intelligent being can do anything unless it makes effort to do something. It may try to do one thing and really do something else. A man may attempt to take a flower; and, for that purpose, by the requisite volition move the hand, but, instead of reaching the flower, may overturn a vase, which he did not observe. His plan did not embrace all the essential facts, or circumstances; his knowledge, at least as applied, was defective, and the effect did not conform to the preconception. Still, but for the effort to reach the flower, he would not have overturned the vase. If *his* power does it and yet he does not exert his own power, the power must exert itself, or be exerted by something without him and not of him; and, in either case, it is not his power, and he has no agency either in putting forth the power, or in producing the effect. He does not even make the signal for some other cause to put the power which produces the effect into action. If, then, the power of an intelligent being is put forth at all, it must be by the being to which such power pertains; and the condition which makes the difference between the non-exercise and the exercise of its power is that of effort; and hence, its effort is necessary to its doing or being the cause of anything, even of that which it does not intend to do. But, when an intelligent being makes an effort to do *something*, it is with an intent and design to do it; and it will not try, endeavor, make effort to do anything which it does not *want* to do. So that, the *want to do something* is essential to its doing anything, even that which it does not want to do.

But, though the want rouses the mind to effort, it does not make or direct the effort. The intelligent agent that perceives the relation of the anticipated sequences of the effort to the want, must do this; though, without the want, these sequences would not be sought. If Napoleon, on the morning of the battle of Austerlitz, had not been aroused from his slumber, he would not then have fought that battle; but the page, the drum-beat, the cannon's roar, or the want of food, of activity, or of glory, which aroused him, had nothing to do with the direction or order of the battle. So the want arouses the mind to effort, but does not, and, being unintelligent, *cannot* direct, or even indicate, what effort. This must be determined by the mind, which uses its knowledge, intuitive or acquired, for that purpose.*

But, admitting that want is in all cases a necessary prerequisite to effort, some may suppose that effort is a condition of *cause* only in a finite being; and that infinite power accomplishes its ends without effort. Such, however, do not imagine that He produces effects or changes without an act of His will; and, if our definition of will is correct, this is an effort. To suppose any intelligence to become the cause of any change without some action of its own, is to suppose intelligence to be cause and a necessary cause, merely in virtue of its existence. But all the effects of such a cause must be simultaneous with its existence, and its causative power must cease at the moment of its birth. Now, at any given moment of time, all the causes which can influence the immediate succession of events must exist; and, if the effects of all these causes are *necessary* consequences of their *existence*, then these effects must all be coexistent with such existence; and, even if we suppose one or more of these effects to be the creation of a new cause, if *its* effects, too, are necessary consequences of its existence, they, also, would be coexistent with its creation; and the causative power of the first cause, with that of all subsequent created causes, would be exhausted at the same instant and no effects could be produced in the future. Hence the necessity

* See Appendix, Note XXVII.

of some cause, the effects of which do not, of necessity, result from its *existence*, but which retains a power of producing change that it does not, of *necessity*, exert at the instant—which is not cause merely in virtue of its existence.

Matter, retaining, or extending its power in time by means of motion; and intelligence, with power which it puts in action when it perceives a reason, or has a want; are the only such conceivable causes. Of these, we have already shown that intelligence, in its powers of effort and of preconception, has a special adaptation to future effects; and that matter in motion can now be, at most, only its instrument in producing these effects.

That God, with His infinite attributes, *exists* cannot, as already shown, of itself, be a cause of any changes subsequent to the commencement of such existence; and hence, if such existence embraces a past eternity, His mere *existence* cannot, of itself, be, or ever have been, the cause of anything which has had a beginning.

If the power exerts itself without any effort of the being of which it is an attribute, then that being has no more agency in producing the effect, than if it took place without any exercise of its power whatever. There must be a distinction between that condition of any being, finite or infinite, in which it actively produces, or endeavors to produce change; and that condition of repose, in which, satisfied with things as they are, or as it perceives they will be, by the agency of other causes, it remains inactive and has no agency in producing change. The former must be a condition of effort. If, in the Supreme Being, there is no such distinction, then the effects must be independent of His action, and are not caused by Him, for they come to pass as well without as with His action. Hence, whatever has its origin in His agency must require His effort.

Much of the reasoning which I have just before this applied to show the necessity of effort to the producing of any effect by a finite being, as man, is applicable to any order of intelligent being. The Infinite, however, would never, by its effort, produce effects counter to its intention; although, through self-active free agents of its own creation, it might be the remote cause, or rather the cause of the cause, of what it did not decree, or even foreknow.

The idea that Omnipotence may be creative without effort is, perhaps, induced by observing that with every increase of our own power we accomplish any given work with less effort; and it seems to be a mathematical deduction, that when the power becomes infinite, the effort must become nothing. But if the magnitude of the effect, or the power required to produce it, keeps pace with the magnitude of the power applicable to its production, no such consequence is deducible from increase of power. We look upon Newton and Napoleon, each in their respective spheres of action, as having had more power in themselves than most men; but no one supposes they made less effort. On the contrary, we are apt to consider the efforts of such men as commensurate with the effects of the exercise of their powers. So, also, if the works of a being of infinite power are infinite, there is at least no reason to suppose that His efforts are not as great as those of a being of finite power producing finite effects. Even Omnipotence has its bound in the absolutely impossible;

and there may be effects, just within the verge of possibility, approaching so near the impossible as to task even infinite power to accomplish them. There is, however, in the case supposed, no power at all without the effort. If we should speak of a dormant power, we could only mean, not that there is now power, but that there would be power if exerted; *i. e.*, in a self-active being, with effort there would be power; and attributing Omnipotence to any being could only mean that the efforts of such a being may be all-powerful.

Effort, then, to which want and knowledge are prerequisites, is an essential element of a creative being; and He who governs and controls all the "vast, stupendous scheme of things," and reconciles the various and conflicting efforts of numberless free agents in harmonious results, cannot be an inert being, passively looking upon the gradual development of His designs, but must put forth an active energy, must make effort, —must will these results.

We have already remarked that want involves the idea, or knowledge of future change, though not of the means of producing change. Want, then, which, in the system we are asserting, lies at the foundation as a prerequisite of effort or will, is also the first incipient, chaotic, but still inchoate stage of those preconceptions of the future by which the mind eventually determines these efforts; and the want thus has with it the germ of the element of its own gratification. In this we may recognize something of that harmony, or unity which usually pertains only to truth and which ever marks the designs of Infinite Wisdom.

But, for the gratification of the want, the mere knowledge that change is necessary is not sufficient. We must know *what* change; and, however small and simple the want, or however easy and obvious the means, a creative preconception of them is required. I am hungry, and seek to gratify the want for food. I see bread before me, and know that, by various movements of my hand, mouth, tongue, &c. &c. in a certain consecutive order, *and only in that order*, the want may be gratified. I may want a house to give me shelter, and for this a more complicated creation must be designed and a more extended creative power must be put forth, and with the same regard to the order of the efforts, to actualize the creative conception. Still, the mind could design or form such creation within itself, and will, or make effort, to actualize it without itself, if there were no other intelligence or power in existence, or if all other existence were entirely passive; and hence, feeling the want and having the knowledge required to determine the mode of gratifying it, could by its own inherent powers, unaided and unrestrained by any other power, determine, or put forth a corresponding volition, could will the creation it has conceived, and, if there is a direct connection between its volitions and their sequences, the mind can thus actualize its conceptions in a real external creation. Nor, so far as relates to the act of will itself, is the mode of that connection important. If the mind only knows that the consequences will, or may follow its volitions, this knowledge is a sufficient basis for its own effort; for an effort directed by its use of its own knowledge is self-directed and therefore free. Whether there is any direct connection between volition and its final sequences, is a question which we have already considered, though more especially in relation to external phenomena. The same question arises in regard to internal changes, and this will be considered in the next chapter.

CHAPTER XIV.

OF EFFORT FOR INTERNAL CHANGE.

In regard to the relation of effort to internal changes; as, can we of ourselves put our internal powers in action? or, can we repent of evil and change our affections and dispositions solely by our own efforts? we will first remark that, though we may very reasonably suppose that our own mental efforts are more closely connected with mental than with external material changes, still, as it appears not improbable that our efforts are made effective in the external by the intermediate agency of the Omnipresent Intelligence, so, in like manner, it may be that the Divine influence is necessary to give efficacy to our efforts for internal change. The question here raised is whether the sequences of volition are the immediate effects of our effort to produce them, or if there is some intervening power or cause, to the action of which our own efforts are either necessary, or uniform antecedents. In both cases, however, the important fact that our efforts are necessary antecedents or conditions precedent to the changes is known, and furnishes a good foundation for effort, let the subsequent effects be brought about as they may. If the effort is essential to a desirable result, the reason for the effort is the same, whether the result be proximate or remote. Though this is all that is strictly within the scope of our present inquiry, yet; as germane to the subject, we may be permitted to remark, that the action of those internal faculties by which we *do* follows our efforts to use them to increase our knowledge, or to effect other internal change, as uniformly as the bodily movements follow our efforts to produce external change; the connection between the effort and the sequence of it is in both cases equally uniform and equally inscrutable. External circumstances may affect us both internally and externally, may produce sensation and emotion; and may, also, move our bodies without our volition and even against it.

We cannot directly will a change in our mental affections any more than we can directly will what are termed bodily sensations. We cannot *directly* will the emotions of hope, or fear, or to be pure and noble, or even to want to become pure and noble, any more than we can directly will to be hungry, or to want to be hungry. If we want to take food we are already hungry, and if we want to perform pure and noble actions and to avoid the impure and ignoble, while this want, or disposition prevails, we are already pure and noble. If we want to be hungry, i. e. want to want food, and know that by exercise, or by the use of certain stimulants, or by other means we may become hungry, we may by effort induce this, in such case, a cultivated want; and if we want to want to be pure and noble and know the means, we may, in like manner, by effort gratify the exciting want, and induce the want, which in such case is a cultivated want, to become pure and noble.

If, from seeing the pleasure which admiring a beautiful flower affords to others, or from any other cause, we want to admire it, we would readily perceive that some additional knowledge is essential to that end; and that the first step is to find, by examination, what in it is admirable. To examine, then, becomes a secondary want, and we will to examine. The result of this examination *may* be, that its before unknown beauties excite our admiration and make it, or the gazing upon it, an object of want; so we may also will to examine what is pure and noble till its developed loveliness excites in us, or increases, the want to be pure and noble, and induces a corresponding aversion to what is gross and base.

It may be that increasing our knowledge of the flower will have an opposite effect, and produce disgust, or confirm our indifference. We cannot, by will, determine what the knowledge, or the effect of the knowledge on us will be; but still, as we cannot by effort directly discard, or *lessen*, the knowledge we already have, the only way in which we can by effort change our present intelligential relations to the flower is to *increase* our knowledge; and hence, herein lies our only chance and hope to come to admire it.* If there is anything really admirable, or lovely in a flower, or in a moral emotion or sentiment, examination may reveal it, and our admiration follow the discovery. If holiness were something which it were well for us to want and to have, and yet repulsive in its nature, examination could not help the matter. We never could thus make it a *primary* want; but, in such case, increasing our knowledge might even eradicate such

* See Appendix, Note XXVIII.

want if innately existing. If repulsive, it could only be wanted as a means of something else, and then, as a nauseous dose, the less thought of the better. But God has not so ordered it; on the contrary, by the constitution of our being, virtue in all its forms, in itself, appears more harmonious and beautiful, more lovely and attractive, the more it is examined; and hence, with the power to examine, may be made the object of a cultivated want and of consequent effort to attain it.

We said the result of the examination,—the newly discovered beauties of a flower, or of a moral virtue—*excites*, or *increases* the want; for the purely mental wants, as well as those associated with our physical nature, have their roots in the constitution of our being; and the recurrence of the former, if not so regular in their periods, or so imperative in their demands as the latter, is still amply provided for without any special effort of our own. God has so constituted us that the want of progress—of something better than the present attainment—is an universal want, occurring in our spiritual, even more certainly than the appropriate wants in our physical constitution. The occurrence of them in both and our providing not only for their immediate gratification, but for their recurrence in the future, make conflicting wants, between which we have to decide; and though our decisions in such cases may become habitual, and be almost unnoticeable, yet the occasions for such decisions will continue to arise.

The occurrence and recurrence of our spiritual wants are as certain as those of hunger. We are continually reminded of them by our own thoughts and acts, by comparison with those of others, and by those external appearances, which result from God's thought and action; and He has placed within us the moral sense, as a sentinel, with its intuitions more certainly warning us of what, in wants, or means, is noxious to our moral nature, than the senses of taste and smell do of what is injurious to our physical.

These remarks, with our previous reasoning, lead us to the conclusion that want, constitutional, acquired, or cultivated, is the source of effort for internal, as well as external change, and that this is true of every order of intelligent, active being.

God directs His efforts with infinite knowledge, perfectly considered, or comprehended—perfect wisdom; man, his with finite knowledge, imperfectly considered, or only partially comprehended—fallible judgment, or imperfect wisdom. Infinite wisdom always reconciles its wants, or the mode of gratifying them, with what is right; and hence, moral perfection. Man's finite wisdom does not always reconcile his wants, or the mode of gratifying them, with absolute right; and hence, moral evil, or imperfection, in his general condition as exhibited in aggregated social combination; nor yet with *his own* conceptions of right; and hence, individual moral depravity, which can only exist when his efforts are not put forth in conformity to his knowledge or sense of right.

As a man cannot do any moral wrong in doing what he believes to be right, his knowledge, though finite, is infallible as to what it is morally right for him to do;* and his fallibility in morals must consist in his liability to act at variance with his knowledge, or conviction of right, and never in deficiency of knowledge, or even in belief. In this view, his *knowledge* in the sphere of his

* See Appendix, Note XXIX.

moral nature is infallible, and were he infinitely wise, or certain to act in conformity to his knowledge of the right, he would be infallible in his moral sphere of action.

It is also evident that the mind must direct its efforts for internal change by means of those preconceptions of the future effects of its efforts, which its knowledge enables it to form.

Now a preconception is an imaginary construction,* an incipient creation of the mind in the future. In forming it, the mind does not, of necessity, even consider, or recognize the already existing external circumstances. In "castle-building" it often voluntarily discards these circumstances and forms a construction entirely from its own internal being. Retaining its knowledge of the past, and having the power of abstraction, it could just as well conceive even an external creation, if all external existences, facts, and circumstances were annihilated. A man thus isolated may imagine a universe in which all is, in his view, beautiful and good; or, confining himself to his own being and prompted by his physical wants, he may, in imagination, revel in all the luxuries of sense. He may not even intend to make the additional effort to actualize these combinations, and make them palpable to others, or permanent within himself. If he makes such effort he, perhaps, finds that it is unavailing, and that he cannot give external reality to his creative conception of such a universe, and that he has not the means to obtain the luxuries he has imagined. Yet he has formed these ideal constructions as freely and as independently of all other existing causes, as though he had

* See Appendix, Note XXX.

OF EFFORT FOR INTERNAL CHANGE. 151

omnipotent power to realize the conceptions in an outward creation.

So, too, if moved by the aspirations of his spiritual being, he may conceive in himself a moral nature, pure and noble, resisting all temptation to evil and conforming with energetic and persevering effort to all virtuous impulses and suggestions. Though we may make no effort and not even intend to make any to realize such ideal conceptions, they are not without their influence on our moral nature. They appear sometimes to be formed merely for the exercise of our faculties in constructing, and sometimes for the pleasure of contemplating new and varied forms of harmony and beauty; and, in both cases, they are not without utility. The preconceptions thus sportively made add to our knowledge and to our skill in combining, and furnish models which may be available for future practical use. Poetry presents us with such constructions ready formed by others. These purely ideal conceptions have this advantage, that, in forming them, the mind being free from the excitements and selfish inducements, from the temptations of actual affairs, is more disinterested in its judgment of right and wrong and acquires experience and forms habits, which, without its actually encountering, prepare it for the exigencies of real life. The making of such constructions as harmonize with our conceptions of moral excellence is itself improving; a determination in advance, by persevering effort to make them manifest in action upon proper occasion, is a greater step in progress; and the mere willing to actualize them, when the occasion presents, is, so far as the moral nature is concerned, really their final consummation; for, whether the effort be exhibited in external manifestation or not, makes no difference to the condition of the moral nature. The external act or effect is but the tangible evidence to others of the internal effort, which is the real manifestation of the moral element. This is in harmony with our statement that, producing the intended effect is not material to our freedom in willing it. If a man wills to do an act which is good and noble, it matters not, concerning his virtue, whether his effort be successful or otherwise; the effort is, itself, the triumph in him of the good and noble over the bad and base. If the object of the effort, instead of external good and noble action, is the direct improvement of his own moral nature, then the persevering effort to be good and noble is, itself, being good and noble.

It follows from these positions that, as regards the moral nature, there can be no failure except the failure to will, or to make the proper effort. The human mind, with its want, knowledge and power of abstraction, having the power within and from itself to form its creative preconceptions and to will their actual realization independently of any other cause, power, or existence of any kind, up to the *point of willing*, is, in its own sphere, an independent creative first cause. Exterior to itself it may have no power whatever to execute what it wills, or, having some power, it may be frustrated, or counteracted by other external forces; and hence, in the *external*, the contemplated creative consummation of volition may not be reached; but, as in the *moral nature*, the willing, the persevering effort is itself the consummation, there can, in it, be no such failure; and the mind, in it, is therefore not only a creative, but a SUPREME CREATIVE FIRST CAUSE.

We have then, between effort in the sphere of the moral nature and in that sphere which is external to it, this marked difference: that while in the external there must be something beyond the effort; *i. e.*, there must be that subsequent change, which is the object of the effort, before the creation is consummated; in the sphere of the moral nature, the effort is itself the consummation, and all that follows but manifests the condition, or the want of that nature, which, though innate and originally developed by the actual occurrences of life, may yet have been cultivated by the mind in contemplating its ideal preconceptions, without the interference of external causes, or of circumstances, except so far as those externals may have suggested this cultivation, or have added to the knowledge of the means of effecting it.

In the *sphere of its own moral nature*, then, whatever the finite mind really wills is as immediately and as certainly executed, as is the will of Omnipotence in its sphere of action; for the willing, in such case, is itself the final accomplishment of the creative preconception which the mind has formed in and of itself. We must here be careful to distinguish between that mere abstract judgment, or knowledge of what is desirable in our moral nature, and the want, which leads to the actual willing, or effort to attain it. A man may know that it is best for him to be pure and noble and yet, in view of some expected, or habitual gratification, not only not want to be *then* pure and noble, but be absolutely opposed to being made so, even if some external power could and would effect it for him. We may, however, remark that, as the moral quality of the action lies wholly in the will and no

7*

other being can will for him, to be morally good without his own efforts is an impossibility; all that any other being can do for him in this respect is to use means to excite his wants and increase his knowledge, and thus induce him to put forth his own efforts. Even Omnipotence can do no more than this; for doing more, —the making a man virtuous without voluntary effort of his own—involves a contradiction. The accumulations of virtuous effort are manifested in the knowledge which indicates, and the cultivated wants which require right action. The influence of such knowledge and wants becoming persistent and fixed by habit forms, as it were, the substance of virtuous character.

A man, who does not want to be pure and noble, may yet begin one step lower in the scale of moral advancement, with the want to want to be pure and noble; and, here commencing the cultivation of his moral nature, ascend from this lower point, through the want to be pure and noble, to the free effort to gratify this want.

The *effort* of a man to be good and noble is the consummation, is actually being good and noble. The virtue, in the time of that effort, all lies in, or in and within the effort, and not in its *success or failure*, which is beyond, or without the effort. It is, for the time, being just as perfect if no external, or no permanent results follow the effort. If the good effort is transitory, the moral goodness is equally so, and may be as mere flashes of light upon the gloom of a settled moral depravity.

Nor does the nature of the resulting effect make any difference to the moral quality, or character of the effort. A man's intentions may be most virtuous, and yet the actual consequences of his efforts be most pernicious. On the other hand, a man may be as selfish in doing acts beneficent to others, may do good to others with as narrow calculations of personal benefit, as in doing those acts which he knows will be most injurious to his fellow-men; and doing such acts for selfish ends manifests no virtue, whether that end be making money, or reaching Heaven,* and brings with it neither the self-approval, nor the elevating influences of generous, self-forgetting, or self-sacrificing action.† The moral nature of a volition is not, then, in any way affected by what actually follows that volition.

Again, no moral wrong can pertain to a man for any event in which he has had, and could have no agency, which he could neither promote, nor prevent. Until he has put forth effort, against his knowledge of duty, or omitted to put it forth in conformity with this knowledge, there can be no moral wrong. There is no present moral wrong, either in the knowledge now in his mind, or in the exciting want which he now feels. There may have been moral wrong in the acquisition of any knowledge, or in the omission to acquire any, which required an effort. Such acquisition or omission may have then been counter to his conviction of right. There can be no moral wrong in the acquisition of that knowledge, which he unintentionally acquires by observation. That a man involuntarily knows that the sun shines, or that a drum is beating, cannot be morally wrong in itself. So likewise, that any knowledge now actually has place in his mind can, of itself, involve no present moral wrong doing, though the fact that it is there may be evidence of a previous

* See Appendix, Note XXXI.   † See Appendix, Note XXXII.

moral wrong committed in its acquisition. This he cannot *now* prevent. Such knowledge may have so polluted his moral nature, that it will require an effort to purify it. The polluting arose from the previous effort to acquire, or, negatively, from not making the effort to prevent acquiring, and not from the mere fact of possessing the knowledge, which is now beyond his control, and does not, of itself, alter the moral condition from that state in which the wrong of acquisition left it, though every wrong application of it may do so.

So also in regard to the natural wants. There is no moral wrong in the mere fact of their recurrence. There may be moral wrong in our willing to gratify a want, which should not be gratified, or in entertaining, or cultivating one, which should be discarded, or eradicated, or in the time, or the mode of the gratification. That such want exists at all, or that it should recur at such time, may be proof of a previous wrong effort in cultivating the wants, or of an omission to cultivate some conflicting want; but, if its present recurrence is not by our own effort, such recurrence, of itself, can involve no present moral wrong, and merely furnishes the occasion for virtuous effort to resist what is wrong, or to foster and strengthen what is right. The want may indicate the present condition of the moral nature, while it also supplies the opportunities which make both improvement and degeneracy possible. Though that condition may be comparatively low in the scale, yet an effort to advance from this point may be as truly and purely virtuous as a like effort at any higher point in the scale.

In the *present moment*, then, the knowledge and the want, which exist prior to the effort, involve no present moral right and wrong; and, as we have already shown that the sequence of the effort does not, it follows that the moral right and wrong are all concentrated in the effort, or act of will, which is our own free act.

Efforts to be pure and noble, and for corresponding external action, may become habitual, and hence comparatively easy; habit, as before explained, in this as in other cases, retaining, or holding fast what is acquired in action, and thus leaving the mind at liberty to employ itself in new acquisitions,—new progress in action.

We may further observe in this connection that our moral wants differ from our physical, in existing in *thought*, which is more under the control of the mind's acts of will than the physical conditions of bodily wants; and though we cannot directly will not to think of anything, yet by willing to think of something else we may displace and banish the first thought; so, though we cannot directly will the removal of a want, yet we can will to direct our attention to something else, and also use our knowledge of means to call up, or induce another want, and thus be unmindful of, or discard the first want. And though this is especially true of the moral wants, it partially applies also to the physical. We know, for instance, that by exercise and fasting we can induce hunger; and we may find means of inducing any moral want and by the use of these means, some of which we have already suggested, may give some one moral want a preponderance over others, which, by repetition becoming habitual, will go far to eradicate a discarded moral want and to modify the influence even of the physical.

If entirely eradicated there can be no corresponding

volition and a man habitually holy, who has eradicated the conflicting wants, loses the power to will what is unholy; and, as he cannot be unholy, except by his own voluntary act, he has then no power to be unholy. This is, perhaps, a condition to which a finite moral nature may forever approximate, but never actually reach, never attain that condition of perfection in which it is absolutely unable to will what is impure and ignoble.*

A being infinitely wise, pure and noble cannot, while in that condition, will what is in any degree unwise, impure, or ignoble, this being contradictory ; and, if such a being has no want and no susceptibility to want what is unwise, impure and ignoble, such being cannot freely will what is unwise, impure and ignoble; and if, as we have endeavored to show, the will cannot act otherwise than freely, such a being cannot will what is thus contradictory to its nature.

Our moral wants, like our physical, are many of them wholly innate, while for others there is only an adaptive preparation. As we may, from our acquired knowledge, come to want and to cultivate some particular physical want, so we may also come to want and to cultivate any of our moral wants ; as, for instance, from our observation of others, or our own past experience, or from reflection, may want to want to progress in holiness—want to want to be holy—and, if we have the requisite knowledge, we may adopt means to gratify the exciting want, which, in this case, is an acquired want, and thus induce the want to be holy, which though a natural, or innate want, by this process becomes, also, a cultivated want. Through this knowledge of the means of giving to some of our internal

* See Appendix, Note XXXIII.

wants a predominance over others, we are enabled by effort to influence our moral characteristics at their very source. Even under circumstances least favorable to the recognition of our spiritual condition, amid the engrossments of sense, the excitements of passion, or the turmoil of absorbing business, external events will often suggest our moral wants, while in calm and thoughtful moments they present themselves as spontaneously as thirst in a summer's day.* But as a prudent man will anticipate his bodily wants and look around to provide for their recurrence, and thus maintain his physical vigor, it is also wise to keep our moral wants in view and to bestow on them such attention as will sustain our moral energy. The intuitive knowledge *to examine* avails in both cases. Whatever of moral improvement we effect in this way, must be from the want; from the preconception, or knowledge, reduced to a form available to the gratification of the want; and by the effort.

Having now shown that, by means of such knowledge, we can cultivate our wants and thus give one or the other of conflicting wants the ascendancy and promote one to the, at least, partial exclusion of others; *that* the knowledge of each individual as to what is morally right for him is infallible; *that* the mind can form an ideal construction, or preconception within itself, without reference to any external existence; *that* it can freely make effort to realize such construction; and *that*, nothing *beyond the effort* has any influence upon the moral nature of the effort, or of the agent making the effort; we may, more confidently than before, deduce the conclusion, that the mind in the sphere

* See Appendix, Note XXXIV.

of its own moral nature, applying an infallible knowledge which it possesses, to material purely its own, may conceive an ideal moral creation and then realize the ideal construction in an actual creation by and in its own act of will; and hence, when willing in the sphere of his own moral nature, man is not only a creative first cause, but a *supreme* creative First Cause; and, as his moral nature can be affected only by his own act of will, and no other power can will, or produce his own act of will, he is, in it, also a *sole* creative first cause, though still a finite cause. Other intelligences may aid him by imparting knowledge; may, by word, or action, instruct him in the architecture; but the application of this knowledge, the actual building, must be by himself alone. Though finite, his efficiency as cause in this sphere is limited only by that limit of all creative power, the incompatible, or contradictory; and by his conceptions of change in his moral nature, which are dependent upon the *extent* of his knowledge; and, in this view, the will itself having no bounds of its own, may be regarded as infinite, though the range for its action is finite; or, in other words, within the sphere of its moral nature, the finite mind can will any *possible* change of which it can conceive, or of which it can form a preconception; and, as the willing it is the consummation of this preconception, there is no change in our moral being, which we can conceive of, that we have not the ability to consummate by effort; and as, so far as we know, our power to conceive of new progress, to form new conceptions of change, enlarges with every consummation of a previous conception, there is no reason to suppose that there is any *absolute* limit to our moral sphere of effort, but that it is only relatively and temporarily circumscribed by our finite perceptions, which, having a finite rate of increase, may forever continue to expand in it without pressing on its outermost bound; and, if all these positions are true, every intelligent being, with power of abstraction and a moral nature, has in his own moral nature for the exercise of his creative powers an infinite sphere, within which, with knowledge there infallible, he is the supreme disposer; and in which, without his free will, nothing is made, but all the creations in it are as singly and solely his as if no other intelligent cause existed; and for which he is, of course, as singly and solely responsible as God is for the creations in that sphere in which He manifests His creative power; though, as a finite, created being, even in this, his own allotted sphere, man may still be properly accountable for the use of his creative powers to Him who gave them.

CHAPTER XV.

CONCLUSION.

I have now endeavored to show, in the first place, That it is, at least, doubtful whether there can be any unintelligent cause.

That, be this as it may, every intelligent being that wills, is itself cause, in a sphere which is commensurate with its knowledge.

That the finite intelligence, in the lowest form of instinctive action in which it merely acts out an intuitive plan furnished to it ready formed, which is the only one it knows and of which it may know only one step at a time, is still a first cause.

That, when its knowledge embraces the whole plan, so that it works with a view to an end, it enters the sphere of a designing first cause.

And that, when, with still increased knowledge, it forms its own plans of action, it becomes an *originating* first cause, by the exercise of its finite powers within the sphere of its finite knowledge, in which it has a finite presence, *freely creating*, as God, by the exercise of His infinite powers, creates in that infinite sphere in which He is Omniscient and Omnipresent.

That such creative action is, in some cases, rendered more easy to the finite mind by its adopting through memory and association the plans it has before formed in similar cases, and thus, in *habitual actions*, saving itself the labor of forming new plans.

That the mind has innately, as a part of its constitutional existence, the knowledge which enables it to will, or by effort either directly to do certain things, or to put its own powers for doing them in action; and also to cause muscular movements, which are its first step in producing changes external to itself.

And that, having this ability to be active and by its knowledge to direct its activity, it is incited to effort by want, also, at least, in the first and in most instances, constitutional.

That this effort in each case is a beginning, which, except in the case of habitual modes, applied to like occasions, or through some change in its knowledge, is in no wise dependent upon its own former activity, nor related to the external results of that activity, any more than to such results brought about by any other activity, or cause.

That the effort cannot be connected with anything in the past as a necessary effect, but can only be so connected at all by the action of the mind.

That, at each effort, the mind takes things as they actually present themselves to it at the moment of willing, as the basis of new action, using this, or any other available knowledge it may have, to form preconceptions of the effect of any contemplated action on the future, including also the condition of that future in case it does not act, and then, by a preliminary exercise of its faculties, comparing these preconceptions and judging, or, as we may otherwise express it, by deliberation applying its knowledge to a judgment,—and thus determines, for itself, by what mode it will endeavor to gratify the exciting want, and makes the corresponding final effort, or efforts ; or if it favors that preconception in which the element of its own effort is not, it makes no effort ; the deciding between these preconceptions is, itself, the determination of the mind as to its course ; its determined plan of action, its idea of the change it will produce and of the mode in which it will produce it, are thereby completed ; the creation it would will into existence is conceived, is separated from all other conceivable combinations, and a successful *effort* to realize, or to actualize that preconception, or, in other words, producing by an effort that change in the future which the mind in virtue of its intelligence perceives in advance to be required by its want, finishes the creation which that want demanded ; and the mind will create no more until it has another want, and conceives, or designs some new creation to gratify it.

That innate wants and intuitive knowledge thus furnish a basis for the beginning of voluntary action, which is further developed and its sphere of action enlarged by increase of knowledge.

That man, having a power to will and a want to will, may will, or that, having a want, for the gratification of which an act of will, or a series of acts is necessary, he wills in such a particular way, rather than in any other, because, being *intelligent*, he *knows*, or judges that particular way to be best adapted to the end.

That every particular, or distinct existence must have some peculiar characteristic, to distinguish it from other existence, as, without such distinctions, all existence would be one existence ; and that the pre-requisites of effort, want, knowledge and faculty of will, are a part of the characteristics, attributes, or conditions, which distinguish active, intelligent beings from other existences.

That the object of the effort, is always to produce some change in the future; and that, in this work of producing some change and thus creating the future, every being, that designs and wills, is a creative first cause—a co-worker with God—to the extent of its finite power, freely and independently putting forth its efforts to modify that future, which is the composite result of the combined action of all efficient causes.*

I have also endeavored to show:

That man, having a power of abstraction, may form and vary his preconceptions, or incipient creations, purely from his own internal ideas, without any reference whatever to any other existence; and may freely and independently make effort to actualize these preconceptions.

That the effort to actualize them is, so far as relates to his *own moral nature*, the consummation of his creative conceptions, and that hence, in the sphere of his own moral nature, man is not only a creative first cause, but a supreme creative first cause, limited in the effects he may there produce only by that limit of his knowledge, within which his creative preconceptions are of necessity circumscribed and by the impossibility of working contradictions, which applies to the Infinite as well as to the finite intelligence.

And further, that of the only pre-requisite antecedents of his creations, want, knowledge and faculty of will, the want, though it excites to action, or is the oc-

* See Appendix, Note XXXV.

casion for it, does not direct, or even indicate the direction of the effort, which the *mind* must do by means of its knowledge, and that, in regard to its moral action, this knowledge being infallible, man can there only err by *knowingly* willing what is wrong, and as this wrong willing must be his own free act, an act which no other being or power can do for him, he is, as a sole first cause, solely responsible for it and for all the results he intended, or which he might have foreseen and prevented, and is himself the real author of all the necessary consequences of such action.

That, as his only possible moral wrong is in his *freely* willing counter to his knowledge of moral right, and the knowledge by which he directs his efforts is here as infallible as that of Omniscience, and his power of will, within the sphere of that knowledge, unlimited, he cannot excuse himself on the ground of his own fallible nature, or even urge it in mitigation of a wrong effort. He must have known the wrong at the time he willed, or it would not be a moral wrong. He must have been able to will rightly, for his knowledge, which is the only limit to this ability, embraced all that was essential to action morally right.

In this system, then, wants are pre-requisites of all intelligent activity. In the most common affairs of life, we put forth effort to provide food, raiment, and shelter; and in those more important, or rather those more extended, they still lie at the foundation of the greater, or more complicated movements; and he who contends for the mastery of empires, may really be stimulated only by the innate and seemingly insignificant wants of his animal being, aggravated by an exclusive cultivation. From this low condition he begins to rise as soon as such wants as those of the approbation of himself or of others, have influence and the love of glory finds place. This is perhaps the first stage in that moral progress, of which the harmonious blending of love and duty in our wants is the last term.

With wants thus essential to the development of his active nature, man is most bountifully provided. They permeate his whole being. He has numerous physical wants; his intellect wants knowledge, truth; his æsthetic nature requires the beautiful; his moral qualities demand all that is right and just in principle, or noble in sentiment, with corresponding action; and his religious element requires the contemplation of the ethereal, pure and holy, with a relying faith in the protecting power and sympathy of some adorable object of gratitude, reverence, and love.

Besides all these particular wants, he has the general want of improvement in his physical condition and of progress for his whole spiritual nature. The pervading want of exercise for *all* his faculties is an important addition to the system; and, as if to perfect this apparatus within himself and make his efforts independent of suggestion from without, even of his own physical organism, his activity begets the want of repose and his repose the want of activity; and nearly allied to this the want of variety, of novelty, of change merely as change, by which the very transitoriness of our enjoyments becomes a source of pleasurable activity.

A being, with no other wants than those which spring from the appetites, would be lower than most brutes, for they evince wants for superiority of some kinds.

The gratification of some of the physical wants, however, being essential to our present form of existence, they are most imperative; but they are, in their nature, limited and temporary, when gratified ceasing to exist; and, if there were no other wants, there would be an end of all active energy till they again recurred, as seems to be the case in some animals.

The influence of these temporal wants is, however, made less inconstant by the secondary want of acquisition, or the want to provide, in advance, the means of gratifying the primary wants, when they shall recur. To this acquisitiveness, even when gratification of the temporal wants is the sole object, there seems to be no limit, and it may permanently become the habitual object of effort.

The physical wants in their normal condition seem to be only preliminary, to teach, or form habits of persevering effort, and thus fit the mind to exert its powers in the gratification of those nobler wants which the soul's progress demands.

In these views we may observe the moral beauty of that arrangement by which the physical wants, while almost irresistibly inviting us to action and teaching us persevering effort, between their lessons, naturally withdraw themselves for a season and leave the soul free to exert its powers upon its own higher and nobler wants, and thus anticipate and prepare itself for an exclusive spiritual progress. And we may also observe how this beautiful provision is counteracted and perverted, when the acquisitiveness, which, as a want to secure the continuous or future well being, is a beneficent provision, is cultivated only in its adaptation to the physical—a condition so fatal and to which we are so obnoxious, that the idea of a material Hell seems to have been devised and inculcated to meet and combat the evil on its own ground. In striking contrast with our physical wants, those of our spiritual nature are only further incited by gratification ; the pleasure from them is in the progress, and the more they are gratified, the more steadily they require gratification.

The insatiable, or rather boundless wants of man's spiritual nature ; his want for progress, his aspiration for something better than he has yet attained, in the effort for which his activity finds its appropriate sphere, and his *want* of activity, a proper and exhaustless source of gratification, are essential to the harmonious and uninterrupted working of the system. Exclude these, and the mind, absorbed by debasing physical gratification, or satiated with sensuality, loses its vitality and becomes the prey of *ennui*. The mind, when relieved from the immediate pressing cares of physical existence, naturally turns to the spiritual for the employment of its activities. It seeks to lay up stores of knowledge as a basis for its future creative efforts, or as a means of present mental improvement in the acquisition.

The child early shows a disposition to form ideal constructions, and with mud or blocks, to give them a tangible external existence. Though our first creative efforts are probably in the material, they are early transferred to the moral ; and visions of glory, renown, honor, as the results of lofty character and noble action, find place in the imagination, furnishing us with the materials for constructing the airy castles which flit before the fancy and, in vanishing, leave us models of grace, beauty, and purity. We are thus, at an early period of life, introduced into the moral sphere of constructive effort, and the quickening influence, which the soul receives in this direction, when the first revelations of unselfish, ennobling and romantic passion fill it with ideals of loveliness, grace and elevation, and inspire it with lofty sentiment and energetic virtue, attests the beneficent provision for moral culture.

The ideal constructions, the incipient creations of the mind, are sometimes themselves the proper end, or final object of effort; as, for instance, when by their imagined beauty, or perfection, which they may embody as an actual creation in thought, they gratify an æsthetic want; and sometimes serve as a substitute partially gratifying a want which demands their outward realization, but which is perhaps difficult or impossible. The mere castle-building, however, is often but a pleasurable exercise of the mind, which, like the sports of youth, is a preparation for that sterner work which becomes necessary, when, from the inflexible material of principles, we would make a construction which will possess the elements of durability, and be worthy of preservation. To fit these unpliant materials to each other in a harmonious system requires the labor of severe thought, and to protect it from the assaults to which, when constructed, it is ever exposed, demands constant, persevering energy and unremitting vigilance. But here another admirable provision of our nature comes to our aid. It is the interest which attaches to everything, which we have produced by much labor and care. When, by earnest effort, we have built up within us a moral structure, and by careful thought gradually conformed it to our ideal of moral harmony and beauty, we acquire that interest in its preservation, which nerves the energies and stimulates the vigilance, which are needed to sustain it against the gusts of passion, or the wily and insidious approaches of temptation.*

The provision which has been made for the *influence* of our wants is, in this connection, not unworthy of note. The varied observation of material phenomena, or the flow of mental perceptions and ideas, may suggest a want, but this essential element of our voluntary activity has not been left to any accidental occurrences. Such occurrences may suggest, or provoke our physical wants, and present the occasions for their gratification; but, without any such provocation and without any effort of our own, they will, through *sensation*, recur by an innate constitutional provision of our being. And there seems to be no reason to doubt that, by means of the *moral sense*, or some other constitutional provision of our moral nature, the wants with which the spiritual being is innately and bountifully furnished, also recur without our bidding, and that, for these, too, God has amply provided suggestion in the external, by the significant beauty, harmony and grandeur of His own works, with their ever varying expression appealing to the soul in that poetic language of imagery and analogy, which is intuitively comprehended by all, and on all exerts its persuasive and elevating influences. For no one capable of reflection can look upon the exquisite models, the vast, the grand, the beautiful, the perfect, everywhere presented in the external universe and not feel that to it there is a counterpart; that there is something which perceives and appreciates, as well as something which is perceived and appreciated; that within his own being there is an inchoate universe to him as boundless, and which is his

* See Appendix, Note XXXVI.

especial sphere of creative action. Here is opened to his efforts an infinity of space in which, as already shown, he is a supreme creative first cause, a sphere already canopied with twinkling thoughts, dimly revealing the chaotic elements requiring his efforts to reduce to order and cultivate into beauty; and making visible a darkness, which continually demands from him the fiat, "*Let there be light.*" Constructing this universe within is the great object of existence, the principal, if not the sole end of life. Happy he who, faithfully working in the seclusion of his own allotted space, so constructs this internal universe, that when from the recent void it breaks upon the gaze of superior intelligences, all the sons of God will shout for joy; and when the appointed days of his work are completed, the Great Architect shall Himself pronounce it GOOD.

BOOK II.

REVIEW OF EDWARDS ON THE WILL.

BOOK II.

REVIEW OF EDWARDS ON THE WILL.

INTRODUCTION.

THE prominence which has been accorded to the work of Edwards " On the Will," marks it as the text for our comments on the doctrines of the necessarians. They regard it as the great bulwark of their creed, and confidently assert that the severest scrutiny of their opponents has discovered in it no vulnerable point. The soundness of the premises, and the cogency of the logic, by which he reaches his conclusions, seem indeed to be very generally admitted, so that, almost by common consent, his positions are deemed impregnable, and the hope of subverting them by direct attack abandoned.

This is the more remarkable as he wholly fails to convince a large portion of his readers, who, thus unconvinced and yet unable to detect the fallacies of the argument, come to regard it as an inexplicable puzzle, and rely on their consciousness, or appeal to revelation, to sanction the belief in their own free agency.

These may furnish rational grounds for belief, but

avail little in the controversy. The first is merely saying, I know because I know, or I believe because I believe; and both parties, with equal earnestness and confidence, claim that their respective views are confirmed by the records of inspiration.

In a conflict between the dicta, even of infallible authority, and an apparently conclusive demonstration, we can only infer, either that there is error in the demonstration, or that the dicta are not truly interpreted. This still leaves error, on the one hand or the other, to confuse our vision and obstruct our progress. Discarding then the method of attempting to show that this "iron-linked and irrefutable argument," as it has been termed, is unsound because its conclusions are in conflict with beliefs more generally accepted, or even with demonstrated truth, I shall seek to point out the particular errors and fallacies by which it is vitiated and rendered wholly unavailing.

Edwards's argument is threefold. First, he aims to prove that the mind in willing *cannot* determine itself. Next, that in willing it *is* determined or controlled by something other than itself; and then, that, as a matter of fact, its volitions are and must be foreknown, and therefore necessitated.

These positions seem to imply an admission that self-control is, as I have asserted, the distinguishing characteristic of free action, and yet Edwards also assumes, in some of his arguments, that if the will, or the mind in willing, determines or controls its own action, it is still controlled, and hence not free. Upon this false notion of freedom, in connection with his definition of will, and the assumption (not strictly deducible from it) that will and choice are the same thing, a large portion of his reasoning on the first two named points is founded.

Edwards also asserts that "choice is a comparative act," and argues as if it were the *result* of the comparative act. By means of these various definitions of the one word choice, he can argue that choice, as the result of a comparison, is not subject to our control, and then, will being the same as choice, it follows that will is not subject to such control, and hence is not free. I have endeavored to prove that choice is knowledge and not will, and thus to remove this fruitful source of error in Edwards's argument. He also on these points treats events, natural laws, habits, motives, &c., as if they were real independent powers causing certain effects. The errors of these views I have sought to exhibit.

The assumed axiom that *the same causes of necessity produce the same effects*, is also made to perform an important part in Edwards's system, and the almost universal admission of this dogma has tended much to give currency to his argument.

I have attempted to show that, even in the material world, this law of uniformity is not one of necessity, or even of universal application, while in regard to mind it has no proper application whatever.

For the proof that our volitions are in fact necessitated, Edwards relies on the assumption that they are and must be foreknown by Omniscience. In doing this, he has, in my view, attributed to Omniscience a necessity which could only be predicated of a being of very limited powers, and the argument, resting on such presumption, is invalid.

Many advocates of liberty having accepted the erroneous definitions and unfounded assumptions of the necessarians, most of which appear to be sustained by the authority of profound investigators, have, by such acceptance, been forced into false and indefensible positions, and hence their cause has suffered in the conflict.

If it shall be found that the system I have elaborated dispels the difficulties and surmounts the obstacles presented by the necessarians, and that the logical conclusions are thus brought into harmony with the common sense and the almost universal convictions of mankind, such result will in turn tend to confirm the views I have advanced in the direct argument in proof of liberty. Among these I would particularly note, as useful in the discussion upon which we are about to enter, the definitions of Will and of Liberty; the remarks in regard to Cause; the nature and influence of Habit; the position that knowledge in the last analysis is always a simple passive perception of the mind; that the mind directs its action by means of its knowledge, and finds the reason for it, not in the past, but in the preconception of the effects of its effort in the future.

By this last position the past is cut off from present action, and is in no wise connected with it, except as the mind may in the past have acquired the knowledge which enables it to form more accurate preconceptions of the future effects of various efforts, and more wisely to select among them, and among the various modes of producing the desired result.

All these were more or less important to the reasoning in proof of liberty, and I trust will now be found efficacious in refuting the arguments which are adduced against it.

CHAPTER I.

EDWARDS'S DEFINITION OF WILL.

EDWARDS defines Will to be "that by which the mind chooses anything," and adds, "The faculty of the will is that faculty, or power, or principle of mind, by which it is capable of choosing: an act of the will is the same as an act of *choosing or choice.*" (Part I. Sec. 1, p. 1.)*

He also identifies volition with *choice* and *preference,* and willing, with choosing and preferring. Alluding to a distinction made by Locke, he says, "But the instance he mentions does not prove that there is anything else in *willing* but merely *preferring.*" (Sec. 1, p. 2.) "And his willing such an alteration in his body in the present moment, is nothing else but his choosing, or preferring such an alteration in his body at such a moment, or his liking it better than the forbearance of it." * * * * "It will not appear by this, and such like instances, that there is any difference between *volition* and *preference.*" (Sec. 1, p. 3.)

This definition with its explanation seems to admit of various constructions. From the definition itself it might appear that the will is a distinct entity, which

---

* The quotations are from the edition of Edwards's work on the "Freedom of Will," published in Albany, A. D., 1804.

the mind uses as an instrument with which to choose, or when it makes a choice; or that the *mind's act of will* is a cause of which *its choice* is an effect. The explanations, however, seem to indicate that the definition is only intended to assert that the *act of will* and the *choosing or choice* are one and the same act of the mind. The instances in which he thus uses these terms as equivalent are very numerous, and he expressly says, " to will and to choose are the same thing." (Part I. Sec. 7, p. 91.) It is not, however, clear whether in Edwards's view the act of will embraces the process of choosing, or is concentrated in the choice, which is the result of the process. When he says, "An act of choice or preference is a comparative act, wherein the mind acts in reference to two or more things, that are compared and stand in competition in the mind's view," (Part II. Sec. 10, p. 119,) he states the *process* and makes *it* the act of choice, or the act of will. It is BY this process—this comparing—that the mind chooses, and hence his definition of will also, in terms, embraces it. On the other hand it is obvious that the object, or intent of this comparative act, is always to *obtain knowledge* as to the merits of the things compared, and that, to this end, the mind must come to a conclusion, a decision, or judgment as to these things, otherwise the comparative act ends in nothing, leaving the mind as it began it, and there can then be no choice. Hence the comparing is not itself the choice, nor the act of comparing, the act of choice, for there may be no choice in any way connected with such comparing. That the comparative act is separable from, and distinct from choice, is further manifest from the consideration, that, when the object of comparison is merely to obtain knowledge, as when I compare two triangles to ascertain which is the greater, although there is *comparison* and a final decision or judgment, there is *no choice*. Some other element is yet required. If on comparing their merits as food, I find beef superior to veal, and yet neither now *want* food, nor *want* to provide against hunger in the future, I do not *choose* beef. The whole process as completely ends with the *knowledge*, as in the case of comparing the triangles. If, however, I *want* food for present or future use, I choose beef. Choice then is knowledge with a co-existing want to which it has a certain relation. It is that condition of the mind, in which, with a *want*, it has found and *knows* which of two or more things is best adapted to its want.

These considerations serve to show that the comparative act is not the choice ; and such an hypothesis is contrary to other of Edwards's statements. In distinguishing the understanding and will, he classes all the knowing abilities with the former, and says, " In some sense the will always follows the last dictate of the understanding," &c. (Part I. Sec. 2, p. 16.) If will and choice are identical, this is to say that choice follows the last dictate of the understanding. The object of the comparative act being to obtain knowledge, it is obvious that choice, if it be not itself the last dictate of the understanding, but something that follows the last dictate, must come after the *comparison*, and hence cannot itself be the comparison, or the act of comparing, and the assertion of Edwards that " choice is a comparative act," is incompatible with his assertion that it *follows* the last dictate of the understanding.

The mind's comparative *act* is obviously always an act of will. It is always its effort, or act of will to obtain knowledge as to the things compared; and if the comparative act is not itself an act of choice, here is an act of will, which is not an act of choice, but is a preliminary act, from which choice may or may not result. Choice being but the perception, the knowledge, that one thing is superior to another, never is an act any more than the knowledge that $2+2=4$ is an act. The end sought by this effort, or act of will, sometimes, and only sometimes, is selection, or choice; and even then, to make the act of will itself the choice, confounds the act with its object. That the comparative act, made for the purpose of choosing, is an act of will, sustains Edwards's assertion that, "*the will is that by which the mind chooses,*" but makes it futile as a definition; for it thus *chooses* only in the same sense as it *does* any other thing. It is by the mind's effort, or act of will, that we remember, or move our hand; and hence, in this view, it would be as pertinent to say, the will is that by which the mind remembers, or by which it moves the hand, as to say it is that by which it chooses. This shows that, though in this view it may be true that the mind, in its act of will,—using will as an instrument, or otherwise,—is a cause of which choice is sometimes an effect, yet, with such construction, Edwards's definition is wholly unavailing.

It may be said that in every act of will, or effort to compare, or to remember, or to do anything else, there is a choice of that act. But this must be an *antecedent* choice; and the act of will, in comparing or in remembering, cannot itself be the choice, *which preceded it*, but is the object or thing chosen. If it be said that the choosing to compare or to remember, is itself the act of will, it brings us to the remaining construction of

Edwards's definition, and raises the question as to whether the act of choice and the act of will, or choosing and willing, are one and the same.

Every choice must be preceded by a comparison; and if this comparison is a comparative act of the mind, it is an act of will, and if will is the same as choice, this comparative act is itself a choice, which also must have been preceded by a comparative act, which again is a choice, which also must have been preceded by a comparative act, and so on, ad infinitum, involving the absurdity, which Edwards so often charges on his opponents, of a series of acts of will, or choice, to which there could be no first act. If then in saying that, " an act of choice is a comparative act wherein the mind acts in reference to two or more things compared," &c., he means that there is only one act of the mind, that of comparing, and that this is itself the act of choice, the statement is manifestly incorrect and contradictory to other of his own statements; and if he means that "the mind's act in reference to the two or more things that are compared," &c. is another act distinct from the act of comparing, of which it is a result, and that this is the mind's act of choice, then, as this act of choice requires a prior act of comparison, which prior act is an act of will, and, of course, in his system, also an act of choice, it must require a prior act of comparison, and so on, ad infinitum, involving the absurdity before mentioned.

To avoid this difficulty of action in a finite being, without the possibility of any first act, which is thus involved in Edwards's definitions, and grows immediately out of using choice, in the popular sense, as the result of a comparison, and also as a synonym for will, it may be said, that though choice implies comparison, such comparison is not of necessity a comparative *act;* but that the comparison, and its resulting choice, may be immediately perceived and apprehended by the mind, without any previous effort, or act of will. Such hypothesis is not only quite conceivable, but seems to be in harmony with what I have asserted in Book 1st, as to the mind's sense of knowing by simple mental perception, without effort or act of will. But, Edwards says, "An act of choice or preference, is a comparative *act* wherein the mind acts;" and though the mind may passively be the subject of sensation and emotion, or the recipient of knowledge, it cannot be *passive* in its own *act.* Supposing, however, that calling the comparison an *act* is an inadvertence or error, and that, without any action, the mind may passively perceive the relative merits of the things in themselves, and thus arrive at the knowledge of their equality, or inequality; or may thus perceive, or apprehend the superior adaptation of one of the things compared, to its want, and thus passively reach a choice, still such choice is then admitted to be a perception, and not an *act* of the mind, and hence cannot be the mind's act of will; it can only be knowledge, or, at most, knowledge combined with feeling, which would still prove that choice and will are not the same. Edwards, however, denies that the mind can thus passively decide as to the things compared. To show this, I quote one of his own arguments, changing the word *volition* to *choice*, which he uses as its synonym. "To say the faculty, or the soul determines its own *choice*, but not by any act, is a contradiction. Because for the soul to *direct, decide,* or *determine* anything, is to act; and this is supposed; for the soul is here spoken of as being a cause in this affair, bringing something to pass, or doing something; or, which is the same thing, exerting itself in order to an effect, which effect is the determination of *choice*, or the particular kind and manner of an act of will. But certainly this exertion or action is not the same with the effect, in order to the production of which it is exerted, but must be something prior to it." (Part II. Sec. 2, p. 48.) The last sentence also seems to lead directly to the conclusion that, "the comparative act" is not the "act of choice," but must be prior to it, which confirms the position I have just taken in regard to the quotation that "an act of choice is a comparative act," &c. After this, however, he says, "Volition in this case, is a comparative ACT *attending* and *following* a comparative view." (Part II. Sec. 10, p. 120.) The comparison may be an act of will, and the choice is sometimes a result of such an act. It is manifest that every act of comparison does not result in a choice, or in a subsequent act of will; and Edwards, though he does not specifically distinguish between those which do and those which do not, has probably indicated the kinds of cases he had in view as the ground of his definitions, in this statement:—" yet I trust it will be allowed by all, that in every act of will there is an act of choice; that in every volition there is a preference, or a prevailing inclination of the soul, whereby the soul, at that instant, is out of a state of perfect indifference, with respect to the direct object of the volition. So that in every act, or going forth of the will, there is some preponderation of the mind, or inclination, one way rather than another; and the soul had rather *have*, or *do* one thing than another, or than not to have, or do that thing; and that then, where there is absolutely no preferring, or choosing, but a perfect continuing equilibrium, there is no volition." (Part I. Sec. 1, pp. 5, 6.) Here the condition of every act of will is an act of comparison, resulting in the mind's preferring, or choosing to "*have*, or *do* one thing rather than another, or not to have, or do that thing."

In making an act of choice the same as an act of will, Edwards, of course, makes the choice the last act of the mind in relation to the effect, or the change it seeks to produce. He thus expressly asserts this: "And God has so made and established the human nature, the soul being united to a body in proper state, that the soul preferring or choosing such an immediate exertion, or alteration of the body, such an alteration instantaneously follows." (Part I. Sec. 1, p. 3.)

Our *immediate* object or intent in every act of will is to effect change in some portion of our own being. The above quotation relates to and asserts this only of bodily movement; in other places this truth is recognized with regard to mental action also. The act of choice then, in Edwards's system, as the act of will, is our last act or agency in producing an effect, or in doing anything; and, so far as we are concerned, our act of will is the doing of that thing.

The cases in which, as already quoted, Edwards makes the preferring, or choosing, when the soul "had rather *have*, or *do*," &c. are distinguishable.

When I prefer or would *rather have* one thing than another thing, I have, on comparison, decided or judged, i. e. come to the knowledge that the one thing is better adapted to my want than the other; and when I would rather have this one thing than not to have it, I have, on comparing the having with not having, decided or judged, that the advantages of having are greater than of not having, and that, as between mere having and not having, I would rather have. So far I choose to have, and, if choice were my last agency in the matter, then, so far as I am concerned, I would immediately have. But it is obvious that to have, I may still be obliged *to do*. The comparing the having with not having is itself the mind's effort or act of will, but is not itself a choice. And the choice, when reached as a result of comparing, has none of the characteristics of an act of will. It is not that last agency which is immediately followed by the effect; and this choosing to have does not immediately move, or change any portion of our being. The choice to have is not immediately followed by our having, or even by our trying to have, or doing anything to have. As in other cases, in the act of comparing the having with the not having, we have an act of will which is not a choice; and, in the result of the comparison, we have a choice, which is not an act of will. To extend the choice to the corresponding effect, we must *do*. And if we do not know how to produce that effect, our first doing may be to examine and find how to do it. That to thus examine is the mode in such cases, I have before suggested is intuitively known, and thus becomes a primary foundation of action. But if, as to the manner of doing, we already have sufficient intuitive, or habitual knowledge, the preliminary examination may not be resorted to, and, in that case, the act to be done is not, as compared with other acts, the subject of choice, and we come directly to the question, whether, in view of the advantages of having, and of any pain or other expected consequence of the doing, we will choose to *do*.

The thing may be preferred to any other thing, and we may have chosen to have rather than not have it, and know what to do in order to have, and yet, for good reasons, we may still decide, or choose, not to do. The comparison is now between doing and not doing, with the advantages of the results of doing—the having—on the one hand, contrasted with any pain or unpleasantness attending the doing, on the other. The question, as to whether choice in any case is an act of will, is now narrowed down to the case of choosing between doing and not doing. This is really the same case as that of the mind's deciding between acting and not acting, to which I have alluded (Book I. p. 69), as the result of a preliminary act to obtain knowledge, preceding the mind's final act of will, and liable to be confounded with it; and, in conformity to what was then argued, I will here observe that, if the choice between doing and not doing is the last act of the mind prior to the effect or end sought, then the choosing to do concludes our agency in the matter as completely as would choosing not to do, and that, if so, there can be no difference between that condition of mind which succeeds a choice to do and a choice not to do, which is contrary to observed fact. The act of will, by which we compare one contemplated action with another or with non-action, is not itself that contemplated action, but is a preliminary effort to obtain knowledge in reference to such contemplated action or non-action. When we choose to *have*, our choice may be realized by some other agency than our own, though on such agency our mere choosing, not externally manifested, can have no influence; but, when we will to *do*, or to try to do, we must ourselves be the agent; and when, in such a case, we choose the doing, rather than the not doing, if our choice, as the last agency of the mind, is itself the doing, then the choice and the thing chosen are one and the same, which is absurd. This makes it evident that, as the choosing an apple among various fruits is not itself the apple, or the choosing an act among various acts is not itself the act, so choosing a *doing* is not itself the doing; and hence even the choice to do, that choice which most nearly approaches the effect, never reaches the doing, or trying to do; but that that action, that effort or energy by which the mind accomplishes or executes its decision, judgments, preferences, choices, &c., comes between these decisions, &c., and the effect, and, of course, is something distinct from the choice; and, if we look a little beyond the *choice to do* to the act of will, which is the trying to do, and which when successful, always moves some portion of our own being, we find that, as to this moving, we know, and can know, only one mode of doing it, and that is by willing it; so that in this, the peculiar and exclusive province of the will, there is neither occasion, opportunity, or possibility of any choice. It may further be observed, as at least conceivable, that, in some cases, the question of doing, or not doing, may be so settled, either intuitively or habitually, that no comparison is needed; and in this case, we proceed to the doing without comparing it with not doing, or choosing between them. If, as just suggested, the particular act to be done, or not done, has been in like manner intuitively or habitually settled, then the action follows the choice of the effect to be produced without any subsequent choice; and the choice of an effect requiring an intermediate act, cannot itself be that intermediate act, i. e. the choosing is not the willing.

As already intimated, one objection to using the word *choice* as *will*, and, also, as an act, or the result of an act of comparison, is that it confounds the understanding and the will; or knowledge, and we may add, feeling, with effort. In applying some of the numerous terms and phrases, which Edwards uses as equivalents for choice, this becomes more apparent. For instance, " So that, whatever names we call the act of the will by, choosing, refusing, approving, disapproving, liking, disliking, embracing, rejecting, determining, directing, commanding, forbidding, inclining, or being averse, a being pleased, or displeased with; all may be reduced to this of choosing." (Part I. Sec. 1, p. 2.) To use the one term *choosing* for " commanding," or " forbidding," and also for " being pleased, or displeased with," is giving a wide range to a word intended to be applied with philosophical accuracy. Our " being pleased, or displeased with," may perhaps be the same as *choosing*, but cannot be an act of will any more than our hearing the sound of a cannon is an act of will. The pleasure, or displeasure, and the sound, are all perceptions, emotions, or sensations, and not acts of will, or even subject to the mind's control by its acts of will.

The equality or superiority of one thing, as compared with another, is a fact found, not made, or done. It is apprehended or perceived, not willed; and hence, such *final result* of a comparison is not an act of will, but knowledge acquired, at least in most cases, by an act of will. And choice is but the final result of a comparison in which the mind has *found* or come to *know* the fact, that one thing, in its adaptation to a personal want, is superior to some other. It too is a fact found, not made or done, and it too is knowledge and not will, nor an act of will. The essential element of choice is that result of a comparison which is a decision or judgment that one thing suits us better than another; which decision or judgment, in all its degrees of certainty or probability, is a perception and not an effort. It is in the sphere of knowledge and not of will. We cannot by an act of will directly choose, or alter our choice. When we speak of *making* a choice, we allude to the act of will by which we compare to ascertain which is best adapted to our want,—which suits us best,—and *finding* this is said to be *making* our choice. In comparing, the mind is active; but in the final result, the *perception* that one thing is greater than another, as that the whole is greater than its part, or that one thing is better adapted to our want than another, making, in the latter case, our choice, the mind is passive, as much so in the one case as in the others, and can no more alter the one by a mere act of will, than it can the other. So too, we can as freely will that mental action by which we compare, as that muscular action by which we seek to move a heavy weight; but cannot, in either case, by willing determine the result. This using as a synonym for will, the term choice, which means knowledge, of a particular kind, opens the way for various forms of the sophism that, as will is choice, and choice is knowledge, and the mind cannot control its knowledge, *i. e.* cannot vary the facts or truths it finds, it cannot control or determine its will, because it, being choice, is also knowledge. This is perhaps even more clear in that other expression for the act of will and of choosing, " a being pleased, or displeased with," already alluded to; and also in that similar expression, "appearing most agreeable, or pleasing to the mind," which Edwards thus fully identifies with choice :—" I have rather chosen to express myself thus, *that the will always is as the greatest apparent good*, or, *as what appears most agreeable, is*, than to say that the will *is determined by* the greatest apparent good, or by what seems most agreeable; because an appearing most agreeable or pleasing to the mind, and the mind's preferring and choosing, seem hardly to be properly and perfectly distinct. If strict propriety of speech be insisted on, it may more properly be said, that the *voluntary action* which is the immediate consequence and fruit of the mind's volition or choice, is *determined* by that which appears most agreeable, than that the preference or choice itself is." (Part I. Sec. 1, p. 11.) This directly asserts that the voluntary action is the *immediate consequence* of the mind's volition, or choice. It also, less directly, identifies *an appearing most agreeable to the mind* with choice; hence making " this appearing most agreeable " the determiner, and also the immediate antecedent of the " voluntary action;" and, in harmony with this, in the concluding sentence, refers the act of volition (choice) and the appearing most agreeable to the same cause—to that " which causes it to appear most agreeable." But this appearing most agreeable to the mind, and, of course, that choice, or preference, which is identified with it, is not, as Edwards assumes, the mind's act of will, but its perception, which is knowledge, or, in this case, knowledge combined with sensation or emotion. The mind, after having by the comparison come to *know* what is most agreeable, may passively enjoy the "appearing most agreeable," without any act of will. Now it is evident that the mind by its own action cannot control this "being pleased, or displeased with," nor this "appearing most agreeable to the mind," and, if these are the same as choosing, and choosing is the same as an act of will, then the mind cannot control its act of will. If these terms and phrases are really synonymous, then by substituting equivalents, we may deduce from the simple expression, *a man's willing is as he wills*, that, *his being pleased is as he wills*, and other like erroneous consequences.

It might however still be urged that this making the act of choice or choosing, itself the act of will, does not conflict with the mind's freedom in willing; for if, as Edwards says, "For the soul to *act voluntarily* is evermore to act *electively;*" and if, in electing and choosing its act, it directs and determines its own act, it is then free in such action; for this directing its own action is the very essence of freedom. Still to this, under Edwards's definition, it might be replied, that the choosing is not selecting an act, but is itself the act, and as such is the last agency of the mind, and that, after this, there is no act for it to do; and hence, the mind's liberty to direct its action, as above stated, begins just when there is no action to direct, and amounts to nothing.

In thus shutting out the effort, which I suppose to follow our choice of the modes of doing, or our choice to do rather than not to do, and to constitute the doing, Edwards consistently asserts that our only freedom consists in producing the effect we choose to produce. But as he makes choice the last agency of the mind in producing this effect, this is to say that, whenever choice is followed by the effect chosen, the mind, in its action, is free; and, when our choice is not so followed, the mind's action is not free; thus making a subsequent event change, or make an existence in the past, which is absurd.

In making choice and preference and their equivalents identical with will, Edwards immediately encounters some of the difficulties to which I have alluded; and among the first, that of there being preliminary acts of comparing, resulting in choices or preferences, which have no tendency to move mind or body, which is always the characteristic of an act of will, as recognized by himself; and, if any one doubts it, he can easily satisfy himself by seeking to produce some effect, without commencing with some change in his own being. Alluding to a statement of Locke, that "the word *preferring* seems best to express the act of volition," but that "it does it not precisely; for," says he, "though a man may prefer flying to walking, yet who can say he ever wills it?" Edwards remarks, "But the instance he mentions does not prove that there is anything else in *willing*, but merely *preferring;* for it should be considered what is the next and immediate object of the will, with respect to a man's walking, or any other external action; which is not being removed from one place to another, on the earth, or through the air; these are remoter objects of preference; but such or such an immediate exertion of himself. The thing nextly chosen or preferred when a man wills to walk, is not his being removed to such a place where he would be, but such an exertion and motion of his legs and feet, &c., in order to it. And his willing such an alteration in his body in the present moment, is nothing else but his choosing or preferring an alteration in his body at such a moment, or his liking it better than the forbearance of it." (Part I. Sec. 1, pp. 2, 3.) But, from this statement, it appears that, before the man had " chosen, or preferred such an exertion and motion of his legs and feet," he had already chosen or preferred to be moved to another place; and, if choice or preference is the same as will, he must, at the same time, have willed to be moved to that other place; but, instead of this, Edwards asserts that he *willed* something, which, as he suggests, is entirely distinct and different from such *choice*, viz. : " an exertion and motion of his legs and feet;" and " not his being removed to such a place, where he would be;" so, also, he says, " though a man may be said *remotely* to choose or prefer flying; yet he does not choose or prefer, incline to or desire, under circumstances in view, any immediate exertion of the members of the body in order to it; because he has no expectation that he should obtain the desired end by any such exertion; and he does not prefer, or incline to, any bodily exertion or effort under this apprehended circumstance, of its being wholly in vain." (Part I. Sec. 1, p. 3.) By "remotely to choose, or prefer flying," Edwards cannot mean remotely in regard to time. If he does, certainly such a choice or preference cannot be an act of will; for, though we may perceive that an occasion for action in the future will arise, and may intend such action then, action itself must always be in the present. If I am not *now* acting, I am not acting at all. I may now be active in comparing various conceivable future results, and in laying plans to effect those which I deem most desirable, or choose; and those plans may involve action at some future time, but cannot now be an act in that future. All this is only providing knowledge for future use, if the occasion for it occurs. The choice, too, as between the various results, is in the present, though the subjects of the comparison may only be perceived in the *future*.

But even if a man may choose in the future, it is at least equally certain, that a man may choose at the present time, to fly; and the subsequent remark shows that Edwards merely means, that the choice or preference for flying is *remote from an action;* that there is not " any *immediate exertion* of the members of his body in order to it;" that is, the *mind* makes no exertion to move the members of the body in order to fly; for by " exertion of the members of the body," he cannot mean exertion made by these *members*, but only, that they are the *subjects* of the *mind's* exertions. The statement of Edwards, then, amounts to this, that the difference between a man's preferring to walk, and walking, and preferring to fly, and *not* flying, is, that in the former case, the preferring is followed by *an exertion*, and, in the latter, it is not; thus substantially confirming my views and definitions. But, as, even in Edwards's view, this preferring the exertion of the members of the body in order to *flying*, is distinct from preferring to fly, then, though a man willed such an exertion, he would be willing a distinct thing from the flying which he preferred; and his preferring flying was still a preferring, growing out of a comparison of different modes of bodily movement, without any *willing*. But, in Edwards's system, when the mind had compared and judged, or decided, and the *preference* for flying was reached, the flying was already willed, and the subsequent fact of flying, or not flying, could not alter the prior fact of preferring or willing, which had already existed. All this difficulty and confusion evidently grow out of the attempt to make choice and will identical.

It is obvious that a man, on comparing flying with walking, may prefer the former, as apparently a more graceful and rapid mode of moving. Up to the point of preference, or choice, there is no difference—touching subsequent action, or non-action—between his preferring to walk and his preferring to fly, and that difference, by which, in the one case, he does or tries to do what he prefers, and, in the other, does not, must come after this preference is decided and established. The *exertion*, which Edwards practically admits as constituting the difference in the two cases of choosing to walk and choosing to fly, must then come after the choice. He has, however, as before shown, placed choice in immediate contiguity with the effect, and thus, having left no room between, must of necessity crowd this exertion either into the choice, on the one hand, or into the effect, on the other; and though his views generally favor the former, in this particular case, he speaks of the *exertion* as the *thing chosen*, which, of course, is not the same as the choice, but, on his statements, must be the immediate *effect* of the choice. His expression, " exertion AND motion of his legs and feet," seems to imply that the exertion is something distinct from the motion, and that both are of the *legs and feet;* while his other expression, " exertion, OR alteration of the body," admits of the inference that they are one and the same thing, or that one is a substitute for the other. It is, however, certain that exertion must be of the mind, and that " bodily exertion," and similar phrases, only designate the subject of the exertion, and not the agent making the effort. Exertion, then, as used by Edwards, must be that action of the mind, which is the immediate antecedent of the effect; and Edwards has thus practically, though unconsciously, been obliged to admit into his system if not into his own mind, the element which I have placed between the judgment, or choice, and the effect, or change indicated by that judgment, or choice; and, in some way, probably by the constraining forms of conventional language, we have been led to apply to it, the very similar terms, EXERTION and EFFORT.

As he also makes the act of will, by whatever name he may designate it, the immediate antecedent of the effect, he must, in admitting a mental exertion which must come after the choice, also virtually admit, that this exertion by the mind is the mind's act of will. Having, however, in his system, no space between the choice and the effect, he is compelled, as a logical necessity, to include this exertion either in choice, and thus, in some instances, as before stated, make the choice the same as the thing chosen; or, to avoid this, put the *exertion* into the effect, including it in the same category with *bodily motion*, thus confounding things so widely different, so very distinct, as the motion of matter, and effort, or endeavor; and here again also confounding the choice with the things chosen.

Under the views which I have asserted in Book I, we would find the distinction in the two cases of choosing to walk and choosing to fly, in the difference of our knowledge of the two. The *want* may be, to be moved to another place, and a man not knowing which mode of movement to adopt, on comparing the motion of a bird with that of an ox, may prefer the flying to the walking; but if he knows no mode of flying he cannot practically even attempt it, any more than one who, comparing the past and present, should prefer living in the last century, can make effort to live in it. That his want of knowledge of a mode makes the real difference in the two cases is obvious from the fact, that if a man has any faith, the slightest belief, that, by swinging his arms and kicking the air, or by any other acts in his power, he can fly, he can make the effort, can will to fly, as well as will to walk, and that many persons, having faith in some conceivable mode, have made very earnest and persistent efforts to fly, bringing all their knowledge of materials and mechanical combinations into requisition for that object; and the effort itself was as real and as perfect as though it had been successful. In birds this knowledge is probably intuitive, and they, no doubt, will flying as readily as walking.

Edwards, in defining will, as he says, " without any metaphysical refining," evidently intended to use the term choice in its popular sense; but if, in this use, it admits of such latitudinous and various application, it is manifestly unfit for philosophical analysis. But even if choice is sometimes popularly used as an equivalent for will, such use is by no means universal, as it should be to make it even one ground of identity. We say choose, or choosing an apple; but never will, or willing an apple; and, generally, the term choice seems applicable to external objects, while an act of will can relate only to changes in our own being. If, when we say, a man does a thing, because he chooses to do it, or a man does a thing, because he wills to do it, we intend to express the same thing, we may still mean in each expression to combine both choice and will, as distinct subjects. Both expressions may be elliptical; choice being unstated in the one, and the act of will in the other. But more generally, I think the former expression implies an examination, a comparison, the result of which furnishes a reason for the doing; while the latter applies to that hasty, or capricious doing, which is not founded on such reason.

To recapitulate : Edwards makes willing and choosing, or an act of will and an act of choice, identical; and also makes the willing the last agency of the mind in producing an effect. He also makes choice either a comparative act, or the result of a comparative act. These two definitions of the term choice seem to me philosophically incompatible, and as unwarranted even by vulgar use. In the first place, the comparative act is not itself the choice, but a preliminary act of mind, of which choice is in some cases the object; and hence there is an act of will, which is not itself a choice. Again, if choice is the result of an act of comparison, and this result is, as Edwards says, also an act of will, or the last agency of the mind in producing an effect, then this choice must have been preceded by an act of comparison, which was an act of will, and, as such, being also choice, it too must have been preceded by another act of comparison, and so on ad infinitum. If it be admitted that the series may be traced back till we come to a comparison and choice which are simple perceptions of the mind and not acts of will, then we have a choice which is not an act of will, and which evidently pertains to the sphere of knowledge, or, in Edwards's division, to that of the understanding, and not to that of the will. And when we trace the series forward to where the mind has decided as to what change it would have, or what its want indicates, and also as to the mode of effecting it, and come to the last decision, or choice, as to whether to do, or not to do; then, if choice is the last agency of the mind, the choice to do, to it as completely ends the matter as the choice not to do, leaving no room for the subsequent difference in the conditions of the mind in the two cases; and further, if this choice is itself the act of will, or the last agency of the mind, it is, so far as the mind is concerned, also the doing, and the choice and the thing chosen are one and the same thing. If it be said that the definition, "the will is that by which the mind chooses anything," means that the act of comparing by which the mind chooses is an act of will, then this definition is futile, because we could, in the same sense, say that the will is that by which we remember, or move our muscles, or *do* any thing else; and besides, this is not the sense in which Edwards uses it. Even as regards the act to be done, we do not always select or choose it by a preliminary act comparing it with the other acts; for, in all those cases of instinctive, or habitual action, in which the one mode, and only the one, is intuitively known, or has been determined by previous and repeated experience, we do not delay action to compare and choose; and in every act of will, as it must have for its object to move some portion of mind or body, for which we know only the one mode of will, or effort, there can be no choice *as to the mode*.

And finally, Edwards himself, in using choice as will, and identifying choosing with willing, meets with the very difficulties we have indicated, and is obliged practically to admit exertion,—effort—as intervening between the choice and the effect chosen. That these errors in definition, or varied application of the same terms, lead to important errors, I trust, already appears, and will become more palpable as we proceed in the examination of his argument. I will only add, that, if the arguments I have here presented are found to be fallacious, or insufficient, and it shall still appear that choice is not a mere perception, or is not that *knowledge* which results from a prior comparison ; but is an *action* of the mind, deciding by an *act of will*, in conformity to the knowledge it acquired by comparing ; then, as it is not this *knowledge* which thus acts, but the active agent—*the mind*—directing its own action by means of this knowledge, if we carry back the domain of action, or will, to choice, we also extend the mind's freedom in action over the same ground ; for, the mind's directing its own action constitutes its freedom.

CHAPTER II.

LIBERTY AS DEFINED BY EDWARDS.

Of the term liberty, so important in this inquiry, Edwards says, "The plain and obvious meaning of the words *Freedom* and *Liberty*, in common speech, is *power, opportunity,* or *advantage, that any one has to do as he pleases ;* or, in other words, his being free from hindrance, or impediment in the way of *doing, or conducting in any respect as he wills.** And the contrary to liberty, whatever name we call that by, is a person's being hindered, or unable to conduct *as he will,* or being necessitated to do otherwise." (Part I. Sec. 5, p. 36.) It is manifest that the *willing* is not here deemed a *doing*, nor the doing a willing, for this would make Edwards say that freedom is power to do as one does, or to will as one wills. This power to do as one wills, must then mean power to produce the effect for which the act of will is put forth.

This power that any one has of *doing as he wills*, he subsequently contends, is the only liberty which man possesses; and, in the same section with the above, he says, "but the word as used by Arminians, Pelagians and others, who oppose the *Calvinists*, has an entirely different signification" (p. 38); thus clearly intimating,

* See Appendix, Note XXXVII.

as he defends the Calvinistic view, that only his opponents use it in a different sense. Now, it seems somewhat remarkable, that this human liberty, if it exists, should be placed, not in the acts of willing, of which the willing agent is conscious as his own acts, but, in a subsequent performance, in which Edwards admits and asserts the human being is not conscious of being an actor at all, and does not know who, or what the performers are. Such a liberty is but the liberty which a man, powerless to move himself, may have in being actually moved by some other power, which to him is unknown. If the willing is not considered as a doing, and this liberty in doing *as one wills* is the *only* human liberty, then, of course, the mind of man has no liberty in willing; and the decision of the main inquiry as to the liberty of the mind in willing is involved in that of the correctness of Edwards's definition of the word liberty; the assertion of which begs the question, for if the *only* liberty comes after the willing, the act of the mind in willing is excluded from it.

If, on the other hand, the willing is considered as a doing, then, in the act of willing, the liberty, which, by the terms of this definition, is *power to do as one wills*, becomes, power to will as one wills, or do as one does, and, as this power must be admitted, liberty in such act of will is immediately deducible from the definition. In his Sec. 4, p. 35, Edwards directly aserts that "in this case," (*i. e.* when willing is also the doing,) "not only is it true that it is easy for a man to do the thing if he will, but the very willing is the doing; when once he has willed, the thing is performed, and nothing else remains to be done." One's liberty in willing may be a power to will as he pleases, which is self-direction of effort, by means of knowledge in the form of a perception of what will suit him best, and the confusion in Edwards's argument here arises from his assuming that the phrase "as he pleases" is equivalent to "as he wills," which he has before asserted in his definition of will. It is one form of the difficulty which continually arises from his making will synonymous with choice, preference, and other terms or phrases of like import.

When we have a want, and contemplate the means of gratifying it, we find what *change* will gratify; what *action or effort* will effect the change; and then *whether to make the effort* or not. In all these cases the knowledge thus found is, at least very generally, a choice among things compared, and it seems obvious that if freedom in doing is defined to be *doing as one pleases or chooses*, freedom in willing should, in analogy to it, be *willing as one chooses*. From this harmonious order Edwards excluded himself by his definitions making will and choice identical; though in his reasoning, as will hereafter appear, he assumes that the distinguishing feature of a *free* act of will is its conformity to a previous choice of the act; and this, as choosing the act is the consummation of our knowledge relating to that act, is in conformity to the views I have stated in Book I.

CHAPTER III.

NATURAL AND MORAL NECESSITY.

EDWARDS makes much use of the distinction between natural and moral necessity, which phrases he thus defines :—" And sometimes by moral necessity is meant that necessity of connection and consequence, which arises from such *moral causes* as the strength of inclination, or motives, and the connection which there is in many cases between these and such certain volitions and actions. And it is in this sense, that I use the phrase *moral necessity* in the following discourse. By *natural necessity*, as applied to men, I mean such necessity as men are under, through the force of natural causes, as distinguished from what are called moral causes; such as habits and dispositions of the heart and moral motives and inducements. Thus men placed in certain circumstances are the subjects of particular sensations by necessity; they feel pain when their bodies are wounded; they see the objects presented before them in a clear light, when their eyes are opened; so they assent to the truth of certain propositions, as soon as the terms are understood, as that two and two make four, that black is not white, that two parallel lines can never cross one another; so, by a natural necessity, men's bodies move downwards, when there is nothing to support them." (Part I. Sec. 4, pp. 27, 28.)

Edwards further says, "When I use this distinction of *moral* and *natural necessity*, I would not be understood to suppose, that if anything comes to pass by the former kind of necessity, the *nature* of things is not concerned in it, as well as in the latter. I do not mean to determine that where a *moral* habit or motive is so strong that the act of the will infallibly follows, this is not owing to the *nature of things*." (Sec. 4, p. 29.) And again, "I suppose that necessity which is called *natural*, in distinction from *moral* necessity, is so called because *mere nature*, as the word is vulgarly used, is concerned, without anything of *choice*. The word *nature* is often used in opposition to *choice;* not because nature has indeed never any hand in our choice; but this probably comes to pass by means that we first get our notion of nature from that discernible and obvious course of events, which we observe in many things that our choice has no concern in; and especially in the material world; which, in very many parts of it, we easily perceive to be in a settled course; the stated order and manner of succession being very apparent. But where we do not readily discern the rule and connection, (though there be a connection, according to an established law, truly taking place,) we signify the manner of event by some other name. Even in many things which are seen in the material and inanimate world, which do not discernibly and obviously come to pass according to any settled course, men do not call the manner of the event by the name of *nature*, but by such names as *accident, chance, contingent*, &c. So men make a distinction between nature and choice; as though they were completely and universally distinct.. Whereas, I suppose none will deny but that choice, *in many cases*, arises from nature, as truly as other events. But the dependence and connection between acts of volition or choice, and their causes, according to established laws, is not so sensible and obvious. And we observe, that choice is, as it were, a new principle of motion and action, different from that established law and order of things which is most obvious, that is seen especially in corporeal and sensible things; and also the choice often interposes, interrupts and alters the chain of events in these external objects, and causes them to proceed otherwise than they would do, if let alone, and left to go on according to the laws of motion among themselves. Hence, it is spoken of as if it were a principle of motion entirely distinct from nature and properly set in opposition to it: names being commonly given to things, according to what is most obvious, and is suggested by what appears to the senses without reflection and research." (Sec. 4, pp. 30, 31.)

There is in all this much confusion, growing out of a vague use of the terms "nature," "nature of things," and "natural causes," by which Edwards seems to distinguish natural from moral necessity, and yet asserts that they have the same relation to both. As he argues elsewhere that every volition is an event, which is indissolubly connected with some other event in the past, on which it is dependent as an effect upon its cause, and hence, must of necessity come to pass; he must, to sustain this, assert that choice,—volition—" arises from nature as truly as other events," and is embraced in that "course of events," though "the dependence and connection," " according to established laws is not so sensible and obvious." But this is in opposition to his other views which make *choice* " a principle of motion entirely distinct from nature and properly set in opposition to it," and which he seems, at least partially, to adopt. I think, however, that it is *will*, and not *choice*, that is popularly " spoken of as if it were a principle of motion entirely distinct from nature," &c.; and though this speaking is not accurate, there is a foundation for it in the views I have already stated in Book First of this treatise.

In conformity to those views, every intelligent being, acting through its will, is a distinct cause, modifying that future, which is the joint product, or effect, of all causes combined; and the object of effort in each intelligent cause is to change, or make that future different in some respect from what it would, or might be, but for its own agency; and hence, each will is, in some sense, in opposition to all other wills and to any other causes external to itself, and especially to those of which it can anticipate such consequences as it would modify. When it perceives such consequences, it may strive to vary their effects by its own act of will,—its own causative agency. It may, however, coöperate with all other causes as to any effect which it does not seek, or wish to change; in such case putting forth its own effort, only to become an agent in producing such effect; which agency is, so far, still a change, or difference wrought by its own effort, or act of will.

What Edwards says of *choice* is true of *will*, that it " often interposes, interrupts, and alters the chain of events in these external objects, and causes them to proceed otherwise than they would do, if let alone, and left to go on according to the laws of motion in themselves."

If these *laws of motion*, or the uniform course of events, which we observe in external things, are but manifestations of the will of God, then, when we seek to alter them, we are, in the sense before alluded to, opposing His action, or striving to modify its effects. In the same way, each finite mind may oppose other finite minds, when it perceives that their action is leading to results which it does not wish.

This independent and distinct action of each intelligent agent to modify the action of all other causes, argues that each determines its own course of action and consequently is free in such action. If the individual will is controlled by these other external causes, then these external causes oppose their own action, through the will which they thus control; or convert the will of another to their own use; and this control over another will, as before shown, can only be exerted *directly*, by making the willing by it, their own willing; and indirectly, only when the willing by the agent thus used is free.

Edwards's argument from natural and moral necessity rests upon that vague, popular notion, which leads men to impute certain events, for which they know no secondary causes, to the "nature of things," which really means nothing more than that such events are of common or uniform occurrence. He has told us that "*mere nature*, as the word is vulgarly used, is concerned, *without* anything of choice." Had he looked beyond this vulgar use to what it is concerned with,— to the will, or, as he would say, the choice of God, he could hardly have failed to perceive, that the choice, or human will, could not change the course of nature at all, except by being an independent cause; and that, if it is controlled by nature in its acts of will, any opposition of it to nature must really be nature opposing itself, by means of the act which it controls. If the human mind, acting by its faculty of will, can produce such changes in the course of nature as Edwards represents, it must, so far, be a power independent of nature; and as he virtually divides all power or cause into nature and human will, the human will, must, so far, be independent of all other power or cause; and hence, in producing these changes is subject only to its own control; which is but an expression for its freedom *in willing*.

In regard to the limit of what Edwards calls " natural necessity as applied to men," and by which, as already explained, must be meant the paramount will of God, which, though it may not interfere with man's freedom in willing, frustrates his efforts, we may remark, that the same necessity occurs to us in reference to the counter willing of the finite mind. We may not be able to prevent, or to counteract its will or effort, any more than we can that of the infinite; either may frustrate the execution of what we will, without interfering with our freedom in willing. The wound inflicted on me by an act of violence willed by another *man*, may be as unavoidable to me as the consequent pain, which results from " the nature of things,"—from that constitution of my being which is willed by God. In either case, it is a question, not of freedom in willing, but of power to execute by willing; the sufficiency or insufficiency of which may only become known by the trial, by the result, which follows the willing; and, of course, cannot affect the willing, which has already been, or now is. If these views are correct, the argument which Edwards exhibits, in treating of natural and moral necessity, is against that liberty of *doing as we will*, which he deems the only human liberty, rather than against that *freedom in willing*, which he seeks to disprove.

The classification, by Edwards, of all cause into nature and the human will, admits of three distinct intelligent causes of effects,—the will of God,—my own will,—the wills of other intelligent beings, all of which may be independent of each other; no one directly interfering with the other, but each directing its own power, and yet, each, in virtue of its own intelligence, freely modifying its exercise of its own powers, in consequence of what it perceives the others have done, are doing, or may be expected to do. The result of their former efforts, sometimes coöperating, sometimes opposing, have produced the present state of things, in view of which each now acts, and the composition of the effects of their several efforts with material causes, if any, creates the future.

We may now observe that, in the definitions of moral and natural necessity, the term necessity is used in very different senses, or relations. Moral necessity, as stated by Edwards, means a supposed necessary connection between the action of a mind in willing and something else, which is of, or in that mind, " as inclination, motive," &c., while natural necessity, which, to correspond, should mean the action of external causes on the will, does not relate to the act of willing at all, but only to what follows the act of will, to the want of human *power*, in some cases, to influence the will of God, or change that which He has willed.

In the same way, the phrase "moral inability" is applied to willing, while "natural inability" relates to the effect which is the sequence, or object of willing; to the want of power in all cases to control, or alter that condition, or course of nature, which is the manifestation of God's will. Natural necessity, and natural inability, both imply that a man cannot avoid feeling pain, when wounded; cannot overturn the Alps, or change the course of the stars which God has ordained. The definition also asserts, that the human mind must believe in conformity to evidence presented to it; which is merely asserting, that the human mind cannot by effort alter what already is or has been, nor prevent the future effect of any power superior to its own; or, being intelligent, cannot by the exercise of its intelligence, divest itself of the necessary attributes of intelligence, and not perceive and know that which it does perceive and know; the whole statement, so far as it bears upon the question of human freedom, amounting to this, that the power which a finite being exerts by will is not paramount to that of Omnipotence, and cannot work contradictions.

If by "nature," or "the nature of things," Edwards does not mean the will of God, then in saying, "I suppose none will deny but that choice, *in many cases*, arises from nature, as truly as other events. But the dependence and connection between acts of volition or choice, and their causes, according to established laws, is not so sensible and obvious," he makes "nature" an unintelligent cause, producing, among other effects, human volitions, "according to established laws," without showing how it can know, or conform to such law, or how be cause at all. Or, if he makes " nature " the will of God, acting in conformity to His own laws, he asserts that human volitions arise, like external natural effects, or changes, from His direct action, and is mistaken in supposing that none will deny this position, which really begs the whole question. It is, however, upon the assumed " necessity of connection " of the acts of will with " such moral causes as the strength of inclination, or motive," that Edwards mainly founds the argument against freedom in willing, which he deduces from his definition of moral necessity, and which he thus initiates: " Moral necessity may be as absolute as natural necessity. That is, the effect may be as perfectly connected with its moral cause, as a natural necessary effect is with its natural cause. Whether the will in every case is necessarily determined by the strongest motive, or whether the will ever makes any resistance to such a motive, or can oppose the strongest present inclination, or not; if that matter should be controverted, yet I suppose none will deny but that, in some cases, a previous bias and inclination, or the motive presented, may be so powerful that the act of the will may be certainly and indissolubly connected therewith. Where motives, or previous bias are very strong, all will allow that there is some *difficulty* in going against them. And if they were yet stronger, the difficulty would be still greater. And, therefore, if more were still added to their strength, to a certain degree, it would make the difficulty so great that it would be wholly *impossible* to surmount it; for this plain reason, because whatever power men may be supposed to have to surmount difficulties, yet that power is not infinite; and so goes not beyond certain limits. If a man can surmount ten degrees of difficulty of this kind with twenty degrees of strength, because the degrees of strength are beyond the degrees of difficulty; yet, if the difficulty be increased to thirty or an hundred, or a thousand degrees and his strength not also increased, his strength will be wholly insufficient to surmount the difficulty. As, therefore, it must be allowed that there may be such a thing as a *sure* and *perfect* connection between moral causes and effects, so this only is what I call by the name of moral *necessity*." (Sec. 4, pp. 28, 29.)

One essential support of this argument is the hypothesis that the same causes *necessarily* produce the same effects, which I will consider hereafter; as, also, the relation of motives generally to the will, which Edwards here introduces, but states more fully in a subsequent chapter.

The first statement in the quotation just made merely asserts that the connection between the human *volition* and *its moral cause* is as perfect as the connection between other causes and their effects; for instance, that between the *volition of God* and its *effects*. It in fact asumes that human volitions are a part of a chain, or "course of events, that we observe in many things that our choice has no concern in." This, as Edwards uses volition and choice, seems self-contradictory; but even if admitted, it would still not avail to prove the necessity of volitions, or their dependence on preceding links of the chain, unless he also shows that volitions are not included among those events of which he says, "choice (will) often interposes, interrupts and alters the chain of events." It is true, he seems to confine this power of choice to "interpose," &c., to an interposition in regard to external objects, causing "them to proceed otherwise than they would do if let alone, and left to go on according to the *laws of motion* among themselves." Whether the antecedent links of the chain, assumed by Edwards as reaching to volition, are external, or internal, does not yet appear, but there is no reason to suppose that such chain, if internal, may not be interfered with by the power of the mind, as much as though it were external, but rather the contrary.

The latter part of the quotation is an attempt to prove that the mind, in the act of willing, sometimes meets with difficulties, which it cannot surmount. This seems in conflict with Edwards's other position, that the act of will is a necessary part of a chain or course of events, which the mind not only does not have to aid into existence, but which will of necessity come to pass without its aid, and hence, in coming to pass, can present no difficulty for the mind to overcome. If, however, Edwards hereby intends to assert that such difficulties *prevent* the volition, then there would be no act of will to be the subject of freedom or of necessity. This might show that, under certain conditions, the mind has not power to will, but not that it is not free when it does will. Or, if he asserts that these difficulties prevent the mind from effecting what it wills, it still does not effect the freedom or any other condition, or characteristic of the act of will, which already is, or has been. His design, however, seems to be to argue that, notwithstanding such difficulties, the mind does still will in the premises, but by these difficulties is constrained or compelled to will in a particular way and cannot, by the exercise of its own power, will in any other. It is not easy to conceive of a case in which the mind cannot *try* either to surmount, or to avoid a difficulty; and this trying to do either, whether successful or not, is an act of will. The argument assumes that the ability to *try to do* is limited—that the human will is finite. I have already considered this point in Book First, but will here add, that, under Edwards's assertion that the will is the same as choice and, also, as desire, it seems even more difficult to conceive of any limit to it. An absolute limit to the power to choose among objects of choice, whether they be things or acts, or to will changes, seems indeed to be as inconceivable as a limit to space. We may always choose, and may will or try to do anything within the limits of the conceivable, as we may wish anything conceivable. The limit cannot be in the magnitude, or the multiplicity of the objects presented, for the mind can choose between one portion of the universe and the other, or between as many universes on the one hand, and as many on the other, as it can conceive of; and, having the requisite knowledge, can do it as easily as it can choose between two apples. It can choose or refuse anything conceivable, and hence, so far as the objects of choice are concerned, has no conceivable limits. As the power required to choose or to refuse, does not increase with the magnitude, multiplicity, or any other property or quality of the objects of choice, there is no reason to suppose that, in this respect, this faculty of mind is not adequate to the infinite as well as the finite. The only cases which Edwards here states of this difficulty are those in which " a previous bias and inclination, or the motive presented," are " so powerful " that the will cannot overcome them. As the only tangible notion he gives us of motive, is that of *a perception of what is agreeable or pleasing prior to the act of will;* which, in his system, is the same as " previous inclination," and bias being but a synonym for inclination, this statement amounts to saying that the difficulty consists in " a previous inclination," which again under his definitions, and as the phrase is generally used, is a *previous choice.* Edwards elsewhere assumes (Part II. Sec. 7, p. 92) that " antecedent choice " of the act must be the distinguishing characteristic of a *free* act of will. This too accords with the common belief, and the only possible exception I have suggested to it is, that in some cases of instinctive or habitual action, the mind perceiving that a certain act will accomplish its object, may adopt it without comparison with any other act, or with non-action. When such comparison is instituted, the choice is the summation of the mind's knowledge by which it directs its effort. Admitting then the two positions of Edwards, that " previous inclination " may be so strong that the mind in willing cannot go counter to it; and that an act of will to be free must conform to " antecedent choice," it follows that as the act of will must conform to this " previous inclination," and previous inclination is the same as antecedent choice, that the act of will *must*, in such cases, be a *free* act. These insurmountable difficulties, thus in connection with other of his assumptions, furnish Edwards with proof of *a necessity*, but it is that the mind's act in willing is of *necessity free.*

The supposed cases of the mind's want of power to overcome a previous inclination, would seem to come under the head of moral inability rather than of moral necessity; but Edwards's argument upon it really is, that the previous inclination "may be so powerful that the act of will may be indissolubly connected therewith," and hence necessitated by this "previous inclination" as a moral cause in the past. In this form, however, the inference that the mind's act in willing must of necessity be free, which I just deduced from this certain connection of such acts with "previous inclination" or choice, is quite as obvious as upon the simple statement that there is in previous inclination a difficulty which the mind has not sufficient power to overcome. By making this inclination a cause of inevitable volition, Edwards consistently makes the case one of moral necessity rather than of moral inability, but at the same time exposes his position to other objections which, if necessary, might be urged against them.

That in regard to our actions we meet with cases of difficulty, requiring effort to determine what we will do, or attempt to do, must be admitted. But this difficulty never occurs in *immediate* connection with the willing. The mind is always ready to will whenever it has a want, and knows or conceives some mode by which it deems it possible to gratify that want. When it has no want there is nothing for which to put forth effort, or to will; but there being no conceivable limit to our wants, there is no conceivable limit to the will in that element. We can suppose that a child may want to make its three oranges six, and if it can conceive of any possible means, as by piling them one on another, or dividing and recombining them, it can choose, and can also try, make effort, or will to do so. In these views we reach the result, already stated in Book First, that the mind's power to will is limited only by its sphere of knowledge, and that the faculty of will is, in itself, unlimited. The difficulties exist only in regard to the mind's obtaining the knowledge it needs to determine its final action, and this is really a difficulty, not in its willing, but in its power to execute what it wills, for even in such extreme cases as that of making three oranges six, or of a man's wanting to live in the last century, one may try, make effort, or will to *find* some mode of doing it, however fruitless; and any inability to will to live in the last century arises from our being unable to execute what we attempt by this preliminary act of will, the object of which is to obtain the knowledge of means, or modes, for its final action to that end. All such cases of difficulty as Edwards alludes to, must be those in which the circumstances are so obscure, or so complicated, that the mind has not a clear perception or knowledge of what is best to be done, or of the best mode of doing it, or knows no mode whatever of doing what it wants done; and the obtaining this knowledge constitutes the difficulty, which it *freely* puts forth its *efforts* to overcome, but in which it may or may not be successful. When the mind acts upon its previous knowledge of some mode adapted to the occasion, whether that knowledge be intuitive or acquired, it never can have any difficulty in the willing. If we know it will be pleasant or unpleasant to do a certain thing, we take this into view in deciding whether to do it or not. It is in seeking to learn or know what to do, or the mode of doing, that we encounter difficulty, and this difficulty is not in making the effort—not in willing to learn—but in the learning of these things, which we may freely make effort, or will to do, yet may not have the power to accomplish.

It is also to deficiency of power to do what we will, and not to our power, or freedom to will, or to try to do, that Edwards's "natural necessity" applies, and our inability to overcome the difficulties of learning or deciding what to do, really belongs, in his classification, to natural and not to moral necessity or moral inability.

Another case of peculiar difficulty is supposed to arise in determining the particular act, when of several acts there is no perceivable ground for preferring, choosing, or willing one rather than another. The difficulty in willing, is here a factitious one, being *inferred* from the assumed identity of willing and choosing. Even under this assumption, such difficulty must arise from our not knowing which of two or more things is preferable, *i. e.* from a want of knowledge. This knowledge is of course incompatible with the hypothesis that "there is no perceivable ground for preferring."

Edwards, however, admits that in such cases the mind does adopt some one of the acts—that it does will. Now, in this, and in all the other cases mentioned, the question which concerns the mind's freedom, is not how much difficulty it encounters in determining its actions, nor how much knowledge it wants or can obtain for this purpose, but does it determine them. If the mind determines its own action, it must be free in such action. If, on examination, all the modes of gratifying a want appear to be attended with such disadvantages or difficulties that the mind concludes not to try to gratify it, or if no mode whatever can be found, then the mind's effort for this object ends with the preliminary examination, which, though unsuccessful, was, for aught that appears, a free act of will; and in such case there is no subsequent act of will, free or otherwise. There is a subsequent act only when the mind by its examination has determined the act, and, of course, it then acts freely.

Still another, and perhaps the greatest, source of difficulty is in conflicting wants. We may want a certain gratification, which we may perceive will bring with it or entail some unpleasant consequences. The mind examines, that is, seeks more knowledge, seeks clearer views of the effects of certain actions, to enable it to decide between such conflicting wants.

It is in such efforts that virtue and vice are mainly manifested in action: and it is here that the mischievous tendency of a system which makes such efforts but necessary links in a chain of events, beginning before the existence of the active agent, and hence beyond his control, becomes most apparent. There are things, the doing of which will afford us present pleasure, but which, being injurious to others or to ourselves, make them morally wrong; or which, involving future pain to ourselves, the doing of them is unwise; and conversely, there are things, the doing of which is attended with present pain or discomfort, but which we know ought to be done as a moral duty, or as required by a wise regard for the future. Were it otherwise there would be no room for the exercise and increase of virtue, by self-restraint, or generous effort. I would here observe that, the fact that an action is morally right or wrong, or that it may influence our future well-being, is but *one* of the circumstances, which the mind considers in determining its effort; that it can will against its moral convictions of right; and even against what it knows to be for its own ultimate good, is certainly no proof of a want of freedom in willing, but rather the contrary.

That a man does not always will in conformity to what he knows to be right, or that he knowingly wills against his own ultimate benefit, only proves that he is not wholly pure in morals, or perfect in wisdom, and not that he does not will freely. The martyr, who nobly dies by torture, rather than renounce truth or principle, and the base wretch, who shrinks from any sacrifice to duty, and, for present personal gratification, violates all his convictions of right; both act, or will, with equal freedom.

From their actions, we infer that they are beings with very different characters, and if, with this difference, we should find them acting alike, we might suspect that their actions were influenced or determined, by some common cause, external to the one or the other, or to both of them; so that this diversity of action is an indication of self-control or freedom, rather than of necessity. How this difference in character came about, is not strictly material to the question,— does the intelligent being, such as he is, will freely? To make or influence his own character, might argue a wider range of action, and with it a more extended sphere of freedom, which, in conformity to the views stated in Book I, would imply an extension of knowledge also. In unison with this, we find that the mode in which the character can be effected, is by increase of knowledge, for which man, if not the lower animals, can put forth intelligent efforts. In the first place, through the moral sense, we all know what, for us, is right or wrong; and with this knowledge it is universally admitted, that it is always most wise and beneficial to do the right, but, as before observed, such general abstract propositions have little influence on our voluntary actions. We may not be quite sure that the case in hand is not an exception to the general rule. We may not perceive how the rule can apply and distrust it. We are wanting in faith. The faith is acquired by increase of knowledge; for the general proposition being admitted, it follows, that with sufficient knowledge, it will become obvious in each particular case, that doing right is most wise and beneficial. We may thus come to perceive and know the particular benefits which will accrue from right action, and when, by mature reflection, our faith in the certainty of such future benefits is made perfect, we submit to present privation and suffering to attain them, as readily as the merchant foregoes present enjoyments purchasable with his money, and parts with it, in the confident belief of large future gains; or, as a man in a ship on fire, leaps into mid ocean, when he perceives that if he does not, a worse fate is inevitable. When we have settled a number of individual cases sustaining the general rule, have clearly perceived the particular advantages of each, and then, by the test of actual experience, found that the results of actions morally right are most satisfactory to us, our faith in the general proposition is confirmed and its influence increased. By such investigations, and such actual experience, we may come to associate moral right in our efforts with the most beneficial results, till right action becomes habitual.

Actual experience is in some respects most effective; but mature reflection, or the abstract investigation of conceivable cases will fulfil the same intention, and has the advantage which calm and disinterested thought has over the hasty processes required by the emergencies of action, in which we are often unduly influenced by what appears prominent and important only because it is imminent. Such investigations will aid us to overcome the difficulty which there often is in our concluding to sacrifice present pleasure, or to suffer present pain, to secure the prospective benefits of right action. By repeatedly assuring ourselves of these benefits, and dwelling upon them, they are so brought home to our affection that the right actions, with which they are thus familiarly associated, become the subjects of cultivated secondary wants, and, as such, conflict with and at least tend to countervail the immediate temptations and inducements to wrong action. It is thus that the knowledge acquired by our own efforts, or imparted to us by any extrinsic agency, human or divine, becomes a means of influencing our actions at their source in want. As before observed, what we may have accomplished in this way by our own efforts, has, from the greater value which we attach to the results of our own care and labor, the advantage over what may have been otherwise obtained. From these views it appears not only that man, being what he is, is free; but that what he morally is, or may become, in a great measure depends on his own efforts, though he may be aided by extrinsic intelligences. Among these aids we may note the influence of the moral sense, and our desire to preserve our own self-respect, both of which are implanted in us by the Creator, and through which the mutilation and degradation of the soul, by intended wrong doing, are preconceived and painfully felt in advance of the act; while our desire for the esteem of others makes way for a virtuous influence by their approval of right and reprobation of wrong, a duty which all should fearlessly and honestly perform.

By means of the mind's ability to create and to contemplate imaginary cases, its power of forming its own character, may in a great measure be removed from the influence of these extrinsic circumstances which furnish the occasions for outward action, and from the exciting and selfish inducements which often attend it.

Now returning to our argument it appears that the difficulties which we have considered are not in the province of the will, but of the understanding, and that they arise from our deficiency in the knowledge required to find the comparative measure of various existing circumstances, or future effects, or conflicting wants; or, to reconcile some of these wants, or the mode of their gratification, with moral right; which deficiency we may in some degree supply by effort,—though sometimes we cannot surmount this difficulty, and often cannot do it in time to apply the knowledge or the truth found to direct our actions.

We come now to consider the particular cases by which Edwards illustrates moral ability, or what may be termed a negative moral necessity. "To give some instances of this *moral inability*. A woman of great honor and chastity may have a moral inability to prostitute herself to her slave,—a child, of great love and duty to his parents, may be unable to be willing to kill his father. A very lascivious man, in case of certain opportunities and temptations, and in the absence of such and such restraints, may be unable to forbear gratifying his lust. A drunkard, under such and such circumstances, may be unable to forbear taking of strong drink. A very malicious man may be unable to exert benevolent acts to an enemy, or to desire his prosperity; yea, some may be so under the power of a vile disposition, that they may be unable to love those who are most worthy of their esteem and affection. A strong habit of virtue and great degree of holiness may cause a moral inability to love wickedness in general, may render a man unable to take complacence in wicked persons, or things; or to choose a wicked life and prefer it to a virtuous life. And, on the other hand, a great degree of habitual wickedness may lay a man under an inability to love and choose holiness; and render him utterly unable to love an infinitely holy being, or to choose and cleave to him as his chief good." (Sec. 4, pp. 32, 33.)

Preparatory to an examination of these cases it is important to know what Edwards means by "Moral Inability." He says, "Moral Inability consists * * * either in the want of inclination; or the strength of a contrary inclination; or the want of sufficient motives in view to induce and excite the act of the will, or the strength of apparent motives to the contrary. Or both these may be resolved into one; and it may be said in one word, that *moral inability consists in the opposition or want of inclination.* For when a person is unable to will or choose such a thing, through a defect of motives, or the prevalence of contrary motives, it is the same thing as being unable through the want of an inclination, or the prevalence of a contrary inclination." (Part I. Sec. 4, p. 32.)

This quotation fully confirms my previous statement that Edwards uses motive as an equivalent for inclination.

We must also still bear in mind that he uses the

words inclination, preference and choice, as synonyms of will. Inclination can only exist in connection with some want, and as a consequence, though not a necessary consequence of it, other conditions being requisite.

In the second of the cases just quoted from Edwards, he uses the phrase "unable to *be willing*," and he must mean to imply the same in the other cases, and not an inability to *do the thing* spoken of, as otherwise they would be irrelevant. His first case is perhaps the strongest. Supplying this ellipsis it reads thus, "A woman · of great honor and chastity may have a moral inability *to be willing* to prostitute herself to her slave." In this, for "moral inability" substitute its equivalent as above defined by Edwards, "opposition or want of inclination," and again for inclination, his equivalent for it, *will* (choice or preference), and the assertion reads, A woman of great honor or chastity, may have an opposition, or want of will, to be willing to prostitute herself to her slave; that is, she cannot will what she does not will, or what she opposes by will. The same thing appears more directly, by taking the words in their ordinary import without tracing them through Edwards's peculiar definitions. "A woman of great honor and chastity" is a woman, who is unwilling to prostitute herself; and to will to prostitute herself would be to will and not will, or to be willing and unwilling at the same time; or, still shorter, to be chaste and unchaste at the same time, contradictions which Omnipotence and Omniscience could not reconcile, and which, could they be reconciled, would militate, at least as little against, as in favor of, freedom in willing.

In Edwards's second case, the denial of his statement does not, of necessity, involve any contradiction in terms. Nor is the statement of necessity true. The contrary is not only conceivable, but it is conceded as a fact, that in a portion of India it is deemed a filial duty of the child to kill his father, when suffering from the infirmities of age. The belief or ideas, the *knowledge* of the child, there indicates this act, which to him may be so unpleasant, that only " great love and duty to his parent" would induce him to perform it. The child here *knows* a mode of action, which reconciles the killing of his father with his own sense of " love and duty " to him, and, even though he encounter the difficulty of reconciling it with conflicting wants, he may adopt it. The other cases would only call forth analogous remarks.

All these cases are more or less analogous to that of a being, pure and noble, being unable to will what is impure and ignoble, because he has no want which will be gratified thereby, or because he has a conflicting want, which, in his judgment, should be gratified. If, then, the absence of the *want*, or the presence of an equivalent conflicting want, is the reason of the moral inability in the instances given by Edwards, such inability does not conflict with freedom in willing. When there is no willing, there cannot be either freedom or necessity in willing; and a man's having freedom to will what, or when he does not want to will, or to will in opposition to his paramount want, or to his inclination, were it possible, would not be freedom at all; and the inability to will what, or when he does not want to will, is not opposed to freedom. Such ideas of freedom are absurd and contradictory. It must be borne in mind, that we are not now considering the question how a man comes to be virtuous or vicious, or whatever he may be, but the freedom of his mind in willing, under all the conditions and circumstances existing at the time of willing, whether that be at the time of the first act of will to gratify an innate want by means intuitively known; or subsequently, when other wants have been developed and other knowledge acquired, and conflicting combinations of them have arisen, requiring much preliminary effort to fully apprehend and wisely to judge or decide.

If the foregoing views are correct, the whole of the argument of Edwards in regard to increasing the difficulty, until it surmounts the power of the mind to choose, prefer, or will, is unavailing to prove *necessity;* nor have his illustrations of moral necessity or of moral inability any such tendency, but on the contrary, both arguments, and the illustrations of them, really indicate that the mind is of necessity free in willing.

I would here further observe, that in regard to such internal motives, as "previous bias or inclination," which must be either previous conclusions or preferences, there is no reason to suppose, until the mind has actually willed, or at least has finished its preparatory deliberation, and while it is yet opposing, or comparing, or seeking new views, new knowledge, to oppose to or to compare with the old, that, by this process, it may not change any previous bias or inclination, and vary the result, or the act of will, so that it will conform to such change; there is no NECESSITY to the contrary. "Previous bias, or inclination," though not, as Edwards's definitions would make it, already a state of willing, is such knowledge as the mind may immediately act upon, and is then closely connected with the act of will. In some cases our acting from previous bias or inclination is merely substituting the memory of a preference, or of a reason, or of a mode of action, which has before been perceived and approved for present investigation. But if the mind does not will freely, there is no reason to suppose that its previous state or condition, by which must be meant, previous to the act of will, will influence it at all in willing. The *bias* and *inclination* are of the mind, and can affect the mind in willing only as this biassed or inclined mind itself controls its will. If something else than this mind controls its will, its *own* bias or inclination can have no necessary influence whatever upon its will.

Again, " a previous bias or inclination or the motive presented," must be a previous preference; and Edwards virtually says so. (Part I. pp. 2 and 32.) Hence as he uses the terms, this previous preference or inclination is a previous choice, or act of will; and we have in one choice or preference, the motives for another choice or preference, the first or motive choice, requiring a cause for its existence as much as the latter, and no advance is thus made toward a solution of the problem as to what determines the mind in choosing or willing.

It will be perceived that much of the argument which Edwards deduces from the instances we have quoted, rests upon a supposed power in *habit*. As in the case of "nature of things," and "inclination," or "motive," Edwards seems to have adopted this term as representing a power or cause, without defining what it is, or showing any attributes by which it can become cause of any effects. I would here also suggest that there is no certainty that habits, however long established, will continue; and, of course, they imply no *necessity* of continuance. There is no *necessity* that the acts of a man, heretofore uniformly vicious, will continue to be vicious; and the only ground of *probability* that they will be vicious is that *he wills freely*. If the willing is not the free act of the vicious man, but is controlled by some other being or power, then the vicious habits or propensities of the vicious man can have no necessary connection with the willing of the vicious acts, and his will, being controlled, constrained, or coerced, will as probably be opposed to his habits and propensities as in conformity to them. The result we arrived at (Book I. chap. xi.), that habit is but the mind's using a plan of action, formed on some previous like occasion, instead of making a new plan each time, takes from habit even the appearance of a distinct power, controlling our voluntary actions. It shows that it has no other effect than to obviate the necessity of present investigation. The results thus previously obtained, become a part of the knowledge of the mind, which it uses in determining its mode of action, as it does any other knowledge. Such use of its knowledge, we have already shown, does not conflict with its freedom in willing. If it is peculiar to this memory of former results, and the familiar association of previous action with consequent gratification, that the want is thereby intensified, and, at the same time, more promptly and easily gratified by the mind's being relieved from the labor of new investigation as to the mode, these facts become but a portion of the known circumstances which the mind considers preparatory to deciding in regard to its final effort; and the existence of circumstances among and with which to exercise its powers of comparing, judging, &c., in selecting, we have already shown, does not conflict with the freedom of the mind in willing, but only furnishes occasion for its exercise. That it wills to adopt the results of former investigation, or to copy former action, rather than resort to new inquiry, or seek new modes, is no reason to infer that, in so doing, it does not will freely. It manifests as much freedom in adopting these former results as it could in reinvestigation. Adopting the habitual mode will be more easy and generally quicker; and, these are so far inducements or reasons to the mind for adopting it, when it wants to save labor and time; but if the mind *wants* exercise and to occupy its time, or to acquire, or test new modes, their influences will be reversed. There is nothing then, in habit, conflicting with the freedom of the mind in willing. That, by a figure of speech, a man is often said to be a slave to his habits, arises from two distinct reasons. By habitual gratification, some of our wants constitutionally acquire great intensity. When, for instance, the nervous system has long been habitually excited, its constitution is so changed, that remission of the excitement produces the most painful sensations; and, in aggravated cases, delirium and death. The want, in such cases, becomes intense and its demand for relief, as the demand for safety in case of extreme danger, usually overbalances all other considerations. The common saying, that, *a man is a slave to his habits*, has a foundation also in the fact that it often happens, that when a man has habitually adopted certain modes of action, he ceases to make effort for further progress in that direction; but this indicates not an absence of freedom in the effort which is made, but the absence of any effort to learn new or better modes.

As the consciousness of our own acting lessens as the effort diminishes, it is not surprising that we should fail to recognize our own agency in those efforts, which habit has made so easy, *so natural*, that we are hardly aware that they require from us any mental exertion whatever; and hence we are easily led to attribute them to some extrinsic power, or to consider habit itself as such a power.

The only case, other than habit, which Edwards gives of moral necessity, is that of "previous bias or inclination," and this, as before shown, being in his system the same as preference, choice and will, the argument or assertion that a man must will in conformity to such moral motives as "bias or inclination," in that system only proves that, under the influence of moral necessity, he must will in conformity to what he wills.

I have already shown that Edwards's views and assertions on this point together involve a necessary freedom of the mind in willing, and having founded the reasoning, not upon the erroneous dogma that will, choice, preference and inclination are identical; but only upon such of his positions as are admitted, the conclusion does not merely convict him of inconsistency in such views and assertions, but argues the actual existence of such freedom. It has also been shown that the influence of natural necessity, or the action of causes other than our own will, can only frustrate our effort; and this *subsequent result* cannot militate against the freedom of the *mind's act* of willing.

CHAPTER IV.

SELF-DETERMINATION.

In regard to the argument of Edwards in his Part II. Sec. 1, against the WILL's *self-determining power*, I would remark that it is irrelevant to my position, which not only does not involve that dogma, but asserts, not that the WILL, but that the mind, the active being, determines its own volition, and that it does this by means of its knowledge; and further, that the choice, which, it is admitted in most if not in all cases, precedes the effort, or act of will, is not, as Edwards asserts, itself an act of will, but is the knowledge of the mind that one thing is superior to another, or suits us better than other things; this knowledge being always a simple mental perception, to which previous effort may, or may not have been requisite; and that every act of will is a beginning of new action, independent of all previous actions, which in no wise of *themselves* affect, or influence the new action; though the *knowledge acquired* in, or by such previous actions, being used by the mind to direct this new action, may be to it the reason for its acting, or for the manner of its acting; and that, in the use of such knowledge, to direct, or adapt its action to the occasion, or to its want, it begins with the intuitive knowledge, that it can, by effort or will, put its own being in action and use and give direction to its own powers. But some of his reasoning seems to imply, that the mind itself, in choosing or willing, is subject to external constraint or control; and, in this view, it is important to examine it. After stating the position of his opponents, " that the *person* IN the exercise of a power of willing and choosing, or the soul, acting voluntarily, determines" all the free acts of the will, Edwards says, "Therefore, if the will determines all its own free acts, the soul determines all the free acts of the will, IN the exercise of a power of willing and choosing; or, which is the same thing, it determines them of choice; it determines its own acts BY choosing its own acts. If the will determines the will, then choice orders, and determines the choice; and acts of choice are subject to the decision and follow the conduct of other acts of choice. And, therefore, if the will determines all its own free acts, then every free act of choice is determined by a preceding act of choice, choosing that act. And if that preceding act of the will or choice be also a free act, then, by these principles in this act too, the will is self-determined; that is, this, in like manner, is an act that the soul voluntarily chooses; or, which is the same thing, it is an act determined still by a preceding act of the will, choosing that. And the like may again be observed of the last mentioned act; which brings us directly to a contradiction; for it supposes an act of the will, preceding the first act in the whole train, directing and determining the rest; or a free act of the will, before the first free act of the will. Or else, we must come at last to an act of the will, determining the consequent acts, wherein the will is not self-determined, and so is not a free act in this notion of freedom; but if the first act in the train, determining and fixing the rest, be not free, none of them all can be free; as is manifest at first view, but shall be demonstrated presently" (p. 44). To the statement of his opponents, he herein only adds, as a postulate, that acts of choice and acts of will are equivalent expressions; and if he adopts the axiom, that, if a statement when expressed in one set of terms is true, it is also true when, for any of those terms, their equivalents are substituted, he might, under the postulate, argue that whatever was truly asserted of acts of will, might likewise be asserted of acts of choice, and vice versa; but it is not easy to conceive how, with such data, he can get beyond this. His changing of the word *in* to *by* may affect the whole course of the argument. To illustrate this, let it be said, that a body changes its position in moving, and moves *in* changing its position. This may imply only that the body may be moved, or, which is the same thing, that its position may be changed, or, if the body has a self-moving faculty, that it may move itself. The two phrases really, only reciprocally define or explain each other, but if we connect them with the term *by* instead of *in*, and use *by* as an abbreviation of *by means of* or, *by reason of*, or *by cause of*, as is not uncommon, though we never say *in* means of, &c., we might infer that the cause of the body's motion was its change of position, and, vice versa, that the cause of its change of position was its motion; and hence, infer that the cause must be both before and after the effect, or each alternately before the other, in an infinite series, so that a body never could begin to move, or to be moved; and even, if under such conditions, motion could be conceived of as existing from eternity, it would seem to be impossible for it to be continued; for a body, though in motion, could not change its position before it moved, nor move before it changed its position. It does one *in* doing the other, not *by* doing the other; and it does one in doing the other, only because the one and the other are the same thing. So, if we admit, with Edwards, that an act of willing and choosing are the same thing, all that he can legitimately deduce from the statement of his opponents, that "the soul determines all the free acts of the will, *in* the exercise of a power of willing," is that, if so, the soul freely wills *in* choosing, or freely chooses *in* willing, or freely chooses *in* freely choosing.

Edwards defines will to be that *by* which the mind chooses anything, and then says, "an act of the *will* is the same as an act of *choosing*, or *choice;*" and by other expressions completely identifies will and choice. Hence, he may as well say that the mind wills by choosing, or by the choice, as that it chooses by the will; and from these two positions of his it might be argued that, as the mind wills *by* choosing, or chooses by willing, the willing and choosing must alternately precede each other, as cause without limit, and that there could be no first willing or choosing; thus involving in his own statement the very absurdity which he charges upon his opponents, and which they seem to have avoided by the use of the word IN, which Edwards, in making out his position against them, changes to BY.

The position of his opponents which Edwards undertakes to disprove, is, as quoted by himself, that "the soul determines all the free acts of the will IN the exercise of a power of willing, or choosing," which is equivalent to saying that *the soul, in its own free act of will, determines itself* IN *that act;* whereas, the position, which he really combats, is the very different one, that *the soul, in its own* free act of will, *determines itself* BY *a previous act of will;* the disproving of which does not at all affect the position of his opponents, as above stated, though it may apply to some other of their assertions. This changing IN to BY is repeated and runs through the whole argument. We may also observe in it much ambiguity and confusion from using the words *choice* or *choosing*, as sometimes meaning the *process of choosing*, and sometimes as the final *result of the process;* and also using the terms *mind and will* sometimes as equivalents, and sometimes in a manner implying doubt as to whether it is the MIND, *or the* WILL, *which determines, or is determined.*

Edwards appears not to recognize that intelligence, mind, may itself be cause. He says, " but to say that the will or mind orders, influences, or determines itself to exert such an act as it does, BY the very exertion itself, is to make the *exertion* both cause and effect." This whole phraseology is founded on the idea that mind is not itself a cause *directly* producing effects by its activity or power in willing; but that it must first order something, in itself, to will them; and further, it is only by the use of the word BY, that he infers, even from that phraseology, that the exertion is the cause of the exertion. It would seem to be proper to call that which " orders, influences and determines" the exertion, *i. e.* the mind itself, the cause of that exertion, rather than make another exertion of that same mind the cause; and if the term IN had been used in place of BY, this would have become so apparent, that it could hardly have escaped observation. I trust that what I have said, in Book First of this work, on the subjects of spirit and matter as cause, is sufficient to show, that it may be at least as proper to refer any effect directly to mind as cause, as to any material or other conceivable cause.

It is true, that before an act of will, there must be something to move the mind to action, for, though the mind is cause, it is a cause which, being intelligent, does not act without a reason. Edwards finds this prime mover in his "motives," which he not only supposes to move the mind, but to determine or give direction to its movement in the act of willing. I have supposed that want arouses the mind to action, and that the mind directs that action by means of its knowledge already possessed, adding to it, when it seems needed, that obtained by its preliminary efforts or acts of will for that object. Of the knowledge thus acquired for the particular occasion, we may particularly note that obtained by the mind's preliminary efforts in comparing and judging of those preconceptions of the effects of its volitions, which, by its knowledge, innate or acquired, and its prophetic power, it is enabled to form in the future. I shall have occasion to speak of this difference in our views hereafter; and will now only remark, that as already shown, neither the want, nor the knowledge, whether it be of the past, present or future, innate or acquired, is a volition; and hence, as already intimated, even if the argument of Edwards establishes the absurdity of one volition being willed by another, in which I do not differ with him, it does not affect my position.

The doctrine, that the mind, being in virtue of its intelligence a creative first cause, can originate change, and direct that change by its present prophetic perceptions of the future effects of its act of will, is directly opposed to that which asserts, that the mind in willing is " determined, directed and commanded " by a *previous* act of will, which, being in the past, is now entirely beyond reach of the mind's faculty of will, and hence control by such previous act would be as fatal to the mind's freedom in its present willing, as if such control were by another being; if it be not wholly destructive, also, of the admitted power of the mind to will. Even admitting that choice is always a pre-requisite of every free act of will, and that it is by such choice that the mind determines its free act, still, if I have succeeded in showing that, in fact, choice is not itself the act of will, but is only a certain kind of knowledge; such admission would still leave the case within my general position, that the mind directs its power in willing by means of its knowledge, while that fact leaves no ground for the infinite series with no possibility of a first act, which Edwards deduces from the assumption that choice and will are the same; and the argument he derives from this infinite series, in the form of a reductio ad absurdum, and so often applies, is then shown to be entirely fallacious.

CHAPTER V.

NO EVENT WITHOUT A CAUSE.

In Part II. Sec. 3, Edwards says he uses the word cause "in a sense, which is more extensive, than that in which it is sometimes used," applying it to that which has no "positive efficiency, or influence to produce a thing, or bring it to pass," but which "has truly the nature of a ground or reason why some things are, rather than others, or why they are as they are, rather than otherwise;" and after saying, " that when I speak of *connection of causes and effects* I have respect to *moral* causes as well as those that are called *natural* in distinction from them, " he further says, " Therefore I sometimes use the word *cause* in this inquiry to signify any *antecedent*, either natural or moral, positive or negative, on which an event, either a thing, or the manner and circumstance of a thing, so depends, that it is the ground and reason, either in whole, or in part, why it is, rather than not; or why it is as it is, rather than otherwise; or, in other words, any antecedent with which a consequent event is so connected, that it truly belongs to the reason why the proposition, which affirms that event, is true; whether it has any positive influence or not. And in an agreeableness to this, I sometimes use the word *effect* for the consequence of another thing, which is perhaps rather an occasion than a cause, most properly speaking." Edwards then applies this definition to prove that no "event whatsoever, and volition in particular, can come to pass without a cause of its existence" (p. 54); or, as he afterwards says, "whatsoever begins to be, which before was not, must have a cause, why it then begins to exist" (p. 56). And again, "*what is not necessary in itself, must have a cause*" (p. 58).*

The *extended* meaning, which he gives to the word cause, facilitates this proof, but, at the same time, makes it doubtful whether such proof will be available for the purpose he intends. His object is to argue from it, that as volition is an "event," or a "whatsoever that begins to be," it must have a cause, it must be an effect, which is so connected with the cause by which it is brought to pass, that it is of necessity controlled and determined by that cause. But when he has shown a connection of *a thing* with *that cause* in which, by his definition, he includes what "has *no* positive efficiency, or influence to *produce a thing*, or bring it to pass," he cannot properly argue that such cause necessitates the thing, in the production of which it thus has no "positive efficiency or influence."

In the previous section, he thus states the proposition to which he applies the argument derived from the necessary dependence of an effect upon its cause: "But certainly, those things which have a prior ground and reason of their particular existence, a cause, which antecedently determines them to be, and determines them

* See Appendix, Note XXXVIII.

to be just as they are, do not happen contingently. If something foregoing, by a causal influence and connection, determines and fixes precisely their coming to pass and the manner of it, then it does not remain a contingent thing whether they shall come to pass, or no" (pp. 53, 54). Though this may be strictly true, the necessity for a *thing* coming to pass is evidently not to be inferred from such proposition, by showing that, that thing is connected with a cause, which may have no causal or other influence to produce *the thing, or bring it to pass;* for the very foundation of the general proposition is, that the "causal influence" "determines and fixes precisely [the thing] coming to pass and the manner of it." But, though Edwards's definition of cause will not bear the argument he rests upon it, and his attempted demonstration wholly fails; we are not disposed to question the necessary dependence of an effect upon its proper cause, or that a volition is such an event as must have a cause that determines it; but we deem it a sufficient answer to any application of the argument against the freedom of the mind in willing, to say that the mind is itself the cause of its volitions, and that this necessary dependence of the volition, as an effect, upon the mind as a cause, only proves that the mind controls and determines its volitions, or its own acts in willing; and hence, in them, acts freely.

The whole question is involved in that of the mind's being itself cause, or not. Edwards seems to deny, or, at least, to ignore mind as cause, and though his assertion that "as to all things *that begin to be*, they are not self-existent and therefore must have some foundation of their existence *without themselves*," (p. 56) may really only admit of the inference that the *volition* must have a *cause without itself*, he treats it as if this cause must also be without the mind that wills. He asserts that volition is an act of mind and, if he admits that mind, in the act of willing, acts as cause, and still insists that this *act of cause*, being a "whatsoever" that "begins to be, which before was not, must have a cause, why it then begins to exist," he must mean to assert, that for every such act of cause there *must* be another act of cause; and not merely that for every act of cause, there must be a cause to act, which would be the merest truism. He must then assert, that for every act of the mind as cause of its volition, there must be another act of cause; and this, as he before says "to say it [the will] is caused, influenced and determined by something and yet not determined by anything *antecedent*, either in order of time or nature, is a contradiction" (p. 52), must mean, that for every such act of cause, there must be a prior act of cause; which, also, must have required another prior act of cause, and there never could be a first act of cause. Or, if he makes a distinction, and says that the act of the will of God is an event which has no such prior cause, then the whole argument fails, for it must prove that, as a metaphysical necessity, there can be no event that begins to be, without such a previous act of cause extrinsic to itself, or it avails him nothing; and if it can be said that the mind of God is a cause, which is extrinsic to its volition, the same may be asserted of the human mind, or of mind generally; and even if, in any sense whatever, it could be said that the Divine volitions may be without a cause; then, as it has become evident that there may be events without a cause, the question immediately arises as to whether human volitions are not such events. I, by no means, intend to assert that they are. And when, in the next section (p. 62), Edwards inquires "whether volition *can arise without a cause*, through the activity *of the nature* of the soul," I think it would have been more pertinent to the subject to have asked, whether *the soul through the activity of its nature* can be *a cause of volition*. He proceeds to argue against the position of some writers, who, it seems, assert the affirmative of the inquiry as he states it; and, in so doing, he thus gives an affirmative answer to the question as I have stated it. "*The activity of the soul may enable it to be the cause of effects;* but it does not at all enable or help it to be the subject of effects which have no cause" (p. 63). The first portion of this admits all that is essential to prove, that the soul may itself be the cause of its volitions. The latter portion seems to indicate a difficulty, which is, in fact, wholly removed by the first; for the soul being itself the cause of its volitions, it is not in them, "the subject of effects, *which have no cause.*" The next sentences explain the latter portion of the above quotation. "Activity of nature will no more enable a being to produce effects and determine the manner of their existence *within* itself, without a cause, than *out of* itself, in some other being. But if an active being should, through its activity, produce and determine an effect in some external object, how absurd would it be to say, that the effect was produced without a cause" (p. 63).

In reply to these positions: the activity of the soul being itself admitted to be cause, we may say conversely, that the activity of the soul may produce effects *in itself* as well as *without itself*. And that, if an active being should thus, through its active nature, produce and determine an effect *in itself*, how absurd would it be to say, that the effect was produced without a cause. The argument on this point is, however, directed to the proof that the "*activity*" is not itself the cause, rather than that the *active agent*, or the agent which exercises this activity, cannot be; and as this latter is really all that is important in this position of the inquiry, as to the freedom of that active agent in willing, we might pass the reasoning on the other point, but, that dwelling a little further upon it may serve to elucidate the subject generally. In the course of the argument, Edwards says: " 2. The question is not so much, how a spirit endowed with activity comes to act, as why it exerts such an act, and not another; or why it acts with such a particular determination? If activity of nature be the cause why a spirit (the soul of man, for instance) acts, and does not lie still; yet that alone is not the cause why its action is thus and thus limited, directed and determined. Active nature is a general thing; it is an ability or tendency of nature to action, generally taken; which may be a cause why the soul acts as occasion, or reason is given; but this alone cannot be a sufficient cause why the soul exerts such a *particular* act, at such a time, rather than others. In order to this, there must be something besides a *general* tendency to action; there must also be a *particular* tendency to that individual action. If it should be asked, why the soul of man uses its activity in such a manner as it does; and it should be answered, that the soul uses its activity thus rather than otherwise, because it has activity; would such an answer satisfy a rational man? Would it not rather be looked upon as a very impertinent one?" (pp. 63, 64.) It seems a sufficient answer to this question, "why the soul of man uses its activity in such a manner as it does," that the soul is intelligent; and hence, is able to determine which action will suit it best; and, in virtue of this intelligence and, especially, of its power to foresee, or preconceive the future, as before explained, it is a creative *first* cause, requiring no propulsion from the past, or no prior cause for its action.

Edwards proceeds with his argument to show that "activity of nature" cannot be the cause why the mind's "action is thus and thus limited, directed and determined," as follows: " 3. An active being can bring no effects to pass by his activity but what are consequent upon his acting; he produces nothing by his activity, any other way than by the exercise of his activity, and so nothing but the fruits of its exercise; he brings nothing to pass by a dormant activity. But the exercise of his activity is action; and so his action or exercise of his activity, must be prior to the effects of his activity. If an active being produces an effect in another being, about which his activity is conversant, the effect being the fruit of his activity, his activity must be first exercised, or exerted, and the effect of it must follow. So it must be, with equal reason, if the active being is his own object and his activity conversant about himself, to produce and determine some effect in himself; still the exercise of his activity must go before the effect, which he brings to pass and determines by it. And therefore his activity cannot be the cause of the determination of the first action, or exercise of activity itself, whence the effects of activity arise; for that would imply a contradiction; it would be to say, the first exercise of activity is before the first exercise of activity and is the cause of it" (pp. 64, 65).

So far, in this chapter, I have virtually conceded the assertion of Edwards, that "the activity of the soul may enable it to be the *cause* of effects;" and hence inferred that it may, through its activity, be the *cause* of its own volitions. I have done this, in order to show that, even on that hypothesis, the argument really favors freedom and not necessity. It seems to me, however, more correct to say that the activity of the soul is itself the willing; or, at least, that willing is itself one mode of its activity. Edwards's argument, virtually, both admits and denies this. He admits the exercise of the soul's activity generally, and argues that this cannot produce a volition, because volition is an exercise of its activity; and therefore, as the exercise of its activity cannot be before itself, it cannot be the cause of its activity, *i. e.* the thing does exist, but it is impossible that it should exist, because it cannot be before itself. He is arguing about the exercise of activity *generally ;* and, therefore, this objection to his mode of reasoning cannot be met by saying that, when he speaks of the *exercise of activity generally*, he does not mean that *exercise of activity*, which is a *volition*, and if it could be so said, the argument, that the exercise of activity cannot be before itself, would then have no relation to the volition, which is *not that* exercise of activity. The argument, even if tenable, would apply only to activity *generally*, or in the abstract, and not to activity, which has a particular direction, or which is directed in some particular way by intelligence or other power. I agree with him as to the impotence of activity *generally*, and think he has even gone too far in saying that "the activity of the soul may enable it to be the cause of effects" (p. 63). He argues, "That the soul, though an active substance, cannot diversify its own acts but by *first acting*" (p. 65), because "the substance of the soul before it acts, and its active nature before it is exerted are the same without variation," and the "same causal power without variation" cannot "produce different effects at different times" (p. 65). But the same argument proves that it cannot diversify its "first acting." *Activity of nature generally* would, alone, admit of no variation; uncombined with knowledge, or with intelligence, if it could be cause at all, it would be but *one* invariable, blind cause; and hence, could produce only one effect; but it could not even be this. Mere active nature alone, or the knowledge alone, would be powerless; neither alone could be cause, any more than weight or velocity alone can be momentum. A mere activity *generally* must act equally in all directions; must act equally in favor of and against any movement or doing, and neutralize itself.

Activity generally expresses, not a power in itself, but only what may become power, a something, which may be used by whatever can apply and direct it; and when Edwards asserts that "active nature is a general thing; it is an ability, or tendency of nature to action generally taken, which may be a cause why the soul acts as *occasion or reason is given*" (p. 64), he virtually admits all that is essential to my system; *i. e.* that the soul has an ability to action, which it may use when it sees a reason, and that its effort, or act of will, is but an exercise of this *general ability* or power of action, which it directs and determines to some *particular* act, by means of its knowledge. In such case, however, the active nature is not the cause of the soul's acts, but is only the soul's ability to act, in itself as passive as the ability to smell. By means of the combination of the soul's ability to be active with its knowledge as a means of directing that activity, it becomes itself cause, or can produce change, whenever the "*occasion is given;*" that is, when it *wants* to produce change, and knows some means of doing it by its power to act. If the willing is not, in fact, the soul's only activity, it is conceivable that it might be, and in that case we might say the mind is active in willing; or that, in willing, it is active; the willing being no more the effect of its activity, than the activity is of its willing, nor one the cause of the other, any more than the other is the cause of it. It raises the same question as that to which we before alluded, as raised by Edwards's changing the word IN to BY in his first section (Part II.) on self-determination. In this aspect, the mind in willing, has a striking analogy to that of a body in motion. In defining will, I have, in explanation, said that it is the "mode in which intelligence exerts its power;" and that "the willing is the condition of the mind *in* effort; and is the only effort of which we are conscious." So of a moving body, motion is the mode in which it exerts its power and is the condition of a body in changing place. Activity is the mode in which spirit, or matter, exerts its power. In the case of intelligence this is manifested in willing; and in that of matter by moving, or changing its place; and though the body may move *in* moving, it cannot move *by* moving; for this making its move the cause of its moving or change of place, or the change of place the cause of its moving, implies that, that which is thus deemed the cause is prior to the other; but, as before intimated, they are really the same thing; and hence, to make one the cause of the other, is to make a thing the cause of itself. So, also, if the willing by the mind is but a certain activity, that activity cannot be the cause of the willing, nor the willing the cause of the activity; for this activity and the willing are one and the same thing, or express the same condition of the mind. The logic by which Edwards, in such cases, makes his favorite reductio ad absurdum, in an infinite series, may be applied to any case, in which two equivalent terms, expressing action, are used to define each other; as, for instance, the mind is in a certain way *active* in willing; or, in willing is in a certain way active; or the mind *wills* in *choosing*, or *chooses* in *willing;* choosing and willing being taken, as in Edwards's system, as equivalents; or a body moves in changing its position, or changes its position in moving. Between either pair of equivalents substitute BY for IN, making one the cause of the other; and then, being really the same thing, they must be simultaneous, and thus the cause must be both before and at the same time; or, each may in turn, with equal reason, be alternately made the cause, and then the infinite series, admitting of no beginning or first action or cause, is reached.

When Edwards says, "the question is not so much, How a spirit endowed with activity comes to act, as why it exerts such an act and not another, or why it acts with a particular determination;" he really raises the main question as to whether the mind in willing a certain act, rather than any other of the many conceivable acts, is constrained to determine to adopt that act by power extrinsic to itself; for, if the determining or controlling power is not extrinsic to itself, it determines and controls itself in the act of will, which, as we have already shown, is only another expression for its freedom in willing. He subsequently puts the question in this form: "Why the soul of man uses its activity as it does," admitting that it is the *soul*, which *uses* its activity, but still leaving open the question as to whether, in such use, its act of volition is constrained by some external power, or is its own action induced by considerations or causes within and of itself.

If it is asked why God did not make $2 + 2 = 4$, we can say that He may not have had any want to do it, and hence, would not make any effort to that end; and further, that even with such want, the thing would have been impossible. The impossibility of reconciling contradictions is a condition of action, even to Infinite Power.* If asked, why He made the earth to revolve in a particular orbit, rather than in any other of the infinite number conceivable, we can only say, that He must have determined this from considerations purely His own, from His own perception or knowledge of its fitness, in other words, that it was self-determined. There may have been conditions required by His want to create and by what already existed. For instance, if matter was already in motion, and in virtue of its motion, was an extraneous blind power or force, it would furnish certain circumstances to be dealt with. It is conceivable that there may have been only the one particular orbit, which would fulfil the purposes of the Creator, and at the same time conform to the other or external conditions. The perception or the

* See Appendix, Note XXXIX.

knowledge of this fact, must be the immediate reason for the selection and subsequent effort; and this knowledge may have been the result of previous effort, or series of efforts, springing directly out of the want and such perceptions or knowledge as required no previous act of will. All such knowledge, combining with the knowledge of existing external and internal conditions, makes the sum of the circumstances which the mind has to consider in its decision as to its action, and which the mind alone can decide upon.

If there is no application of knowledge required, the effort would be but that of a blind cause, which is to say, there could be no effort. To suppose that no effort is required, is to suppose that the conditions may themselves produce the effect. If the conditions themselves necessitate one certain volition, then, as the absolute conditions at any moment are the same to all, all must have the same volition at the same moment, and if a volition is one of the necessary effects, not of all existing conditions, but of those only of which the mind willing is cognizant, then, at the very moment in which the mind recognizes that such conditions exist, and is thus prepared to direct or to select its act in conformity with this new knowledge, the volition and any necessary sequence of it must already have been; for, by this hypothesis, the mind's action, even in examining, is not essential to the direction of the act, which is controlled by the pre-existing and extrinsic conditions, all the effects of the mere existence of which must already have been brought about. If the volition in each being, varies with the particular conditions of which it is cognizant, there must be something which knows what conditions are recognized, and adapts the volition to them, and if it be admitted that these conditions include the circumstance that the mind itself perceives and conforms its act to them, then the mind, by that process, does determine its own act, and of course is free in that act. The examination by the mind, of the conditions under which it is about to act, is a preliminary effort to obtain the knowledge by which to direct its final action ; and its first act of examining is directed, not by the conditions, as yet unknown, but by means of its knowledge, intuitive or acquired, that such examination is a proper preparation for further action. It feels a want and knows that the best mode of proceeding to gratify or to determine whether to gratify it or not, is to *examine ;* and, having this want and this knowledge of means, it directs its action accordingly, *i. e.* on recognizing the want, it begins its action by an examination. If it already has a knowledge of the means by former experience, or by intuition, and has no expectation of finding any better means, it needs to examine only so far as to ascertain the existence of the circumstances, or conditions, which make the occasion for the application of such knowledge. If, in such cases, the mind acts directly upon its intuitive knowledge of the mode, or means, its action is instinctive ; but if it acts from memory of past experience its action is habitual. It is manifest that the pre-existing and extrinsic conditions do not influence the volition, except as they may arouse want, or contribute to the knowledge by which the mind is enabled to decide what it will do, in regard to that want.

If, to the question proposed by Edwards, " why the soul of man uses its activity as it does," it should be replied, that intelligence, from its very nature, has a faculty to determine, or to direct its activity, it would be in conformity to his own previous statements, that the mind has a faculty by which it wills, and that an act of volition is a determination of the mind. If, thereafter, he asks for a cause of the determination of the determination, or volition, it is like asking for the end of the end; and to make a case analogous to that by which he has just argued that the nature of the activity of the soul cannot be the cause of its determination let it be asked, what is the cause, or reason that, a finite right line has an end; and let it be replied, that a finite line is limited in its nature and that, on this, the end or "thing so depends, that it is the ground and reason, either in whole, or in part, why it is rather than not, or why it is as it is rather than otherwise," and that this "truly belongs to the reason, why the proposition which affirms that event (or thing), is true;" and therefore this is the *cause* of the end. To this reasoning it might be objected that, the line's limited nature cannot be the cause of its having an end, because the cause must be exerted before the effect; and its limited nature can have no effect, as cause, till it is exerted; but the exercise, or application of its limited nature is a limit, or end; and this exercise, or application must be before the limit, or end; but the limited nature arises from there being a limit, or end; and therefore, it must be before the limit, or end: and hence, cannot be the cause of the end: and this is parallel to Edwards's saying, "But the exercise of his activity, is action; and so, his action, or exercise of his activity must be prior to the effects of his activity," &c. (p. 64), and to the reasoning, which follows it. In the same way, too, it may be said that, the existence of the line is not a cause, or reason why the ends of the line exist; because, if so, the existence of the line must be before the existence of its ends, which again is absurd. But the existence of the line and its being finite, are the only two things or conditions upon which the existence, and even the manner of the existence, of the ends depend. If it now be said that the existence of the line and its limited nature are not cause, under Edwards's definition, for the reason that it requires that cause should be antecedent to the effect; then, it follows, that the existence of the end and the manner of the end may be determined by what, *under Edwards's definition*, is not a cause; which renders nugatory all his argument that the will must be determined by such a cause; for that, he makes but one inference from his general proposition, that everything which begins to be, must have such a cause.*

But it cannot be urged that, under Edwards's definitions, anything is not a cause, for the reason that it is not *antecedent* to the effect; for he thus defines what he means by being antecedent: "To say, it is caused, influenced and determined by something, and yet not determined by anything *antecedent*, either in order of time or nature, is a contradiction. For that is what is meant by a thing's being *prior* in the order of nature, that it is some way the cause or reason of the thing, with respect to which it is said to be prior" (p. 52). So that, a thing being prior to another, or not, may depend on the fact of its being the cause of that other, or not; and hence, whenever Edwards argues, as he frequently does, that one thing cannot be the cause of another, because it is not prior to it, he begs the question; for, under his definition, its being prior or

* See Appendix, Note XL.

not, depends on whether it is the cause or not. Its being cause depends upon its being antecedent; and its being antecedent depends upon its being cause.

I have thus commented upon that portion of his argument which relates to cause, not so much to disprove its particular results, as to show *generally*, that the consequences, deduced from such a definition of cause, are not reliable, and really prove nothing. It must be borne in mind, that I do not deny the positions of Edwards that every event, which begins to be, must have a cause; or the necessary dependence of that event upon its cause; which I have endeavored to show, in their proper application, prove that the mind, itself being cause, wills freely. The prevailing tendency of most men to apply the results of their observation of the connection of cause and effect in the material, to the spiritual, leads them to seek a cause, in the *past*, for every change, and hence, to overlook the important fact, that intelligence, in virtue of its power to anticipate its effects in the future, is a *first* cause. We may follow the course of cause backward through a train of consecutive consequences and antecedents, till it comes to an intelligent will, as a first cause, when it doubles on its track and the *reason* of its action (the effect it preconceived) is found in the line over which we have been pursuing it; thus eluding those, who still look for it beyond or in the past.

Every act of will is the beginning of a series of which all the other terms are in the future; and all its connection with the past is but the knowledge, which the mind uses in directing its own action, as an intelligent cause of future effects; and this knowledge, at the time of the willing, is in the mind's view, is then in the present and not in the past. If from an intelligent being we cut off, or annihilate all the past, or if to such being there never had been any past; if it came into existence with want, and the knowledge of the mode of gratifying that want by acts of will or effort having reference only to the future, it could still determine and direct its efforts as well as if it were conscious of a past in which it had obtained some or all of this knowledge.

It may be said, that a being's coming into existence *with such want and knowledge*, is an event which must have a cause in the past, with which it is necessarily connected and which determines the manner and mode of its existence; but this does not affect the question of its freedom. If, from any cause, a being has come into existence with power to control and direct its own efforts, such being is free in such efforts, so that the question, is such being free, is not affected by the cause through which it came to exist. If it be said that the want and knowledge, which are necessary conditions of such a being, control the act of will, it may be replied, that neither of these, nor both combined, can make effort or will, unless they constitute the intelligent being that wills; and, in that case, they also constitute a free agent.

If every act of will is determined by the whole past, then that whole past is the cause of such act of will; and being, at every instant, the same to all, if the same causes necessarily produce the same effects, every mind would will at the same instant and will the same thing. If the act of will in each is determined by that portion of the past of which he is cognizant, then there must be something to adapt the act, in each case, to this variation in the knowledge of the past; and this can only be done by something which knows what this portion of the past is to which the act of will is to be adapted. This the "past" or other unintelligent cause cannot do.

We shall have occasion to notice this supposed dependence of volition on a cause in the past, in examining other portions of Edwards's argument, and especially that in which he treats of motive as such a cause.

CHAPTER VI.

OF THE WILL DETERMINING IN THINGS INDIFFERENT.

EDWARDS says, "A great argument for self-determining power is the supposed experience we universally have of an ability to determine our wills, in cases wherein no prevailing motive is presented. The will, as is supposed, has its choice to make between two, or more things, that are perfectly equal in the view of the mind, and the will is apparently altogether indifferent; and yet we find no difficulty in coming to a choice; the will can instantly determine itself to one, by a sovereign power, which it has over itself, without being moved by any preponderating inducement." (Sec. 6, p. 73.) This mode of stating the case seems to be warranted by the extracts which he makes from the writings of some of his opponents, but I think it is not well stated. Among other objections, it supposes the *will to choose* and, also, virtually assumes that the mind determines its act of will by a previous act of will; and, as in Edwards's system, an act of will and choice are the same, it is not difficult under it to elaborate much absurdity from such a statement. In putting their argument into his own terms, he makes them say, that the WILL is apparently altogether indifferent, and yet, WE find no difficulty in coming to a choice. Now, if WILL and WE are not the same thing, if he does not embrace our whole being in will, this is merely saying that A is indifferent, and yet B finds no difficulty. In reply to one whom Edwards supposes to advocate the position as above stated, he says, "The very supposition which is here made, directly contradicts and overthrows itself. For the thing supposed, wherein this grand argument consists, is that among several things the will actually chooses one before another, at the same time that it is perfectly indifferent; which is the very same thing as to say, the mind has a preference at the same time that it has no preference." (Sec. 6, p. 74.) And again, "If it be possible for the understanding to act in indifference, yet to be sure the will never does; because the will's beginning to act is the very same thing as its beginning to choose or prefer. And if, in the very first act of the will, the mind prefers something, then the idea of that thing preferred does, at that time, preponderate or prevail in the mind; or, which is the same thing, the idea of it has a prevailing influence on the will. So that this wholly destroys the thing supposed, viz.: that the mind can, by a sovereign power, choose one of two, or more things, which in the view of the mind are, in every respect, perfectly equal, one of which does not at all preponderate, nor has any prevailing influence on the mind above another." (Séc. 6, p. 76.)

The whole force of this objection is subsequently more concisely thus stated: "To suppose the will to act at all in a state of perfect indifference, either to determine itself, or to do anything else, is to assert that the mind chooses without choosing" (sec. 6, p. 77); and he might have added, in view of his definition, that this is to assert that there is an act of the will, when there is no act of the will. His opponents, however, taking his own statement, really make no such assertion; and it is obvious that these objections to them, repeated as they are in various forms, are but logical deductions from the assumption that the choosing by the mind is an act of will, or that an act of will and choice are identical; upon which I have already commented. In Edwards's statement of the views of his opponents, as quoted at the commencement of this chapter, it is not clear what is meant by the phrase, "self-determining power." If it means only self-determining power of the will, or that the mind determines its acts of will by other acts of will, it is, as before stated, wholly irrelevant to my position, which does not rest upon, or involve that dogma; but if, as some of the subsequent remarks indicate, it also means a power in the mind to control its acts of will, it is proper that we should notice the arguments which deny this.

In view of these several objections to the statement, as made by Edwards, I think the argument would be more fairly stated thus: A great argument for the self-determining power of the *mind* is the supposed experience we universally have of an ability to will in cases where the mind is indifferent as to the several objects of choice, and has no preference among the several movements or modes by any one of which it perceives that it can accomplish some one of the several objects among which it is indifferent as to which one. This statement excludes all preference among several objects, some one of which it is desirable to obtain or to accomplish; also, all preference as to several modes of obtaining or accomplishing that object, some one of which must be adopted in order to accomplish it. It will be perceived that if the statement went farther than this, and made the mind also indifferent as to the accomplishment of this one object, that, then, the mind would have no inducement in the premises to act, no want, and in such case there would be no act of will to reason about; and if it went farther in another direction, and made the mind also indifferent as to its willing or not *willing*, thus assuming that it can have no *preference* even in that act, it would, in view of Edwards's definition, entirely shut out the admitted act of will in the premises, and exclude the very question, which he really raises in this connection, viz. : how that act of will, or preference, or effort, which we put forth to make this movement or action, by which to obtain the object, is determined when there are several such objects and several such movements all equal in the mind's view, and among which it has no preference and can find no ground for any. It would virtually assert that the mind did not, in such case, will at all; and especially would it do this, under the system of Edwards, which makes preference and will the same. In the system I have advanced, this same result would also be reached; for, if the mind is indifferent as to whether to will or not, it has no want to will; or, at least, none which is not neutralized by a conflicting want, and it will not will. The statement I have suggested then, affirms all the indifference in regard to an act of will, which it can, without being self-contradictory. To illustrate the statement, suppose a man wants only one egg of which there are several before him, each in his view equally good and equally easy to be obtained; no choice either in the eggs, or in the several movements, or actions necessary to obtain some one to gratify the want; and yet the mind does will one of the many equal movements or actions, to obtain one of the many eggs, which are all equal in its view, and thus gratifies its want to have some one of them. It cannot be intended by the advocates of a self-determining power of the *mind* to say, that the mind determines to will when it has no object in willing; when it has no desire to produce any effect and is wholly indifferent as to exercising its will; and yet, the last objection quoted from Edwards, seems to assume that some of them take this position. If he merely refutes this position, as thus assumed, it cannot affect the system I have stated in Book First, for such an indifference wholly excludes the existence of a *want*, which, in that system, is a prerequisite of the action of the mind in willing; and, of course, in it, volition is precluded when there is no want. And if, when Edwards argues that the mind cannot will in a state of indifference, he means that it cannot will when there is not only no choice as to the several objects, or the several actions presented, but, also, no choice as to whether it acts at all in regard to any one of the equal objects or actions, he merely asserts that the mind cannot will when it has no want for will, or cannot exert its power to influence the future when it does not want to exert it; and, in this, the advocates of freedom certainly need not differ with him. The particular cases which he cites, however, do permit the existence of such *want*, and, in other respects, conform to the supposed indifference as I have stated it. He admits too, that in such cases, the mind does actually will; and to get over the difficulty, which, under his system, arises from the existence of a volition, when there is nothing in the mind's view, no motive, to induce the *particular preference*, which, by his theory, is that volition, he supposes the mind itself to devise a way of getting itself out of this state of indifference, or this equilibrium, as to the objects of choice ; and thus to obtain the preference—the volition—which he admits does occur. He says : "Thus, supposing I have a chess board before me ; and because I am required by a superior, or desired by a friend, to make some experiment concerning my own ability and liberty, or on some other consideration, I am determined to touch some one of the spots or squares on the board with my finger ; not being limited or directed in the first proposal, or my own first purpose, which is general to any one in particular; and there being nothing in the squares in themselves considered, that recommends any one of all the sixty-four more than another " (pp. 77, 78). The difficulty here presented is, that the mind has determined to touch some one of the sixty-four squares, but perceives no ground of choice, and hence, cannot choose between them, or will to touch any one. To get over this difficulty Edwards goes on to say, " In this case, my mind gives itself up to what is vulgarly called *accident*, by determining to touch that square, which happens to be most in view, which my eye is especially upon at that moment, or which happens to be then most in my mind, or which I shall be directed to by some other such like accident. Here are several steps of the mind's proceeding, though all may be done as it were in a moment ; the *first* step is its *general* determination, that it will touch one of the squares. The *next* step is another *general* determination to give itself up to accident, in some certain way; as to touch that which shall be most in the eye or mind, at that time, or to some other such like accident. The *third* and last step is a *particular* determination to touch a certain individual spot, even that square, which, by that sort of accident, the mind has pitched upon, has actually offered itself beyond others." (Sec. 6, p. 78.) In a note, he defines " what is vulgarly called accident," as " something that comes to pass in the course of things in some affair that men are concerned in, unforeseen and not owing to their designs." The object of this position seems to be, to show that, in such cases, admitting that the mind does will, yet it does not determine its own act of will, or preference; but, that the act is determined by something extraneous to the mind and which, by it, is " unforeseen and not owing to its design," and, if it could be established that the will, in such cases, is determined by *force* of this " something," over which the mind has no control, it would seem to establish necessity at least in such cases. The argument, however, appears to be unfortunate in many respects. While denying that the mind can by its own action, and without this " something," over which it has no control, get itself out of this state of indifference, it begins by showing how it can do so; for when it says, " in this case the *mind determines* to give itself up to what is vulgarly called accident," it is the mind that does it. And more especially is it intended to deny, that the mind can get itself out of this dilemma by an act of volition. But in Edwards's system, and in any system to be of any avail, this *determining* of the *mind* " to give itself up to what is vulgarly called accident," must either be itself a volition, or be followed by a *volition* of that mind, which is thus made to get itself out of a state of indifference by means most especially denied to it. That it does this by its own act of will, cannot, of course, be an argument against the liberty of the mind in willing. I have before remarked that the mind's forming a plan, in which, by successive acts of will, in a certain order, it reaches ends which it cannot reach by a direct act of will, is one of the ways in which it manifests its creative power; and if, in cases of indifference, like those above cited, it plans to do that by indirection which it cannot do directly, it no more militates against its freedom, than does its successive acts in obtaining, chewing and swallowing food to satisfy the hunger it cannot appease by a direct act of will.

But it does not apppear to be at all certain, that the mind, in this case, is under any necessity to adopt this indirect mode, or even that it is thereby relieved of any of the supposed difficulty of willing directly. Even if the mind in willing, or choosing the particular square, is determined by the accident; still, in determining to give itself up to accident, it is not determined by the accident; for the accident itself is not yet determined, and may not even be *in the view of the mind*, which Edwards holds to be essential to every motive; and hence, if the mind does not *directly* determine to give itself up to the accident and thus determine its own act, instead of the one question, as to how the mind determines the particular square, we have two other questions, firstly, how the mind determines to give itself up to accident, and, secondly, how it determines the particular accident by which its choice of the square is to be determined. By the hypothesis, the only object

OF WILLING IN THINGS INDIFFERENT. 267

the mind can have in giving itself up to the accident is to determine thereby which particular square it will touch; and there must be many of these accidents among which the mind can have no possible preference, as one will answer the purpose exactly as well as another; and the question arises, how the mind can prefer or choose one of these rather than another, any more than it can prefer or choose one of the sixty-four squares of the chess board. The mind's ability to make such choice, cannot arise from the nature of the accident; for, if we conceive of two accidents exactly opposite in their nature in every respect, still one will answer the purpose just as well as the other. It may be the passing of a cloud; the shooting of a star; the advent of a comet; or the NOT happening of any of these events. That the occurring of one accident may be more agreeable than another can be no reason for the selection, for such selection has no more influence to cause it to occur, than to cause it not to occur. As to the place of its occurrence, it is only essential to the purpose intended, that it should be within the limits of the mind's observation; as to time, it is conceivable that the mind may have a preference; it may prefer to be out of the state of indifference as quickly as possible, and hence, prefer to select such an accident as its knowledge indicates may soonest happen; but if the application of this knowledge, by the mind, is not precluded by the condition that this accident is "something unforeseen and not owing to *its* design," still, even with such conditions, there must be a great number of such accidents, the chances of an early occurrence of which are in the mind's view just equal; and hence affording no ground of preference among them in this respect. The ground of preference cannot be in the effect of the accident, not even in the preconception of the effect, for the only effect that can come into notice at all, is the determining that, in regard to the determination of which the mind is indifferent; and this consideration of itself seems to preclude all ground of preference among the conceivable accidents, except that in regard to time, as just mentioned; and, any such preference must, under Edwards's system, be an act of will; and determination of a subsequent act of will by it would be the will's determining itself, which is the thing he denies. But, however this may be, it is certain that the mind may be as indifferent as to the selection of a particular accident from among a number of accidents, any one of which will answer its purpose equally well, as it can be in regard to the particular square on the chess board; and hence, will be as unable to determine the particular accident to be selected for use, as to determine the particular square to be touched, and we have a recurrence of the difficulty in the very means devised to surmount it.

In the particular case which Edwards selects, he *seems* to avoid some of these difficulties. He says, "by determining to touch that square which happens to be most in view, which my eye is especially upon at that moment," &c. &c. This, however, is not such an accident as he defines, "as unforeseen," for it has *already occurred, is seen,* and is a part of the certain knowledge of the mind; and if he should adopt such events, instead of the accidents just considered, and thus avoid some of the difficulties which arise with *them,* he would immediately encounter another; for, if the certain knowledge of the mind can be used, in place of the accident, to determine the case of indifference, one can as well say, I will touch a certain square because $2+2=4$, as because my eye happens to rest upon it; for, if the indifference actually existed while the eye was thus resting upon it, that fact, of itself, could not prevent the indifference any more than the fact that $2+2=4$, could prevent it; and the same of any other fact known at the time of the indifference. If I know that by *accident* I cut my finger yesterday, it will no more help me out of a present case of indifference, than any other known fact. I know that on the chess board there is a square in one particular corner, and I can just as well determine to touch that particular square without the knowledge of any previous accident as with it. To do this, one of the preparatory steps is to direct the eye to that square, and, when the indifference is only as to what square is touched, selecting one to which the eye is already directed, saves one preparatory step in the process; but, if this is the consideration which prevails, then it ceases to be a case of indifference; for the mind, though still indifferent as to the *square touched*, is not indifferent as to the *action in touching*. Among the circumstances already existing, and in that examination of them, which the mind habitually, and perhaps, in the first instance instinctively makes, it then perceives a reason for one act rather than any other, and it is not such a case of indifference as the argument supposes; it does not differ from cases comprehending a large proportion of those practically arising, in which the mind by a preliminary particular effort examines before it decides, or even inclines to any particular final action. But, be this as it may, it must be admitted that an event of which the existence is already certain is not such an accident as Edwards contemplates or defines; and, if he means that the movement of the eye is to be subsequent to the determination of the mind to give itself up to the accident of its movement; then he has selected an event which is dependent on that mind's will, which it can foresee and must design; *and the difficulty is solved by the mind's own self-determined act of will.* It is making the act of the mind in willing to touch a particular square, depend upon the act of the mind in willing the movement of the eye; and such a solution of the difficulty becomes an argument for the self-direction or freedom of the mind in willing.

If it be said that the movement of the eye, though the effect of design and volition, is still so far accidental that the mind can direct it to the board without directing it to any particular square, the same may also be said of the movement of the finger. Why not, then, make the movement of the finger, in the act of touching it, the means of determining? I apprehend that the movement of the eye has been selected rather than that of the finger, only because we are less *sensible* of the uncertainty of a muscular effort upon the hand, than upon the eye. The movement of either to a particular point, requires care; and to do it with facility, that skill or ready apprehension of the required muscular movements and their successive order, which results from practice, inducing habit. It must be learned. The child is not at once able to direct the movement of its hand to a particular spot; and though we may learn to do it with great certainty and facility, we never do it without *some* care and attention. We learn about what amount and what kind of muscular movement are required to move the hand to a particular point, but still, we are generally obliged to watch the result and to modify the movement as it approaches the destined spot. This is evident from the fact that if we close one eye, so that we cannot so readily see the position of the finger and measure the relative distances of it and the spot to be touched, we must move it much more slowly as it approaches the spot, than we need to do with both eyes open, or we shall be very liable to miss it altogether. The movements of the eye are, no doubt, subject to a similar uncertainty and require similar care properly to direct them, though such care is less observable than in the case of the finger.

If, on the other hand, it be said that the movement of the finger is too certain and, therefore, not sufficiently *accidental* to answer the purpose of the mind in getting itself out of a state of equilibrium, it may withhold this care; or the eyes may be partially or wholly closed, and thus any required degree of uncertainty obtained in the movement of the finger. The movement of the finger thus, under certain obtainable circumstances, partakes as much of the nature of an accident as the movement of the eye; and hence, Edwards might as well have made the movement of the finger and its resting on a particular spot the reason for touching that spot, as to have made use of the movement of the eye for that purpose; and this would be to make the mind determine the act of touching IN the act of touching; or to determine its act directly instead of indirectly through, or BY another act; and this, so far as the act has reference to touching a *particular* square, excludes Edwards's idea that the act is determined by that "motive," which "has some sort or degree of tendency or advantage to excite the will *previous* to the effect."

It is however obvious that the finger, in its approach to, or in its first contact with the board, may come into a position, which, in the view of the mind, is just equal as to some two, or some four squares, and that the same is also true of the eye; and hence, in either case, the difficulty of indifference may again occur; and Edwards has evidently selected that, which, so far as it is an accident, is liable to the difficulty of indifference in its application, even after the difficulty of indifference in selecting it has been surmounted. But, supposing the difficulty of indifference in selecting the accident to be gotten over, and that, in some way, the mind " has *pitched* upon " " that sort of accident " by which " a certain individual spot " " has actually *offered itself* beyond others; " in what way does the " accident," a passing cloud, for instance, determine the particular square to be touched, or the action by which it is to be touched? In what way can it be cause at all, and, especially, in what way can it be the cause of the determination by the mind to touch a *particular* square, or of its act of will to touch, or of its *choosing or preferring* a particular square to be touched? There manifestly may be nothing in the event or accident itself, tending to such effects or results any more than there is in the fact that $2 + 2 = 4$; as well suppose the *square itself* to determine, as the *event itself* to determine. There is evidently no less difficulty in selecting one particular accident from among myriads of accidents, all equal for its purpose, than in selecting one particular square from the sixty-four, all likewise equal. There is then no more difficulty in selecting the square, than in selecting the accident, to say nothing of the difficulties of indifference, before suggested, in applying the accident after it is selected. It is obvious that the whole causal efficacy in the case must subsist, not in the event, or accident, but in some rule which the *mind* itself makes in the premises ; as, for instance, that if the *cloud* passes *easterly* a certain square shall be touched ; and if westerly, then another certain square. Such a rule would conform to Edwards's hypothesis " that it will touch that square, which happens to be most in view," &c. But how does the mind determine this rule as to the square to be touched ? It has no less indifference and no more preference as to which of the sixty-four squares each division of the rule shall be applicable, nor to which two of the sixty-four the whole rule shall apply, than it has as to which one shall be touched. Again, supposing this difficulty surmounted ; if the mind makes a mere arbitrary rule, that, if the cloud passes easterly it will touch a certain square, and, if westerly, another certain square, being still indifferent as to which of the squares is touched, it can certainly just as well make the rule that, if it passes westerly, the *same* and not *another* certain square is to be touched, thus making it certain that, let it pass which way it will, one particular square is to be touched ; and this being the same as determining, in *any event*, to touch one certain square, it follows that the event and the rule of its application may be dispensed with altogether ; or, in other words, the mind can as well *directly* determine the particular square to be touched, as it can the particular square to the touching of which the event and rule shall apply when it is indifferent as to which it will touch ; and, consequently, as to which the event and rule shall apply. Suppose, however, we in some way overcome all these difficulties of making and applying a rule to a certain square in preference to other squares, when, by the hypothesis, there is not and cannot be any ground for such preference, and that the rule is actually made and applied, the whole efficacy, the whole causative power or influence to determine the mind in willing to one particular square, is in the mind's making the rule and abiding by it; or, which is the same thing, the mind's *governing itself* by an arbitrary rule of its own creation, which is to assert for it a freedom equal to that of Omnipotence. It is a freedom apparently even beyond that which I have asserted for it, in governing itself by the knowledge, intuitive or acquired, which it has merely found and has not itself created; and the mind, in the supposed *indirect* mode of determining in cases of indifference, would exhibit not only more creative power and more contrivance, but give stronger expression of its freedom than it could do in *directly* determining its acts of will in such cases. Again, the rule, even after it has been created by the mind, has in itself no causative power. It is the mind's abiding by it and thus executing it, that gives it all its efficacy and causality; and hence, the hypothesis of Edwards, that the mind gives itself up to accident, if true, only proves that the mind adopts a course by which it determines its own volitions under the circumstances which are supposed to present the greatest difficulties to its so doing; and by a means as arbitrary and self-originated, as a direct determination of the act of willing to touch the particular square would be; and nothing is lost to the argument in favor of freedom, or gained to that in favor of necessity by the indirection.

The supposed cases of indifference, however, do seem

to militate against the theory of Edwards, for they admit an act of will, when there is nothing without the mind, and no *previous* bias or inclination in it, to direct its action. All that Edwards calls motive is, therefore, excluded by the hypothesis; and his attempt to bring in some extraneous event, and thus get a *constructive* motive, entirely failing, the whole decision has to be referred directly to the intelligence that wills, acting without that preference or choice in regard to the objects presented, which usually is a portion of the knowledge by which the mind determines its action. So far as relates to a particular square or act, neither the motive which in his system is essential to the willing, nor the preference which, in it, is the willing itself, appears to have any existence, or to be possible in his supposed cases of indifference. The argument of Edwards assumes that it is necessary that the mind should not only choose to touch, but that it should also choose *among the objects of touch*. In his system, to will is to choose, and there can be no act of will but as an act of choice. If this choice must be a choice among the extrinsic *objects* of effort, in the sense in which he applies it to the square of the chess board, then a man never could thus will, when there was only one such object; a man could not will to take one egg unless there were at least two eggs to *choose* from, for with less than two, there could be no choice among the objects of choice.

It not only is not necessary to the final action to deliberate and decide, or to choose among *objects* which we immediately perceive to be equal, but it is not necessary that we should so choose among those in which we know or suppose there is a difference. I may, with my eyes open, thrust my hand into an uncovered basket of apples with as little regard to selection as if a cover, or my eyelids concealed them from my sight. In such cases, and in cases in which there is obviously no choice, I take as if there were but one, without choice, and bestow no more care upon the act than is necessary to direct my hand to the mass, and not to grasp more than one.

In reference to the bearing of the views, elicited in Book First, upon such cases of indifference, I would observe that, in the case we have been considering, the *want* to touch one and only one of the squares, is the whole ground of the mind's acting at all; that deliberation is not, perhaps, entirely excluded; but that, at the moment of commencing the examination, the mind perceives that there is no difference in the objects presented; and hence, dispenses with any further exercise of its power of comparing and judging; it being, as before stated, for the mind to decide, by the exercise of its judgment, how long it will examine a subject before deciding its final action in regard to it. That it must possess the power to thus end an examination and to judge of how far it will examine, is evident in almost every act of will, and even in cases of indifference, which, comparison as to the objects being useless, seem more nearly to exclude the exercise of the judgment than any other. For instance, in the act of touching a square on the chess board, the movements of the hand by which this may be accomplished are absolutely infinite, for there is no limit to the straight, curved and zigzag lines by which the hand may be moved to the board; and if the mind must examine each one and compare it with the others before it decides in which one it will move its hand to the board, it would never get ready to will to move at all; and as it does will, it must have the power to will, not only without choosing among all the objects of choice, but even without that examination and comparison which are essential to choosing among them all. The fact seems to be that the mind having perceived some mode of action, which will gratify its want, determines of itself by the preliminary exercise of its judgment, whether to adopt that mode, or look further for a better mode before adopting it; and that it often acts in doubt as to whether it has made a sufficient examination. How much time may be devoted to such examination, as already stated, is a matter of which the mind, in view of the circumstances, must judge. A man who has not long fasted, may seek the stalled ox and pass the dinner of herbs, which one famishing with hunger could not prudently do. When the mind comes to the conclusion—judges or knows—that the chances of advantage by further examination are balanced by the chances of disadvantage from the incident delay, it will cease to examine and will decide and act with such knowledge as it has; but more especially, as in cases of indifference, when it knows that no examination will reveal any advantage, will it cut off the examination and immediately determine its action. It would seem to be natural, or in conformity to that constitution which God has given to the finite mind, that it should will immediately on perceiving any mode of gratifying a want that it feels; though it is quite conceivable that the knowledge of deliberation as a means of adapting its acts to circumstances, or as essential to safety, may be intuitive. An animal with only one want and with no other knowledge than that of one means of gratifying it, would immediately will;

but in a being with conflicting wants and a knowledge of various modes of gratifying them, and also of various consequences of the gratification, to will becomes a more complicated matter. Even then, as before suggested, want may become so imperative, as in the case of imminent danger, sudden and violent excitement, and of appetites habitually unrestrained and nurtured into passion, that it shuts out all secondary considerations, all the results of its acquired knowledge and experience, all deliberation as to consequences; and acts as if it knew but the one want and the one mode of its gratification; and in such case, is reduced to a condition similar to that of an animal with mere intuitive knowledge and consequent instinctive action. But it may be asserted as a matter of fact, that in most cases the human mind avails itself of a variety of knowledge in the mode of gratifying its wants; and especially of its past experience as to the subsequent effect of different modes, which requires examination and an exercise of its powers of conceiving, comparing and judging;. and this examination is an element which the mind itself, in virtue of its intelligence, its knowledge, intuitive or acquired, introduces between its want and its final action.* But in a case in which, by the hypothesis, there can be no difference in the proposed modes of gratifying the want and no use in such examination, the mind in recognizing this fact, dispenses with the examination; and thus instead of adding a new process to aid its determination in such cases, as Edwards supposes, it merely omits, wholly or partially, one to which it is accustomed to resort in other cases. The mind wanting to touch *one* of the squares and perceiving that there can be no

* See Appendix, Note XLI.

OF WILLING IN THINGS INDIFFERENT. 279

preference between them, omits the preliminary effort to judge and decide as to such preference, and decides arbitrarily as between them, or as to some known modes by which the finger can be placed on some one of these squares without having found any ground for preference, for the reason that such a decision is necessary to gratify its want.

In other cases the mind may be aware that there may be reasons for one act rather than another, which it cannot take time to ascertain, because of the necessity of immediate action; or will not, because in its judgment, the time required can be more advantageously employed; and it cuts short the deliberation, deciding with such knowledge as it has. In the case of indifference we cut short this deliberation the moment we perceive that it cannot possibly reveal any new or better ground of action, and determine the matter in a direct act of will. It may be said, that at the moment of coming to the decision not, or no longer to deliberate, some one square must be in the mind's view, or which, as Edwards supposes, "the eye is especially upon at that moment." But suppose the attention or the eye is at that moment directed to the line common to two, or to the point common to four squares, it is still a case of indifference, to be determined by the direct and arbitrary act of the mind, when there is nothing external to it to control or direct, or even influence its choice or its effort, making a strong case of the exercise of its free creative power, as an originating first cause of change in the future; and as already stated, if the mind does this, as asserted by Edwards, by means of an arbitrary rule of its own making or adopting, it is a still stronger manifestation of its power and of its freedom.

It may not be wholly irrelevant here to observe that these supposed cases of selecting in things indifferent are somewhat analogous to that we have before suggested, in which the mind wants to will for the mere exercise of its faculty of will, without reference or preference as to what it wills; and as, in that case, after deciding to gratify its want, there is neither object, present or future, nor mode of obtaining the object between the want and the willing, which is itself the object, there is no room for deliberation between, and the want to will is gratified by a direct act of will, without the preliminary processes of comparing and judging to select among the objects and modes. So, in the case of *indifference* as to the object and the modes of attaining it, the mind having determined to attain one of the objects, by one of the modes, as soon as it perceives that, as supposed, there is really nothing to examine, no room for deliberation between its *want* to touch and its will to touch, nothing but this act of will needed between its want and the effect, which is to gratify its want; it wills directly in the premises.

It may throw some further light on this curious problem to remark that Edwards's hypothesis of an arbitrary rule in these cases of indifference seems to derive some plausibility from an apparent analogy to the deciding between two parties having equal rights. For instance, two persons have equal claims to something which is indivisible and must be possessed wholly and at all times by one and not by the other, any division of the substance of the thing, or of the time of its possession destroying its value. In such cases the circumstances suggest a decision by what Edwards calls accident; something which neither of the interested parties can foresee or control, as the drawing of lots, throwing of dice, &c.; but here the elements of justice and of two conflicting wills to be reconciled, really make all the necessity for resorting to an accident which is beyond their prescience and control, that each may have, under the rule adopted, an equal chance. If the matter were referred to *one* other will, to an impartial judge, the action of whose mind, in such case no human intelligence could prognosticate, his decision, or rather his action, a mere arbitrary act of his will—there being by the hypothesis no possible reason why he should decide one way rather than another,—would be such an *accident* as Edwards suggests, and do just as well as drawing lots, or throwing dice. If the judge should order the case decided by lot, he would still have to make an arbitrary rule, as that he who draws number one shall have the thing; or that he who draws number two, shall have it. It is evident that he could just as well decide between the two equal claimants, as between the two equal rules. He must resort to this mode then, not because it is any easier, but for some other reason, as, for instance, to satisfy the parties or himself, that the decision is impartial, or that each really had an equal chance; or to avoid the unpleasant duty of depriving, by his own direct act, one or the other of his equal right. The analogy, then, furnishes no ground for the supposed necessity of resorting to an "accident" to determine the will in cases of indifference, where there is no question of personal right or interest. Still another reason for the supposed difficulty, or inability of the mind to determine in cases of "indifference," as urged by Edwards, is its apparent analogy to cases of mere matter, kept at rest by external forces acting equally upon it in all directions. An argument from such analogy really begs the question; for the only reason why mere matter is thus kept at rest is that it has no self-moving power or faculty within it, no means of moving itself, which is the very thing asserted and denied of intelligence or mind, in this controversy as to its freedom in willing. If we suppose mere matter to have a self-impelling force imparted to it, by motion or otherwise, then, if acted upon equally in all directions by other forces, it moves by its self-impelling force, precisely as if these other equal and conflicting forces were annihilated; they neutralize each other. And so, if the mind has a self-determining power in itself, then, if equally acted upon in all directions by external forces, its internal force would be unimpaired, and the moment it *knows* that the various objects or modes of its action presented to it are all exactly equal, it decides among them as readily and as easily as if there were only one such object or mode, and the sole question was as to adopting it, or not acting at all. We before reached this same result which seems to be attested by observation, indicating the existence of such a power. A man wanting one egg, and having decided to gratify the want, may particularly examine every one of a number before him, and having satisfied himself that, so far as he can know, all are equal, he takes one without further hesitation. Among the infinite modes of taking it, he decides among those apparently equal, in the same way. So, also, a man wanting to touch one of the squares on the chess board, has already, in virtue of the constitution of his being, his faculty of effort, his want and his knowledge, a certain inherent force which is not

OF WILLING IN THINGS INDIFFERENT. 283

affected by the presence of sixty-four squares in all respects equal; and the moment he perceives their certain equality, he touches one of them as readily as if there were only one to touch, having first decided to touch one rather than not to touch. If there were only one, the same supposed difficulties might arise as to what particular spot upon that one to touch; or by which of the infinite lines of movement to approach it. In all these cases, as already intimated, it is not necessary that the mind should even ascertain that the objects and modes are all equal; but only, that the chances of advantage by its finding any ground of preference or otherwise, are, in its judgment, not sufficient to warrant the application of further time and labor to the investigation.

CHAPTER VII.

RELATION OF INDIFFERENCE TO FREEDOM IN WILLING.

In his seventh section (Part II), Edwards considers the notion of "Liberty of Will consisting in indifference," using the term *indifference* as directly opposed to preference. He argues that "to make out this scheme of liberty the indifference must be *perfect* and *absolute*. * * * Because, if the will be already inclined before it exerts its own sovereign power on itself, then its inclination is not wholly owing to itself" (p. 85). By will Edwards asserts he means *the soul willing* (p. 43). He also makes inclination, choice and preference each synonymous with act of will (p. 2). The statements on the same page with the above quotation also clearly show that Edwards here uses the terms inclination, choice and preference as synonyms, viz.: "Surely the will cannot act or choose contrary to a remaining prevailing inclination of the will. To suppose otherwise, would be the same thing as to suppose that the will is *inclined* contrary to its present prevailing *inclination*, or contrary to what it is *inclined* to. That which the will chooses and prefers, that, all things considered, it preponderates and inclines to. It is equally impossible for the will to choose contrary to its own remaining and present preponderating inclination, as it is to *prefer* contrary to its own present *preference*, or *choose* contrary to its own present *choice*" (p. 85). By substitution of these equivalents, the argument just quoted will stand thus: *Because, if the soul willing be already willing, before it exerts its own sovereign power on itself, then its willing is not wholly owing to itself.* It is obvious that such statements must be fruitless. But further, by the *will* exerting its own sovereign power on itself, he must mean the *soul willing*, exerting, &c.; and the argument then amounts only to this: *Because if the soul willing be already willing before it wills, then its willing is not wholly owing to itself; that is, if the soul wills when it is not willing, or does not will, then its willing is not wholly owing to itself.* The inference which Edwards himself draws from these positions is: "Therefore, if there be the least degree of preponderation of the will, it must be perfectly abolished, before the will be at liberty to determine itself the contrary way;" which, though somewhat obscured by introducing new terms, as preponderation for inclination, really, under his definitions, only asserts that, while the soul is in any degree willing one way, it cannot be willing the contrary way. Throughout this section there is much confusion and sophistry from using the term inclination as identical with will, and yet as something which goes before and influences the will. The same, to some extent, may also be remarked of the terms choice and preference. This confusion is further increased by the frequent use of the term will, as a synonym for mind or soul. After assuming "as an axiom of undoubted truth that every free act is done in a state of freedom and not only after such a state," he says, " Now the question is, whether ever the soul of man puts forth an act of will, while it yet remains in a state of liberty, in that notion of a state of liberty, *viz.*: as implying a state of indifference, or whether the soul ever exerts an act of choice or preference, while at that very time the will is in a perfect equilibrium, not inclining one way more than another. The very putting of the question is sufficient to show the absurdity of the affirmative answer; for how ridiculous would it be for anybody to insist, that the soul chooses one thing before another, when, at the very same instant, it is perfectly indifferent with respect to each! This is the same thing as to say the soul prefers one thing to another at the very same time that it has no preference. Choice and preference can no more be in a state of indifference, than motion can be in a state of rest, or than the preponderation of the scale of a balance can be in a state of equilibrium. Motion may be the next moment after rest; but cannot co-exist with it, in *any*, even the *least* part of it. So choice may be immediately after a state of indifference, but has no co-existence with it; even the very beginning of it is not in a state of indifference. And therefore, if this be liberty, no act of will in any degree, is ever performed in a state of liberty, or in the time of liberty." (p. 88). This portion of the argument now stands thus: The soul of man never puts forth an act of will while it is in a state of indifference, or not choosing or preferring; for this is to will when it does not will; and as, if the freedom of the act of will consists in indifference, the act of will must be in the time of such indifference, there can be no such free act of will. If any, using the terms in the sense that Edwards uses them, have asserted such freedom, *i. e.*, that the freedom of the mind in willing consists in its willing when it is in a state of indifference, or not willing at all, their position is sufficiently refuted. Edwards also considers the position of those who, " to evade the reasoning should say that, the thing wherein the will exercises its liberty, is not in the act of choice or preponderation itself, but in *determining* itself to a certain choice or preference; that the act of the will wherein it is free and uses its own sovereignty, consists in its *causing* or *determining* the *change*, or *transition* from a state of indifference to a certain preference, or determining to give a certain turn to the balance, which has hitherto been even " (p. 90). This is only a *particular* case of the *general* proposition just mentioned, involving, under Edwards's definition, the same absurdity of the mind's *willing* the " change or transition," when, being in a state of indifference, it is not *willing* at all; and so far this argument only proves that the mind cannot both will, and not will, at the same time, which no one will dispute.

Edwards further asserts that a *free* act of will cannot " directly and immediately arise out of a state of indifference." Now, under his definitions, every act of will, choice or preference, which begins to be must spring directly from a state of indifference; for, as he uses the terms, the mind must be either in a state of indifference or of preference, and never can be in both; so that, the instant it ceases to be in one of these states, it is of necessity in the other; and if any particular preference was not preceded by a state of indifference as to what is thus preferred, the mind must always have had that preference and been engaged from all eternity in that act of will, which, in Edwards's system, is designated by this particular preference. It is evident that no such act of will is possible to a being, whose existence has had a beginning; and as, under the assumed conditions, every other act must have sprung directly from a state of indifference, when it is proved that a *free* act of will cannot directly and immediately spring out of a state of indifference, it will also have been proved, under these definitions and assumptions, that no free act of will is possible to a being whose past existence has been finite. Edwards thus attempts this proof: " If any to evade these things should own that a state of liberty and a state of indifference are not the same, and that the former may be without the latter, but should say that indifference is still *essential to* the freedom of an act of will, in some sort, namely, as it is necessary to go immediately *before it;* it being essential to the freedom of an act of will that it should directly and immediately *arise out* of a state of indifference; still this will not help the cause of *Arminian* liberty, or make it consistent with itself. For if the act springs immediately out of a state of indifference, then it does not arise from *antecedent* choice or preference. But if the act arises directly out of a state of indifference, without any intervening choice to choose and determine it, then the act, not being determined by choice, is not determined by the will; the mind exercises no free choice in the affair, and free choice and free will have no hand in the determination of the act, which is entirely inconsistent with their notion of the freedom of volition " (pp. 91, 92). It will be observed that this argument assumes that choice is a necessary element of free will, and is that element which distinguishes it from *un*free will, which, if asserted generally and taken in connection with the assertion of Edwards that, " to will and to choose are the same thing" (p. 91), is analogous to saying that water is a necessary element of hot water, and is that element which distinguishes it from cold water. That the free act of will must be *immediately preceded* and determined by choice is here assumed; and this, if choice is also deemed an act of will, involves the notion, attributed by Edwards to the Arminians, that a free act of will must be determined by a preceding act of will; and hence, Edwards's inference that the position, that a free act of will is immediately preceded by indifference and not by choice or act of will, is inconsistent with their notion of liberty. It is obvious that this reasoning is directed only against those who assert that a free act of will must co-exist with, or " immediately arise *out* of a state of indifference;" and that it avails even as against those, only on the assumption that indifference is that state of the mind in which it has no choice or preference; that choice is a necessary antecedent and *the immediate antecedent* of *free* will; and that to will is the same thing as to prefer or choose.

I infer, from Edwards's statements, that the Arminians hold that the choice of the mind, is a prerequisite of a *free* act of will; and yet that choice and act of will are the same; and thus, in asserting the mind's freedom in willing, were forced to the position that the freedom was exercised in a state preceding that of choice; a state, which was *not* that of choice; and consequently, in his and their use of terms, was a state of indifference. As I do not assert what this argument opposes, and deny some of the propositions which are essential to its conclusions, it has little application to my positions.

I see no objection to Edwards's use of the term indifference, as the antithesis of choice or preference, but I hold that every act of will is immediately preceded by a perception, by the knowledge that such act will, or may produce the effect *wanted;* and this perception or knowledge may be a preference or choice, as among various modes of action, or as between action and non-action; that, except in those cases of hasty action in which at once perceiving that a certain action will produce a certain desirable result, we adopt it without stopping to compare it with other possible modes of action, or with non-action, this perception is a choice or preference, and hence, for the purposes of this argument, Edwards's assumption that a free act of will is an act of will which is preceded by the mind's choice or preference, and is in conformity to such choice, may also be admitted. But, then, such a perception, choice or preference, is not an act of will, but knowledge; and this knowledge or choice, is not a distinct power or entity, which itself determines the act of will, but is merely that acquisition by which the mind determines its act, in adapting it to the desired end; and the freedom of the mind in such case consists as before argued, in its determining its own acts by means of its own knowledge. This addition to our knowledge is always an immediate perception, but may have required preliminary acts of will to make it obvious to the mind's knowing sense. It may be the result of an effort, in or by which the mind compares various things or modes, till it judges or decides among them, that is, perceives or knows which is best; but the *effort* and the decision or judgment which is its *result*, are two distinct and very different things; the effort is an act of will and, in this case, the result is a choice.

The form in which an admission that choice is a necessary antecedent of *free* will, could be most plausibly used against the freedom of the mind in willing, seems to me to be this: Even supposing the mind's choice to be something distinct from its act of will, still the choice in that case, is the result of a comparison, which was itself an act of will, and, if a free act, must also have been preceded by a choice, which, in turn, must be the result of a previous act of will, and so on ad infinitum, leaving no possibility of a first free act. It will be observed that this argument is the same as that of Edwards, except that, instead of making choice itself an act of will, it makes it the result of an act of will and avails only on the assumption that *every* choice requires an antecedent act of will. This assumption I deem unfounded. When I, at the same time, see an ox and a mouse, I know at once without any effort or act of will, that the ox is larger than the mouse. It is a fact obvious to simple perception requiring no preliminary effort to arrange either objects or ideas to make it apparent. In the same way I may at once perceive that one thing is better than others; and when I thus perceive that one thing is *better adapted to my want* than others, and that it is better to have, than not to have it, it is a choice of that thing, which is thus recognized by the mind's sense of knowing, without any preliminary effort; and such choice, even under our admission, may be the basis of free action.

But it does not appear certain that choice, either as the result of an act of the will in comparing, or even as a simple perception of the mind, is a necessary antecedent to a free act of will. The mind may perceive some good result of an effort, and make that effort without comparing it with other efforts, as we may decide to take an apple immediately before us, without comparing it with others in the same basket. In walking, for instance, a man, having by previous action decided, knows that he wants to move in a certain direction, and that the mode of doing it is at each point of his progress to take another step in the same direction. The facility with which a man in walking thinks of other subjects, and the little interruption of his thoughts, seem to indicate that he does not, at each act of will, or effort to take a step, without which the step would not be taken, compare the act of stepping in a certain direction with that of stepping in other directions, or with the swinging of the arms, or any other conceivable act, or even with not acting at all; but, as before suggested, acts immediately upon the perception, the knowledge, that such act tends to a desirable result. The essential element or fundamental condition of free action is not that it is chosen, but that it is self-directed; and it would be proper to bear this in mind even if it should on investigation appear that choice of the action is still an essential element of this self-direction, because choice has a more general application, signifying selection among other things, as well as acts of will; and hence, even if choice is always the immediate antecedent of free action, a free action is not always the *immediate* consequence of choice; and this even though the mind in choosing always has a view to future action, either proximate or remote.

The latter portion of his seventh section (Part II.)

Edwards devotes to those who "should suppose that these difficulties may be avoided by saying that the liberty of the mind consists in a power to *suspend* the act of the will, and so to keep it in a state of indifference until there has been opportunity for consideration; and so shall say * * * that liberty consists in a power of the mind to forbear or suspend the act of volition and keep the mind in a state of indifference for the present, until there has been opportunity for proper deliberation." (P. 92.) Edwards assumes that those who say this, mean to assert that this power to suspend its volition is the *only* liberty of the mind in willing; and argues as if they had said, the liberty of the mind consists in its *actually suspending* the act of the will. He further assumes that "this suspending volition, *if there be properly any such thing*, is itself an act of volition," and, on these assumptions, his argument runs thus: the only free volition is the volition to suspend an act of will, and the freedom of this volition, in turn, consists in a volition to suspend it, and so on *ad infinitum*, admitting of no first free act of will. This reasoning, availing only against those who assert that the ·*only* liberty of the mind in willing consists in its suspending its act of will, and then being also founded on assumptions which do not enter into my system, and which I deem erroneous, does not really affect the argument I have presented in favor of freedom. Edwards in the above quotation seems to question " if there be properly any such thing " as " suspending volition," and, if there is, asserts that the suspending " is itself an act of volition." The question, can the mind suspend volition, really involves that of its ability to determine as to whether to act, or not to act. For, if the mind cannot even *suspend* a volition, it must, of course and of necessity, make or have the volition and have it immediately. On the other hand, if it has power to suspend volition, it must be for an indefinite time, otherwise there is a time when it has not power to suspend, and power to suspend for an indefinite time is power not to put forth nor have the volition at all. On the first hypothesis, when there was only one cause, and that cause then able to produce all the effects it has since produced, as, if omnipotent, it must have been—and if suspending volition involves such contradictions as Edwards supposes, even omnipotence could not suspend its volition, but must immediately have actually created and done everything possible. And, if a part of this doing was the creating of other causes acting by will, they, too, at the same instant, must have exhausted all their causative power, making all cause end the instant it came into existence, or the moment the first cause of all acted. As the influence of matter, if made cause by being in motion, may be retained, or continued in time, from the circumstance that to move from one point of space to another requires time, so the influence of spirit, as cause in virtue of its intelligence, is continued in time from the circumstance that, by its intelligence, it may think, examine, compare, and judge, or decide as to the proper time of ending the preliminary examination, and proceed to the final action.* The assertion that " suspending volition is itself an act of volition," I deem unfounded; but Edwards thus attempts to prove it : " If the mind determines to suspend its act, it determines it voluntarily ; it chooses, on some consideration, to suspend it. And this choice or determination

* See Appendix, Note XLII.

is an act of the will; and indeed it is supposed to be so in the very hypothesis; for it is supposed that the liberty *of the will* consists in its power to do this, and that its doing it is the very thing wherein *the will exercises its liberty.* But how can the will exercise liberty in it, if it be not an act of the will? The liberty of the will is not exercised in anything but what the will does." (Pp. 92, 93.) There is a covert sophistry in this, growing out of using the term will as synonymous with mind. The latter portion shouldread thus: "for it is supposed that the liberty of the *mind* consists in its power to do this, and that its doing it is the very thing wherein the mind exercises its liberty. But *how can the mind* exercise liberty in willing, if it be not in an act of will? The liberty of the *mind* is not exercised in anything but what the mind does;" which would prove nothing against the *mind's* freedom in willing. In regard to this last-quoted assertion, as thus altered, we may observe that Edwards's own remarks in defining will, lead to the conclusion that the mind's liberty may be as much exercised in that which it refuses, as in that which it chooses, and, of course, as much in that which it refuses to do, as in that which it chooses to do; in what it does not will as well as in what it does will.

It will be observed that Edwards's proof of the assertion that suspending volition is itself an act of volition rests directly and wholly on the assumption that the mind's choice is the same as its act of will; and if I have succeeded in showing that this is an error, then, not only the above-mentioned assertion, but this whole argument of Edwards against the freedom of the mind in suspending volition, is shown to be fallacious. I would, however, further remark upon it that, if to suspend the mind's act of will requires an act of will of any kind, free or unfree, then once the mind is in action it never can suspend action, or cease to act; for every act must continue till there is another act to suspend it. But even if, against all experience, this be admitted, it still would not prove that the mind is not free in its every act of will; for it is conceivable that the mind may be under a continual necessity to act, and yet that itself as continually directs its every act, and is consequently free in such act. For aught that appears in the argument, if it could will at all, it might still freely will to suspend willing, though its efforts be found to be unavailing. If, for want of a known mode, or any other reason, we could not thus will at all, then, as it is manifest that we might still, as the result of a comparison of willing with not willing, prefer or choose non-willing, the *choosing*, which is possible, cannot be the same thing as the willing, which on this hypothesis is impossible; and the main foundation of the argument is thus destroyed by another essential support of it. The assumption of Edwards, as above stated, would however admit of only the one act suspended, and a series of acts each merely suspending the preceding one; and each of those acts, as his argument virtually asserts, must be without the preliminary act to consider, or get any new knowledge; for this would not be an *act* to suspend the prior act. The mind's sphere of action would thus be curtailed to very narrow limits. That when we perceive that a contemplated effort may be better made at some future time, we may, in conformity to this perception, delay action till then, is a matter of fact, which I presume will be admitted, and hence, in this sense, a contemplated act of will may be suspended. In such case, we may have compared the advantage of present with future action, and come to a conclusion, a decision in favor of the latter, *i. e.*, that at a certain time, or when another expected event occurs, we will make a certain effort; but such decision is not itself the future effort, but only present knowledge regarding that effort. But we may thus suspend for an indefinite time, or for all time, and thus wholly abandon and contemplated volition, or any portion of an act or series of acts. To will to suspend an act of will is then the same as willing not to will, either for the time being, or at all. Indifference being that condition of the mind in which it is not willing, to say that the mind wills to keep itself in this condition is to say that the mind wills not to will, which, if asserted generally, involves the absurdity of supposing that, for the mind to cease willing, or not to will, it must still will; that after having once willed, non-willing is still only another willing. The assertion that the mind cannot suspend its willing by an act of will, if made in general terms and as applicable to *all* willing, must be as true as that thought is not suspended by thinking, or motion by moving. This all amounts to saying that we cannot do a thing by not doing it, or by doing the contrary to it. But, even if it be admitted that, in this general sense, the mind can only suspend its willing by willing to suspend, it would be a sufficient answer to this position to say that the mind never wills thus *generally;* never wills *will*, but always, when willing, wills some particular act; and that, though it cannot stop action by acting, it can still, even while acting, suspend one particular act by directing its power to another particular act, as, even though we could not stop moving, we might still suspend motion in one direction by moving in another. The liberty of the mind in directing all its actions might thus still be maintained under the hypothesis, that to suspend action *generally*, required an act to suspend, though the exercise of liberty as to acting, or not acting, might then be denied. But the particular jurisdiction of the mind, which is questioned by this denial of its power to suspend willing, is not derived from any *negative* attribute of its power *not to will*, but from its positive ability to will, which is its own effort, or the exercise of its own power; and without such exercise there is no act of will. The mind has then only to refrain from any positive effort, which it will do whenever it sees reason for it, and the condition of non-action, or general suspension of its willing, is reached. To suppose the mind to will when *itself* does not will—and this non-willing is its condition whenever it does not perceive any object, or reason for willing—involves the hypothesis that it is compelled by some extraneous power to will; and this, again, as before shown, involves the contradiction of supposing it to will, when it is not willing, when it is not exercising its power, or making any effort whatever. If the mind, by extrinsic power, can be moved to will, when itself perceives no reason for such willing, it is not, in such case, either an intelligent or willing agent any more than an axe or other instrument, which is moved by extrinsic effort directed by extrinsic intelligence.

From these general considerations, turning to particular or individual acts of will, in which alone they can find *practical* application, we would remark that, by the phrase "suspending an act of will" cannot be meant suspending an act, or that portion of an act, or of a series of acts already accomplished; nor can it apply to an act of which the mind has yet had no idea, but must have reference only to such acts as the mind has already contemplated and intended, determined, or *chosen* to do. But here, under Edwards's definitions, it may be said that what has been *chosen* has already been *willed*, and hence the willing it could not be suspended. The fallacy of this position, resting on the assumed identity of choice and will, has already been exposed. But further to illustrate: suppose a man is reading aloud, and has already pronounced the first syllable of the word " gallows," when a man suddenly enters whose father was hanged. The reader may then perceive a reason for *suspending* the act of pronouncing the last syllable, and do so. His knowledge is altered, and he conforms to it by suspending or abandoning the act he intended. The same thing occurs whenever by any change of knowledge he perceives, not, as in the case just mentioned, that the contemplated act will be injurious, but merely that it will not be in any wise beneficial; there is then no perceived or known reason for action, and without such knowledge, an intelligent being does not exert its power to produce change. Again, suppose that, when the reader had pronounced the first syllable, a man enters, whose presence suggests no direct reason for not finishing the word, but with whom he has urgent business; he may, for this reason, suspend the contemplated act to finish the word, that by another act he may attend to something more pressing. In this case one act is suspended to make room for another act. The mind suspends its intended act, in the first instance above stated, because it perceives a reason against such action. In the second instance, because it perceives that there is no good reason for the act; and in the third instance, because it perceives there is a reason for preferring another act. Whether, in this last case, the suspension of the one act is the consequence of the other act, or only a necessary preliminary to it, may be a question; if the former, then the mind suspends the first act *by*, or as a consequence of its second; and if the latter, it first suspends one act, ceasing to act in it, that it may afterward do another. The question is not here material, as the first contemplated act of will is in either event suspended. If this suspension is a consequence of the mind's effort to do something else, the doing something else is a mode in which the mind, by its own action, suspends a contemplated volition; and if there is a preliminary act suspending this contemplated volition, then the mind thus suspends because, in the more urgent demand for another act, it perceives a reason for such preliminary act to suspend; and then, in the instances above stated, the third becomes the same as the first, in which the mind suspends an act because it perceives a reason for such suspension. All these reasons may be simple perceptions of the mind, without any effort to reach them; and when the mind perceives a reason for not acting, it can, in the aggregate of its knowledge, perceive no reason for acting; and when it does not perceive a reason to act it does not act; and *not* to perceive a reason requires *no* act, so that this suspension may take place without *an act* to suspend.

As already shown, to *will* to suspend an act of will is equivalent to willing not to will. We have also stated that a man never wills to will generally. If the will is a faculty for which the mind *wants* exercise, it may seek to gratify that want, but, in doing so, must will, not generally, but some particular act. This position is easily brought to the test of experiment. There is obviously no way in which the mind can will generally. Will is the mode in which the mind manifests its power; and to will generally would be to exert power for no object and with no preponderance in one direction rather than another, which would be to exert it equally in all directions; and power exerted equally in all directions must neutralize itself, and there would then be no manifestation of power whatever in any direction. So far from the mind's being able to will thus generally, it cannot even will distinct genera of acts. If we want and even decide upon or choose bodily movement generally, we must know what portion of the body to move and in what direction, before we can *will* the movement. To will movement in no direction, or equally in all directions, would be to will no movement. If we want to reason, we must know something to reason about, and, at each step of the reasoning, must get a perception, find—not make—the logical sequence. Nor do we ever *will* to *will* a particular act, but *directly* will the act. To say a man wills *an act of will*, or thinks thoughts, or knows knowledge, expresses no more than to say he *wills*, he *thinks*, he *knows*. To will to will is to make effort to make effort, *i. e.*, to do the thing to be done in order to the doing it. The nearest approach we can make to willing to will, is when we want exercise for the faculty of will, *i. e.*, to exert our power without reference to any benefit to be derived from the effort; as we may want exercise for the body without any reference to any ulterior result. If we want such exercise for the will, and especially if we want that peculiar exercise of selecting objects or acts arbitrarily, without a preliminary act to compare, or judge of consequences, we will, in gratifying such want, display the characteristics of caprice. We, however, still directly will particular acts, and do not merely will to will. The mind, then, in no case, either general or particular, wills to will; and for stronger reasons it does not will to not will. To will not to will, in a general sense, would be doing a thing in order not to do it; and, in regard to a particular act, the mind may decide not to do it, and not doing requires no effort. The mind's act of will is based directly upon its perceptions of a reason for such act; and its non-action results from its not perceiving any reason to act, or from its perceiving a reason to suspend any contemplated act. In all these cases, it is the intelligent being that governs; in all, the mind, by means of its knowledge, determines how to act, or whether to act or not.

To suppose that to suspend an act of will, or to stop willing, requires an act of will, or, in other words, that to stop making effort requires an effort, is to suppose some power acting on the mind to cause it to will. But the only other things necessarily involved in its volition are its want and its knowledge: neither of these, as distinct entities, can, singly or combined, will, or direct the act of will; this must be done by the mind, the active being, that wants and knows. But even supposing a power to inhere in this want and knowledge to produce an act of will, the moment the want ceases, or the moment the knowledge changes and the mind perceives that the contemplated act will not tend to gratify its want, such power ceases; and, in that case, the contemplated act of will would be suspended, not by an act of will, but simply by non-action. If the knowledge is so changed that the mind, instead of merely perceiving that a contemplated act will not effect its object, or is not preferable to non-action, or perceives that another act is preferable, then still, as regards the first contemplated act, there is only non-action, and not an act to suspend it before the other act becomes possible.

I would here further observe, that a want demanding effort may be more than neutralized by the simple perception that repose is more wanted, and no effort be made, the mind still conforming its conduct to its knowledge. We always will, put forth our power, make effort for some object, and this object always is to make the future different from what it otherwise would be. If we already *are not willing*, we do not will not to will, for we seek no change in that respect. Even if, in such case, we could conceive that there might still be a want not to will, what we want already is, and no effort is required to gratify the want. If we *are willing*, we cease the willing, we cease to make effort, as soon as the end is accomplished, or as soon as we perceive any other sufficient reason for ceasing; and without a special effort to cease making effort, without a special act of will to stop willing. So far from our willing not to will, it is, at least, very doubtful whether we ever will, or ever can will *not* to do, or *not* to try to do. We will to do something, and not to do nothing. If the case of willing not to do differs from that of willing not to will, or is anything more than a particular case of it, still, either generally, or in each particular case of doing, it may be said that, if we already are not

doing, we do not will non-doing, for we seek no change
in that respect, and the argument we have just stated
in regard to willing not to will, applies to willing not
to do, both generally and in any particular case. When
the question is between doing one thing or another
thing, we seek knowledge, and our conclusion is a
choice, a decision as between them; and when it is
between doing and not doing anything, we also choose,
decide, as between doing and not doing; but in neither
case is the decision, the conclusion, or choice itself, the
act of will, or the trying to do, but only the knowledge,
found by a preliminary act for that purpose. In the
first case we have found—come to know *what* to try to
do; and in the second, we have come to know whether
to try to do, or to refrain from trying to do; and if the
decision is in favor of the latter, that knowledge ends
the matter. In this the mind conforms to its knowledge,
its decision, by refraining from further action. In all
these cases, the decision of the mind may be the result
of previous effort to obtain knowledge; but if the question arises as between action and non-action generally,
or even as between a particular act and such non-action;
i. e., whether, when a case arises in which we perceive
action may in some respects be advantageous, we will
give any attention, any thought whatever to it; the
decision of such question must be an immediate perception of the mind; for any preliminary effort to obtain
more knowledge, including any effort to recall and
apply what we know, or to arrange it so as to aid our
perception, is another action, manifesting that the mind
has already decided, in view of the premises, to act.
The whole phenomena in such case is perhaps expressed
by saying, the mind immediately perceives, knows,

without effort, whether action or repose suits it best; and its freedom, in this, as in other cases, lies in its ability to conform itself to this knowledge, without extrinsic constraint or restraint. Hence, even if it could be shown that this question, as between action and non-action, arises with every want or occasion for action, it would not argue necessity, for the mind still decides the question with such view, such knowledge, as it already has; and, in so doing, determines upon its own action, or non-action; and the arising of such question only furnishes an occasion for the exercise of its liberty, in exerting, or not exerting its powers, as the question between various acts furnishes the occasion for the exercise of its liberty in directing its efforts; though the latter case admits of preliminary effort to discover the mode or direction, while the former does not; non-action has no mode or direction.

I have before suggested that the *choice* by the mind may be its immediate perception that one thing is better than another. If, however, the decision of the question between action and repose, involves a comparison, requiring preliminary effort, then the non-action of the mind, or its refraining from action in such cases, must always arise from an immediate perception of some positive and not comparative advantages, or disadvantages of repose, or of action. In themselves, repose or action may be either pleasurable or painful. It appears, then, that though the mind can both will and suspend its act of will, or not will, it requires no distinct act of will, either to will, or not to will; that, in willing, it directly wills the particular act, and does not first will to will it; and that, in not willing, it as directly refrains from the particular action, and does not will not to will it: it merely does not act at all.

If our action is to be reënforced, strengthened, or made persistent, it is not by willing to will, but by means of knowledge, which may be inculcated by others, or found by our own efforts and dwelt upon till our perceptions of the benefit or pleasure expected from the act become so vivid, that a want, not in itself urgent, glows in desire, or is inflamed to passion; and the mind then wills without reference to any collateral or remote consequences, and without comparing the advantages, which so absorb it, with those which might be derived from other action, or from non-action. Those cases of action in which the mind is absorbed by one view, or one object, though the absorption is the result of its previous action, or attention, or thought devoted to the subject, become, in some respects, similar to those in which the mind acts on an immediate perception, without seeking more knowledge to direct its action. In them it has sought more knowledge, but only in one direction, and still acts upon a single idea. It is in such cases that the aid of others, in presenting their views and imparting their knowledge, may most obviously be useful; and especially in those cases in which the absorbing object, or the immediate perception, upon which the mind is about to act, is the gratification of some want which ought not to be gratified. When this is in conflict with our own knowledge of what is morally right, it becomes so important, that God never permits such action without a monition through the moral sense, warning us to refrain from the mutilation, or degradation of our being, and suggesting search of that knowledge, which, by a faith in the wisdom and goodness of the Supreme Intelligence, intuitive, or early acquired, we know will reconcile gratification and duty.

There are some cases in which the mind really decides its action upon an immediate perception of the gratification to be derived from such action, and still, to avoid the painful sensation of self-reproach in doing what it knows to be wrong, seeks by preliminary act to find reason to reconcile the act with its sense of duty; and, for this purpose, by its power to direct its efforts, seeks the arguments which favor, and excludes attention to those which oppose the act; or it may do the same thing to find a reason to convince others, and thus avoid or mitigate their censure. Such dishonest mind, in the first case, makes the vain effort to deceive itself. In the latter case, it seeks to deceive others; and in this may possibly succeed.

The reasoning of Edwards, which we have just been considering in this chapter, has little bearing upon my position, except that his denial of the liberty of the mind to suspend a volition, denies the mind's liberty in this one particular. This denial is associated with indifference only by the assertion of his opponents that the object of the suspension is to keep the mind "in a state of indifference until there has been opportunity for consideration." This, on the grounds I have stated, is merely to say, until there has been time to obtain more knowledge; and, if that knowledge is sought by effort, it is only one case of the mind's suspending one act of will to make room for another. It was not, then, important to my own position to have thus followed the whole of this argument "concerning the notion of the liberty of will *consisting* in indifference;" but the examination may serve to illustrate my own views, and at the same time to show how thoroughly the reasoning of Edwards is based on his two irreconcilable definitions, the one making choice the act of will, and the other making it the result of a comparative act, which is only knowledge sought and obtained by that act. As before observed, he also confounds the choice with the act of comparing of which it is the result; and thus produces additional confusion and error. I may further remark that, in conformity to his assumption that to choose and to will are the same, he inverts his definition, and instead of making the "will that by which the mind chooses," makes the *choice that by which the mind wills.*

No real progress could logically be made by this use of identical terms, and it is only by using one of them in a different sense, or as both identical and not identical with the other, that any conclusion, beyond *what is, is,* can be reached, and then with all the liability to error involved in the double and incompatible definitions.

There is, however, in this word *indifference,* as used by Edwards to denote that state in which we are not willing and have no choice, an important significance, indicating the point of the mind's departure from the passive to the active condition. In profound sleep it is thus indifferent, and being then unconscious of any want, or any reason for willing, it does not will; and any change which takes place in itself, or in other things, must then be produced by other agencies. Its waking, or being roused from this unconscious state, must be brought about by agencies external to itself. It must, however, be still susceptible, at least to some sensations, for it cannot change itself; and if it could not know any changes produced by extraneous agencies, it never could be awakened. The sensation could produce no effect upon the mind until the mind recognized it. If this passive state is not itself profound sleep; if, when awake, the mind is even entirely inactive, its condition can then vary from that of profound sleep only in its greater susceptibility to the effects of extrinsic activities. Without action it cannot change either its own passive condition or anything else. It may, however, in its passive condition, be acted upon, and the first step in this change from the passive to the active condition is a perception of some change; and in its feelings or perceptions growing out of such change, it may find reason for acting itself. If this change is from a satisfied condition to that of a want, for instance, to that of hunger, or thirst, arising without our volition, we act in reference to its relief. When we are fatigued and need sleep, we require greater inducements to act, and in proportion to our exhaustion; for this exhaustion is a reason or want not to act, and must be overbalanced by a counter reason or want; but so long as we are conscious, so long as we *know*, we can, for perceived reason, resist the change to sleep, or seek to produce some other change, though, from causes beyond our control, we may not have the power; from exhaustion, the *instruments* of the mind may have become too weak, as a decayed lever will not, by the application of the same power, raise the weight for which it once would have sufficed. But, with every change about us, we either intuitively or habitually know that some action on our part *may* be required to avail of beneficial, or to protect ourselves from evil consequences; and we *usually* give enough effort by thought, to every such change, to enable us to form a judgment, sometimes a too hasty one, as to the necessity or expediency of further effort, by thought or otherwise.

The effort of the mind, by thought or observation, to find what is transpiring and what further efforts the changes around it may require, is called ATTENTION; and this generally marks the first change from the passive to the active mental condition. It does not, however, always require an effort of any kind to know the changes which are taking place. It requires no effort to know the sensation, which itself is a change indicating some other change. We know we are hungry, and we hear the discharge of a gun, without effort; and with the sensation, the knowledge, not only as to whether the change indicated by it demands effort, or not; but, if it does, the knowledge of the particular effort demanded may be an immediate perception, without any preliminary effort; and, if this ever happens, the mind's activity then commences with the effort, the reason for which is thus perceived without a preliminary effort of attention in examining the changed or changing events. The circumstances most favorable to this immediate perception of the requirement or non-requirement of effort, are when the change is one of frequent occurrence, so that the application of our knowledge has become habitual, and especially when the change is one in which we perceive and have usually before perceived no reason for effort. In such cases it may be difficult to determine whether the decision is an immediate perception, or the result of an effort; but the probability seems to be that, with observed change, the mind generally puts forth an effort of attention to find if any action, or change of action, is thereby required, and if not, that it again relapses into a state of repose, or resumes its previous course of action. It thus suspends one action, till, by another, it ascertains whether the changed circumstances require the first to be longer delayed, or wholly abandoned. In cases like those just alluded to, the time and effort required for this are hardly appreciable, and if we are, at the moment, conscious of an effort, it is presently obliterated from the memory. The striking of a clock, which, a moment afterward, we are unconscious of having heard, is a familiar illustration. The striking has before frequently occurred, and, with exceptional cases, as when marking that the time for some action has arrived, we have in it found no reason for effort. But the mind must have recognized the sensation at the moment, for it would have heard the faintest whisper; nothing external to the mind causes it to hear the one and not the other, and itself could not make this distinction without first knowing what it was distinguishing between. The sensation produced by the striking has furnished no ground for action, has given us neither pleasure nor pain; we have not even drawn any inference from it as to the time, present or past; and the whole phenomenon is thus reduced almost to nothingness, leaving very little that could be remembered, and this so isolated, so free from association with other knowledge, that it is immediately left out and lost. The striking of a clock, leaving a sensation which merely marks the passage of time, is in some respects peculiar. Our mere progress through time has little more effect upon us than our movement with the earth through space, which, even when recognized, does not usually induce any effort, though, as in the exceptional cases in regard to the striking of the clock, the inferences from it, as that short days and cold weather are approaching, may be a reason for some effort, or change of effort. The constant murmur of the forest, or the roar of ocean, though indicating no such change as calls for action, and seemingly unheeded by those accustomed to it, is yet recognized by the mind; for if it suddenly ceases we know it, and we could not know of the cessation of the sound, without first knowing the sound that ceased. In such cases, the sensation not only does not indicate any change *requiring action*, but the continuous monotony of sound is an assurance to the mind that, so far, no such change is taking place. This partially relieves the mind from its wonted watchfulness in regard to the external, and favors its becoming absorbed in reverie, or concentrated upon abstract speculation.

CHAPTER VIII.

CONTINGENCE.

In the eighth and ninth sections of Part II., Edwards, treating of "the supposed liberty of the will as opposite to all necessity," and "the connection of the acts of the will with the dictates of the understanding," says: "I would inquire whether there is, or can be any such thing as a volition which is contingent in such a sense, as not only to come to pass without any necessity of constraint, or coaction, but also without a *necessity of consequence*, or an infallible connection with anything foregoing" (p. 96); and soon after, referring to this, says: "And here it must be remembered that it has been already shown, that nothing can ever come to pass without a cause, or reason why it exists in this manner rather than another; and the evidence of this has been particularly applied to the acts of the will. Now, if this be so, it will demonstrably follow that the acts of the will are never contingent, or without necessity, in the sense spoken of; inasmuch as those things which have a cause, or reason of their existence, must be connected with their cause. This appears by the following consideration: for an event to have a cause and ground of its existence, and yet not be connected with its cause, is an inconsistence" (p. 96). He then proceeds to prove this last proposition. Admitting it, still, as already intimated in my remarks on "No Event without a Cause" (Part II., Sec. 3), if mind itself is the cause of the event, it only proves in reference to such events, "the acts of the will," that they are connected with the mind, but does not at all tend to show whether that mind, the active power, which produces them and is their cause, acts freely, or otherwise. It is a mere abstract proposition involved in the notions, or definitions of cause and effect, and just as true of one kind of cause as of another; and hence, indicating no distinguishing quality or property of that cause; of course this cannot indicate whether that cause is free or not free. That mind may be such a cause, and especially under the great latitude with which Edwards says he uses the term cause, I trust I have already sufficiently shown.

At the commencement of section ninth, he thus reiterates the conclusion at which he arrives in section eighth, and applies it to his argument: "It is manifest that the acts of the will are none of them contingent in such a sense as to be without all necessity, or so as not to be necessary with a necessity of consequence and connection; because every act of the will is some way connected with the understanding, and is as the greatest apparent good is, in the manner which has already been explained; namely, that the soul always wills, or chooses that which, in the present view of the mind, considered in the whole of that view and all that belongs to it, appears most agreeable. Because, as was observed before, nothing is more evident than that, when men act voluntarily, and do what they please, then they do what appears most agreeable to them; and to say otherwise would be as much as to affirm that men do not choose what appears to suit them best, or what seems most pleasing to them; or that they do not choose what they prefer, which brings the matter to a contradiction" (p. 100).

So far as regards the volition, this contradiction appears only when will and choice are deemed identical. I do not mean to assert or to deny that "acts of the will are none of them contingent," in some of the various senses in which that term seems to be used. If the above argument only implies that acts of the will, taking will to be a distinct entity, capable itself of action, are necessary because they " in some way are connected with the understanding, and are as the greatest apparent good is," I shall only object that, there is no such will and no such acts of will to be subject to such necessity; or, if the argument implies that the will, considered as a mere faculty of the mind and itself incapable of action, is not free because it is controlled by the mind, then it does not even tend to prove any necessity of *mind* in willing; but is one step toward the proof of its freedom. But if, by the acts of the will, Edwards means, as he repeatedly claims to do, "the acts of the mind or soul in willing," then the argument is self-contradictory and absurd; for, as before observed, the understanding, in his system generally, and especially in its present application, embraces all the powers and faculties of the mind, except that of the will; and hence, to say that the *mind*, in the act of willing, does not will freely, or acts from necessity, because the act of will is, in some way, connected with the understanding, is to say that the mind, in the act of willing, does not act freely because the act of willing is, in some way, connected with the mind, which is absurd. And to say that, in the act of willing, the mind does not act freely, because every act of its will is in conformity to its views of the greatest apparent good, or because it "always wills, or chooses that which in the present view of the mind " " appears most agreeable ; " and that this is so, because when men act voluntarily and do what they please, then they do what appears most agreeable to them, is contradictory. It is, in effect, saying that the mind does not act freely in willing, because, in willing, it cannot do otherwise than direct its own action, which is to act freely; and hence, is subject to this *necessity*, or is *constrained* to be free in its action. It is like saying, *freedom is not free, because it cannot be otherwise than free;* and hence, is subject to the necessity, or is constrained to be free; and this is asserting that, *what is, is not;* and that it is not for the very reason that it is; than which, I apprehend, it would be difficult to involve more absurdity and contradiction in the same space. All those arguments which attempt to prove necessity from the dependence of the act of will upon other faculties of the mind, among them that quoted from Edwards (p. 96), more or less involve this absurdity. If the object were to prove that the *will itself* as an entity, distinct from the *willing agent*, is not free, because the will is dependent upon and controlled by the willing agent, the argument would be valid; but Edwards avows that, by will he means the " soul in willing ; " and that such willing is dependent upon and controlled by the soul, or by the understanding, whether viewed as a distinct portion of the mind, or as a mere mode of its effort, goes to prove the freedom of the soul in willing. In section thirteenth, he applies a similar course of reasoning, or an extension of it, to show that, even if the will itself is the cause of the acts of the will, still the will is not free, because being an effect it must still be controlled by its cause, though that cause be itself; that is to say, if the will, as cause, controls itself, it is not free, which confounds all distinction between what is free and what is not free. For, as I intimated in defining freedom, if that which controls itself is not free, and it must be admitted that, that which is controlled by something else is also not free, then, as everything in action must either control itself, or be controlled by something besides itself, there is no such thing possible as free action; and the term free being wholly unmeaning in such application, we could then as well reason about violet, or triangular time, or $dxfg$ will, as about free will. The fallacy of this, and of the argument before quoted from Edwards (p. 100), is in the assumption that, *whatever is directed and controlled in its movement or action is not free;* and, as everything that moves or acts, must be directed and controlled in its movement or action, either by itself, or by something else, it follows, from this *assumption*, that nothing can be free. If it directs and controls itself, it is still directed and controlled; and hence, under this assumption, not free; and if directed and controlled by something else, it is not free in the accepted notion of freedom. If it be granted that that which directs and controls its own movement or action is free, the argument as against the freedom of the mind in the act of willing wholly fails. The argument in section thirteenth is, then, obviously and wholly fallacious; and, also, as before intimated, that quoted from page 100. At most, they only tend to prove that the will, considered as a distinct entity, is not free; and not that the active agent, the mind willing, is not free; but, on the contrary, both of those arguments go to show, or admit that mind, in willing, controls its own act of will, which, as before shown, is but another expression for the freedom of the mind in willing. The position here, as elsewhere, really taken by Edwards, or involved in his arguments is, that every event is an effect of some cause on which it is dependent and by which it is controlled, and, therefore, a *necessary effect;* that volition is an effect of which the action of the mind, in willing, is the cause; but, instead of inferring that the *effect,* the volition, is necessary, he infers that the *cause,* the action of the mind in willing, is necessary, which is wholly illogical. He generally speaks of the *freedom of the will,* and not of the *freedom of the mind in willing,* though he asserts that by the former he means the latter, and occasionally expresses it, or its equivalent, as, " The question is wherein consists the *mind's liberty* in any *particular act* of volition ? " (p. 95). The utter futility of all attempts to reach any new truth by reasoning on the statement we have quoted from page 100, may be shown by substituting in it the word " choice," wherever its admitted equivalents are used, which would make the latter half of it read thus: "*Because,* as was observed before, nothing is more evident than that when men act as they choose, and do what they *choose,* then they do what they *choose;* and to say otherwise would be as much as to affirm that men do not choose what appears to suit them best, or what they choose, or that they do not choose what they choose;" or thus, the argument of Edwards, as there stated is, "that the acts of the will are none of them contingent," &c., "because every act of the will is some way connected with the understanding," &c., and "the soul always wills or chooses that which, in the present view of the mind, * * * appears most agreeable." But, as he says, "an appearing most agreeable and the mind's preferring or choosing, seem hardly to be properly and perfectly distinct," and elsewhere identifies will and choice with what is most agreeable or most pleasing, the above argument merely amounts to saying that acts of will are none of them contingent, because the mind wills what it wills.

The question which Edwards asks as to a volition having "an infallible connection with anything foregoing" (p. 96), has already been considered. The arguments I have adduced go to prove that, even admitting the hypothesis that the mind has other faculties which influence the will and yet are independent of it, which Edwards seems to adopt, his reasoning does not establish necessity; for in this case the mind still controls its own action. If, however, the action of those other faculties requires an act of will, then the act of will which they influence, is really influenced by the mind's previous act of will; and the same, if such faculties are, as I have supposed, only varied modes of effort or will; or efforts or acts of will for varied objects. In either case this would be influencing or determining the final act of will by a preliminary act of will, and if this were the end of it, the final act of will would be determined by a previous act of will, and the active agent, whether it be the mind, or the will itself, thus determining its own action, is free; but in all such cases, we must trace the series of efforts back to an exciting want and a *perception* of some mode of trying to gratify it, which are independent of the will. If by such other faculties Edwards means the capacity for simple perception, then it is the mind directing itself, not by means of such capacity itself, but by means of the *knowledge* which it acquires through this capacity, which brings the whole matter to our position, that the mind directs its efforts to the gratification of its want by means of its knowledge. The argument of Edwards seems to assert that any freedom in willing is impossible; but it might, with more reason, be asserted that *all cause* is free and cannot even be conceived of as otherwise than free. If I direct and control the movement of a ball, and, while so directed and controlled, it impinges against and affects another body, I, and not the ball, am the cause of that effect. If I throw the ball, and, after I have withdrawn all effort from it, it continues in motion by a principle inherent in matter itself, and not by the will, or effort of any other being, then, that which makes it cause is its own motion, which is not restrained, constrained, or in any wise interfered with, *till it comes to produce an effect*, by coming in collision with some other body, or in conflict with some other force; and then comes the trial, as to what, as a consequence of its own free movement, it has *power* to accomplish. If matter is ever cause, the motion, the *activity*, which constitutes its only conceivable causative power, must be uncontrolled; so the effort, through which the mind has causative power, must also be free from external control, even though the effect be frustrated by some other power; and, the moment matter is controlled in its movement, or mind in its effort, by some other power, it ceases to be cause, and becomes only an instrument, used by the power which controls it, which is then the real cause. In either case, too, it is only when it comes to the effect, that the causative agent can be frustrated or controlled in its action for want of sufficient force or power; but this cannot affect its *previous* condition as cause—cannot change its *previous* freedom of motion or of effort. There is, however, this essential difference between the two cases; that, although the movement of the matter in motion, till it comes to produce its effect, is free in the sense that it is not impeded or controlled by other external force at the instant, its freedom stops here, and it has no power, no liberty, *to control itself*. It cannot alter any direction given to it; and, if such direction has no extraneous cause, it must have been from eternity, and every successive motion have been controlled by past movements; there never could have been any initial force or movement which was self-controlled and directed, for matter never could begin to move itself. The term liberty, in the sense in which we apply it to intelligent cause, seems inapplicable to matter; for all its freedom consists in not being impeded in doing that which some other force has compelled it to do. It has no self-control. A body now moving is, therefore, rather an instrument, by which some prior cause extends its effects in time, than a cause itself; or, more properly, a link in a chain of instrumentalities, which cannot be traced to any beginning, or *real cause* in matter, for it never could have directed or moved itself. On the other hand, mind, perceiving the future varies its efforts from consideration of the future effects, and thus escaping the control of the past, acts as *final cause*, making such efforts as it perceives in advance to be requisite to the *future* effect it seeks to produce.

CHAPTER IX.

CONNECTION OF THE WILL WITH THE UNDERSTANDING.

IN the preceding chapter I have already noticed some of Edwards's remarks upon the connection of the will with the understanding, and will now observe that, if will is choice, it cannot always, as Edwards asserts, "follow the last dictate of the understanding," which itself may be a choice; and, of course, by his definition, in such case the last dictate would itself be the willing. On this point I would further remark, that this last dictate is often neither a choice, nor an act of will, nor followed by an act of will. If we investigate abstract truth, the last dictate of the understanding is that the result is so, or so; or, perhaps, that it is yet undetermined; and, in either case, no volition follows. Suppose, for instance, we want to ascertain the quantity in 3×7, and, having applied the proper modes, rest in the conclusion that it is 21. We have, in this result, a last dictate of the understanding, but no volition, or act of will follows: the matter is finished, there is no further *want* and no further *effort;* for the want was merely to obtain, and is fully gratified by obtaining, this "last dictate of the understanding." In regard to our actions, however, the object of examination is always to determine either between different modes of acting, or between acting and not acting; and, in either case, the result, or last dictate of the understanding, is *always* a choice or preference as to that particular action, or as to action or non-action; and hence, as the choice or preference cannot follow itself, it is evident that, if this choice is the act of will or volition, it *never* follows the last dictate of the understanding. But even admitting that Edwards means that the will—volition—which *always* follows the last dictate, is something distinct from that last dictate or choice of the understanding, still, as the understanding, in his system, embraces certain faculties which pertain to mind, it merely follows that the mind exerts some of its other faculties in order to an exercise of its will, or to decide what the exercise of the will shall be. But this involves the absurdity of supposing that, before an act of will there must *always* be an act of will; for this preliminary exercise of the other faculties must be by an act of will; and even if this were possible, it would argue nothing against either the freedom of the mind in willing, or its own, or even the will's self-determining power, but quite the contrary. In reply to Dr. Whitby, Edwards thus applies the doctor's admission that the will follows the last dictate of the understanding: "For if the determination of the will, evermore, in this manner, follows the light, conviction, and view of the understanding, concerning the greatest good and evil, and this be that alone which moves the will, and it be a contradiction to suppose otherwise; then it is *necessarily* so, the will necessarily follows this light, or view of the understanding; and not only in some of its acts, but in every act of choosing and refusing. So that the will does not determine itself in any one of its own acts, but all its acts, every act of choice and refusal depends on and is necessarily connected with some antecedent cause, which cause is not the will itself, nor any act of its own, nor anything pertaining to that faculty; but something belonging to another faculty, whose acts go before the will in all its acts, and govern and determine them every one" (p. 104). Here it is evident that Edwards makes the will a distinct entity, the freedom of which, and not the freedom of the mind in using or exercising it, is the matter in question; and that he also treats the understanding as if it were also an entity distinct from mind; and, as a distinct power, controlling the distinct entity of will; arguing that the will is not free, because it is controlled by the understanding; which is more erroneous than to assert that it is not free because of its dependence on the action of the mind through its other faculties; and this attempt to prove, not the mind in willing, but the will, as distinct from mind, necessitated, and thus necessitated because of its subjection to the mind's control, pervades the section. Upon such reasoning I have already sufficiently commented, and shown that it really confirms, or assumes, the freedom of the mind in willing.

In regard to what is said by Edwards (Part II., Sec. 9) of the necessity of an act of will to *attention by the mind*, I would remark that it is not an act of will by which, when the eyes are open, we see the sun and other external objects and their relations. The external objects cannot compel, or cause an act of will, producing that attention by which these objects are themselves first recognized; for they could produce no effect on the mind to make it will, or do anything whatever until it recognized them. So also it may not be by an act of will that the mind, when aroused and made sensible by want, perceives its knowledge, now present to it, and the relations of that knowledge, intuitive or acquired, to its want, also present with its knowledge, and all in the mind's view. I do not, however, deem it important to the views I have put forth, whether the mind, when aroused from a state of inactivity by a want, begins by an effort to get the requisite knowledge to gratify the want, or by a simple perception of that knowledge; it may begin in either mode, and sometimes in one and sometimes in the other. In the case of instinctive action, it is probably always a mere perception of its intuitive knowledge, and of the relations of that knowledge to its want, naturally associated; and, in the case of habit, similar perceptions of its knowledge, artificially associated with its want by repetition. In other cases, the mind may have to make an effort to find in its memory, or even newly and for the first time to obtain, the knowledge essential to the gratification of its want. Its intelligence enables it to conform its action, in this respect, to the existing circumstances; and, by effort, to put that portion of its body or that faculty of its mind in action, which, in view of existing circumstances, it *perceives* to be best for accomplishing its object. This whole matter of the will's following the last dictate of the understanding amounts then merely to this, that often, when the mind *wants* to produce any change, it makes preliminary effort to obtain knowledge as to the mode of producing such change, or obtains it by simple perception, and then determines its action by means of such knowledge, which, as we have already shown, is acting freely.

CHAPTER X.

MOTIVE.

One argument of Edwards, and, perhaps, that which he most relies upon, may be thus stated: There is no event without a cause; the determination of an act of will is an event, and must have a cause; this cause must be motive, for without motive the mind would have no inclination or preference toward anything; and, as the cause must of necessity produce one certain effect and no other, the act of the will is, of necessity, determined by the motive to be one particular volition, and can be no other. He not only makes motive determine the will, but he makes it the cause of the act of will itself. We give his own words from the commencement of section tenth: "That every act of the will has some cause, and consequently (by what has been already proved) has a necessary connection with its cause, and so is necessary by a necessity of connection and consequence, is evident by this, that every act of the will whatsoever is excited by some motive; which is manifest, because, if the will, or mind, in willing and choosing after the manner that it does, is excited so to do by no motive, or inducement, then it has no end, which it proposes to itself, or pursues in so doing; it aims at nothing and seeks nothing. And if it seeks nothing, then it does not go after anything, or exert any inclination or preference toward anything; which brings the matter to a contradiction; because for the mind to will something, and for it to go after something by an act of preference and inclination, are the same thing.

" But if every act of the will is excited by a motive, then that motive is the cause of the act of the will. If the acts of the will are excited by motives, then motives are the causes of their being excited; or, which is the same thing, the cause of their being put forth into act and existence. And if so, the existence of the acts of the will is properly the effect of their motives. Motives do nothing as motives, or inducements, but by their influence; and so much as is done by their influence is the effect of them. For that is the notion of an effect, something that is brought to pass by the influence of another thing.

" And if volitions are properly the effects of their motives, then they are necessarily connected with their motives. Every effect and event being, as proved before, necessarily connected with that which is the proper ground and reason of its existence. Thus it is manifest that volition is necessary, and is not from any self-determining power in the will."

In passing, I would remark upon this statement, that when in it Edwards says, "for the mind to will something, and *for it to go after something by an act of preference and inclination*, are the same thing," he, in fact, materially varies his definition of will, under which he could only say, "for the mind to will something, and to prefer something, are the same thing;" and the addition makes the act of choosing or preferring, include the *going after the thing chosen or preferred*, and is one of many instances of the difficulty to which he is reduced, from not recognizing, by a distinct term, that action of the mind, which sometimes follows its choice, and which I have called *effort;* and which he here virtually admits as coming between the choice and the effect, and characterizes as " the going after the thing chosen," and by the remarkable expression, " exerting a preference." In this case, the proof " that every act of the will has some cause," or that every act of the will, whatsoever, is excited by some motive, rests entirely on this new assumption, but for the interpolating of which, the reasoning would be utterly futile. I do not, however, mean to question these propositions when the term motive is properly applied, but will here remark that his statement does not warrant all the inference he draws. If, as he says, "every act of the will is excited by motive," which "is the cause of its being put forth into act and existence," and then further admitting that motive is some power, or cause not of the mind, it would still only follow that *some* act of will is put forth, and not that what that act of will shall be is thus determined ; " not that it is in such a direction rather than another." Again, if the act of will is " put forth," there must be some active agent to put it forth. Edwards virtually assumes that the motive is itself the active agent directly producing acts of will; and having thus put it in the place of the mind, arrives at conclusions, which really apply to mind, and prove that it is the cause of its own volitions and, of course, is free. If the motives, whatever they are, do not directly produce or control the acts of will, or do not directly act with irresistible force upon the will as a distinct entity, but are only *inducements* to the mind to "put forth" some volition, then it may still be for the mind to determine whether to yield to those inducements, or to which of numerous inducements it will yield, or in what way it will "go after something," or whether it will go after it at all, which would still be to *determine* its own action; and by its intelligence conform that action to the existing circumstances, which motive, as a distinct entity, or any other blind cause could not do. In noticing some portions of this argument, I may attempt to show that even upon Edwards's own definition, that "volition is choice," it is fallacious.

As to what determines the will, he says, "*It is that motive, which as it stands in the view of the mind is the strongest, that determines the will.*" (p. 7.) He also says, "By *motive*, I mean the whole of that which moves, excites, or invites the mind to volition, whether that be one thing singly, or many things conjunctly." (p. 7.) He previously says, "The will is said to be determined, when, in consequence of some action, or influence, *its* choice is directed to and fixed upon a particular object. As, when we speak of the determination of motion, we mean causing the motion of the body to be such a way, or in such a direction rather than another." (p. 6.) The word "*action*" here seems to be superfluous; for, if the action does not influence the will it has nothing to do with it; and if it does, it is an influence. The above statements then assert that the motive which moves, excites, or invites the mind to volition, determines the will, and identify motive and influence. The phrase, "the whole of that which moves, excites, or invites" must include everything past, present, or future, which has any possible influence on the mind in willing. There is an apparent limitation in the statement that, it must "stand in the view of the mind;" but as Edwards says, "Nothing can induce, or invite the mind to will, or act anything, any further than it is perceived," this apparent limitation only excludes what does not influence, and still leaves the phrase to include all that does influence the mind in willing.

This definition of motive then amounts simply to this: that whatever influences the mind in willing is a *motive*; and what does not influence it is not *a motive*. There is, also, the condition that it must be the "strongest motive," and this, of course, must mean *that* motive, which has the most influence on the mind in willing. The whole of the three statements, then, as quoted, and especially if taken in connection with his idea that *influence* is that which produces an effect, amounts to this, that the mind, in willing, is influenced by that which most influences it to will, or that the mind, *in being moved to will*—we must use this form of expression if it does not move itself—is moved by that which moves it, or is moved in the direction in which it is moved by that which moves it in that direction; or that the mind in willing, "the will," is determined by that which determines it. The whole statement amounts to nothing, ending where it began. It is as impossible, logically, to deduce any new truth from such statements and definitions as from the expression "whatever is, is." In this instance we learn from them, in the first place, that the will is determined by that which influences it; next, that what so influences it is a certain motive; and when we inquire what a motive is, we are told that it is anything and everything which influences the will. It seems to be an unsuccessful attempt to apply the mathematical mode, and make the definition give existence to the thing defined, instead of describing something which already exists. But, in this case, we have to deal with realities and not with mere hypothesis. The argument, as Edwards states it, really fixes nothing, determines nothing; it confirms nothing, it opposes nothing. If, as some of his opponents assert, the will determines the will, then that strongest motive, which moves the mind to will, is the will itself; and, under his definition, the only way in which it can be shown that the will itself is not such a motive, or that it does not conform to his definition of it, is to show that the will itself does not determine the will; and, having done this, there is no need of travelling backward to apply the rule that the will is determined by the strongest motive, to prove that the will does not determine itself; for that is then already proved, and nothing is gained in the argument by the introduction of the motive.

So, also, if it be asserted that the mind, by means of its knowledge, or by any other means, determines its acts of will, this is to assert that the mind, by such means, becomes such a motive as Edwards defines; and this assertion, if sustained, would make his own positions proof of the freedom of the mind in willing; for if the mind determined its own acts of will, it is not important to the question of its freedom by what means it does it; and the assertion would only be proved or disproved as in the former case, by first proceeding without any reference to the general idea or definition of motive.* And, if it were asserted that anything else

* See Appendix, Note XLIII.

determined the will, the introduction of motive, as thus defined, would really avail nothing to prove or disprove it; for, in every case, under Edwards's definitions, the only way to prove that this *anything* is, or is not the strongest motive, is first to ascertain whether it does, or does not determine the will. Whether, then, this notion of motive sustains freedom or necessity, depends on the *character* of the motive; which does not appear in the definition. The difficulty is a radical one, and arises from defining "strongest motive" not by what *it is*, or *must be*, but by something that it *may*, or *must do*, doing which it is the strongest motive, but otherwise it is not the strongest motive. Let one take what position he may as to what determines the will, he need not deny that it is the "strongest motive" that determines it, *i. e.* as Edwards defines "strongest motive;" for, to assert that *anything whatever* determines the will, is to assert that *this anything* exactly corresponds to Edwards's definition of " strongest motive," for there must then be asserted of it the only distinguishing characteristic, which he attributed to the "strongest motive," viz.: *that of determining the will.* If freedom determines the will, then freedom is the strongest motive; if necessity determines the will, then necessity is the strongest motive; and we have only got a new name ready for whatever is proved, or proves itself to be entitled to it. As a philosophical discovery of what determines the will, it is much as if a man should say, "I have invented a machine by which men can fly. My invention consists in such a combination and application of mechanical motors, as will enable men to fly!" Nor would it much enhance its merit, if he should add, "The mechanism of this, my invention, *must be visible,* or *be known* to the man who is to fly; and, of the different kinds of motors, that which is the strongest, or which appears to him the strongest, or which by its effects proves itself the strongest, must be used." An inventor could hardly hope to obtain a patent upon the merits of such a specification. On reading it, a man would be very apt to think that this gave him very little aid in designing and constructing a flying machine, but really left it all for him to find out for himself. The same of the motive, one of the difficulties in the specification of which, as already intimated, is, that it does not really define what the motive is. Edwards says, " It must be something that is *extant in the view or apprehension of the understanding*, or perceiving faculty " (p. 7). It is obvious that, to conform to this definition, and, at the same time, admit the deduction of necessity, the motive must be something, which not only is not controlled by the mind, but which in some way has power to control it. But why, then, is it essential that it should be " in the view of the mind," and why, if not in view of the mind, is it wholly without influence? If the flying machine just alluded to, is to be used by some agent or power extrinsic to the man who flies, and he is to be taken up by it, and carried through the air without any agency of his own, there can be no possible necessity that he should see or feel the machine when he is being moved by it. The effect would be accomplished just as well if his eyes were closed, or he asleep and wholly unconscious of its action. And, if this motive is something, which is itself to move the mind to will and not something which the mind is to use to move, or direct its will, there can be no necessity that it should " be in the view of the mind ; " and such necessity indicates that the mind must use the motive to determine its will, and not be used or determined by it; that the *power* is in the mind, or active agent, and not in the motive, which is only something which that agent perceives or knows.

Again, this motive must also be one particular motive. The motives may be numerous, but only one, simple or complex, *i. e.*, made up of " one thing singly, or many things conjunctly," determines the will. Now, this prevailing motive is not that which from *anything in itself* is the strongest, but that *which in the view of the mind* is the strongest. As the motive cannot itself determine that it is the "strongest motive," and, more especially, that *in the view of the mind*, it is the strongest, this must mean that the motive, which the mind perceives or judges to be the strongest, determines the will. But, if the mind, by the exercise of its faculty of judging, or by its capacity to perceive, acquires that knowledge by which itself determines the strongest motive, and the strongest motive determines the will, then the mind, in fact, determines the will; for to determine the strongest motive is to determine which motive shall prevail; and, without such exercise of judgment, or such application of our knowledge, the motive would have no power and would not prevail. But the mind determining itself in willing, by means of its intelligence, or by the exercise of any of its faculties, is only another expression for the freedom of the mind in willing. It is very certain that the motive cannot itself determine that itself is the strongest motive, unless it be an intelligent being with faculties for perceiving, comparing, and judging, and if, in that case, it is the same being whose will is to be controlled, then that being, as its own motive, directly controls its own will, and hence wills freely. It cannot be another intelligent being that determines which is the strongest motive, for then, it is not "in the mind's view" of the one to be influenced, and on him has no influence. If this other being has determined which is the strongest motive, it must still be so presented to the mind of the one to be influenced by it, that he shall also perceive and decide or judge that it is the strongest, or it can have no influence in determining his will. To compare and determine which is the strongest of several motives frequently requires a preliminary effort, or act of will, and the "strongest motive" is not effective till this is done, and we may then have a series interminable unless terminated by a simple mental perception requiring no preliminary effort. If it be said that one having ascertained which is the strongest motive, may thereby *directly* control the will of another, who has not ascertained it, we reply that the controlled will, though in another, is really then the will of the controlling being, and the controlled has no will in the matter to be controlled. If the one being indirectly influences the other, by so changing the circumstances that the latter will perceive a certain motive to be the strongest, then this other is still influenced by his own perceptions, his own knowledge, which, as before shown, does not conflict with his freedom in willing. Or, if the one, in any way, changes the mind's view of the other, with or without changing the circumstances or object viewed, then the mind influenced is still governed by its own views, its own perceptions, own knowledge, otherwise the change in its views would not influence it in willing; so that, if such a motive as Edwards suggests be really found, it will not militate against the position that, if the mind wills, it must will freely.

When Edwards says, "An act of the *will* is the same as an act of *choosing or choice*" (p. 1), and that "the will is always determined by the strongest motive" (p. 8), which again is that "which, as it stands in the mind's view, suits it best and pleases it most" (p. 9), he, in effect, says, that the choice is determined by a choice, if not by the same choice, which is itself determined; for that "*which suits the mind best and pleases it most*," must, as he asserts, be that which the mind prefers or chooses, rather than that which does not suit it so well, or please it so much; and, as he says, the will is *always* so determined, we have either the act of will or choice always determining itself; or every act of will or choice, determined by a preceding act of will or choice, *ad infinitum;* for, if each choice in the chain does not determine itself, it must, under these statements, be determined by some preceding choice or preference for that "which, in the mind's view, suited it best," &c., constituting the determining motive.

That the mind has in itself, or in its own view, a motive for action, is no reason that it does not act freely; but rather the contrary, as without motive, adopting Edwards's view of it, the mind could not be said to decide as to its own actions, having no reason whatever to make such decision one way rather than another, or to decide at all; and hence would not will at all, freely or otherwise. Motives, then, being necessary to the mind's willing freely, cannot, merely in virtue of their existence, be a reason why it does *not* will freely. The existence of that thing, which is a necessary condition to the existence of something else, cannot, of itself, be a reason why that something else does not exist, but, on the contrary, prepares the way for its existence. To have shown that the mind wills without any motive, would have better subserved the argument for necessity.

These views and objections are suggested by Edwards's definition of motives and his remarks upon them; and seem to show that they admit of no such application to the mind in willing as can furnish a foundation for necessity; and that, in attempting so to apply them, he involves views contradictory to his own positions, and which, virtually, or by implication, affirm freedom. If this is asserting too much for the argument which we have just presented, we think it will not be denied that whether the motives prove necessity or freedom, must, as before stated, depend on their character. Hence it becomes important to know what they are, that their character may be ascertained; and, if Edwards had in view some actual motives, which would make this important link in his argument, it is much to be regretted that he did not so define them, that others could readily find and test them. If he had any idea of such, his definition, as before shown, will give us little aid in finding them; and the illustrations he subsequently uses do very little to relieve us from the difficulty of searching them out in that almost boundless expanse, " the whole of that, which moves, excites, or invites the mind to volition," limited only by the one condition that it is "in the view of the mind." This may embrace everything of which the mind has cognizance, within or without itself, making it difficult to examine the whole ground; but, by a classification of the objects, some approximation to it may be possible. Before attempting this, however, we will remark that Edwards, warranted perhaps by the latitude of his definition, uses the term motive in two very different senses; sometimes as meaning the mind's view of any objects or things, and at others, any *objects or things* which the mind views. His definition, " By motive I mean * * * one *thing* singly, or many things conjunctly," favors the latter, as also the expression, " a motive is *something* which is extant in the view or apprehension of the understanding, or perceiving faculty." And when he says, " the will is determined by that motive, which, as it stands in the view of the mind, is the strongest," we should hardly suppose him to mean that the *view of the mind* is itself the motive that *stands in the view of the mind.* This could only mean, that the mind views what it views, or that it views another of its views. But he subsequently says, " if strict propriety of speech be insisted on," the act of volition itself is always determined by that in, or about *the* MIND'S VIEW *of the object,* which causes it to appear most agreeable " (p. 11), *i. e.*, not by the *object,* but by the mind's view of it; and again, " the *idea* of the thing preferred has a prevailing influence " (p. 76), and still more strongly to this point, " *the will is always determined by the strongest motive,* or by that VIEW *of the mind,* which has the greatest degree of *previous* tendency to excite volition " (p. 16). Here, as he cannot mean that the view of the mind is something else than the strongest motive, which may also determine the will, motive has got to be nothing else but a *view of the mind.* It may be said that this expression is elliptical, as there must be something which the mind views. Still there remains the important distinction between the mind's being influenced in willing by *its view* of the object, or by the *object* viewed. Confounding the two in the one word "*motive*," leads to much confusion in Edwards's argument, but as he really thus uses it, we must, to give all the scope he assumes for his position, concede to him the double meaning, and consider motive as embracing not only the *mind's view* of objects, but also the *objects viewed*.

But to return: asserting that the volition is determined by the *view of the mind*, let that which is viewed be what it may, is merely saying that the mind, in willing, is determined by its own views; and, as it must be the mind itself which makes the application of these views, it is saying that the mind determines its own act of will by *means* of its own views, which is but another expression for its freedom in willing; so that, if the essence of the motive is in the *view of the mind*, the influence which Edwards ascribes to the motive confirms the freedom of the mind in willing; and it would not be necessary to inquire as to the objects viewed.

If, however, it be said, that although the mind in willing determines itself by its own view, yet the object viewed is essential to that view, and, therefore, essential to the determination; it may, in conformity with the views I have asserted, be replied that, to have any influence, the object which the mind views must either be its own want, or an object which may be selected to gratify that want, or some knowledge to enable it to decide as to that selection and its subsequent action. If it is a want, it furnishes a foundation for action to gratify it; if it is an object of choice, it adds to the subjects from among which the mind may select to gratify the want. If it is knowledge of any kind, it adds to the power of the mind to adapt the objects of choice to its wants, enabling it to decide more intelligently or wisely as to its own acts. The first furnishes the occasion or opportunity for the act of will; the two last are merely cases of the knowledge of the mind being increased, either as to the objects wanted, or the means of obtaining them, by which freedom in willing is facilitated, and its sphere of action enlarged.

In regard to the other position, that the motive is the *object viewed*, Edwards admits that the object itself, unless in *the view of the mind*, can have no influence. He says: " Nothing can induce, or invite the mind to will, or act anything, any further than it is perceived, or is some way or other in the mind's view; for what is wholly unperceived and perfectly out of the mind's view, cannot affect the mind at all" (p. 7). These views of the mind, of any objects or circumstances whatever, are, as just stated, but portions of its knowledge of things, upon which to exercise its powers to produce change, or of truths enabling it to exercise these powers intelligently; and, as such, are essential to such exercise. Without them it would not make effort, or will at all; and the existence of the things viewed or objects of effort, or of the mind's view, or knowledge in regard to them, which thus facilitates and aids the mind in willing, cannot be a reason why it does not will freely. The power existing in the mind to avail itself, in its contemplated action, of certain conceivable objects or circumstances, may be limited or made nugatory in consequence of those objects and circumstances being absent, or, from any cause, unattainable; but this does not prevent its willing freely in regard to those which it deems attainable. Suppose, for instance, a man is hungry and seeks to gratify his want for food. He *knows* that for copper he can obtain food; for silver, better food, and, for gold, the best, or that food which he likes best; but he perceives that the present circumstances are such that he cannot obtain the gold; only silver and copper are possible. He acts just as freely in the preliminary effort to ascertain which of these two it is best to strive for, and in his subsequent efforts to obtain and apply the one selected by the preliminary act, as he would have done had all the three been attainable. His freedom consists, not in his having power to make the circumstances already existing different from what they are at the time, which is a contradiction, and hence not within the province even of Infinite Power to accomplish, but in directing his efforts, by virtue of his own intelligence, to effect desired changes among the circumstances as they are at the moment of his action. If the circumstances had been different, he might have acted differently, and yet have willed freely, because—and even supposing the same circumstances to necessarily produce the same effect—a free act of will may be as different from what it would be under different circumstances, as if it were necessitated by the circumstances; and no inference against its freedom can be drawn from this variety of action under different circumstances. If the power to effect the change were directly exerted by the circumstances, it would argue in favor of necessity; but as these circumstances can only change the knowledge of the mind—the mind's view—which the mind must itself apply in its action, it argues self-government or freedom. In this latter case, the influence of the motives amounts only to the mind's applying its knowledge and efforts to make these circumstances subservient to its own designs, and thus available in gratifying its wants. To say that the mind does not will freely because various objects of effort exist, and the mind has the faculty of perceiving, or of finding reasons for preferring one or more of them to others, and has a motive to act in conformity to that preference; is to say, that the mind does not act freely, because it has the opportunity and ability to choose its action, and to conform its action to such choice. It is obvious that this variety of objects or of circumstances is essential to the preliminary effort of the mind in choosing. It wants to produce a certain effect in the future. If the mode of doing it is not already known, or immediately perceived, it examines, *i. e.*, makes a preliminary effort to find a mode; and if more than one mode is found, it compares and ascertains which is preferable; it chooses among them; and may then, by yet another preliminary act, ascertain whether action or non-action is preferable; it chooses as between action and non-action. In all these preliminary efforts it has obtained only knowledge; and if having chosen thus to act, it does not so act, or make such effort, it must be because it is constrained or restrained from controlling and directing its own action. But no external power can control or restrain the effort, though it may frustrate the design and defeat the object of it. Much that I have before said of the relation of circumstances to the mind in willing, is especially applicable to preliminary efforts of the mind in choosing; and all goes to show that volition, both as a final act and as a preliminary, by examination, to choice, *is an* original act of the mind, which, but for its action, would not be; and which might be, though there were no activity or power besides itself in existence at the time of such choice, or such volition; and hence, nothing to constrain and nothing to restrain or limit it but the consciousness of its own finite nature. And, even this cannot be said to be a limit to its power of choosing or of willing; but only a limit to its power of conceiving of things to be chosen or acts to be willed or done, and of its knowledge of modes or means to do them. Whenever it can conceive of anything to be done and that there may be a possible mode of doing it, it can make the effort, although, from its finite nature, it is liable to be mistaken in the relation of means to the end; and to be frustrated in the execution of its design. It is not in the willing to do, but in the doing what we will, that we are liable to be frustated or disappointed by the circumstances which are extrinsic to the mind, and those circumstances which are independent of the mind only fix what the mind is to choose among, and do not influence its freedom in the act by which it chooses among them, nor in its action in regard to attaining that which is chosen.

In seeking for such a motive as Edwards uses in his argument, I would suggest the following classification of the "somethings which may exist in the view of the mind," in which phrase he gives the only clue to his idea of motive. As classing some of these as motives may appear contradictory and futile, I may, in justice to Edwards, observe that many of them are such as he does not seem to contemplate; though his definitions and statements are broad enough to cover everything conceivable, and I wish to give to the argument all he can possibly claim for it. I suggest, then, the following objects as possibly coming within his *definition* of motives.

1. The mind itself.
2. Its attributes, or faculties.
3. Its emotions. } Constituting its feeling.
4. Its sensations.
5. Its innate knowledge.*
6. Its memories of things and thoughts in the past. } Constituting its knowledge.
7. Its perceptions of the present.
8. Its conceptions of the future.
9. Its imaginings.
10. Its associations.
11. Other mind; representing all intelligences, other than the mind to be determined.
12. The faculties of these other minds.
13. Its emotions.
14. Its sensations.
15. Its knowledge, past, present and future.
16. Material phenomena; including any circumstances, which are extrinsic to mind.

We will consider these in their respective order.

1. If the mind itself is the motive that *determines its own act* of will, then, as before shown, the mind in such an act of will is free.

2. If the attributes or faculties of the mind are the motives, then, as these attributes or faculties can do nothing except as they are exercised or exerted by the mind, it must be the *mind*, in the exercise of its faculties, *that determines the will;* which, again, would prove the mind's freedom in willing.

3. An emotion, which is not in itself a want, and

* See Appendix, Note XLIV.

which does not produce want, is not a motive. As we have already suggested that no want arises, so no act of will can spring from that joy, which so satisfies the mind that it desires no change, or from that holy and unselfish grief which it would not banish nor modify; and, of that anguish which arises from the consciousness of error, the cause is in the past, and cannot be reached by any act of will; while admiration, wonder, and awe compose or still, rather than excite, the active faculty. All these but make a part of the past experience, adding to that present knowledge which aids the mind in determining its course in the future. But with these and other emotions, as love, hope, fear, anger, the mind may have corresponding wants, if only the want to derive pleasure, variety, or excitement from them. These wants, and the sensation or perception of these wants, may induce the mind to act for its own gratification or relief. But the wants cannot themselves determine that action, for that must depend on the perception by the mind of the means of gratifying the want; and the perception must include, or be the preconception of, the relation of the future effect of its own act to its want, which brings it to the case of the mind determining its action by its own view, which we have before considered. If it has no such perception of a means of gratifying the want by an act of will, and that the want may thereby be gratified, there is no act of will put forth; which shows that the mind, in gratifying any want which may arise from the emotions, still directs its action by means of its preconception or knowledge of the future effect of its effort, which it only can apply, and hence in such effort acts freely.

4. Sensation, as before stated, may, with knowledge,

produce want, suggesting some change for its gratification; or, it may be but a perception of an external fact in the present, involving no want of change in the future. The effect of want as a motive, and of the incidental addition of another fact to our knowledge, have both been already sufficiently considered in their respective relations to the determination of the mind in willing, and shown not to militate against its freedom.

5. Innate knowledge is that knowledge which is directly communicated by the Creator to the creature, but, becoming a portion of its own knowledge, in no respect differs in its effects or influence on the will from other or acquired knowledge. That, as suggested in our chapter on instinct, it may be in such a form as not to require any contrivance to adapt it to use, in the act of willing, and thus facilitates the action of the mind in willing, does not conflict with the mind's freedom in the act which is thus facilitated.

6. The mind's memory of the past, including its own thoughts, and embracing, of course, the knowledge of things, events, and abstract truths which it has acquired in that past. The things and events from being in the past, and the abstract truths from their nature, are unchangeable, and hence not subjects for the action of the will, and only make a portion of the knowledge of the mind, by which it is enabled to decide its future course.

7. The result of the mind's perceptions of the present is a knowledge of existing things. These may admit of a succession differing from themselves—of change—and this change be the object of the mind's act of will; but the mind will not will, or make effort to change them, unless it has some want to be gratified by such change. The things themselves cannot indi-

cate what changes will gratify the want, for they cannot even know what the want is. To do this requires intelligence. To adapt things, or the changes in things, which are effected by volition, to the simplest want, requires not only knowledge, but contrivance, which *things* have not. For instance, hunger is the want of food in the stomach: we cannot immediately will the food there, but have to apply our knowledge and power of thought or examination, in adapting and devising means and ways of doing it; even after it is in the mouth, it is not the food that knows that it must be masticated and swallowed, and the order of these two processes. It is the mind's perception, that by the various acts, from the procuring the food to the swallowing of it, and by these acts, in a certain order, the sensation of hunger may be relieved, that enables it intelligently to determine its successive efforts to that end; and this preconception of the effect of its efforts it is enabled to form by its faculty of conceiving of the future—its finite prophetic power—which is aided and rendered less fallible by every increase of its knowledge. In such case, neither the mind's perceptions nor that which is perceived can determine; but the perception or knowledge enables the mind to determine.

8. The mind's conception of the future is itself a view by the mind, and, as such, embraced in our remarks on the mind in willing being determined by its own views. We are admitting the largest possible latitude to what may be conceived to be motive, but the mind's own view or conception of the future, of something which as yet has no *objective* reality, but is exclusively a view of the mind within itself, seems hardly

such a motive as Edwards speaks of as "standing in the mind's view;" for the mind's perception of that future is the mind's view itself, and not *something* which stands in that view. If this be the motive, we need not repeat our reasoning to show that such views of the mind, such motives, are the essential element which enables the mind to determine its own acts of will as an independent, creative, first cause.

The motive cannot be that future which the mind views, for it, as yet, has no actual existence, and can have no influence on the mind except by or through the mind's anticipation of it, which is the mind's view just considered, and makes a portion of its knowledge.

9. The mind's imaginings being such combinations as have no objective existence, past or present, but supposed capable of existence, may also be regarded as in the future, and be classed with those conceptions which are incipient creations of the mind. Being palpable and tangible to itself, they gratify some want of the mind, as the love of knowledge, the sentiment of beauty, &c. If, for convenience, we take some circumstances of the past, and in imagination vary them, or add some new feature, the new combination really has no past existence, and, as present, exists only as a view of the mind without any objective existence; and, whether we locate it in the past, present, or future, or give it no particular place in time, makes no more difference than the locating of a geometrical diagram in time. In both cases they are but constructions, affording pleasure by their harmony, symmetry, and beauty, or aiding the mind to solve some problem and thus to increase its knowledge.

10. The associations of the mind are only other portions of its knowledge, suggested by that portion which

is immediately in its view; and, though very important in giving the mind a ready use of its knowledge in the formation of its plans, which are prerequisites of rational action, and yet more especially, in that recalling of former plans, which is the basis of habitual action, still association is but, in this connection, a means by which the mind uses its knowledge in directing its will, and requires here no further comment.

11. Any other mind or intelligence, as a mere object, viewed or apprehended by the mind, can have no influence differing in *kind* from that of the mind's view of any other extrinsic object, and this we have already considered. If this other mind has in it anything which will gratify a want in the mind that views it, this mind may put forth an effort to obtain that thing. We have before considered in a similar connection the case of the will of one mind being controlled directly or indirectly by another mind by means of the exercise of any of its powers, or otherwise, and need not repeat the reasoning or the result; and this, with the consideration that those powers cannot exert themselves or have any influence except as exerted by the mind to which they appertain, disposes, also, of

12. The attributes and faculties of one mind, as a motive, determining the will of another mind.

13, 14, 15. The emotions, sensations, and knowledge of another mind can have no influence, except as they are made manifest to the mind to be influenced in that case, becoming but portions of its own knowledge, and, as such, already shown not to interfere with its freedom in willing. We may, however, further remark that the knowledge which one mind acquires from another coordinate or like mind, must be of the same character as that which it acquires or has from other sources; and that the knowledge which the finite mind derives from the Infinite when directly imparted is intuitive; and when *indirectly*, by the written expression of His thoughts in nature, they are but the knowledge of material phenomena or that which is extrinsic to the mind, which belongs under our next and last division.

16. Material phenomena, including any circumstances which are extrinsic to the mind. Material objects cannot, of themselves, be such a motive, for they may have existed from all eternity, and yet never have produced or determined a volition, and even may have been in the mind's view for any length of time and yet never have moved it to will, or determined its will; but if they are a necessary cause in themselves, then the moment they exist they must produce their effect, or if the additional circumstance that they must be " in the mind's view," makes them the cause of volition in that mind, then, as soon as they are in that mind's view, the volition should follow. That this is not the fact, proves that there is something besides the material object and the fact that it is in the mind's view, which produces the effect, or determines the will. The same is true of extrinsic circumstances. Nor can any changes in these extrinsic objects and circumstances, whether produced by the motion of matter, or by intelligent action, of itself, move the mind to will. Increase or vary the circumstances ever so much, they could no more produce any volition in themselves or in others —a volition having reference to an effect which as yet is not—than the extension of the multiplication table could make it know itself or feel hungry. However blindly active among themselves, they cannot embrace

that design, that intention, to produce a preconceived result, which is an essential characteristic of volition, and which distinguishes the action of intelligent from blind causes. For this they avail nothing until the mind uses them as its knowledge to determine its action; and the mind is itself really the efficient cause of that determination, freely adapting its action to the circumstances in its view. There is, evidently, no way in which these circumstances can *directly* produce a volition in the human mind, and if they could, it would be the volition of the circumstances, and not of the human being. These extrinsic circumstances can influence the mind in willing only as they are perceived or apprehended by the mind, and, as such, become but a part of the mind's knowledge, and, of course, subject to our previous conclusions, that knowledge, however acquired, is used by the mind to enable it to determine its acts; and hence, is essential to its freedom in willing; every increase in knowledge enlarging its sphere for the exercise of such freedom.

There are vague notions, in the popular mind, in regard to the influence of circumstances upon us, often bordering on fatalism, if not really involving it, and which find expression in such phrases as "man is the sport," or "he is the creature of circumstances." One reason for this is, that we are liable to be frustrated by circumstances in the execution of what we will. This, it will be observed, is such an effect, after the act of willing, as can have no influence backward upon it. I will to walk in a certain direction, but am obstructed by a rushing torrent, which God has caused to flow there, or by a wall erected through human agency. The circumstance prevents my doing what I intended, and what, from want of sufficient knowledge, I decided to do. The new knowledge thus acquired, leads me to alter my course, and I may never again fall into the same track that I would otherwise have pursued. I go on to produce some change, but what that change will be depends upon the use which my mind makes of this new, combined with its previous knowledge, in directing its subsequent action. Though I cannot, as now ascertained, go in the direction intended, there are still an infinite number of ways in which I can go; and among these my mind, in virtue of its intelligence, judges which is best. It may do this by a preliminary free act, and then, being free, conform its final action to its judgment; and hence, this influence of circumstances does not argue that the mind does not act freely in *willing*, but only that it cannot always *execute* its decrees; not that it does not freely try, or make effort, but that its power is not always adequate to the effect designed, or its knowledge sufficient to direct its efforts most wisely, and the *want of freedom*, if such this *want of power* may be termed, is just where Edwards asserts the only freedom of man exists.

As the mind's being liable to be frustrated in the execution of what it wills by the *existence* of circumstances of which it did not know, is one reason of the popular idea in regard to the influence of circumstances, so, on the other hand, another reason for it may be found in the *limitation* of the circumstances—in the *absence* or non-existence of some that are essential to the execution—to the doing what is attempted—or of some which are prerequisites of the effort, which it would or might make, if they were present and available, and for the want of which the mind either does not will, or wills differently from what it would if they were present and available as a portion of its knowledge. In their absence, the mind knows no mode of obtaining the object for which such circumstances are prerequisite. This does not affect its freedom in willing as to what, under the circumstances, is attainable, but only lessens the sphere in which it can exercise that freedom. This sphere, as before stated, is always commensurate with its knowledge; and it matters not whether the knowledge requisite to any effort—the knowledge of some mode—is deficient, because such knowledge *cannot* exist, or simply because it *does not* exist in the mind. The limitation of the sphere of effort is the same in either case. I may know not only that *I* cannot now make $2+2=5$, but that it is an impossibility, and hence, will not seek any mode of doing it. I may also know that I have no knowledge of any geometrical process by which to trisect an arc, and, as I do not know that this is an impossibility, I may seek to *increase my knowledge*, and by means of such increase devise some mode in conformity to which I may direct my efforts to trisect the arc. So that, whether the thing to be done be absolutely impossible, from there being no possible mode of doing it, or only relatively to me impossible, because I know of no way, the formula heretofore adopted, that *the mind's sphere of free activity, or for the exercise of its creative powers by will or effort, is commensurate with its knowledge*, covers the whole ground. If the mind of every human being at all times embraced all knowledge, then, all the circumstances presented to every mind would, of necessity, be the same, but by the limitation of human knowledge different circumstances are presented to different minds.

Of two persons wanting a metal, one may have, within his power, lead, zinc, and gold; another only lead and zinc; but the latter chooses and conforms his effort to his choice as freely in regard to the two, as the former in regard to the three. If a man with all the natural endowments of Newton, and with his acquired habits of industrious and persevering study, had always lived in the Sandwich Islands, he would not have had, in the surrounding circumstances, the opportunities essential to such discoveries as Newton made. The requisite books and instruments—the means of knowledge—would not have been there accessible, or to him possible; but he would have been equally *free* by effort to avail himself of such means as were there in his power.

The mind varies its own action to conform to the relations which it perceives between the circumstances and the preconception of the effect by which it seeks to gratify its want, and it does this in virtue of that intelligence, which, perceiving this relation, makes self-control and freedom, or self-action free from extrinsic control, possible to it.

We find then, in all this conceivable range, no motive that so determines the will as to warrant the inference of necessity; none to which the mind itself is subordinated, or which will admit of dispensing with the mind itself as the cause, which determines its own acts of will.

Let us now see if Edwards has himself indicated any such actual motive. In the *general statement*, already quoted, he affirms that without motive the mind in willing " has no *end* which it *proposes to itself*, or pursues in so doing ; it aims at nothing, and seeks nothing, and, if it seeks nothing, then *it does not go after any-*

thing." These expressions indicate that the essence of the motive is in the end which the mind seeks, something which as yet is not, but which will be the effect of its volition, and that which is in the view of the mind as the motive to the volition, is the idea of the effect of the volition. But the idea or preconception of the *effect* of a volition could have no influence toward a volition, if the mind did not want to produce the *effect* it preconceived. The want is the incitement to effort; and the mind's judgment or knowledge as to the adaptation of the effect, which it anticipates in the future, to the want and of the effort to the effect, enables it to determine as to the particular effort or volition it will put forth.

So, also, in the *particular case* by which he illustrates the influence of the strongest motive, he says: "Thus, when a drunkard has his liquor before him, and he has to choose whether to drink it or no; the proper and immediate objects, about which his present volition is conversant, and between which his choice now decides, are his own acts in drinking the liquor, or letting it alone; and this will certainly be done according to what, in the present view of his mind taken in the whole of it, is most agreeable to him. If he chooses or wills to drink it, and not to let it alone, then this action, as it stands in the view of his mind, with all that belongs to its appearance there, is more agreeable and pleasing, than letting it alone" (p. 10).

The expression "between which his choice now decides," must mean, *between which he by an act of choice now decides* (otherwise he makes choice decide the choice), and, taking this as his meaning, the objects contemplated by the drunkard are his own acts in "drinking or letting alone," either of which is yet in the future.

It is true that Edwards immediately says, "But the objects to which this act of volition may relate more remotely, and between which his choice may determine more indirectly, are the *present* pleasure the man *expects* by drinking, and the future misery which he judges will be the consequence of it;" but, at the time of this judgment, both the drinking and its consequences are in the future—still expected—and the anticipated conception of them is all that "is in the mind's view." The mind by its judgment is to weigh its preconception of the effect of "drinking the liquor," against its preconception of the consequences of "letting it alone," which, Edwards has just said, are the acts between which the drunkard's choice now decides; and though Edwards does not expressly say so, yet, to give the illustration any force or meaning, we must suppose that, of the two acts about which he says "the present volition is conversant," that one which, "as it stands in the view of his mind with all that belongs to its appearance there," is most agreeable, or suits it best, is the strongest motive; and this is but a preconception of the effects of a certain act, which the mind decides to be in accordance with that want which it seeks to gratify. As already remarked, Edwards does not say this, nor does he appear to have had any clear thought of it; but it seems difficult to make the facts he states, or the case he cites, illustrate any other position than that his motive is, in fact, the mind's view of the future effect of its own action, and this is the mind's knowledge by which it perceives a reason for acting and for the particular direction of its action, and not a motive power putting the mind in action. Such view is but the reason why the mind, as cause, acts in one particular manner, instead of another, rather than a cause itself of the action, or of the particular manner of the action. His " motive," however, as illustrated in this instance, corresponds to the influence which I have assigned to the mind's preconception of the effects of its effort, and " the mind's view " is but a portion of its knowledge, which it uses to determine its action, as it uses any other knowledge it may have, and which knowledge, as already indicated, by a preliminary effort to examine, or to consider, by deliberation, and sometimes perhaps by an immediate mental perception, becomes the judgment of the mind. As he uses "motive" in some other places, it indicates the influence which I have assigned to *want;* and, in this instance, just quoted, the decision of the mind is really to be between two conflicting wants—the want to enjoy the pleasure of "drinking the liquor," and the want, "by letting it alone," to avoid the unpleasant consequences of drinking it— both of which, under Edwards's view, must be motives; and that, the gratification of which *in the mind's view suits it best,* is the strongest motive.

Even admitting, then, that *the same causes necessarily produce the same effects,* which is still an essential link in this argument for necessity, this doctrine of motives; from its inception in the definition and statements of it to its conclusion, reveals nothing which really conflicts with the results attained in Book First of this Treatise; and, on examination, it turns out that the motive which, by a mere hypothesis, is made the *cause* of the determination of the will, can be in reality nothing but the mind itself, or the mind's own views; and, in either case, as the application of the views must be made by the mind that views, it is the mind which determines its own volitions or efforts. And this expression for its freedom is made more emphatic by the development which comes out in the illustration and in the final summing up of the argument by Edwards, that the mind in willing is not only determined by its own views, but by its view of the future effects of its own action, as yet having no existence except in its own preconception, which is its own creation; or rather, by the relations which it perceives between its own created preconception and its own want; and the consideration that these relations do not inhere either in the want or in the preconception, but are in the mind's view wholly by the exercise of its intelligent faculties—its own thought—directed to the examination by means of its own previous knowledge, intuitive or acquired; that such examination is essential to a wise action; and that it is by such knowledge that Supreme Intelligence itself must direct its action; serve at once to illustrate and strengthen our position. It would, indeed, seem that there could be no stronger expression of the freedom of an intelligent agent in willing, than that it determines its own acts of will, by means of the knowledge obtained by the exercise of its own faculties, of the relation between its own creations—the preconceptions of the future effects of its efforts—and its own wants. The whole process and all the elements of the act of will in such case are in and of the being that wills.

But, supposing all these difficulties and objections to these positions of Edwards to be, in some way, surmounted, we have still to inquire as to the meaning of that "previous tendency," which is an all-important element in motive, as applied in his argument for necessity. He says: "Everything that is properly called a motive * * * has some sort and degree of *tendency*, or *advantage* to move, or excite the will *previous to the effect, or to the act of will excited.* This previous tendency of the motive is what I *call the strength of the motive*" (p. 7). And again: "Whatever is perceived or apprehended by an intelligent and voluntary agent, which has the nature and influence of a motive to volition or choice, is considered or viewed as *good*," i. e., the mind perceives or judges it to be good. And, immediately after the above, he says: "I use the term *good*, namely, as of the same import with agreeable;" and hence, the strongest motive is that which appears *most agreeable*, as he thus more fully states: "But if it tends to draw the inclination and move the will, it must be under the notion of that which *suits* the mind. And, therefore, that must have the greatest tendency to attract and engage it, which, as it stands in the mind's view, suits it best and pleases it most" (p. 9). The prevailing motive then, is that which, as it stands in the mind's view, suits it best and pleases it most. But, "a being pleased with" is the phrase which he uses (p. 2) as identical with "an act of will," and which he subsequently identifies with *choice* or *preference*, by saying, "it will not appear by this and such like instances, that there is any difference between *volition* and *preference*, or that a man's choosing, liking best, or being *best pleased with a thing* are not the *same with his willing that thing*," and by many other expressions of like import. So that this strongest motive, or "that which appears most inviting, and has, by what appears concerning it to the understanding or apprehension, the greatest degree of previous tendency to excite and induce the choice," must be that motive for which the mind has a choice or preference over all others, and it is this choice or preference of the mind, which gives it *all* its influence or tendency to move the will; but as its tendency to move the will is *previous to the act of will*, or *choice*, or *preference*, we have the choice, or preference, which gives this previous tendency, not only before itself, but under the definition, that "the *will*" is "*that by which the mind chooses anything*" (p. 1). We have, in this *previous tendency of the motive*, a choice before that by which the mind chooses has acted, which is absurd.

These results follow from the fact that the *terms* by which Edwards defines "the previous tendency of motive," are the same as those by which he designates choice or preference; and if, instead of seeking the relation of the things in the substituted terms or definitions, we look directly to the things themselves, it seems evident that nothing, whatever, has any influence to move the mind till it has some preference or choice for it. This makes the previous tendency to choice, a choice itself, which, by Edwards's hypothesis, would require a previous tendency or choice to excite *it*, and so on *ad infinitum*.

This difficulty is not obviated by supposing the previous tendency of the motive to inhere in something which is extrinsic to the mind, for it is not a motive at all until it is in the mind's view, and strongest motive is still that which in the mind's view suits it best; and, whether it be in the *mind's view* itself, or in the *object viewed*, it can exert no influence until the mind has some choice or preference for it, which still makes the choice previous to the act of will or choice, and before that by which the mind chooses has acted. We here again observe how this, the main argument of Edwards, is made fallacious by being founded on the two incompatible definitions of choice.

In the unsettled state of metaphysical language, it is, perhaps, allowable for a writer to define his own terms, and even in some instances, like the mathematicians, to bring the subjects into existence by the definitions. But, in such cases, he must not involve incompatible conditions. If a mathematician should say, "a triplogon is a plane rectilineal figure included within three sides and with three right angles;" or a machinist should *plan* a flying machine, or a perpetual motion, one element of which should be a revolving wheel with a weight on one side just equal to one on the other, but that on the other a little heavier than it; though one might reason ingeniously and even correctly upon such hypotheses, yet no practical result, no new reality, could be evolved from it ; and so, if motive, by the definition of it, is that which is before itself, or that which comes into being before the existence of that which gives it being, however subtle the reasoning upon it, no practical result, no solution of any question of realities, can be evolved from it. All reasoning from such hypotheses must take this form : " If a triplogon is contained by three sides, and has three right angles, then some quadrilaterals must have four sides and six right angles ; " and, though this should be shown to be a logical consequence, the truth of it would still depend upon the possible existence of such a figure as a " triplogon " has been defined to be.

We before had occasion to show that, in Edwards's system, there is no room for anything between a state of indifference—a not willing or choosing—and the act of choice or will; and, if that conclusion was correct, there is in his system no room for this motive, or previous tendency of motive, between total indifference, or not choosing, or not willing, and the act of choosing or willing; but, as appears by the preceding reasoning, the motive, or the previous tendency of motive, must itself be an act of choice, in his system also an act of will, springing directly out of a state of indifference.

Beyond all these, there exists the same difficulty in regard to the determining power of motive, which Edwards finds in regard to the will's self-determining power. In his system, everything must have an antecedent cause; and these motives, and even the previous tendency of motives, must have a cause as much as the volitions of which they are assumed to be the cause. If we pass over intelligence in willing, as a first cause of its own volitions, making it only an intermediate link in the chain of causes, and effects, we never come to a beginning or first cause.

This difficulty must attach to every system, which does not recognize some *self-moving* power, or cause, and which, as it cannot be in matter, must be in spirit. Edwards, in fact, assumes that *motive* is a first, self-acting cause; this denies that every act is necessarily controlled by some cause in the past, which is an indispensable link in his argument for necessity. If this motive is the intelligence that acts, if the mind itself is the motive, or cause of its volitions, then his argument really asserts the freedom of the mind in willing.

CHAPTER XI.

CAUSE AND EFFECT.

IT will be observed that the argument of Edwards, in favor of necessity, rests mainly upon the assumption that *the same causes*, OF NECESSITY, *produce the same effects ;* I say *of necessity*, for if the relation of effect to cause be not one of necessity, no necessity of the effect can be inferred from the relation. If the motive is the cause of the act of choice or volition, and the particular act of choice or volition, is not a necessary effect of its cause, but some other volition might have ensued, then, there is nothing in the relation of cause and effect upon which to predicate necessity in the act of choice or volition ; so that the whole force of this argument rests upon the hypothesis, that the relation of effect to cause is one of *necessity*.

That the same causes necessarily produce the same effects must mean that, if the same causes occur, or are repeated in action any number of times, the same corresponding effect will occur, or be repeated each time. If the same cause never occurred, or acted twice, there could be no occasion for the rule—nothing to which it would apply. It is the same, then, as a case of *uniform-*

ity of cause and effect. Now, this law of the uniformity of cause and effect is known to us only as an empirical law growing out of our observation of the succession of changes in matter, and these changes, as we have already shown, must be controlled wholly, or mostly, by a creative intelligence—by the will of an intelligent being. The law of uniformity in these changes of matter,* then, must depend upon the will of this intelligent being. The acts of the finite intelligence in producing these changes are but infinitesimal, and hence, even if there were no other reason, may be left out of view, and the control of the changes in the material universe be ascribed directly to the will of the Supreme Intelligence. We do not even know that the movement of our own hand, as a sequent of our volition, is not a uniform mode of God's action, and not by our own direct agency. The law, then, that in the material world the same causes produce the same effects, is deduced from our observations of the uniformity of God's action. It cannot be a law of metaphysical necessity, for it is just as conceivable that He should will that the same set of circumstances should be followed by different consequences every time they occurred, as that He should will the same consequences with every such recurrence. There is no causal power in the fact that the cause has before acted, or that the same circumstances have before occurred. Excluding such cases as involve contradiction, and which, of course, even Infinite Power cannot control or affect, there is no reason to presume that the law goes any farther than is indicated by our observations of the facts. We do not *know* that the changes in winds or weather, are subject to any such uniformity; they may, in every

* See Appendix, Note XLV.

individual case, be effected by the will of God acting without reference to any uniformity. Even if in such cases we find that an effect is uniformly preceded by a limited series of antecedents, it does not follow that this series is a part of one which is infinite. It may be isolated, and be in fact but God's *uniform mode of doing that particular thing*, and may have no uniform connection with any prior antecedents. To suppose all the events to be either necessary terms of an infinite series following each other in a necessary order, or even in a pre-ordained order, would leave no room for the continued exercise of God's designing power, and, as we shall have occasion to note more *particularly* hereafter, would deprive Him of the highest attribute of Creative Intelligence.

In regard to matter, then, this uniformity of cause and effect, so far as it goes, is not a necessary but an arbitrary law, which the Supreme Intelligence has adopted for His own government in the management of matter, and which our observation of His modes of action in the material world has revealed to us. There is no reason to suppose that He makes such laws for His own action in *all cases*—as in changes of the weather, for instance—or, that He may not vary from the law of uniformity, which appears to us to be established, and thus produce what we call miracles.

That He is all-wise and omniscient obviates the necessity of trying experiments to which finite intelligences are subject, for he must be able to preconceive the results, and, by a comparison of these preconceptions, to determine the best modes of action in any circumstances without continually trying different modes; and knowing the best mode, will, of course, adopt it in a recurrence of the same circumstances, unless from some cause, the gain of variety makes the new mode of action, with such variety, better than the old one without it.

When in natural phenomena we seek to generalize existing facts, or the succession of events, we do not really seek the consequences of any necessity in the same causes to produce the same effects, but the consequences of God's uniform action. If we find in the premises no evidence of such uniformity in His action, our knowledge will be limited to particular facts in the past.

In regard to the finite mind, observation does not indicate any such law of uniformity, or necessity of cause and effect, for, it is impossible to predict, with certainty, what the action of mind under any circumstances will be; nor, from the act, can we determine the cause or reason of the act, which, in one man, may be the gratification of his want to do good to others, while another man, under the same *apparent* circumstances, does the same act because he perceives that he will eventually thereby be enabled to inflict great injury on others. The fact that we cannot, with *certainty*, predict what the future action of any mind will be under any antecedents, and conversely, from the action cannot, with certainty, tell the antecedents, shows that there is no observable or known uniformity in the relation of this action of the mind to whatever the antecedents of its action may be. It may be said, that this is because we cannot take into view all the circumstances; but, if so, this not only proves that we have no experience proving the rule, but that we cannot have any such experience, and such assertion would thus weaken the position it is intended to support. So far as we have opportunities for observing the action of mind under similar circumstances, the fact seems to be that, not only do different minds act very differently, but that the same mind sometimes changes even its habits and modes of action very suddenly and unexpectedly; and hence observation reveals no rule of uniformity of cause and effect which is of necessity applicable to mind. Edwards says:

"I might further observe, the state of the mind that views a proposed object of choice, is another thing that contributes to the agreeableness, or disagreeableness of that object; the particular temper which the mind has by nature, or that has been introduced and established by education, example, custom, or some other means; or the frame or state that the mind is in on a particular occasion. That object which appears agreeable to one, does not so to another. And the same object does not always appear alike agreeable to the same person at different times. It is most agreeable to some men to follow their reason, and to others to follow their appetites; to some men it is more agreeable to deny a vicious inclination, than to gratify it; others it suits best to gratify the vilest appetites. It is more disagreeable to some men than others to counteract a former resolution. In these respects, and many others which might be mentioned, different things will be most agreeable to different persons; and not only so, but to the same persons at different times" (p. 14).

But, if these "objects of choice" in "the mind that views," and which he treats as motives, produce such different effects on different minds, and, also, on the same mind at different times, where is the evidence of this uniformity, or of this *necessity* of the effect of these motives as cause of the volitions? which is the very foundation of his argument upon motives, as already shown in the quotation from him (p. 116).

It may be said that, in such cases, though all extrinsic circumstances are the same, some change in the mind varies it as a cause. I will consider this point of identity, in its effect on the argument, hereafter, and, for the present, will only remark that in such cases it must be the *changed mind*, which is really the efficient cause of the variation in the effect, and that, if the rule does not apply to two minds acting under the same circumstances because they are not the same cause, nor yet to the same mind, acting a second time with all other circumstances the same, except such as of necessity arise from its being a second and not a first time, no possible case can arise for the application of the rule to mind.

If, as at least appears probable, spirit is the only real cause, and postulating that the finite mind is not co-eternal with the Infinite, there was a time when only one cause existed; and if *the same causes necessarily produce the same effects*, this one cause never could have produced but one effect, or, at farthest, but duplications of the same effect. If it be said that the fact of this cause having once acted and produced one effect, makes such a variation of the circumstances under which it acts, that its subsequent action may differ from the first merely from the fact that it is the second, and not the first causative action; then, we say that this entirely destroys the rule and makes it a nullity; for the same cause cannot act a second time, without having acted a first; and if, from the fact of its having acted once, the effect of the second act may be different, there can be no such *necessary* uniformity of effect as the law supposes.

There must be something to determine if there shall be a difference between the effect of the first and second action, and, if so, what difference. That difference in circumstances, which has arisen from the cause having once acted, cannot itself determine the different action the second time.

We have already shown that the mere existence of the thing created cannot influence the mind that created it, except as a circumstance to be considered by it in determining its next creative act, and as, by the hypothesis, there is nothing else in existence when this second action is to be determined, it must be determined by the cause—by the Infinite Mind—in view of the result of its first action, and of what it wants to do in the future; and hence, as before shown, the Infinite Intelligence is not only an originating creative cause, but, in virtue of its intelligence, can produce different effects by successive acts of volition, and determine what the difference in each of these successive acts shall be.

If we suppose all material creation to be the one effect of the first action of the First Cause, then, under this rule of uniformity of cause and effect, that cause must have then become dormant; and as, whether that creation be the imagery—the conceptions—of the mind of God made directly palpable, or His ordering of matter conformably to His conceptions, it cannot change itself, or be governed or changed by law impressed upon it, it must, so far as Creator and creation are concerned, remain fixed without change; for any subsequent change would be another and different effect produced by the same cause, which is contrary to the assumed law, that the same causes necessarily produce the same effects, and hence, if this law be true, the first effort of the First Cause would destroy itself as cause, leaving no room or possibility for its future activity in new and different creations, or in changing what it had first created.

But there is change—change in our sensations, if in nothing else; changes we do not produce by any action of our own, and hence, we must infer the continued existence of some other power as cause, producing these changes.

If the same cause must necessarily produce the same effects, the effects must be co-existent with the cause; for if the cause can exist without immediately producing the effect, it *may* exist any length of time, and even forever, without the effect, and the effect would not be a necessary effect of such a cause; and, in this view, the First Cause, if the subject of such a necessity of effect, must have immediately exhausted its creative or causative power in a necessary effect.

If, to obtain a continuing causative power, and yet retain the law of necessity in cause and effect, we suppose the effect of the first cause to have been the creation of other cause, then, this other cause, too, must have immediately produced all its necessary effects; and so of any number of duplicate causes, and there would be an end of the power to produce changes, all, being simultaneous, would have no existence in time, and no subsequent changes could be produced. So that the application of this rule to intelligence as cause, denies any continuing power to produce changes in the universe; which, being contrary to the fact, proves the rule untrue, and shows the necessity and the fact of the existence of a cause which is not subject to this law of necessity, or of uniformity of effects, but which has a faculty of producing different effects, or, at least, so far adapting itself to circumstances, that, from the fact that it has once exerted its causative power, and produced an effect, it may, by a subsequent exertion, produce a different effect. This freedom must be an attribute of the Infinite Intelligence, and "uniformity of cause and effect" in regard to It, means nothing more than the uniform modes of willing, or the modes which It voluntarily adopts for Its own government; which is but an expression of Its freedom; for this is controlling Its own action; and that It does this in conformity to a law of Its own creation, or which It voluntarily adopts, cannot lessen this freedom.

With regard to the finite mind, experience indicates that, after having, under any given circumstances, acted in one way, it may, on a recurrence of them, elect, and frequently does elect, to try another way; the fact that it has already tried one way with certain effects, having, by increasing its knowledge, led to a belief that some other way may be productive of more desirable effects, or, at least, again add to its knowledge by practical experience in the new mode. It is enabled to design or conceive these new modes of action, to examine and judge of their expediency, and to execute them in virtue of its being intelligent, originating cause, with a faculty of adapting its action to its view of the circumstances in which it is placed, and by which it is surrounded, which itself only can do.

It may be said, that this change in the view, or

knowledge and want of the mind, makes it, in fact, a different cause. This is merely a question of identity, which it is useless now to discuss, further than to say that, if it be the same cause, producing different effects, it disproves the rule; and if it be a different cause, it cannot logically be inferred from different causes producing different effects, that the same causes must produce the same effects. I may, however, further observe, that this difference in the mind's knowledge in the second case, grows directly out of its experience in the first; and if, as a consequence of intelligent cause or causes having once acted, their recurring action may be different, the rule as to them becomes a nullity; for there is then no necessity that the subsequent action of the same causes shall produce the same effect as they did when they first acted. If it be said, in asserting this necessary uniformity, the phrase " same causes " includes not only the efficient, or active power, but all the co-existing objects and circumstances having any relation whatever to the action of this power, still the rule can then never have any application to intelligent beings acting as cause, for in mind the same circumstances cannot thus occur twice, because, to it, the fact of having occurred a first time, itself makes a difference in the second. It varies the knowledge, which is one of its essential elements as cause. The nearest approach to it is when the mind has forgotten that they have before occurred. In such cases we determine as if they never had before occurred, and the common experience is that we sometimes realize afterward that, from not recalling their previous occurrence, we, in the second case, acted differently without being aware of it, and when, but for this forgetting, we probably would have repeated the first action.

This cause and effect, as used by Edwards, involves the infinite series, which he so often introduces into his arguments. If the same causes necessarily produce the same effects, and everything which begins to be must have a cause, then this new event, this beginning to be, must arise from some *change in the operating causes*, otherwise no new effect could be produced; but this change in the operating causes is an event which must also have a cause, and which, in its beginning, must have arisen from some change in the operating cause of *it*, which change, again, must have had a cause; and so we have a series, which can have no beginning unless there was either an event without a cause, or a different effect from the same unchanged cause. If, to avoid this dilemma, we suppose the series traced back to a necessary self-existent cause, which had no beginning, it may be replied, that such cause, existing from eternity, if acting from necessity, must, of necessity, have produced its proper effect an eternity ago, and could produce no other and new effect, except by some subsequent changes in itself, which it would have no power to produce; for this would be a different effect of the same cause, and hence, we are compelled to infer a cause which has either the power of changing itself as cause, or of varying its effects while it remains the same cause. It may be said that, before this cause produces a different effect, it changes itself, either by direct action, or by producing an effect, which reacts and becomes cause of change in its own cause; but even then, as the *changed* cause would be a *different* cause, one, as before observed, could not argue from different causes producing different effects that the same causes *must* produce the same effects; and, even if we could, if the creative and created cause act only from necessity, all their effects must be coexistent with their existence, and all their causative power be instantaneously exhausted; so that, to continue effects in time, there must be some cause which does not, of *necessity*, produce only one particular effect, but can delay action, and when it does act can produce different effects.

We have no reason, then, either from experience or from the nature of things, to suppose that any such law of uniformity is applicable to spirit causes, but, on the contrary, as already stated, actual existences, or changes in them, at least, in our own sensations, prove that there is now, or must have been some cause, which did not of necessity produce the same effect; and the existence of such a cause, either in the past or present, would disprove the rule of *necessary* uniformity.

I have endeavored to show that we have such causes in intelligent beings,—infinite and finite—with originating, creative power; causes, which, from the very fact of having already produced one effect, are better prepared to go on to produce other and different effects, and that, but for this versatility, only one effect ever could have been produced.

An effect cannot be till its cause exists; but it does not follow that cause must be *before* its effect. That which may become cause may, and, as in the case of intelligent being, generally does exist, before by activity it becomes cause. If matter exists in a state of rest, it too must have activity, motion, imparted to it before it becomes cause. At the same instant, however, that a sufficient cause begins to act, its effect must also begin to be, and if that which may be cause, or in which power may be said to subsist, begins to act at the instant in which it comes into existence, its effect must be simultaneous with its existence; for, as before observed, if the effect can be delayed one instant, it may another, and another, and so may never be, which is to say that the sufficient cause is not a sufficient cause. As used in my argument, however, it is only essential to predicate this co-existence of effect with a *necessary* cause.

If we suppose matter, in the first instance, to have been quiescent, then all changes in it must be traceable to an intelligent will; and, if we suppose matter to have been in motion from eternity, and, as a consequence, to have been producing, in a certain order of succession, such *necessary* effects as arise from the impossibility of two bodies occupying the same space; or, which is the same thing, of one space being two spaces; then, all changes from this *certain order* must, also, be referred to an intelligent will.

In tracing the connection we are but tracing the last effect back to an intelligent cause—in most instances to the will of God as a first cause. We cannot often, if ever, tell how many terms there may be in the series. For aught we know, gravitation may be the immediate *will* of God, acting in conformity to a uniform law, which He has voluntarily adopted, and which we have ascertained, while the changes in the weather may be immediately determined by His will, acting either without uniformity, or in conformity to some law which we have not ascertained.

The present conditions may be different from any which ever before existed, and hence different from any which ever before attended or preceded either a clear or a cloudy sky, and yet either a clear or a cloudy sky will attend or follow them.

Some of these things may have been made not uniform to vary the problems of life, and develop the finite intelligence in their solution, as the concealment of his plans, by one player at chess, makes a necessity for more thought, care and vigilance in the other, to provide for an unascertained amount of variability in his move. It is true, that the same intention might be fulfilled by concealing the law; but greater variety in the problems is obtained by using both means, stimulating the human intellect to discover the law and thus get power to foreknow events arising under it; and, also, forever tasking it to provide for certain contingencies, which it never can thus learn certainly to anticipate.

There is no more difficulty in supposing the finite intelligence to be a first, or originating cause of change in its finite sphere of action, than in supposing the Supreme Intelligence to be first cause in the sphere of the Infinite. Intelligence, in all degrees, may possess the faculty of adapting itself to that change of circumstances, which itself has produced by causing an effect, and go on to produce another and different effect; and this entirely destroys the rule of necessary uniformity of cause and effect as applicable to intelligent cause; for, if such cause, in consequence of having produced one effect, may, from that very circumstance, produce a different effect, no case can possibly arise in which the same intelligent cause MUST produce the same effect.

Without such power of adaptation to the changes which itself has wrought, the First Intelligent Cause must forever have thought the same thought, or performed the same action over and over; and, if the effect of that action was the creation of a finite intelligence with one or more thoughts, then, every other effect must also have been the creation of a finite intelligence, like the first, with only the same thought. But, if it be a characteristic of intelligence that, through its constitutional want for activity, or more directly, its want for knowledge and its intuitive knowledge of the means of acquiring it, one idea is but the precursor of another and different idea, and that these ideas, singly or accumulated, are the means by which the mind adapts its action to the want, both thoughts and muscular movements, internal and external action, may be varied without any other effective cause than the intelligence itself, which wants, thinks and acts, and which is thus, in itself, a creative first cause.

I have already alluded to the fact, that this uniformity of the action of Supreme Intelligence, as observed in many cases, may arise in part from the perfect wisdom by which it determines its acts without the necessity of experiment. The same remark applies in some degree to the action of the finite will, which, with finite wisdom, knowing, or ascertaining by experience, or otherwise, the best modes in certain cases, will adopt them, whenever such cases arise; and this gives some appearance of reason for the application of the law of uniformity and necessity in cause and effect to mind.

It appears then, that a certain uniformity of the effect of intelligent action, on which the argument for necessity is based, is, or at least may be caused by the free action of intelligence, infinite or finite; and, therefore, from the existence of such uniformity, it cannot be inferred that no such free action exists. The existence of an effect cannot be a reason against the existence of that which may be its cause. This uniformity could not have produced itself, nor could it have been produced by blind, undesigning forces, except in cases when some effect must be, and only one effect is possible; *i. e.*, when non-effect and also any other than one particular effect involve a contradiction.* We must refer this uniformity, in all other cases, to the action of intelligence, and to infer from it necessity in the action of intelligence is to make the effect necessitate its own cause.

If the action of the mind is the cause of the volition, then, as before observed, that the volition, as an effect of such action, is necessary, does not prove that the ause—the action of the mind—is necessary, but only proves an infallible power in mind, as such cause, to determine its volitions.

But there may be another reason for this uniformity in the mode of God's action, for, as the finite mind acts more or less through His modes, or is influenced in its action by what it presumes His action under certain circumstances will be, this uniformity of action in Him is essential to the action of finite intelligence—to the existence of finite free agents—for, without this uniformity in God's action, a finite agent could have no knowledge as to what would be the effect of his effort, and would have no inducement to make any effort. If, for instance, an effort to move a heavy body one way was just as likely to move it in a way not intended and counter to the want of the agent, the effort would never be made.

We cannot conceive that the Supreme Intelligence

* See Appendix, Note XLVI.

acts, except from a want of change of some kind—a desire for variety—and this desire, of itself, would seem to be best gratified or accomplished by making every act a new variety, rather than in conformity to some previous act. That God has not done so, but, in many cases, adopted the rule of uniformity of action, seems to indicate a design, which was incompatible with the variety just suggested, and which is not only consistent with, but necessary to, the existence of finite agents freely exercising the finite creative power of will; and in this uniformity, then, instead of the argument which Edwards deduces from it in favor of necessity, we have an argument from final causes in favor of the freedom of the finite mind in its acting or willing.

Before closing this chapter, I will notice an argument derived from the supposed law of uniformity in cause and effect, in connection with the influence of circumstances, which has been thus stated.

If the same circumstances occur a thousand times, and the state of the mind is the same, its action will be the same, and hence, necessary under the circumstances.

This is but a particular application of the general rule, that the same causes necessarily produce the same effects; which, we have already shown, is not a law of metaphysical necessity, and that there is no reason to presume that it applies to mind. The fact that all the circumstances have before occurred, including the condition of the mind, is involved in the statement; and this fact making itself an alteration in the repetition of them, the mind may, from that circumstance, elect to vary its action. If so, as before shown, this destroys the rule, and the inference which is based upon it.

But admit, for the sake of the argument, that this law does apply to mind, and further, that in every one of the thousand cases, one of the conditions of the mind is that of *necessity;* then, the same causes necessarily producing the same effects, the action of the mind is the same. Again, suppose that, in every one of the thousand cases, the condition of the mind is that of *freedom;* then, under the same law of the uniformity of causes and effects, the action of the mind would still be the same in each of these thousand cases; and, as we may thus change this condition of the mind from necessity to freedom, without changing the result, the result cannot possibly indicate which of the two elements was involved; or, in other words, admitting the fact and the application of the law, it applies just as well to mind controlling and directing its own volitions, as to mind in which the volitions are controlled and directed by some external power. If, in every one of the thousand cases, the action of the mind is the same, it can, so far as this case is concerned, just as well be so because it acts freely as because it acts from necessity; and hence, even admitting the law on which the argument is wholly based, and that it does apply to mind, it has no force whatever, and cannot even indicate whether, in each of the thousand cases, the condition of the mind's action is that of necessity or freedom.

Admitting that, in every one of the thousand cases, the mind, even by preliminary effort, or by immediate perception, comes to the same conclusion as to what to do—that, the truth being palpable, it cannot but perceive it—still this perception is not the act of will, but knowledge preparatory to it; and if, with this conclusion or knowledge as to what to do, it were found trying to do something else, this would indicate that the mind was not free, but constrained by some extrinsic power; while, on the other hand, its trying to do that which is in conformity with its knowledge indicates self-direction of its power and consequently freedom in the effort or act of will. It would be a strange and contradictory idea of freedom, which would require, for its realization, that a man might try to do what he decided not to do, and might not try to do that which he decided to do, and thus act contrary to his own views.

The fallacy of the argument from the "thousand cases" lies in supposing that, after the mind has, by a decision or judgment, directed its volition or effort, freedom still requires that *some other* volition or effort should be possible; which, were it so, would really show that the mind might not be free; that is, that it might not direct its own action. The assertion "if the same circumstances occur a thousand times," &c., must include *all* the circumstances; if we stop short of the knowledge or final decision of the mind as to its own action, the rule will be found to have no application, or to be untrue; and, admitting the assertion, it then really shows only that the willing by the mind is always in conformity to its own decision or knowledge as to what to do. If there is, of *necessity*, a connection between this decision and effort, this only proves that the mind is of necessity free in such effort; and to assert the contrary, is again like saying that freedom is not free because it is of *necessity* free.

This view brings the argument home to our definition of freedom, as that condition in which a being directs its own action or movement; while that argument, which, from this necessity of connection between the decision and the volition of a being, would infer necessity, must assume that freedom requires that a being may act counter to itself—to its own directing power.

CHAPTER XII.

GOD'S FOREKNOWLEDGE.

ANOTHER argument of Edwards is, that the acts of the will are necessary because God certainly foreknows them; and that, what is foreknown by Omniscience must as certainly happen as though it were decreed by Omnipotence, and, therefore, such acts cannot be free. Against this it has been contended that, even though God foreknows every event, such prescience does not cause that event, or control the act of will which is foreknown. It may be asserted, with some show of reason, that freedom of the human will is one of the elements of God's foreknowledge; that He knows that such or such an event will happen, because it depends on the foreseen free action of some being, without which it would not happen. On this I would remark, that it does not fulfil the intention of those who urge it. It does not avoid the practical difficulties of fatalism.

A man with this belief might say: "I need not trouble myself with regard to the future. Everything in that future, even my own agency upon it, is already as certainly determined as the past. No effort of mine can change it; or, if effort or volition of mine is to change it, that effort, that volition, will inevitably take place, and no care or thought of mine will prevent it." The position still admits that necessity which it is intended to exclude. With such belief he would make no effort. When a man wills he always intends, as already shown, to produce some effect in the future, to produce some change, or to make that future—internal or external—in some respects different from what it would be without such effort. But, if the fact is that no effort of his can in any way change that future, and he knows it, he will not will at all, freely or otherwise. As just suggested, it may be said that his free act of will is itself one of the events infallibly foreknown, and hence must happen. This, it will be perceived, in the last analysis, involves the contradiction of supposing a free will to be a necessitated will, so that the position assumed, even if it would obviate the difficulty, is untenable, and cannot be urged by the advocates of freedom against this argument for necessity. An event foreknown by infallible prescience must be as certain in the future, as if known by infallible memory in the past, and to say that God foreknows an event, which depends upon the action of an agent, which, acting without His control, may, of itself, freely and independently produce any one of several different results, or none at all, involves a contradiction. I am disposed to yield to the argument of Edwards all the benefit of any doubt on these points, and, waiving any replication which might be founded on the power of God to influence the future *free* action of a finite agent by imparting or withholding knowledge, to admit that what is certainly foreknown by Omniscience must certainly happen, and that, if God foreknows the volitions of men, then they cannot will freely, and for a refutation of his argument for necessity, founded on prescience, rely only upon other considerations.*

One essential link in his argument is that, God *does* foreknow all the future, and, especially, all human volitions; and this Edwards attempts to prove by showing that such knowledge is absolutely necessary to God's proper government of the world. On the point that God *does* foreknow, I would remark that, as in regard to the argument from cause and effect, it appeared that God, having the power to produce infinite variety, had yet chosen to lessen that variety by establishing a certain uniformity between antecedents and consequents, and that the apparent object of this was to make the existence of finite free agents possible; so, also, though God, having the *power* to *determine, could* foreknow all events, He may forego the exercise of such power, and neither control nor foreknow the particular events, which are thus left to be determined by the action of the human mind. That God may certainly foreknow any event, which He has the power to bring to pass, will not, however, militate against the argument in favor of freedom; for, if God, by the direct exercise of His power, produces a volition, it is not the volition of any other being than Himself; and if He indirectly influences the volition by changing the knowledge of a being, then this change of knowledge avails only on the hypothesis that this being *freely* conforms its action to its knowledge. If a being does not will freely, there is no reason to suppose that any inducements to a certain act will avail to produce that act any more than

* See Appendix, Note XLVII.

the contrary. But, as we have already suggested, even supposing God to have this power over every future event, and that either directly or indirectly He can control every volition, and deny freedom to every other being, He may forego the exercise of such power, and thus make the existence of finite free agents possible.

This is not only conceivable, but we are conscious of having and of exercising such power ourselves—that we can refrain from doing and from knowing what we might do and know, in order that another may act freely. For instance, a child is in a room with two doors to it. I know that, by using my superior strength, I can put the child out of the room by a certain one of them, and hence, may foreknow that the child will go out by that door; but I decide not to use my strength for that purpose, and leave the child to its own free action—to go out by either door, or to remain in the room. I may alter the circumstances, as, for instance, by placing some attractive object just without one of the doors in the view of the child, and thus make it probable that the child will leave by that door; and this probability is founded on the presumption that the child, with the *knowledge* of this attractive object, will *want* to move to that object and *freely will* to do so. I may, however, will not to exert any influence—not to change the circumstances, or increase the knowledge of the child—but leave it by its own knowledge freely to determine what to do. In this case I do not even seek to change its final action by imparting knowledge.

Edwards argues that God *must* foreknow the volitions of finite moral agents, for, otherwise, His knowledge of the future would become so imperfect that He could not govern the universe. He says:

" So that, according to this notion of God's not foreseeing the volitions and free actions of men, God could foresee nothing appertaining to the state of the world of mankind in future ages; not so much as the being of one person that should live in it; and could foreknow no events, but only such as He would bring to pass Himself by the extraordinary interposition of His immediate power; or things which should come to pass in the natural material world, by the laws of motion and course of nature, wherein that is independent on the actions, or works of mankind; that is, as He might, like a very able mathematician and astronomer, with great exactness, calculate the revolutions of the heavenly bodies and the greater wheels of the machine of the external creation.

"And if we closely consider the matter, there will appear reason to convince us, that He could not, with any absolute certainty, foresee even these. As to the *first*, namely, things done by the immediate and extraordinary interposition of God's power, these cannot be foreseen, unless it can be foreseen when there shall be occasion for such extraordinary interposition. And that cannot be foreseen unless the state of the moral world can be foreseen. For whenever God thus interposes, it is with regard to the state of the moral world, requiring such divine interposition. Thus, God could not certainly foresee the universal deluge, the calling of Abraham, the destruction of Sodom and Gomorrah, the plagues on Egypt and Israel's redemption out of it, the expelling the seven nations of Canaan, and the bringing Israel into that land; for these all are represented as connected with things belonging to the state of the moral world. Nor can God foreknow the most proper and convenient time of the day of judgment and general conflagration; for that chiefly depends on the course and state of things in the moral world" (pp. 144–5).

"It will also follow from this notion that, as God is liable to be continually repenting what He has done; so He must be exposed to be constantly *changing* His mind and intentions as to His future conduct; altering His measures, relinquishing His old designs, and forming new schemes and projections. For His purposes, even as to the main parts of His scheme, namely, such as belong to the state of His moral kingdom, must be always liable to be broken, through want of foresight; and He must be continually putting His system to rights, as it gets out of order through the contingence of the actions of moral agents. He must be a Being, who, instead of being absolutely immutable, must necessarily be the subject of infinitely the most numerous acts of repentance and changes of intention of any being whatsoever; for this plain reason, that His vastly extensive charge comprehends an infinitely greater number of those things, which are to Him contingent and uncertain. In such a situation, He must have little else to do, but to mend broken links as well as He can, and be rectifying His disjointed frame and disordered movements, in the best manner the case will allow. The Supreme Lord of all things must needs be under great and miserable disadvantages, in governing the world, which He has made, and has the care of, through His being utterly unable to find out things of chief importance, which hereafter shall befall His system; which, if He did but know, He might make seasonable provision for. In many cases, there may be very great necessity that He should make provision, in the manner of His ordering and disposing things, for some great events which are to happen, of vast and extensive influence, and endless consequence to the universe; which He may see afterward when it is too late, and may wish in vain that He had known beforehand, that He might have ordered His affairs accordingly. And it is in the power of man, on these principles, by his devices, purposes, and actions, thus to disappoint God, break His measures, make Him continually to change His mind, subject Him to vexation and bring Him into confusion" (pp. 149–50).

We might, perhaps, argue that these statements rather tend to show that God does not foreknow the volitions and actions of men, or, at least, that if He does, He generally chooses not to interfere with them, but, for long periods of time, leaves them to their own free actions; for it does appear from the record, that "it is in the power of man * * * by his devices, purposes, and actions, thus to disappoint God, break His measures, and make Him continually to change His mind," and that He does not "make seasonable provision" to prevent the necessity of His "rectifying His disjointed frame and disordered movements," as evinced in the necessity of a general destruction by the flood to get rid of a corruption which had arisen from agencies which He did not control, and which, a resort to such a measure by Omnipotence would seem to argue, could not possibly be directly controlled by extrinsic power. We propose, however, to discuss the question on philosophical and not on theological ground, and to treat inferences from Biblical quotations as we would deductions or illustrations from any other statement of fact or belief.

GOD'S FOREKNOWLEDGE. 391

The foregoing reasoning of Edwards asserts, that it is necessary that God should foreknow the volitions of men, because of the influence of those volitions on the affairs of the world. But, it is evident that the supposed difficulty relates less to the *volitions* than to the *effects*, or *actual doings* in which the volitions are executed; and, if the foreknowledge of a volition is thus necessary, the foreknowledge of the sequent effects must, "à fortiori," be, also, necessary; and if the foreknowledge of the volition proves it to be not free, the foreknowledge of the doing must prove it not free, and this would take from man the liberty which Edwards grants him, in doing what he wills. If to this it be replied that, if the volition is controlled, there is no necessity for controlling the consequent effect, or doing, for the volition itself controls it; it would still appear that there is no liberty in the sequent doing, for the reply asserts, that it is controlled by the will, which is, also, controlled, and, of course, whatever controls the will, also controls the doing; so that, if there is no liberty in willing, there can really be none in the consequent doing, and *all* human liberty is denied.

But, even supposing there may be freedom in doing what we will, when there is no freedom in willing, the foregoing difficulty, in respect to God's government, as Edwards states it, is equally obviated, either by supposing that God controls the volition and constrains it to be in conformity to His preordained plan; or that, leaving man to will freely, He frustrates the execution—the doing—making the result different from what the agent willing intended, whenever that intention conflicts with that foreordained plan. Of these two positions, it seems most reasonable to adopt the latter, as it is a fact, well attested by our daily experience, that in the *doing* we are often thus frustrated and overruled, while our consciousness reveals no such interference with our *willing to do*. For aught that appears, the sequences of the volitions may be determined in that inscrutable process, by which our volitions are made efficient, and of which, Edwards truly says, we know nothing. Giving to the argument, then, all the scope which Edwards assigns to it, it disproves the freedom in *doing*, which he asserts, rather than the freedom in willing, which he denies. But, perhaps, the urgencies of the argument do not require that even the freedom in doing should be abandoned; and, even supposing man's volitions to be always executed, I still think that Edwards overrates their influence on the ability of God to control and direct the universe and its affairs. The child's remaining in the room, or going out of it by one door, or the other, does not materially affect that knowledge by which I judge of what I shall do in relation to the future. Knowing all the results possible in the case, viz., that the child will remain in the room, or go out by one door, or by the other, I may use what wisdom I have, in so ordering my own actions, as to insure the most good, or the least possible evil from their combination with any one of the three possible contingent events. Now, the acts of any finite number of finite free agents, must bear a less ratio to the power and wisdom of the Supreme Intelligence, than the act of the child does to even the most wise and powerful of finite intelligences, and as God may know all the acts or effects possible by such finite intelligences, singly or combined, He may, in His infinite wisdom, provide for every possible event which to Him, either by the necessities of the case, or by His own free will, is thus made contingent. Of an arrangement so vast, it is difficult for us to form a conception to reason upon, and I will, therefore, endeavor to illustrate the views just expressed by supposing a case, which, though perfectly conceivable, is beyond the reach of any human calculation, and beyond any human power.

Suppose, then, a chessboard—an automaton chessboard—in which each piece differing in functions, or color, has a different weight, and that each square is separately supported by a spring, so that the different weights will depress each to a different point. If we suppose any one given position of the pieces, it is conceivable that the different degrees of depression may act upon machinery devised for the purpose (say machinery moved by a weight like a clock), so that the best move which the position admits of will be made; and though, even for one movement, it would require very complicated machinery, there is nothing inconceivable or impossible in it; and, as this is conceivable of *any* one combination of the pieces, it is conceivable that it may be applied to every possible combination. Suppose then, such a chessboard, the moves, on one side, made by the automatic machinery, and on the other by an intelligent finite free agent. We will suppose there is nothing else in existence but the board so constructed —(of course, with whatever is requisite to sustain attraction, gravitative and cohesive),—and this free agent playing the other side of the game. The agent moves freely; what particular move he would make, the mechanist who devised the machine did not and could not anticipate, but knowing every possible move which the position admitted of, he has devised the machine in reference to every such possible move; and though no particular move is foreknown, yet, if the mechanist, with full knowledge of every possible combination, has so contrived the machine, that in its turn the best possible move will be made, the result, supposing the mechanist to have his choice in regard to the first move, will certainly be checkmate to the agent, who moves freely, but without this comprehensive knowledge of the whole possibilities of the game. And to effect this result does not require any departure from *uniform modes of action*, but, on the contrary, is produced by the intelligent application of one of the *most uniform* of what we term laws of matter,—that of attraction. The attraction of gravitation, acting through the weight attached to the machinery, imparts the force to move the pieces, and through the difference in the weights and the consequent unequal depression of the squares by the pieces on them, giving direction to that force; while the attraction of cohesion gives the requisite resistance to the springs which support the squares. The combinations on the chessboard, though vast in number, are finite, and may all be comprehended by a finite intelligence. Though no *human* being could in a lifetime accomplish any large part of the calculations and workmanship essential to such a machine as we have described, still, power and intelligence short of the infinite could accomplish it; and, if a mechanist of finite powers could, by modes as *uniform* as the laws of attraction, thus cause to be made all the moves essential to the skilful playing of this complicated game, and that, too, without being able to anticipate a single move on the other side, there can be nothing unreasonable in supposing that God, with a perfect knowledge of all the possible combinations and changes, which His own system will admit of, including all the possible effects of the action of finite free agents, may, without knowing by anticipation the particular acts of those finite agents, so contrive His *uniform* modes of action, that, without varying from such uniformity, every possible contingence will be provided for, " without altering His measures, relinquishing His old designs and forming new schemes and projections." If it be true, or even conceivable, that man, with his finite powers and limited knowledge of the future acts of God and of his fellow beings, which does not include all possible acts, can yet, in his finite sphere, with finite wisdom, adapt his acts with some degree of effectiveness to that future, it is certainly conceivable, that God, with His infinite powers and full knowledge of all that is possible from other causes in the future, may, with infinite wisdom, adapt His acts to *all the possibilities* of that future, so that He will not be liable to be " frustrated of His end."

We have explained how this may be done consistently with uniformity in His modes of action, but He has still in reserve the power of deviating from that uniformity, in miracles, and it appears that the acts of men, in the exercise of their free agency, became so generally perverse and corrupt, that Supreme Wisdom demanded their almost total extinction, and a special act or miraculous interference for that end. Besides miracles, which are deviations from the established uniform modes of God's action, we do not know but that many things are the result of His special actions in regard to which He has established no law of uniformity. We do not know that these things are not dependent, in each case, on His immediate will, without reference to any conformity with acts performed in the past, or contemplated in the future. We do not know but that the storm, which destroyed the Spanish Armada—the winds, which delayed the landing of William of Orange—or the unusually early commencement of cold weather, which frustrated the plans of Napoleon and destroyed his army in Russia, were all as much special acts as the miraculous opening of the waters of the Red Sea, which favored the escape of the Israelites from Egyptian bondage. With these ample means there would seem to be no danger that God, with infinite power and wisdom, could be "frustrated of His end," or, that He would not be able, even without foreknowledge of the particular acts of finite free agents, to bring to pass all that He might deem essential to the proper government of the universe, and to such care or control as He chooses to take of all that He has created.* We will add that the necessity of knowing events in advance, in order to "make seasonable provision for them," arises from the weakness of the agent on whom the making of such provision devolves, and the time required will be somewhat and inversely proportioned to the power and wisdom of the agent. When that power and wisdom become infinite, the time required becomes nought, and God would therefore require less time to consider the most intricate and complicated affairs conceivable, than we would to determine the simplest possible case that could be presented to us.

The foreknowledge of God has the same relation to His action, that the preconceptions of man have to his.

* See Appendix, Note XLVIII.

God perceives what, without His own effort, the course of things in the future may be, and by what effort he can change that course. A finite being may exert all his ability to know the future, and may also exert all his power to influence the course of events, and thus increase the probability that the future will conform to his anticipations: or he may, as in the case of the child just mentioned, forego the exercise of his own power that another may act freely. There is certainly no impossibility that God may do the same. A being of limited powers may know all the *effects* bearing upon his future action, which such single or combined efforts can produce, even if the modes in which they can be produced are infinite, and hence beyond his prescience. For instance, the ways in which a friend may reach a place at which I am to meet him at a given time, may be infinite in number, and yet, the fact that he does reach the place at the appointed time, be all that is material to my plan of future action. In certain states of a game of chess, a man can foresee every possible move, which his antagonist may next make, that can affect the result of the game, and make his own plans accordingly. A man of ordinary skill and discernment may, sometimes, do this even for each of a few moves in advance, and, if he had sufficient capacity, he could do it for the whole game. To one who did this, the game would lose its interest, and he would play it only as a benevolent man plays the simple game of Fox and Geese with a child for its amusement.

Suppose, for instance, that at the commencement of the game, one player, A, having the requisite capacity, perceives that his antagonist, B, has his choice of the twenty different moves. A may plan his play so that he will be ready to move in any one of the twenty cases which can arise, and B, at the commencement, if looking forward, and providing in advance for the whole game, must, for his second move, take into view the four hundred possible contingencies growing out of the two moves to be previously made; and the number of *possible* combinations in a game of ordinary length would be almost innumerable. But even to provide in advance for all these, though far beyond the reach of human faculties, would still be within the scope of even a finite comprehension; and when we contemplate the Supreme Intelligence, as anticipating and providing, or making immediate provision as they occur, for all the possible contingencies which can arise from the free volitions of myriads of free agents, and all their combinations; although we know that, being still finite in number, they cannot exhaust the power, or fill the comprehension, which is infinite; yet, we may perceive that they may furnish ample occasion for the effort— that they may call out the energies of a being, capable of producing all the sublimely vast and minutely perfect combinations, which creative power has exhibited to us; and, perhaps, can hardly avoid the thought that they must, even in such a being, excite that interest, which arises from the necessity of thought, skill, and contrivance, to accomplish its object and avoid being frustrated by the action of other powers.

If, on the other hand, God foreknows, and, as an attribute of Divinity has ever foreknown all the future, then that portion of His creative power which relates to *designing* that future, and which is the highest attribute of Creative Power, has no sphere for its exercise, and never could have had any; it is virtually annihilated, and God becomes a mere *executive* causality working out plans preformed, and requiring in their accomplishment no higher order of intelligence, no more exalted creative talent than is required to copy a painting. On such hypothesis, indeed, still less than this, for, as on it God's own volitions must be foreknown and be manifest to Himself, He does not even have by a present exercise of intelligent power to adapt his effort to the effect, as the copyist must do, and this perfect prescience would degrade the Supreme Power to the same rank as that of one who turns the crank of a mill, knowing that thereby the corn is ground, but also knowing each required volition without any present effort for that object. A prescience which has always included the whole future must be innate, and never have been the occasion for any exercise of intelligent power, which the knowledge required to turn the crank may have been. The acting of a being from the knowledge of a mode which has ever existed ready formed in its own mind is purely instinctive, and action merely from the innate knowledge of its own volitions and of the order of their succession, requiring no exercise of intelligence in applying the known mode to the occasion for it, would be below the ordinary forms of instinctive action.

It is not my purpose now to follow Edwards in his attempt to prove that his system of necessity is consistent with moral agency, with virtue, and with common sense. This, if I have succeeded in showing that his arguments in support of that system are fallacious, and

that it is in fact untrue, would be needless; and, if I
have failed to do this, there would be little ground to
hope that my examination of the subsequent portions
of his work would be attended with any better result.

CHAPTER XIII.

CONCLUSION.

WE have now shown that the Will, instead of being as defined by Edwards " that by which the mind chooses anything," is the mind's faculty or power of making effort, and that, in relation to choice, we make effort to ascertain which of two or more things is preferable only as we do to ascertain any other fact which we want to know ; that Edwards also defines choice to be a comparative act, or the result of such act, and yet makes choice and will synonymous. He also makes will the last agency of the mind in producing an effect, and assumes that choice is a necessary prerequisite and the distinguishing condition of free acts of will. From these various and incompatible definitions of the same terms, and these unfounded assumptions, he argues that as a free act of will must be preceded by a choice, which is itself also an act of will, and hence, if a free act, must have also been preceded by a choice, and this choice as a free act of will again thus preceded, and so on without limit, there could have been no first free act of will, and, if the first act was not free, then the whole subsequent train is not free. But the foundation of this, his favorite *reductio ad absurdum*, which he applies in a variety of modes, is wholly destroyed by correcting the definitions and assumptions as above stated.

In regard to this reasoning I have also remarked that self-direction, and not choice, is the distinguishing characteristic of freedom. The mind thus directs its efforts by means of the knowledge which it has at the moment it makes the effort, including its preconceptions of the effect it seeks to produce. Whether this knowledge has been acquired by previous efforts of comparison resulting in choice, or otherwise, it is, at the time of applying it, but the mind's perception, and the mode of its prior acquisition can make no difference to the freedom of the act which the mind directs by means of the knowledge which it now actually possesses. I have further observed that this confounding will with choice, which as one form of knowledge is not subject to the will, but, as a result of certain comparisons, is as necessarily and passively recognized by the knowing sense as sound is through the ear, opens the way for the argument, that as *choice* is, in this sense, necessary, *will*, being the same as choice, must also be necessary, and this confounding as identical two things so very distinct as will and knowledge leads to intricate confusion and various sophisms, pervading, as already shown, a large portion of Edwards's argument.

In regard to that somewhat simpler form of his *reductio ad absurdum* to prove that the will (free or not free) cannot determine itself, because, if it does, it must determine each act by a prior act of will, admitting of no first act, and which, taken in the view most favorable for Edwards, only proves that the mind cannot always direct its act of will *by a prior act of will*, it has already been remarked that this does not conflict with the position that the *mind* determines its act of will by means of its knowledge, in which act, being thus self-directed, it acts freely. Edwards applies this reasoning to choice, evidently, however, here as elsewhere, using it as a synonym for will, and will, with him, meaning "the soul willing," his inference really is, that the soul willing or choosing cannot determine its act of will or choice. But it is evident that the essence of a choice must be the determining among objects of choice, and if the soul cannot do this it cannot choose at all, but something else must choose for it. From the same position it also follows that as the mind cannot will *generally*, but can only will particular acts which must be determined or decided upon before it can will, *i. e.*, make effort in regard to them, it cannot will until the act of will is elected and determined or decided upon, and if the mind cannot make this election it cannot will till some other power has determined its act for it, and hence cannot of itself make effort or will without this extrinsic aid.

As bearing on this point I have shown that the mind need not and does not will either to will or not to will, nor yet to suspend willing, but that it directly wills or makes effort to do that which it wants done, and remains or becomes passive when it has no want or perceives no reason to be active, and hence a prior act of will is not necessary either to our willing or non-willing. This denies the premise on which the arguments of Edwards just treated of are founded.

Edwards also assumes that freedom means *power to do as one wills*, which, as it can only come after, either does not apply to or denies freedom in the act of willing. In his Part II. Section 13, he asserts that even if the will determines its own act it is not free, because it is still controlled, which, as applied to the argument, as before intimated, is equivalent to saying, the mind in its acts of willing is not free, because in them it must control its own action, and hence is constrained, or is under a necessity, to be free. I need not repeat the reasoning showing that Edwards's definition of freedom, and this assumption that whatever is controlled even by itself is not free, in which the above sophisms have their root, are wholly erroneous, and that self-control or self-direction is the distinguishing characteristic of freedom. Correct these errors, and those before mentioned in regard to will, and a large portion of his reasoning becomes either entirely futile or affirms the freedom, not of *the will*, but of *the mind in willing*.

Edwards's remarks upon "moral necessity" only tend to show that a man must will in conformity to his inclination; but, as he makes inclination synonymous with choice, preference, and will, this only tends to prove that a man must *will* in conformity to his will: or, if he uses this term inclination as designating a choice, and a prior choice, as I think would be proper, then, the argument proves that these acts of will have the condition of previous choice which Edwards assumes to be the essential condition of free acts ; while his remarks on "Moral Inability," going to show that there can be no act of will when this inclination is wanting, merely tend to prove that there can be no act of will without this essential condition of freedom ; the two arguments thus going to prove that every act of will which is *possible* must of *necessity* be free.

In regard to the difficulties which Edwards treats of in connection with "moral necessity" and "moral inability," and which he asserts the will may be unable to surmount, I have shown that the faculty of will is not in itself limited, but that we can will or make effort to do anything which we can conceive any mode of doing, and further, that these difficulties relate not to our willing, but to our obtaining the knowledge by which to direct our efforts or decide what we will try to do, which, as we are not, and cannot be, omniscient, we cannot always acquire. From "Natural Necessity," as Edwards treats it, he can only infer that a man cannot always execute what he wills, or do what he tries to do, which, coming after, cannot affect the freedom of the mind's previous act in willing.

I have also observed, that the existence of difficulties which the mind in its act of will is unable to surmount, goes to prove that the mind is the real agent in such willing, and that if its volitions are necessitated, it could have no difficulty in regard to them : and further, that in all the cases cited by Edwards the supposed difficulty really is the *absence of any want to do*, and if it were possible for the mind to overcome this difficulty, and will what it did not want to will, this would rather indicate that it did not act freely, while the impossibility of its doing so proves that in such cases it cannot possibly be unfree.

After having thus sought to prove that the will, or the soul in willing, cannot determine its own action because of the impossibility of doing it by prior acts of will, or because in the attempt it encounters difficulties which it cannot surmount, Edwards seeks to show that it is determined by some extrinsic cause or power. He argues that every event which begins to be must have a cause, *i. e.*, as he says, a *ground or reason* why it is, and that this cause must be prior to the event; that volition is such an event, and hence must be connected with some *cause in the past* on which its existence depends, and as the same causes must produce the same effects, the volition is determined by this cause to be one particular volition and can be no other. Against this I have urged that the past cannot will—put forth or produce a volition; that mind has an inherent ability to act or make effort, and that this action or effort is its volition, of which itself is the cause, and hence that the necessary connection of the effect with its cause only establishes the mind's power to control its volitions, and thus confirms its freedom in willing. And further, that the volition is in no wise dependent on the past any further than that the mind may have acquired knowledge in that past, which knowledge, however, is now present to it, and that if, from any being having power to act, and in present possession of knowledge to direct its action, the past were entirely cut off, or even if to such being there never had been any past, it could still direct its own action, or make effort to affect the future, which is always the design of effort, and hence such volition is not of necessity controlled by the extrinsic events of the past. I have further observed that, so far as we know, every intelligent being comes into existence with an object of effort—with want—and the knowledge of a means of gratifying this want, and can thus direct its effort without reference to any past.

On this point I have also argued that if the past is a cause of which volition is a necessary effect, then, as to every being there always is a past, every being must of necessity will without any cessation; and further, that if this cause is the whole past, then, as this whole past is at every instant the same to all, and the same causes necessarily produce the same effects (as perhaps any blind causes must do), the same volition must be produced in all at the same time. And if it be said that the volition in each mind is produced only by that portion of the past of which this particular mind is cognizant, then there must be some intelligent power to adapt this volition to the varying circumstances of each mind, which a blind past could not do.

To this controlling cause of volition in the past, Edwards subsequently gives the name of "motive," upon his vague definition of which I have commented. He treats inclination as a motive, but he also makes inclination synonymous with choice and will, which would make the will—the soul willing—the cause of its own act.

He also treats habit as a motive; but, as I have shown (in Book I, Chap. xi), habit is but the mind's acting in conformity to a plan before known to it, rather than to form a new one, and this conforming its action to a mode previously known, being still self-direction, does not militate against its freedom in such action. I have also shown that on analyzing the particular cases cited by Edwards, it appears that motive is but the mind's own view of some desirable effect of its contemplated effort, so that even the "ground or reason" for the act is not found in the past, but in the future, of which the mind has a present preconception. This shows that in these cases, especially selected to prove necessity, the mind directs its acts of will by its own view, *i. e.*, by its own knowledge, thus really affirming its freedom.

As touching this influence of the past, I have further

argued that though that, which by activity may become cause, may and generally does have a prior existence, yet an effect is always simultaneous with the *action* of its cause, for if the effect can be delayed for an instant, it may be for another and another, and so may never be. This would dissolve the connection which must exist between any effect actually produced and its cause, though the terms or things connected may not of necessity be uniform.

In regard to the uniformity of cause and effect, or the rule that *the same causes necessarily produce the same effects*, which is assumed by Edwards, and makes an essential link in some of his arguments for necessity, I have contended that it is not a law of *metaphysical necessity*, but an empirical result of our observations of material phenomena, and that even in them there is no sufficient ground for assuming that it is universal, and no reason to suppose that it applies to mind. That in things material it but indicates that the Supreme Intelligence has voluntarily adopted certain uniform rules for governing or directing His own actions, and that it is quite conceivable that He could have varied this plan so as to have produced a perfect variety or want of uniformity. That even infinite power must be presumed to put forth creative effort from a *want* of variety, and that the only conceivable reason why such variety is partially sacrificed to uniformity, is the absolute necessity of such uniformity to the existence of finite free agents. This uniformity in the material universe, then, instead of favoring the argument for necessity in the action of such agents, as Edwards supposes, really becomes, as a final cause, an argument that they act freely. It is conceivable that this result might have been reached by other modes, as, for instance, by establishing a law of variability, and making this law known to finite agents, but this does not conflict with the argument just deduced from the fact of uniformity, and need not be here dwelt upon.

I have also suggested that this uniformity, in things material, may arise from an infinitely wise being always knowing what is best under certain circumstances and conforming its action in each recurrence of them to this knowledge. Finite mind, too, may freely adopt general rules for its action under certain circumstances, or at each recurrence of the like circumstances may perceive the same action to be best, and freely conforming its action to its knowledge of the general rule, or of the particular fact, produce a certain degree of uniformity in its efforts and in the consequent effects. In none of these cases does the uniformity conflict with the mind's freedom, but such freedom is rather an element in producing the uniformity.

I have further urged that even admitting the rule of uniform causation, and that it applies to mind, we could only infer from it that the volitions as *effects* are necessary, and not that mind, as their *cause*, is necessitated or not free in its action. Such necessity of the *effect* is proof only of the sufficient power of mind as cause to produce it. Hence, though this assumed rule is much relied upon in the argument for necessity, its disproof is not absolutely essential either to the refutation of that argument or to the proof of freedom, and especially if it is established that mind is a first cause, acting from considerations of the *future* and not moved by power in the *past*.

Throughout his "Treatise" Edwards ignores mind

as cause, making such unintelligent things as past events, motives, and habits control and direct the course of events in the future, including human volitions. I have urged that such unintelligent things have no power or tendency to will themselves, or to produce a volition in anything else, and even if they had such power, their causative action and effects must form an infinite series running backward into the past, each link or term requiring a preceding one as its cause without the possibility of ever reaching a first cause; and if the Supreme Intelligence is admitted to be a first cause capable of *beginning* a series of events without reference to a past, then the assumption in regard to the necessity of past causality is destroyed, and cannot be urged against the position that finite intelligence in its finite sphere may act and produce effects in the future without any causative power being exerted by the past.

It appears that some of the advocates of freedom have admitted that will and choice are the same, and also that liberty implies the absence not only of extrinsic, but of self control, and hence were driven to certain positions in regard to "indifference" and "contingence" against which Edwards directs his arguments on these subjects. They are not material to the system I have advanced, and I have remarked upon them only because they afforded opportunity to elucidate my own views, and to expose some of the fallacies opposed to them. Nearly all of Edwards's reasoning upon them rests upon the erroneous definitions and assumptions already mentioned.

Another argument for necessity, adduced by Edwards, is, that the volition always follows the last dictate of the understanding, or is so connected with the understanding, as an antecedent cause, that the volition, as its effect, must be one particular volition, and can be no other. But the last dictate of the understanding is often itself a choice, which in Edwards's system is a volition and cannot follow itself. And if the understanding is a portion, power, faculty, or attribute of the mind, then, that the volition is certainly determined by the understanding only proves the mind's perfect control, and consequent freedom, in its act of willing.

The last dictate of the understanding always is a conclusion as to truths or facts in regard to the subject presented, and may be the result of effort in examining by comparison or otherwise, or may be an immediate perception of the knowing sense. In all cases it is the view or knowledge of the mind, which it can use to direct its action. This last dictate, however, is not always followed by an act of will, but in many cases, as when we compare two triangles merely to ascertain their relative size, the knowledge is itself the end sought, and leads to no subsequent effort—no act of will *follows*.

It appears, also, that the advocates for freedom have relied much upon the asserted ability of the mind to will in cases of indifference, *i. e.*, in cases in which there can be no ground of choice as between two things or two acts, and no motive to choose or do one rather than the other. Edwards attempts to show that in such cases the mind makes for itself a rule of action which becomes to it a *motive* to choose one rather than the other. I have endeavored to prove that the plan he suggests really involves the very difficulties he seeks by it to avoid, and in a greater degree, and that the mind in such cases, instead of doing something additional to construct this motive, really omits the preliminary comparison and judgment as to the things or acts which it already perceives to be equal, or ends its effort to compare with such perception of their equality, as readily as it would do with a perception that one thing is decidedly better than some other, and, in fact, comes to no choice among them. The argument on "choosing in things indifferent" derives much of its supposed importance from the assumption that to choose and to will are the same thing. Under the views I have put forth, choice, even between acting and not acting, may not be of necessity essential to an act of will, much less choice as between different acts or objects. An oyster having the faculty of will and the feeling of hunger, with only an innate knowledge of the mode of opening its bivalves, and that opening them is required to satisfy its hunger, could will to open them without comparing the act of opening with any other act. If it acts at all it must be without such comparison or consequent choice, for it knows no other act with which to compare. It could thus act even though there were no other power in existence, and of course in so doing would then be both uncontrolled and unaided, and hence the act must be wholly its own self-directed act, and, consequently, a free though but an instinctive act. Such an oyster having a faculty of will, and knowledge to direct its effort or act of will to effect what it wants, is in itself complete as a self-acting and self-directing power or cause, is a complete free agent, though with a very limited agency. Its agency is limited like that of every other order of intelligence to the sphere of its knowledge. With the knowledge of one mode of action, preliminary efforts to obtain more knowledge by comparison and consequent choice, are not essential to action, but only to *better* or to varied action, and if such preliminary efforts are unsuccessful and no choice is reached, it leaves the mind to the mode of action previously known to it. As by its own unaided efforts the oyster can to the extent of opening and shutting its bivalves influence the future, it is so far a creative first cause. It can originate action and produce effects—begin and complete a series of effects—for which there is no cause anterior to itself.

Besides the attempts to prove necessity in the mind's acts of will, by showing in the first place that it cannot determine its own action, and in the second, that its action is determined by something extrinsic to itself, Edwards has a third mode of argument seeking to prove that in point of fact volitions must be necessary because God certainly foreknows them. Admitting, for the argument, that foreknowledge of a volition, by an infallible being, involves its necessity, I have contended that for such foreknowledge there is no such necessity as Edwards asserts: that as it appeared probable that God had limited variety, as the object of His action, for the reason that uniformity in it is essential to the existence of finite free agents, so He might for a like reason limit His prescience.

Edwards asserts that foreknowledge, and especially foreknowledge of human volitions, is absolutely necessary to enable the Supreme Intelligence to govern the universe—that without it He could not provide in season for the contingencies which would arise from the unknown volitions. In opposition to this, I have urged that a being of infinite wisdom could, without knowing a single future volition of any finite being, provide in advance for every contingency which could possibly arise from free and independent finite action; and further that a being infinite in wisdom and power has no need thus to provide in advance, as He could both form and execute His plan at the instant that the emergency for it arose; that He could do this and yet conform all His acts to uniform modes, and still have in reserve, for any possible requirement, the power to depart from these uniform modes and work by miracles.

I have also argued that the actual foreknowledge of all future events, including the volitions of Himself and of all other intelligent beings, would deprive God of the highest attributes of creative intelligence, and, in fact, deny that He ever possessed them—that, though still infinite, His creative power would thereby be reduced in rank beneath that of the mere copyist and His voluntary action to the level of the lowest form of the instinctive. As between these two hypotheses, the one attributing to Deity full actual prescience and thereby, as a logical necessity, depriving Him of the highest attribute of creative power, and the other in which a self-imposed limit to His prescience still makes the continued exercise of free creative efforts with intelligent design and adaptation possible both to the finite and the Infinite Intelligence, the reader will judge which is the more reverent, which attributes the greater wisdom, and which most honors the Omniscient.

In here ending my review of this remarkable argument of Edwards, I may be permitted to say that in my efforts to expose its fallacies, as also in the direct argument which I have presented in favor of freedom, I have been actuated by a desire to find truth and to eradicate error, and though I have sought to meet the subtle reasoning of the great advocate for necessity with his own weapons, I am not conscious that either the ardor incident to polemical discussion, the pride of opinion, or any vain ambition for victory has ever diverted me from these objects. On one other point I would make a suggestion. It is in the domain of the spiritual that the highest attributes of Deity are most especially manifested. In entering it, we pass, as it were, from the material workmanship, the magnificent —the stupendous and harmonious grandeur of which so exalts our conceptions and so fills us with wonder, to that inner sanctuary of thought in which all this grandeur is designed, and there find that it is but the massive base of an ethereal superstructure still more admirable and sublime. To explore this domain is the province of the metaphysician, and however reverently he may perform his office, he is often subjected to the imputation of profanely entering the Holy of Holies, and of being rudely familiar with sacred things. How far I have avoided what would justify such imputation, and how far my efforts to advance truth have been successful, that portion of a small class of readers still attracted by the subject, of whom it may be my good fortune to obtain audience, will decide, and they will perhaps indulge me in closing this work with the expression of an earnest hope that it will be conducive to the progress and elevation of man, and a sincere belief that nothing in it will be found to lessen the love, reverence, and homage, which even the most abstract contemplation of the Character of the Most High tends to inspire.

APPENDIX.

APPENDIX.
NOTES TO BOOK I.

NOTE I. P. 7.

These views may explain the difficulty of applying mathematical reasoning to other subjects. In these we have to apply our definitions to something that exists independent of the definitions, and there is great difficulty in doing this accurately. Another difficulty is in comparing the relations of things not homogeneous in their nature. In mathematics we deal with nothing but quantity, and the whole scope of the comparison is as to its equality, or inequality, under different forms. The definitions must be perfect, for they determine the thing defined; and all the truths of Geometry are really involved in these definitions; the demonstrations under them being mere logical processes, showing that they are so involved, or that what is true, when stated in one way in the definitions, is also true when stated in another way in the propositions.

NOTE II. P. 9.

We may also, in some cases, avoid or discard sensations by acts of will. In regard to objects of vision, we may shut our eyes, or direct them to other objects, and may, at least in some degree, modify many other sensations by directing the attention to or from them by direct acts of will. By will we may select from among external objects the subjects of our attention. Though we and other intelligences may be at work altering, at each moment we recognize by the senses only what is and not what will be. What we have now observed of those sensations, which we refer to external objects, is also true of those physical sensations, which arise from our own material organism. Those, too, are external to the mind and independent of the will. We cannot, by will, feel, or avoid feeling hungry; and most persons in a normal condition can very faintly even recall or imagine the sensation of bodily pain. In sleep, that state in which the soul seems most independent of the *external* senses, it has this power; and in some conditions almost perfectly; indicating that we have undeveloped spiritual faculties by which we may retain the physical sensations, without the material organs of sense.

NOTE III. P. 13.

In the bodily movements we are conscious of acting upon distinct members occupying distinct positions in space, and that when we move the hand and when we move the foot there is a difference both in the object and in the effort. There is generally some remoter object of an effort for bodily movement, as to move from one place to another by walking, using our limbs as the instrument for this purpose.

In the efforts for mental change we may perhaps be conscious of using the material organism of the brain as an instrument, but if so, as this occurs in every kind of effort, it furnishes no means of distinguishing the efforts from each other. Perhaps we only resort to the organic brain as a means of exciting sensations in the mind, which we use, as we use language, symbols, or counters, to condense and to mark the progress, positions, or relations of our ideas. If, as the phrenologists assert, we use different portions of the brain for different processes or objects, still these portions have been named from these processes or objects, and have not furnished the name for the corresponding efforts, and what they assert, if established, would not indicate different active agents or powers, but only that the same active agent in its different efforts uses different organic instruments.

NOTE IV. P. 16.

In the first class of these cases, any effort of which we are conscious is to comprehend the meaning of the terms, rather than to judge as to the truth they express when understood; but in the last case, the truth is no less really involved in the terms than in the others, but being less obviously so, effort is required to discover it. If, instead of seeking to know the truth of the expression, that the angles of a plane triangle are equal to two right angles, we seek to find the measure of those angles, the case will more widely differ from the first class. The limit of simple perception, or of the capacity for perceiving truth without previous effort in arranging our knowledge of the subject, varies not only in different individuals, but in the same individual at different times. If this capacity were infinite, the acquisition of any knowledge whatever would require no other effort than that of directing attention to the subject, and if the attention of a being of such capacity could also embrace all objects, every truth would be immediately apprehended by it. Such a being would be, or at least could be, omniscient.

NOTE V. P. 25.

In regard to processes of thought, a question arises somewhat analogous to that hereafter suggested in regard to matter in motion, viz. :—Does it require an effort, an exercise of power, to continue or to stop them? The mind is pursuing a logical train, does it require the exercise of the will at each step to advance it? or can it, by simple perception of the relations of the terms, anticipate the successive steps, and going on without any exercise of the will, require such exercise to stop it at any point short of the final result of the argument, or of the mind's non-perception of any further results? It is obvious that the simple perceptions of the mind at every stage of the logical process, whether such perceptions have or have not required a preliminary effort, have a determinate limit beyond which the mind has not progressed, and that it is here for the instant arrested till, either by its own effort or by some extrinsic power, the obstruction to its mental vision is removed, or such arrangements made of its ideas as will enable it to get another perception reaching farther into the subject. The perception is always immediate and instantaneous; there is no momentum carrying it beyond the point to which the mind actually sees. A gleam from truth may flash upon us and be immediately lost, requiring further search to find the gem; and when found we may deem closer examination requisite to ascertain if it is pure and genuine.

However this may be, it seems certain that the mind cannot directly determine the successive steps by a mere act, or exercise of its will; for these must depend upon the absolute relations which the mind perceives among the terms of the argument; and hence, the *result* is not a product of the will, though the *process* by which the result is reached, or made palpable to simple mental perceptions may be, and generally is. So of those other processes of thought in which the mind examines and searches for truth without the intervention of words; directly analyzing, combining and comparing the *objects* of its thoughts, as originally perceived or apprehended, instead of first putting them in words. The observed relations here, too, control the progress of the thoughts, and the final result is not dependent on the will. The only difference between the two cases is, that in pursuing the one, the logical train, the mind is directed to its conclusions by the relations it perceives among the terms, while in the other, it is directed by the relations it perceives among the things themselves. If we *happen* to see two fragile bodies moving rapidly toward each other in the same right line, we, with our past experience, may perceive, *without any effort of will*, that one or both will be broken; and if we have in view the expression $x - 1 = 5$, we may in like manner perceive that $x = 6$; and so of more complicated forms of expression. Though we may will to seek out the relations, we cannot by will change our perceptions of the relations which we perceive whether sought or unsought. They are real and immutable existences or truths which we cannot alter by will or exclude from our belief any more than on examining the subject we can by will exclude the results that $2+2=4$, or that all the angles of a plane triangle are equal to two right angles. So far then as our knowledge is derived from sensation and from thought, the influence of our exercise of will is limited to the quantity of time and the amount of effort we apply to its acquisition; and to a selection from among the various subjects suggested by external or internal agencies, to which this time and effort shall be directed. These questions as to whether an effort of the mind is required to continue or to stop its train of thought, or whether it can recognize certain consequences of its observations or certain relations of its thoughts without such effort, are really questions as to the limits of simple mental perception, and are still more analogous to those relating to sensation than to matter in motion. I see a tree and a stone before me without any effort. How far I perceive the relations of the two without effort may be a question; and so, also, it may not be ascertained how far the mind perceives the relations of its ideas or of its various knowledge without effort, and this is not essential to our inquiry. For this, the facts that we have some knowledge, intuitive or acquired, without effort, and that by proper effort our knowledge may be increased, are sufficient. We cannot by will vary the facts or truths as they appear to the mind, nor even wholly exclude them. To be able to vary them by will, would be but an ability to destroy our power to find truth. Mind cannot banish any thought or thing from it by direct effort or will, for to will not to think of or not to attend to anything is still to think of or to attend to it, and it is only by directing its thoughts to something else, that it can by effort get rid of its present thoughts or images. It cannot always avoid them. Other intelligences, infinite and finite, have, to some extent the power to impress their thoughts, their creations, upon us, whether we will or not. In regard to the power of the mind to control the results of its investigations, it may, perhaps, be urged that we will to examine only those facts and arguments which lead to the particular result which we wish to establish, avoiding those on the other side. But, in such case, a man conscious of this cannot be said to have acquired any knowledge. He may be prepared to assume and defend a position, but the fact that he has intentionally made his examination a partial one for the very purpose of arriving at the particular result, and done so from apprehension that an impartial examination would not lead to it, is conclusive upon himself that he knows the result is not to be relied upon; and hence, he must be in doubt as to the result,* or rather, just so far as he has interfered by his will, he has entirely failed to obtain any knowledge; and, of course, the result cannot affect the conclusion we have just arrived at in regard to the relations of will

---

* This is probably the foundation of a not uncommon religious belief that, before we can know anything aright, the will must be brought into a state of subjection to God: that we must, in contemplating His manifestations become passive—become as a little child—which having formed no theory, and having no interest to pervert truth, passively perceives and accepts the conclusions from observation and reflection, without any inclination or effort to mould them to its prejudices, pride of opinion, or interest.

to our knowledge. What we have said on this subject is equally applicable to all our beliefs and opinions, of every degree of certainty or probability. We cannot control them in the process of acquisition; and once acquired, they cannot be changed by our merely willing such change. The opposite view that belief is dependent on the will seems to have led to honest persecution for *opinions* deemed heretical.

NOTE VI. P. 25.

As the mind cannot act except by exercising some of its powers, every act of mind is an effort or act of will; and the phrases, acts of will, acts of mind, and mental action are really synonymous. If the mind is moved, except in or by the exercise of its own power, it must be by some extrinsic power, and so far is as passive in such movement as is the stone which is so moved. It is not itself then active, but is the passive subject of action. We may be moved by external agencies and in this be passive; when we move ourselves we must be active and we have no means of moving ourselves except by act of will or effort. We are *moved* by distress to pity, without our own action; the emotion springs directly from knowledge, which may have required no effort; but when we would relieve that distress by any act of our own, we must will—make effort. In acquiring knowledge,—in learning what is—by simple mental perception, either of things or ideas, the mind may make no effort. But when it seeks by the exercise of its own powers to know something which it does not now know, or *to do* anything whatever to change the existing state of things—to influence the future—it must make effort, it must will; and conversely, whatever is done without its effort is not done by it, but must be by some other power of which it can at most be but an instrument.

The deciding and the willing of the mind are sometimes confounded. The phrases *decided to do* and *willed to do* are frequently used as equivalent. This arises from a decision being, at least very generally, preliminary to an act of will; but there are many decisions of the mind which involve no coexisting or subsequent act of will, as its conclusions in regard to abstract truths, or when it decides not to attempt any change, not to interfere by any exercise of its power with the course of events. In this last case, as the willing is the means by which we effect change, if the decision is the willing, we should have to say we willed not to will. There is a manifest distinction between the cases in which the decision is not, and those in which it is, attended or followed by some action to effect change. In the latter we are conscious that the decision is followed by a mental affection, which we term effort, and without which the effect, though we may conceive of it and view it as in itself desirable, would not follow. The decision is the final conclusion or judgment of the mind as to doing; and when it has decided to do, it executes its decision, so far as it has power, by an effort. It does or tries to do what it decided to do. A decision or final judgment is but an addition to our knowledge, in some cases as to what already is or will be, and in others as to what is best for us to do. This decision or judgment may have been an immediate perception, or it may have required a preliminary effort, but this does not conflict with the assertion that the decision is not the willing, but tends to confirm it, as knowledge, whether a simple perception or acquired by effort, is not an act of will.

NOTE VII. P. 32.

Professor Bowen, in his very able "Lowell Lectures," gives a negative reply to all these positions. He rests his conclusions on the premise that matter cannot move itself or direct its own motion, which is also the basis of my reasoning, and I do not perceive that his reaches farther than mine, or proves that matter *in motion* may not be an independent cause or that it could not be used as an instrument to prolong and extend the effects of intelligent action. I much desired to make such proof, but found no way to do it. I desired it not only to simplify the question of free agency, but also to facilitate the proof that God still exists; which we both treat as deducible from the proposition that matter has no causative power.

I may here further observe that the views I have advanced in Book II., in regard to the law of cause and effect, and my inference, from the observed uniformity of things external to us, of a design in the Supreme Intelligence to provide for finite free agents, also closely resemble those put forth by Professor Bowen. My conclusions on all these topics having been reached, written, and discussed with my friends, before his lectures were delivered, could not have been influenced even by the infusion and circulation of his views in the common atmosphere of thought, and hence are entitled to that greater consideration and credence, which are properly accorded to the concurrent results of independent mental action.

NOTE VIII. P. 35.

If bodies in motion produce effects on other bodies by impinging against them, it must be by giving motion to those at rest, or by stopping, retarding, accelerating, or changing the direction of those in motion; and if moving bodies strike on opposite sides of a body at rest, it cannot move both ways at the same time; and hence, a loss of some of the power of matter in motion. If bodies impinge with equal aggregate force on opposite sides of the same body, then the motive power of all such impinging bodies may be destroyed and no new force is communicated to the intervening body. If the bodies thus impinging either on an intervening body or directly against each other, are perfectly elastic, then so far as our observation informs us, they would acquire equal force in the opposite directions, and the result would be the same as though no body had intervened and no direct collision occurred except that the impinging particles would have exchanged with each other and each turned back on the lines on which, but for the collision, the other would have moved. But in case of such elasticity it is demonstrable that the impinging bodies must come to a state of rest, and being but inert matter, they could not put themselves in motion again.

If, as is now asserted, the force of the impinging bodies, when they are arrested, is converted into heat, still that heat often assumes a passive form, as in coal, requiring some active cause to develope and make it efficient, and in this view the heat which is stored in the coal is but an instrument by which this cause makes itself effective. It matters little to our argument whether the active cause produces force by means of the heat reserved in the coal or by putting quiescent matter in motion.

NOTE IX. P. 35.

The apparent power of matter in motion to produce effects, of course without design in the matter, is probably the foundation of those notions of a blind chance in the succession of events, which, in some form or other, seem always to have had a place in the popular mind. Matter once put in motion by intelligence might, after it had produced all the effects intended, go on to produce other effects; or before the completion of the intended effects, it might produce other effects which were not intended. These are said to come to pass by chance or accident, and though frequently used interchangeably, I think that in common discourse the former is more generally applied to effects without or beyond the scope of the design, and the latter to such as incidentally happen within it, and are either unexpected or counter to the design.

NOTE X. P. 38.

It is not necessary to suppose that this energy is really constant *everywhere*. If all changes in matter, and all activity within the universe of our knowledge, were suddenly suspended and to remain so for millions of years, as measured by something without that universe, and all simultaneously put in motion again, beginning where, or as, it left off, we never could know it. The succession would be the same to us as if there had been no interruption.

NOTE XI. P. 39.

It is only by a figure of speech or, perhaps a contraction of language, that matter is said to *do* anything; and the recent change of expression from "moving" to "being moved" is, so far, more strictly philosophical.

NOTE XII. P. 43.

This finite presence, or presence co-extensive with knowledge, answers all the purposes of spirit, for, if we exclude the phenomena of the bodily sensations and muscular action, nothing is gained by our being actually moved in space; and hence, so far as our spiritual nature is concerned, this finite presence of man within the sphere of what he actually knows is as perfect as the omnipresence of the Supreme Being in His infinite sphere of knowledge. Our limited, incomplete and fading knowledge in many things requires to be renewed and augmented by means of the senses which, for this purpose, must be brought within sensible distance of their objects.

NOTE XIII. P. 47.

It seems that by long dwelling on an idea, or from some excited or abnormal sensitiveness of the mind, it sometimes loses the power to change or annihilate its own creations, and they become to it as external realities, producing, if partial, monomania, or, if general, causing one species of insanity.

NOTE XIV. P. 49.

It may be apprehended by some that this ascribing all the creative powers of Deity to man, in however small degree, may unduly arouse his pride and excite his presumption. If there be such a one, let him essay any comparison, even the most trifling. Let him observe yonder towering elm mirthfully rustling its foliage as if titillated by the awkward attempts of its neighboring spire to appear graceful. Or first looking upon nature,—the great picture which God exhibits to us as His own creation,—turn from it to the most exquisite painting of a Claude Lorraine or a Salvator Rosa, perhaps grouping a few trees, a glimpse of water, a speck of green sward, floating clouds and dubious rays of sunshine, &c., &c., and in the comparison, the works of man, even those which, as the highest efforts of his creative genius, excite our profoundest admiration, will appear sufficiently Lilliputian, sufficiently paltry and insignificant, not to say mean and even ludicrous, to induce a becoming modesty, to attemper his pride and humble all that is haughty and arrogant in his nature; and in the comparison he may realize that there is something more than a mere abstraction in the mathematical dogma that no increase of the finite can alter its ratio to the infinite. He may here observe, too, what we have before intimated, that the *conceptions* of the human mind are more perfect, more Godlike, than the *expression*. For ourselves, we apprehend no evil tendency in the exaltation of man to the conscious dignity and responsibility of a being endowed with creative power. We believe he is too apt to take debasing views of himself, to consider meanness and wrong as appropriate or necessary to his condition and attributable to the natural weakness and imperfections of his being, rather than to his own agency, or his own neglect properly to exercise the powers he has at command. We believe, too, that it is essential to even an imperfect conception of any one of God's attributes, that we should ourselves possess it in some measure. Without this, we have no means of estimating the vast difference, and can no more form even a remote conception of how much greater God is than His creatures, than we can tell the proportion between seven acres and three hours. The proper effect then of the finite mind having the same attributes, is to enable it to form more adequate conceptions of the Infinite and make itself more sensible of its inferiority; and if, as we have supposed *may* be the case, its efforts are made effective through the uniform modes of God's action, the finite becomes wholly dependent on the Infinite for the *execution* of *its designs* and for the *effectiveness* of its efforts; and these considerations, in this connection, are eminently calculated to inspire gratitude and imbue us with humility.

NOTE XV. P. 58.

As already remarked, a being, satisfied with things as they are, cannot be said to feel a want, and he makes no effort, he does not will any change. If he perceives that causes external to him are doing what he wants done without his agency, then, if his want is only to have it done or to know that it will be done, his want is gratified by perceiving that it will be done. But perhaps he wants to know that it is actually done by these external causes; and to. this end an effort of attention is still required to gratify his want.

NOTE XVI. P. 61.

Even in cases of instinctive action, though, for reasons hereafter stated, we do not have to seek for knowledge to apply, or even to arrange the order of successive efforts, still it seems impossible that we should conform our action to the perceived circumstances—to the occasion demanding such action—without some intermediate effort, however instantaneous it may be, the need of which effort, as already suggested, may be intuitively known. However this may be, we early learn the importance of considering the circumstances before we yield to instinctive impulses, and of adapting our actions to them, and thus are led to introduce conscious deliberation, either as a wholly new element or as an increase of one already existing, thereby changing the features or character of the action.

NOTE XVII. P. 75.

CONFLICTING WANTS.—There may be conflicting wants between which the mind must decide. If, for instance, a man with only bread and water at command is both hungry and thirsty, he must decide which want he will first make effort to relieve. Or if, with the want to move out of some apprehended danger, there is co-existing the conflicting want of bodily repose, then he must decide between them by a comparison of his preconceptions of the future effects of his conduct. No matter how short the plan of action, or of how few steps it may be composed, he may make the comparison. Even if the conflict is merely between effort and repose, one of the preconceptions being then limited to the mere making of effort, if we perceive in advance that effort will be painful or pleasurable, it furnishes a subject of comparison with the painful or pleasurable effects of not making the effort.

It is conceivable that we may *want* not to make any effort, and that, under the influence of this want, we would not examine as to any effort required by any other conflicting want. This is equivalent to supposing that there is no want of change, or that the want of repose is a conflicting and, in the view of the mind, a permanent want. If, with this supposed and eventually paramount want not to act, there is a co-existing, conflicting want, the mind must recognize it, for that which is not recognized by the mind cannot be its want. It cannot then shut out the presentation of the question, or the petition of its other want;* and its subsequent non-action is proof that it has decided upon it.

It is, however, doubtful whether we can ever properly be said to have a want *not* to act. We may want to make effort, but there are distinctions between the want to make effort, or the want of effort, and the effort itself. In the first place, the distinction between the want and the thing wanted; and in the second place, that between the want of effort generally and a particular effort; we may be disposed to effort and yet some particular efforts be undesirable, and even with this want of effort generally, any particular effort not yet made or determined must be a preconception

---

* The popular idea that the right of petition should be utterly inviolable seems thus to have its origin in the lowest depths of the constitution of our spiritual being. It might be curious to trace out the analogy of its association with the idea of liberty, in its metaphysical and in its political relations.

and not a want. Hence, it can never in the first instance be a conflicting want, but only one of the modes of gratifying our want of effort, and as such, as just intimated, may come into comparison with other preconceived modes. In other words, what may be represented in terms as negatively a want not to make effort, generally is either the absence of all want, or the presence of the positive want of repose. In the one case there is no disposition or indisposition to effort, and in the other, any such indisposition arises from a preconception that the effort if made will conflict with the *want* of repose; and hence, is not the means to be adopted to gratify that want, and is subject to comparison with other preconceptions of the effects of not acting. The forming of the preconceptions of the effect of acting or not acting is itself, for the time being, action; and if with the want of repose a conflicting want is actually presented to the mind, it must decide upon it, at least so far as to dispose of it by considering its merits, or deciding not to consider them.

In the wants of activity and repose we have the last analysis of wants, and here find elements which enter into all our preconceptions for the gratification of other wants. The pleasure or pain of the particular effort, with its anticipated consequences, enters into the comparison of different modes of action. If, when wanting repose, the pain of effort itself, as perceived in advance, either from its proximity or other circumstance, appears greater than the anticipated or apprehended painful results of not acting, or even just equal to them, no further effort than that required to ascertain this fact will be made. So, too, if, when wanting activity, the pleasure of effort itself appears to be just balanced by the anticipated consequent pain of acting, or by the pleasure expected from not acting, no effort will be made. It is then as if the mind had no want to do, and it will not do. In such cases, though it may still know and enjoy or suffer, it is but the passive subject of changes in its own sensations, produced by other and extrinsic causes in which itself had no agency. From this inert or passive state the mind is aroused to effort by want, which may occur and recur without any antecedent effort; and then by means of its knowledge, which also may exist without antecedent effort to obtain it, can direct its effort intelligently.

NOTE XVIII. P. 88.

By memory of a continuity of those changes in our sensations, the sense of identity might still be preserved, even though the will and all its pre-requisite processes of thought were annihilated. Without will, we might still know ourselves as the subjects acted upon, but could never know ourselves as cause. If this view is correct, the personal identity does not of necessity inhere solely in the will.

NOTE XIX. P. 101.

If our first parents had no knowledge of good and evil, in any sense,' they *must* have been in constant communication with God, and as immediately directed and governed by His will as mere matter is.

NOTE XX. P. 109.

These views are in harmony with one indicated in the last chapter, that *deliberation* is superinduced upon some more primitive mental processes.

NOTE XXI. P. 115.

Many brute animals do not know enough to flee from a fire. The horse will not leave his stall, though the stable is burning about him. We might suppose him palsied by terror; but if forced away he runs back again. It seems to be a voluntary act, founded on the association of safety with his stall. Children, when frightened, will in like manner run into danger to seek refuge in their mother's arms.

NOTE XXII. P. 116.

There is no doubt that the intuitive knowledge varies very materially in different animals; and there is, at least, some ground for supposing that it varies also in the individuals of the same species. It seems, however, certain that in all not higher in the scale of intelligence than man, voluntary action has always its base in the instinctive, though the superstructure which constitutes the *plan* of action may be wholly rational. This appears from the consideration that the immediate object of every act of will is to produce muscular or mental activity, for which we only know one mode, and that intuitively, and hence such action is always in itself instinctive. The difference between the instinctive and the rational is not in the knowledge of the mode of acting, but in the mode by which we came to know the *order of the succession* of our acts to reach the end sought.

In regard to the difference in the intuitive knowledge of individuals of the same species it may be remarked that it is not only conceivable, but is matter of common belief, that the *natural* calculators, as the term implies, have an intuitive perception of the relations of numbers, or, at least, an intuitive knowledge of some mode of ascertaining such relation, through which they *instinctively* reach results which others obtain in rational modes only by much time and labor. It is worthy of remark that those who exhibit this knowledge can give no more account of its origin, or even of their mode of obtaining their results, than others can give of their knowledge and modes in regard to muscular movements. If the natural calculator has only such intuitions as enable him easily to *form plans* by which, with very little effort, he reaches his results, his action is still rational. The *amount* of his knowledge, though it may enable him to make his plans more perfect and in less time, does not affect the nature of the act, which is still in conformity to a plan of his own contriving, using his superior knowledge for that purpose. If he only adopts rules or plans which he finds ready formed in his mind, without any investigation of his own, his action is instinctive. If he knows that, by looking for it in his mind, he will there perceive the result as a man perceives it in a table, without going through any process by any rule or plan, the action approaches as nearly as possible to that produced by an external power,—to mere mechanical action. But, as the action still requires an effort to apply the knowledge of this mode of obtaining the result, it is still voluntary and instinctive. So, also, of the natural bone setter. If he has by intuition such knowledge of anatomy as to enable him thereby to *form his own plans*, his action is as rational as if he had learned the same at a medical college. I speak of these phenomena as they exist in popular belief, and have not given to them the examination required to form an intelligent opinion as to their nature or existence. I will, however, observe that it only requires a modified form of one of our senses, an introverted sense of bodily feeling, to enable one to obtain through it, all, and perhaps more than all, the knowledge of the anatomical structure of the system, which can be derived through the sense of sight from dissection, or from the observation of prepared specimens; and that it does not seem more surprising that some men should intuitively have a knowledge of the relations of numbers and the results of their combinations, than that an animal, blindfolded and carried by circuitous and zigzag routes, should know the direct course back to the point from whence it started.

NOTE XXIII. P. 116.

Winking the eye when it needs to be moistened is probably instinctive. The infant knows *when* and *how* to do it as well as the adult, and apparently does it with as much facility. In the adult the attention and the effort required to do it being almost imperceptible, it is liable to be confounded with the involuntary and mechanical on the one hand, while to the more careful analyst it may appear not certain that it does not belong to the rational on the other. If we do not know that moving the lid will relieve the unpleasant feeling in the eye, we will not will to wink for such purpose, and if under such circumstances the lid moves, its movements must be attributed to some cause not of us; and in such case, is as purely mechanical as the movements of the planetary system.*

* The difficulty in applying conventional language to metaphysical inquiries is, perhaps, well illustrated by the fact that the distinction, apparently so broad and palpable as that between mechanical and voluntary, is really not well defined. In some connections the term voluntary would apply only to the volitions. But it has been transferred to the sequences of volitions; and hence, we say the *muscular movement* which we will is voluntary; but, in cases of cramp, or convulsion, it is involuntary or not willed. If we conceive of matter as having been in motion from eternity, and as continuing and producing movements and changes of itself, then these movements and changes are undoubtedly mechanical; but when such changes in matter are produced or directed by a voluntary agent, acting mediately or immediately, their character is more or less changed—we name them from appearances generally—and when we do not recognize the immediate or present acting of a voluntary agent, we call them mechanical. But how close and how *apparent* the connection must be before the term voluntary is applicable, does not seem to be well settled. But all movements of matter must probably be referred to the will of an intelligent being;. and if the universe is the material form with which the Infinite Spirit is associated, as the human frame with its finite spirit, the movement of a planet would, in this view, seem to be as much a voluntary movement, as the movements of our feet, when we will to walk.

On the other hand, it may be said that if a finger is suddenly thrust toward the eye the mind may immediately perceive or judge that there may not be time to consider whether it will reach the eye or not. The injury might be done during the time required to consider this; and hence, it is at once obvious that to insure safety the act of winking must be immediate, without considering any other plan, the future consequences of the action, or even the present necessity for it. Any confidence which we might on reflection have that the finger would not be thrust upon the eye, cannot avail, for the mind has not time to consider this fact. The danger appears imminent and the mind decides almost instantaneously, but its decision may still be a result of the exercise of its rational powers in comparing, &c., or in seeking a mode adapted to the end sought, and, if so, its action by a plan founded upon knowledge thus acquired, or even upon knowledge now acquired by immediate simple perception, and not upon an innate knowledge of the mode, is a rational action. In further confirmation of this view, it may be said that if the finger approaches the eye slowly, it is not immediately closed; but the mind then judging that there is time to adopt the usual precaution of examining the circumstances preparatory to action, does examine; it deliberates as to whether it will be necessary to make any effort to avoid the finger, and if so, what effort. The action must then be in conformity to its own plan, even though its knowledge of the mode it adopts is intuitive; for the adopting of that mode is an exercise of its rational faculties, using the intuitive knowledge of the mode with other knowledge to form its plan of action with reference to a certain future result; and if, when the finger moves slowly, the action is a rational one, it may be difficult to determine at what particular velocity of the finger the action to avoid it becomes instinctive, if it ever does.

But our previous reasoning would go to show that if an external object with the velocity of lightning flashes upon the eye, producing pain or apprehension of injury, and *we* wink for *its* relief or protection, this *may* still be a rational action, though it may not be in time for the purpose intended.

Whether the action be *instinctive* or *rational*, it may become *habitual;* but if the former, nothing is perhaps gained by the transition to the latter, as it may be as easy for the mind to act from the original *intuitive knowledge*, *the innate conception of the mode* of relieving or protecting the eye by moving the lid over it, as from memory of the practice under the same mode, even after any number of repetitions. It is when we know of various modes of action adapted to the same occasions that habit lessens the time and labor of deciding by furnishing a mode before decided upon under similar circumstances.

I have stated what appears to me to be the general rule of distinction between instinctive and rational action. To remove some of the difficulties in applying this rule, to determine to which class certain actions belong, is perhaps rather in the province of the naturalist than of the metaphysician; and by actual observation they may, perhaps, be able to determine whether the movement of the lid to moisten the eye, or to protect it from external violence, is, in either or both cases, *instinctive*. I would, further, here suggest the question, whether the intuitive knowledge of animals leads them to examine the surrounding circumstances before acting, and to conform their instinctive actions to them before they have learned by *experience* to do so? Whether, for instance, if a kid's first want is to walk to its mother's breast, and water intervenes, it will walk into it, or around it, or not walk at all? That there is an adaptation of the intuitive knowledge of the modes of instinctive action to the peculiar wants of the animal is obvious from numerous facts already observed, as that a chicken will not go into water, while a duckling will immediately embrace the first opportunity of doing so.

NOTE XXIV. P. 119.

Though this distinction can be conceived of and expressed in terms, it is yet so slight as to raise a doubt as to whether it practically amounts to anything. The difference in working from direct knowledge, or from the memory of that knowledge, may amount to nothing; though working from a direct knowledge, or from memory of *previous actions*, conformed to that knowledge, may.

NOTE XXV. P. 123.

The influence of this saving of labor in the *plan* is evinced in the fact that when we have a plan ready formed, which may be worked in and made a part of the one now required, we will often use it, though we may know that in all probability less labor will be required to *execute* one entirely new.

NOTE XXVI. P. 130.

Some persons prefer to have these emotions excited without intellectual effort, as in games of mere chance; and those, who are absorbed by the labor of providing for physical subsistence, and who have no intellectual or moral wants demanding effort, may yet want a quasi exercise of those powers, which such wants would call into action, or want the excitement which usually attends such exercise. They may want to be *aroused* by effort, but, degraded by grovelling pursuits, or enervated by luxury, idleness, or dissipation, do not want to make the effort. To such, if not controlled by humane feelings, exhibitions of bullbaits, cockfights, and gladiatorial conflicts afford the required gratification without taxing their own powers. These views indicate that a popular passion for what we call the barbarous sports is not so much the result of that savage state in which the activities have full play in providing for personal defence or security and for the absolute wants of life, as of that highly artificial condition of society in which large portions of the community are overtasked in mere drudgery, and other large portions relieved from the necessity of laboring for physical existence, without the substitution of intellectual or moral objects of effort. It is only one phase of sensualism. The Romans, supported in luxury by their slaves and their conquered provinces, with the love of the coarse and intense excitement engendered in war, would, in times of repose, naturally resort to such exhibitions of effort, intensified to the sanguinary and violent. The rude Indian tortures his captive to increase his own security, or to revenge the wrongs of himself or tribe, and not from that mere wantonness which is the product of a highly artificial and sensual condition of society.

NOTE XXVII. P. 140.

When the knowledge of means is intuitive, it is so closely associated with the want, that it is liable to be taken either for a part or for a necessary consequence of it, and thus the knowledge be confounded with, or attributed to, the want.

NOTE XXVIII. P. 147.

LOGIC.—The knowledge of abstract truth does not necessarily produce any want. It may itself be the object of an effort, which may end in gratifying the want which induced it—the want for some particular knowledge or truth. Hence, as a *want* is essential to voluntary action, a mere conviction of truth does not directly demand such action. A man does not will because he is convinced by demonstrative argument that the angles of a plane triangle are equal to two right angles. The *fact* may gratify a previous want to know, but does not of necessity awaken any new want. A pleasurable *emotion* attending the discovery of the fact, or the exercise of his powers in making it, may induce a want for the repetition of such emotion, and corresponding efforts of the mind to produce it. A perception of some prospective application of such knowledge may also do this. So, too, if he is convinced that a certain act is right and proper, it does not influence his will, unless he *wants* to do what is right and proper. Touch his sensibilities by presenting to him distress, or so portraying it that in imagination it becomes present; enable him to participate in and to anticipate the pleasurable emotions of relieving it, and a want to relieve is induced.*

Hence it is that mere logical results, however high and holy the truths demonstrated, do not touch the springs of voluntary action. In following the demonstrative argument we but perceive the relations between the terms; and before they influence effort, we must make an application of such results to actual existence and dwell upon the new relations evolved by the new results, till they take hold of our affections and assume some form of want. The logic which merely demonstrates, however clearly and forcibly, the *advantages* of holiness, does not of itself move us to effort.

---

* The high morality, the generosity of the act, in such cases, consist in his deriving pleasure from making others happy, or perhaps a higher morality, a purer disinterestedness are evinced in his yielding to an instinctive or innate want to relieve distress without any conscious reference to himself, showing that he has not depraved his moral nature, but that its delicate sympathies make the sufferings of others his own ; and relieving it in others, a relief or gratification to himself; while the man who seeks out occasions for the exercise of such beneficent feelings, shows that he has cultivated this innate want and has come to want the occasions for exercising his generosity, or by vigilant examination to relieve himself even from the apprehension that there is some as yet undiscovered suffering requiring his action to relieve.

For this there must be a want, and to excite such want in our moral nature, one magnanimous act, one exhibition of tenderness, one manifestation of self-sacrificing devotion to principle, one delineation of true, unselfish love, one image of a Redeemer by pure and sublime ideas, so elevated above all vulgar passions and resentments as to look down with a divine love and compassion upon those who reviled and tortured Him, may be more efficacious than all the calculations of utility which selfishness has ever suggested, or all the verbal arguments, which human ingenuity has ever devised.

Hence religion, though she may stoop to meet the attacks of the sceptical logician on his own ground, has a more congenial ally in *taste*, which, in the moral as well as in the physical, is often a precursor and incentive to *want;* in the former generally applied to the more refined and cultivated wants of our spiritual being; and the propagandist finds in the beauties of eloquent expression; in the graces, or the sublimity of poetry; in architectural grandeur; in lifelike delineations of reality, or of ideal conceptions on canvas; in sculptured marble, cold and inflexible as logic itself, but still embodying some lofty conception, or some form of beauty; a more direct and ready emotive influence to arouse the soul with a sense of its own sublime nature and inspire it with devotional feeling, than it can command from the most towering and most successful efforts of the intellect to demonstrate, in terms, the loftiest problems of humanity.

Even in the concord of evanescent sounds, the soul finds an analogy, a moulding or shadowing to the senses, of its own harmonious variety, of its own aspirations, swelling into ecstasy in effort and smoothly subsiding into the luxury of contemplative repose. All these manifestations of art may fitly introduce and induce a want for the development and cultivation of those pure and elevated sentiments of which they but give the first suggestive taste;* and those who have consecrated the power of genius to

---

* I trust that I shall not be suspected of intending lightly to use this word—taste—in a double sense. To my mind there is a profound significance in such relations of a term as I have here attempted to shadow, showing how deep, in the common reason of man, the roots of his form of expression may lie; and suggesting that, even if a merely arbitrary term is used, it is gradually fitted and jostled, by this common reason, into harmonious relations with a whole range of ideas, with only one of which, in its first

the service of truth and virtue, have ever been assigned a high place among the benefactors of their race, while those who pervert it to make vice fascinating and seductive, are justly regarded as vilely treacherous to God and man.

When, instead of the logical or prosaic mode of examining things by means of the relations of the terms by which we represent those things, we look at the actual existences themselves as recognized by the senses, or as made present to the mind by the exercise of its poetic powers, the things are present, or by a scenic illusion appear so, and, in either case, any fact or relation, which does not harmonize with our views or feelings, presents a *want* of change to the mind for its action.

We may remark that, as it is mainly by means of these same poetic faculties that the future effect of an effort in gratifying the want is made present, we here find the wants and the means of their gratification growing side by side in the same common soil. As before remarked, it is in the accuracy of the preconceptions of the future and a proper selection among them, that the mind manifests its ability in action; and hence, the poetic faculty, not only by its power to examine the relation of things as they primarily and naturally exist, instead of the relation of the artificial terms by which those things are represented; but by its prophetic power of imagining, or conceiving of what does not yet exist, is really the basis of that common sense, which is so useful in the conduct of the affairs of life. He, who most clearly imagines, conceives, foresees the future, is, so far, best prepared to act wisely and sagaciously; and, in this respect, the man who perceives has the advantage of him who reasons.

The logician is proverbially liable to great mistakes in practical affairs, to exhibitions of a want of common sense; but it is not so generally admitted that the poetic faculty corrects, or avoids the errors of the reasoning. It seems a desecration to put such noble endowments as our poetic and prophetic faculties to the vulgar, practical uses of daily life. It is taking the lightning from the skies to be the drudge of our workshops; but this is analogous to the influence of electricity, much diluted, in many of the most common and sluggish changes of matter.

adaptation, it had any perceptible affinity; that this common reason perceives and marks in expression those delicate similitudes of thought, which the reasoning of the philosopher is slow in developing

NOTE XXIX. P. 149.

I use the phrases "morally right" and "morally wrong," as applicable to the intelligent being that wills, and not to the good or evil effects of his action generally. Such *effects* may be injurious when the *intentions* were most beneficent and morally right and good.

NOTE XXX. P. 150.

ON FORMING PRECONCEPTIONS AND ACQUIRING IDEAS.—The forming of a preconception preparatory to action is generally a tentative process; the mind noting what will be the effect of one plan of action, and then varying the plan to obviate some defect, or to ascertain if some other is not better. It may, however, sometimes happen that the first plan so completely fulfils all the conditions required, that no further investigation seems necessary.

When the same want has repeatedly existed under the same circumstances, the mind adopts a previous plan from memory and association and acts from habit, saving itself the labor of re-investigation. The investigation, by which the mind determines its preconception, is only one of the cases in which it applies the knowledge it already has to acquire other knowledge. In doing this, it adopts one of two modes. It may examine the facts presented until it is enabled to determine the truth; or, after a partial examination, it may form an hypothesis, which appears probable, or, at least, possible, and then examine whether such hypothesis is compatible with all the facts. In the former case, the mind does not seek to arrive at a particular idea, but to arrive at truth. In the latter, it seeks to ascertain whether the idea it has formed is true. If the object were merely to get a particular idea into the mind without reference to its fulfilling the conditions required in that idea, as, for instance, its being true, no effort for such object could be made; for the idea must then be in the mind before the *want* of it could be determined, and the whole object of the effort would already be accomplished. The want of a particular, definite idea must be a want that is already gratified, and of course is no longer a want. No such want then can exist, and no effort founded on such want is possible. We may have an idea, which we perceive is incomplete and not well defined, and *want* and make *effort* to complete it, or to define it more accurately, that is, to get a more full, or more clear and definite idea of the subject. The mind cannot seek a particular, definite idea, or a particular, definite preconception; but it may seek an idea, or a preconception, which will fulfil certain conditions.

A man may want to know what the truth is, without forming any definite idea as to what that truth is; or having formed a definite idea of what it *may* be—an hypothesis—may want to know if his hypothesis corresponds with the truth. One, who can only count, will know that the product of 7 multiplied by 9 must be some particular number, as yet unknown to him. He wants to know, and, on a partial examination of the facts, he perceives that by the use of his knowledge of counting he can gratify this want to know the product of 7 by 9. He can count out seven piles, each containing nine pebbles; or nine piles, each containing seven pebbles; and then, counting the whole, arrive at a result without having formed any previous hypothesis as to that result. Here, however, are two preconceptions of the mode to be pursued, making seven piles of nine, or nine piles of seven, so obviously equal, that no one could anticipate which another mind would adopt, or which would be first perceived.

The man may, however,—say for the purpose of forming some idea of the number of pebbles required,—prefer to carry his preliminary examination farther. In doing this, he may bring in his knowledge that, in counting, he advances by tens and goes over seven of these divisions of ten each in arriving at seventy; and hence infer that 7×9, being less than 7×10, must be less than seventy, and that sixty-nine pebbles will be sufficient; and, commencing now with this hypothesis, that sixty-nine may be the product of 7×9, he counts out sixty-nine and then makes the experiment to ascertain if he can get just seven piles, of nine each, out of sixty-nine; and varies the number until he can do so.

Though this is not one of them, there are cases in arithmetic and even in geometry, in which the best mode is to begin with an hypothesis and test its truth, or the degree of its variation; and, in the affairs of life, it is generally prudent to test any plan or preconception, as we would a mere hypothesis. They admit of so great variety and the combinations are so numerous, that the application of general rules is not practically reliable. They more nearly resemble the variety and combination of the chessboard, in which it is frequently necessary to consider each of several possible moves and compare the preconceptions of the effects, which we perceive would result. It is not unusual to aid these preconceptions by actually changing the place of the piece as proposed, and thus get, by immediate perception, what, without such move, is but imagined, or conceived.

Persons sometimes, having a vivid conception of the object desired, act hastily to attain it, without having fully matured the plan of the successive efforts required; and are liable to fail in consequence. Some requisite effort may not have been made at the right time, or in proper order, or may have been overlooked entirely.

NOTE. XXXI. P. 155.

There is no selfishness surpassing that of those who, having through life used all their means to obtain for themselves as much as possible of this world, at the last moment seek, by some judicious investment, to make them still available to obtain as much as possible of the next.

NOTE XXXII. P. 155.

Perhaps these views show the metaphysical root of the theological and popular discussions as to the influence of works.

NOTE XXXIII. P. 158.

These truths, vaguely existing in the popular mind, or applied with too much latitude, may have furnished a metaphysical origin for the doctrine of "perseverance"; and the same views, applied to the extermination of the wants morally good, seem to furnish a similar foundation for the belief that a finite moral being may sink to a condition of degradation from which he has no power to rise; and from which nothing but a miraculous intervention of Divine power can elevate him. As above intimated, however, there seems to be good reason to suppose that these wants, especially those more elevated, are so rooted in our being, that they can be actually eradicated only with its annihilation; that even in the lowest stages of depravity, the inferior wants may ever supply temptation and give occasion, on the one hand, for vicious action, or submissive indulgence; and, on the other, for virtuous effort in resistance; thus furnishing the means and inducement for still lower depths of debasement and for more hopeless habitual degradation; and, at the same time, affording the opportunity for reform, or for progress in virtue, to which all the higher aspirations of our nature will be incentives. To these, the Infinite Intelligence ever present and ever palpable in its effects; and ever mediately, or immediately in communion with the finite, may add its Divine influence; and even the aid of one finite being to another be not wholly unavailing in imparting knowledge and exhibiting moral beauty in action, and thus making it a *want*.

NOTE XXXIV. P. 159.

Intervals of such calm thought—of repose from the engrossments and excitements of active temporal pursuits—have ever been deemed conducive to moral well-being, and, when occurring at stated times and places, and especially places set apart for this object, their influence may be enhanced by association and habit. We have stated times to gratify the want of food.

NOTE XXXV. P. 165.

Man, being constituted as he is,—being what our observation of his earliest existence shows him to be,—has the powers and faculties of a first cause. How he became such a being is not within the scope of our inquiry and is probably entirely beyond the reach of the human intellect. Our object is to show what he is, and what capable of, as he is, rather than how he came to be so.

NOTE XXXVI. P. 171.

I know a man, living on a very sterile tract, which to the most unremitted toil yields only a very meagre subsistence, but who, after considering a proposal of his friends to remove to a productive farm upon which much less labor would have given him abundance, said, "When I think how much work I have done on these gravel hills and stone walls, I cannot bear the thought of leaving them." He but expressed a common sentiment of mankind, which is as potential in regard to the results of moral culture as of physical labor, and which has a specific influence in producing consistent and persistent effort, and, of course, upon stability of character, giving to that which amidst adversity and temptation has been built up by effort, an additional advantage over that which has resulted from opportune circumstances.

NOTES TO BOOK II.

NOTE XXXVII.* P. 201.

Edwards adds, in a note, ".I say not only *doing*, but *conducting*, because a voluntary forbearing to do, sitting still, keeping silence, &c., are instances of persons' *conduct*, about which liberty is exercised, though they are not so properly called *doing*."

NOTE XXXVIII. P. 241.

This assertion and the necessary connection of effect with cause make everything necessary; for everything must be embraced in what is necessary in itself, and what is not necessary in itself; and what is not necessary in itself must have a cause, and hence, as an effect of its cause, becomes necessary, so that what is necessary in itself and what is not, being both necessary, everything is necessary.

NOTE XXXIX. P. 251.

In the same way, there may be things relatively impossible to the finite intelligence, which impossibility, when perceived, prevents its efforts to do such things; but when not perceived, has no such influence whatever, though the effort will still be unavailing and the expected effect will not follow it.

NOTE XL. P. 255.

It is, perhaps, worthy of remark that the existence and the nature of a finite line are co-existing and self-existing truths (knowledge), which the mind perceives as the reasons of the determination or end; as the preconception which the mind forms of the effect of its action is rather a *reason*, which it perceives for the determination of its act of will, than a *cause* of it.

* The foot note on p. 201 refers to Note I.; it should read Note XXXVII.

NOTE XLI. P. 278.

The wise, the prudent, the industrious, especially do this;—the foolish, rash, and indolent decide by virtue of their absolute power so to do, without examination. Most men, however, by experience, knowing its importance, do more or less examine, and the results of such examination form the reasons for further action or an addition to those reasons, which were immediately obvious.

NOTE XLII. P. 294.

If it could be shown that cause, or power to produce change, could thus be extended in time, only in the case of matter in motion, and that it, by the changes which it produced, called on the active powers of intelligence as a dormant power, which must wait such opportunity to become cause; then, matter in motion would become essential to the activity of spirit, not merely as something to be acted upon, but to enable intelligence to begin to act and to sustain its action even for a single moment; and, in such case, the existence of matter as a distinct entity would be demonstrated, as also, that it must have existed and been in motion from eternity.

NOTE XLIII. P. 332.

If, as some suppose, the mind has other faculties, as reason, imagination, judgment, &c., which act independently of the will, then, if such action influences the action of the mind, it is still the mind influencing itself. In the view which I have presented in Book I., Chap. iii., these supposed faculties are but varied modes of effort, or effort for varied objects; and any exercise of them bearing on subsequent acts of will are but preliminary acts of will, determining the final act, which would be the mind's determining the final act by its *own* preliminary act. In tracing back the series of such acts, we must eventually come to an act which was induced by a want and directed by the mind's knowledge, in the form of an immediate perception of the means of gratifying it. Such immediate perceptions, in the first instance, must be, and in most subsequent cases probably are, of intuitive knowledge, but may be of knowledge acquired previously, or at the instant. The known fact, most frequently, thus perceived and applied to direct an action, is that the first effort must be to examine the circumstances which, as before intimated, is probably intuitively known. The application of this note to other similar arguments, in which the " other faculties of the mind " are an element, will be obvious without reiterating it.

NOTE XLIV. P. 345.

In the relation of knowledge to acts of will, it is not often necessary to distinguish the innate from the intuitive, the important distinction generally being only between that which requires effort to obtain it and that which does not. In Book I., Chap. xi., I have argued that our knowledge that the mode of effecting movement in our own being is by act of will, must be innate.

NOTE XLV. P. 365.

It is not intended to assert that this knowledge of the fact of uniformity in many cases, may not be intuitive as well as acquired. It is certainly not an idea of universal application, for there are many cases of a frequent recurrence of the same thing, to which we never learn to apply it; and the intuitive knowledge of the fact that in some cases there is a certain uniformity of antecedents and consequences, might be only an innate faith, that God had in such cases established, and would maintain such uniformity, which would be very different from an intuitive conviction that such uniformity must exist as a condition of metaphysical necessity.

NOTE XLVI. P. 379.

Though this may be expressed in terms, it does not seem certain that any such case can be conceived of as practically arising. It cannot occur in regard to the mind in willing, for there is always the alternative of willing or not willing any action. If one body impinges directly against another, there must be some effect (as the two bodies cannot occupy the same space, or one extension cannot possibly be two extensions)—*non-effect*, in this case, involves contradiction; but there are still various conceivable effects, no one of which has been ascertained to be the one necessary effect to the exclusion of the others. The observed effect does in fact vary very materially. It is true, it varies only with varied circumstances, as hardness, inertia, momentum of the impinging body or bodies, &c.; and then, in reference to these circumstances, with a uniformity which has been well ascertained. But, that this or any other uniformity is of metaphysical necessity, that no power could have made it otherwise, has not yet been demonstrated.

NOTE XLVII. P. 386.

I have here intended to give all the scope and weight to the positions of Edwards which could possibly be accorded to them. Nor do I perceive that the admissions here made require any material modification. It may, however, be observed that, in the views I have presented in Book I., any intelligence may *influence* the volition of another by imparting knowledge; but, as before shown, such influence is possible only because the volition of this other is free. This suggestion can have no place in Edwards's system, because he makes knowledge itself the volition, and we thus find that even this argument on the foreknowledge of God is obscured by the confounding of choice and will. If, however, a being has any intelligence of its own—any knowing sense—even its knowledge cannot be wholly controlled by extrinsic power. A man, with eyes to see and ears to hear, must of himself get some knowledge of the external, and with powers of thought must learn some relations of ideas, and cannot be made by extrinsic power to know or believe that $2+2=5$. In virtue of his intelligence he is so far an independent power; and though he may be indirectly influenced by knowledge imparted to him, yet even in this he cannot be coerced or constrained. He may be convinced by skilful presentation of truth; he may be deceived by ingenious falsehood; and freely acting upon the knowledge thus acquired, his action may be different from what it would be if it had not been inculcated. We may suppose the Supreme Intelligence to resort to the first mode, and by imparting truth influence the action of men, or, perhaps, justly withholding divine illumination, permit the perverse to believe a lie. The element of want seems to present another possible mode of influencing the human will. These, as we have before observed, are in the first instance constitutional, and can be cultivated only through the medium of knowledge, which would bring this mode in the same class of influences as that of knowledge itself; and if the constitutional wants are themselves altered by a direct application of power, this would be to change one of the constitutional elements of the being; and either to partially annihilate the being, or add to it by a new creation, making a different being, another free agent, whose acts might, in virtue of being free, be different from those of the former agent. In none of these modes, then, can the wills of finite intelligent beings be directly controlled even by infinite power or infinite knowledge; and the prescience of God furnishes no reason to suppose they can be thus controlled.

NOTE XLVIII. P. 396.

Without entering generally upon a subject for which I am wholly unprepared, I would here merely note the bearing which these views, and some others which I have before stated, appear to have upon the " Science of History." Such a science must have its basis either upon the idea that the events of the future are connected with those in the past, as effects dependent on antecedent causes which must produce such effects and no other; or on the supposition that the Supreme Intelligence brings about results in conformity to certain uniform modes or laws which He has established; by the exercise of His power either making all other effort as nought, or so combining the element of His own action with other causes that the composition of the forces will produce certain uniform results, or at least results which may be anticipated.

In regard to the idea that the events of the future are a necessary consequence of those in the past, our previous reasoning would go to show that, if we eliminate the mere mechanical effects which *may* result from matter in motion, there is no such connection, and that to produce any such requires the action of intelligent cause. The events of the past have no present existence. They may be remembered by an intelligent being, but such memories are but knowledge of the past, which, like any other knowledge, enables such being to direct its efforts upon the future intelligently. The whole influence of such past is, then, through the volition of an intelligent being. Excluding at any moment the mechanical effects of matter in motion, the whole future must depend on these volitions, and the events and circumstances which have already transpired have no more tendency to extend themselves into the future than the wall, which the mason, by his own efforts, is raising brick by brick, has to build itself upward.

The uniformity of the effects of matter in motion, whether as necessary consequences of motion, or as uniform modes of God's action, is established, and furnishes a means of determining from the past something of the future; but this is limited to the mechanical conditions of the material universe, enabling us to anticipate the alternations of day and night and of the seasons—to foreknow the future positions of the planets, and thus to predict eclipses, transits, &c., and so far there is, and has long been, a Science of History.

In regard to thus foreknowing the course of events, which, upon the principles I have stated, is the composite result of all intelligent activity, or of such results combined with the effects of matter in motion as a distinct cause, grave difficulties present themselves. If, as I have argued, God, as a necessity in providing for the existence of finite free agents, foregoes the use of His own power to control every event, and even forms no plan of particulars in the future, but is ever ready by His own action to modify the effects of the free and independent action of all other intelligent beings, then He not only does not foreknow the acts of these finite free agents, but He foregoes the prescience of His own actions, and the student who from past history should seek to deduce these particular future acts, either of the finite or Infinite Intelligence, would be seeking a knowledge which God has proscribed even to Himself.

In any attempt to solve the problem of these particular future events, our data must involve the variable elements of innumerable free wills, each of which may be acted upon and affected by every other, leaving little hope of any solution as to the particular events of volition and their immediate consequences. If it be said that, amidst this almost infinite variety, God yet, by His paramount power, reconciles the divers influences so as to bring about a harmonious result, in conformity to some design which He has preformed, still the particular elements of the combination, including His own agency in it, cannot be foreknown; and in regard to those final or cyclical events, which make a part of this supposed preordained plan, there is manifestly great difficulty. From examination of the past we may learn such very general facts as that God is just, that He will punish iniquity, &c., &c., and hence draw very general conclusions as to His future action; but this still gives little indication of the particular acts by which these ends will be reached, the time when, or even of the cyclical events by which His justice will be manifested, for there may be many events which, so far as we can see, will equally answer the purpose. In this use of His power to do justice or punish iniquity we might expect, not a necessary repetition of former events, but the exhibition of action reaching the same end, making perhaps historic parallels, of which the events now transpiring in our country, compared with those which attended the exodus of the Israelites, when the Egyptians were afflicted with plague after plague, till they were made willing to let the bondsman go free, seem to be a striking illustration. Even in this case it is hardly conceivable that the events could have been inferred, with any particularity, from the past. Perhaps the nearest particular coincidence in this case is, that among those most immediately implicated in the wrong of slavery, it is now asserted that there is hardly a family in which the strife has not brought a death, and then "there was not a house in which there was not one dead." The plague of the locusts devouring the products of labor, is easily typified among either of the belligerents, and perhaps the rod—the law intended to preserve peace and maintain order and justice—was cast down upon the ground and converted into a venomous reptile, in that opinion of our highest judicial tribunal in which it was asserted that, by our fundamental law, as originally intended by its framers, and as it must still be construed, a whole race of men and women had no rights which others were bound to respect. Verily, if such had become our settled principles, there was little reason to expect that the avenging arm of Him whose ears are open to the moan and the prayer of the weak and the oppressed would long be stayed. Such events may indicate general rules or uniformity in God's action; as that the violence and injustice of a people shall react upon themselves, but still throws little light upon the particular modes by which the uniform results will be accomplished. Take for instance, as recorded, the most notable event of His special action since the creation of the world—the destruction of our race because of their corruption. Even supposing that, on a recurrence of such corruption, God would, as an act required by perfect justice, again depopulate the earth, He might still do it by other modes, as fire, famine, pestilence or war. So far, indeed, from our being able from the past to infer that the recurrence of such corruption would be followed by another destroying flood, we cannot even infer that destruction in any form would be resorted to. If there is no change in God, there may be such change in His creatures as will be to Him a reason for a different course of action. Once, among us, the scourge and the gallows were deemed the proper antidotes for depravity; now milder means, with the school and the lyceum, are relied upon, and this change in our views—in our appreciation of means—may be a reason with God for adopting another mode in which He may correct moral evil by imparting more knowledge to the transgressors, and, in case of a resort to miracle, instead of flood or flame, increase the knowledge of our race, either by His own immediate revelations to all, or by inspiring some portion to teach new and elevating truth ; or by sending a special agent with extraordinary or even miraculous power to perform this office. On the grounds I have before suggested, such resort to miracle can seldom if ever become a *necessity*.

Among the prominent difficulties which, in the views I have presented, would appear to impede the Science of History, we have the great variety of events which may intervene between the great general results which mark the footsteps of the Deity in time, and which are perhaps required by His attributes ; the uncertainty as to the periods between such events ; and that there may be many such results which will fulfil the same intention. In a game of chess it may be pretty confidently predicted that a very skilful player will eventually checkmate one unskilled ; but through what particular moves, or how many of them, it will be done, no human being can prognosticate. If now we suppose that, instead of only one result, the object or end in view of the player is to produce either checkmate or stalemate, or some one of a thousand other conditions, the difficulty of foreknowing the final result is vastly increased. In chess the possible combinations are limited ; but by repetitions of them the moves possible in a single game are infinite. If we suppose the possible combinations of the position of the pieces to number a billion, then when a billion and one moves have been made we know that at least some one combination has been repeated. If we assume an arbitrary limit to the

APPENDIX. 453

number of moves in any game, then the variations which arise from changes in the order of the succession of the billion possible combinations will also be limited; and assuming this to be a trillion, we will know that when a trillion and one games have been played some one of the games has been an exact repetition of one of the others; but who would essay the task to tell, in the first case, what *move*, and in the second what *game*, had been repeated; and yet the attempt to conceive or to state the greater difficulty in foreseeing the results of the acts of innumerable free agents would in itself be bewildering.

This main difficulty, arising from the variable element of free volitions, may be thus stated: Excluding, as before, the mechanical effects of matter in motion, the events of the past have no power to generate the future; but that future is the result of intelligent power manifested in efforts or acts of will. Intelligence, thus acting, is a cause which does not, on a repetition of the same circumstances, of necessity produce the same effect, or repeat its own action, but may, in such recurrence, try a new mode, producing a different effect. The influence of this variable element of will is further complicated by each individual acting in reference to what he perceives others are doing, or are expected to do, so that the action even of the Supreme Intelligence may be modified by the action of inferior intelligences, down to the lowest in the scale, and may thus be influenced to elect one rather than another of divers cyclical events, any one of which will fulfil His main design. It must also be borne in mind that the object of every effort is to produce an effect in the future, and change that course of events which, but for such effort, would be established by the influence of other causes; and that efforts which at the time appear to be of little moment often lead to very important consequences. These difficulties appear formidable, leaving little hope that the study of the history of the past will enable us to indicate even any great results by which God, in the exercise of His overruling power, at periods to us uncertain, corrects the aberrations produced by finite efforts, and in the main conforms the course of events and the government of the world to His own attributes. On the other hand, there is encouragement for the prosecution of this lofty science in the fact that every being that wills must have some perception of the future in which there is at least sufficient probability of truth to be the foundation of its action, affording a hope that this prophetic power may be largely increased by study and cultivation. It must not, however, be overlooked, that the probability that the future will conform to our anticipations of it decreases so rapidly, as we increase the distance in time, that our prophetic vision can reach only a very little way into futurity. As favoring the pursuit of this science, I may also refer to the position which (in the text) I have just attempted to illustrate, that God may govern the world and provide compensation for all the aberrations of finite wills without departing from general rules or uniform modes of action; and to the previous positions, that, being perfect in wisdom, His actions, under the same circumstances, will be free from the mutations which attend the experimental efforts of less intelligent beings, and that even the imperfect wisdom of finite free agents leads to a partial uniformity in the actions of the individual, while similarity in the natural wants and intuitive knowledge, and identity in the absolute truths from which we derive our acquired knowledge, tend to produce a corresponding similarity in the actions of different individuals. These tendencies to uniformity encourage the hope that some law or mode of God's action, analogous to that which assures the stability of the material universe, may, within certain limits, regulate the succession of events in the moral. We may also note, that though, in some aspects, the ability which each one has to influence the action of others complicates and obscures the future, in another view it aids us to anticipate it. Our power to influence a future event is so far a power to foreknow it. When the efforts of a large number of persons are directed to the same end, the probability that this end will be accomplished is increased. When these efforts are intended to influence the volition of numerous individuals, though no one can foreknow the effect upon any particular one of them, the probabilities are that, for reasons just stated, a large number will be similarly influenced, and, if the efforts have been wisely directed, that the desired result will be reached. In individual action each adopts the mode which his own knowledge, derived in great measure from past experience, suggests. This leads to diversity of action; and combined action requires a common reason, or at least a common ground for action, and this can often be found in that common or general experience of which history is the record. Hence the obvious application of this science to the enacting of public laws.

In those efforts by which we do our part in creating the future, what we most immediately and pressingly want to know is, what next to do, and the farther we can clearly trace the consequences of our efforts, the better are we prepared to decide what to do. It is evident, however, that in tracing out the consequences of an action in all its subsequent ramifications, the problem as to what is best to be done soon becomes so complicated that the time for action would pass before we could thus decide what to do.

It seems, however, at least probable, that the more systematic study of the past may enable us better to perform our parts in creating the proximate future, may expand our knowledge of the ways of God, and increase our faith in His attributes, and at the same time lead us to some very generic ideas of the modes in which He manifests these attributes in His government of the world; and these are objects well worthy of our highest efforts. In nearly all our efforts to acquire knowledge, our aim is to find out God's ways, and read His character in His works.

The ideas above alluded to, and inculcated in various parts of this work, that in our humblest efforts we are co-workers with God, taking part with Him in the creation of the future, and that our ways change His ways, may to some appear irreverent, and even arrogant, but they seem to me to furnish the only rational ground for hope in effort, or trust in prayer, and that by excluding them we would make our noblest efforts and holiest aspirations the merest mockery. However hallowing and consoling the reflex influences of devout prayer may be, the belief in a system which would exclude us from all influence upon the future, either by our own direct efforts or by petition to the Sovereign power, making us but the subjects of a rigid and inexorable despotism, would degrade humanity and involve all the evils of fatalism.

www.ingramcontent.com/pod-product-compliance
Lightning Source LLC
Chambersburg PA
CBHW051852300426
44117CB00006B/370